THE RISE OF THE

SONS OF GOD

AS JOINT-HEIRS WITH THE KING

MARK D WOOD

ISBN: 979-8-89228-973-3   (Paperback)
ISBN: 979-8-89228-974-0   (Hardcover)
ISBN: 979-8-89228-975-7   (eBook)

Printed in the United States of America

CONTENTS

PREFACE

If you're a Facebook, FaceTime, chatroom, text-message, cell-phone addict, you'll probably never finish this book. But thanks for buying it anyway! I promise, your money won't be squandered! A large portion of the proceeds from this book will be used in the fight against child sex trafficking and related pedophilia, including the rescue of satanic cult victims through organizations like Covenant Rescue Group. I pray a special blessing over you for your contribution to this cause.

Within the many mysteries hidden in the Word of God, like encrypted code, is the mystery of the sons of God. There are many references to these sons of God in Scripture, many of them misunderstood due to our limited spirituality in the cold, dead pews of the post-Constantine church. I am reminded of a Scottish Anglican priest named John Macquarrie who, though his theological views may not resonate well with the full-gospel church, certainly shared some powerful insights that should not be ignored. One of those insights should serve as a wake-up call to contemporary theologians.

> *A theology without spirituality would be a sterile academic exercise.*[1]

How often are scholarly theological commentaries based on sterile academic exercises rather than founded on a solid relationship with the Holy Spirit? How often does a scholar read every other scholar's work before committing to his own commentary because he lacks conviction?

---

1   John Macquarrie, 1917–2007

I believe this is how we have strayed so far from truth in the one religion that offers salvation, called "Christianity," which scarcely resembles her early mother church born in the book of Acts. In many of my personal discussions with Christians, they are quick to tell me what their church or religion believes and insist, "If the church teaches it, do not question it." This is indoctrination and the way cults are formed around one person's views. I never read or write anything without first asking the Holy Spirit to guide my thoughts and words.

Many are quick to disagree with opposing viewpoints, citing something learned from an "academic," or a priest, or church manuals written by YouTube "prophets" or "prophetesses." As much as I have learned from Seventh-day Adventists, I regret to say that they are somewhat of a cult following the late Ellen White. If Ellen White said it, it is treated as though God spoke it. That being said, I love them dearly, and even a broken clock is right twice a day. We should try to learn from everyone through the filter of the Holy Spirit.

When traveling in the days before GPS, we stopped at convenience stores or gas stations to ask directions from someone local, assuming they would know where we needed to go. The clerk began pointing here and there, turning his body, confusing left and right: "Go three blocks, come to a stop sign, and turn left—or wait, maybe it's a right turn." He twisted his entire body to determine whether the turns were left or right. After a few minutes, you realized the clerk had no idea where you're trying to go and left you more confused than before you asked for help.

This is how I felt at the beginning of my spiritual journey, until I realized we have a road map written by the first Surveyor of the earth—the Holy Spirit. Anyone can recite history, but only the influence of the Holy Spirit can reveal the vast network of highways in the spiritual realm that connect the past to the future. For history, we have textbooks. But for spirituality, we pray and fast, seeking the Holy Spirit with all our heart as we consume the Word of God. A new panorama of truth will be revealed on this spiritual highway if we seek it. Asking directions from someone who is also lost will be of no help in finding the right road. Consult the Holy Spirit for directions before taking a wrong turn into a ghetto of demons.

I want to point out something very important in this context of being led by the Spirit, which Paul states very clearly in Romans, chapter 8, as follows:

> *For whosoever are led by the Spirit of God, they are the sons of God.*
>
> *For you have not received the spirit of bondage again in fear; but you have received the spirit of adoption of sons, whereby we cry: Abba (Father).*
>
> *For the Spirit himself giveth testimony to our spirit, that we are the sons of God.*
>
> *And if sons, heirs also; heirs indeed of God, and joint heirs with Christ: yet so, if we suffer with him, that we may be also glorified with him. (Romans 8:14-17)[2]*

I nearly always reference either the King James (KJV), Amplified Bible (AMP), or New American Standard Bible (NASB). In this case, I wanted to scan alternative versions to see if any of them noted a specific point I was searching for. I found that several did. The Douay-Rheims and the Wycliffe, among a few others, captured the differentiation I was looking for in the legal term "sons" versus "children." The King James uses "sons" in verse 14, then shifts to the more general "children" in the rest of the passage.

What difference does it make? In ancient Hebrew culture, it made a huge difference, since daughters were only considered eligible heirs if there were no eligible sons. These "sons" whom the Spirit is leading have a mission from God, ordained by Him to become joint heirs with His only begotten Son (John 3:16). "Children" is equally correct under Christ, since all in Christ will be joint heirs with Him, but the legal aspect of what is being communicated here is critically important, as this book will reveal.

---

2   Douay-Rheims, 1899, American Edition

Romans 8:14 is a legal statement establishing a proper foundation for a legal inheritance.

By the way, the Holy Spirit is the administrator of this inheritance, so you might want to keep that in mind. Don't lose sight of who leads and who follows. It's not a pastor or priest, or YouTube prophet. The Holy Spirit has been sent by God to prepare the bride for the arrival of her King. The sons of God are being led by the Holy Spirit to achieve this purpose.

In my book *The Bride, the Wise Virgins, and the Last Adam*, I present a case for a threefold harvest in harmony with the three agricultural feasts of the Bible. I believe that the wheat harvest, which began with the Feast of Pentecost, will be the bride, without a doubt. The bride is separate from the rest of mankind and closest to the bridegroom. The bride is justified in Christ, set apart from the sons of disobedience. This group will manifest in the future to fulfil Paul's words in Romans, chapter 8. I want to focus on this passage, beginning with verse 16:

> *The Spirit itself beareth witness with our spirit, that we are the children of God:*
>
> *And if children, then heirs; heirs of God, and joint-heirs with Christ; if so be that we suffer with him, that we may be also glorified together.*
>
> *For I reckon that the sufferings of this present time are not worthy to be compared with the glory which shall be revealed in us.*
>
> *For the earnest expectation of the creature waiteth for the manifestation of the sons of God.*
>
> *For the creature was made subject to vanity, not willingly, but by reason of him who hath subjected the same in hope,*
>
> *Because the creature itself also shall be delivered from the bondage of corruption into the glorious liberty of the children of God.*

For we know that the whole creation groaneth and travaileth in pain together until now.

And not only they, but ourselves also, which have the firstfruits of the Spirit, even we ourselves groan within ourselves, waiting for the adoption, to wit, the redemption of our body.

For we are saved by hope: but hope that is seen is not hope: for what a man seeth, why doth he yet hope for?

But if we hope for that we see not, then do we with patience wait for it.

Likewise the Spirit also helpeth our infirmities: for we know not what we should pray for as we ought: but the Spirit itself maketh intercession for us with groanings which cannot be uttered.

And he that searcheth the hearts knoweth what is the mind of the Spirit, because he maketh intercession for the saints according to the will of God.

And we know that all things work together for good to them that love God, to them who are the called according to his purpose.

For whom he did foreknow, he also did predestinate to be conformed to the image of his Son, that he might be the firstborn among many brethren.

Moreover whom he did predestinate, them he also called: and whom he called, them he also justified: and whom he justified, them he also glorified.

What shall we then say to these things? If God be for us, who can be against us?

He that spared not his own Son, but delivered him up for us all, how shall he not with him also freely give us all things?

Who shall lay any thing to the charge of God's elect? It is God that justifieth.

Who is he that condemneth? It is Christ that died, yea rather, that is risen again, who is even at the right hand of God, who also maketh intercession for us. (Romans 8:16-34 KJV)

In verse 19, "sons of God" is translated from the Greek huios (υἱός - Strong's 5207). Verse 16 is translated as "children of God," from the Greek tekna (τέκνα - Strong's 5043). While the Greek tekna can mean "children" or "offspring," depending on the context, I believe its meaning here is the same as huios in verse 19. Why? Because verse 17 is one of the most important points of the New Testament.

And if children, then heirs; heirs of God, and joint-heirs with Christ; if so be that we suffer with him, that we may be also glorified together. (Romans 8:17 KJV)

In ancient Hebrew culture, it was required by law that sons be heirs to their father's estate. Read this note from Strong's word studies:

5207 /hyiós ("son") highlights the (legal) right to the Father's inheritance, i.e. as the believer lives in conformity with the Father's nature (purpose).

This is legal language. Don't worry ladies—you are not being excluded from the sons of God manifestation miracle. Before I provoke a feminist uprising or book-burning party, take note of Paul's words in Galatians 3:28 (KJV):

There is neither Jew nor Greek, there is neither bond nor free, there is neither male nor female: for ye are all one in Christ Jesus.

The bride is a joint heir with her bridegroom in His Father's kingdom. She shares in His inheritance, reigning with Him at His side. The sons of God to whom Paul refers are the bride transfigured (2 Corinthians 3:18).

The focus of this book, then, is anything but a sterile academic exercise in theology. Its focus is a spiritual journey to discover the sons of God who are led by the Holy Spirit. *Who were the sons of God that fell with Lucifer? Who are the sons of God today? Who will become "sons of God" in the future?*

CHAPTER 1

Who Were the Sons of God in Genesis?

Then shall he say also unto them on the left hand, Depart from me, ye cursed, into everlasting fire, prepared for the devil and his angels.

–Matthew 25:41 (KJV)

Satan has angels?

Perhaps the only subject more controversial among Christians than the "Harpazo" is the debate over who were the sons of God mentioned in Genesis, chapter 6. When we approach these biblical themes—saturated with so many opinions that they become confusing, each prefacing their commentaries with pedigreed credentials as if to say, "I am the expert, not you"—remember what Paul says in 1 Thessalonians, chapter 5:5 (AMP) "for you are all sons of light and sons of day. We do not belong to the night nor to darkness." Before opening your Bible or reading any books on the multitude of biblical subjects or insights by different authors or scholars, pray that the Holy Spirit bless you with clarity and discernment on every matter of God's Word. Follow the Holy Spirit, and live by these rules:

Prove all things; hold fast that which is good. (1 Thessalonians 5:21 KJV)

In that they received the word with all readiness of mind, and searched the scriptures daily, whether those things were so. (Acts 17:11 KJV)

The subject of the sons of God taking wives from among the daughters of men opens a wide variety of rabbit holes and conspiracy theories. If we do not clearly understand who is being referred to in Genesis 6, we cannot fully comprehend the extent of this war between God and His adversaries. Always remember: we are at war, we have been at war for millennia, and this war rages on today. A critical point to grasp is that the Bible contains some disturbing history that the "pure in heart" may choose to deny or ignore. Genesis 6 is not where this history began, but where it escalated to a climactic level, compelling God to intervene and shut it down with the Great Flood. Without that intervention, the original DNA of mankind, through Adam's genetic design, would have ceased to exist. The mere suggestion that this may have been the reason for God's intervention—to protect Adam's DNA—reveals the strategic objective of His adversary: *destroy any possibility of a Messiah being born of mankind, one who would elevate mankind's legal authority above that of the "sons of God" through His insuperable authority.*

This is the ugliest war of all wars. We must never lose sight of that fact, or our spirituality will become so diluted that we will pose no threat to demons and be of little use to Yehshua.

Let's now review these verses from Genesis, chapter 6:

And it came to pass, when men began to multiply on the face of the earth, and daughters were born unto them,

That the sons of God saw the daughters of men that they were fair; and they took them wives of all which they chose. (Genesis 6:1-2 KJV)

Regarding verse 2, I want to mention that I scanned numerous translations out of curiosity to see if any rendered the phrase differently than "sons of God." This was a quick search, not exhaustive, but I found that the only variations translated "sons of God" as "divine beings." It is critically important to note that the only difference between translations lies in whether these "sons of God" are considered "divine beings" rather than human in nature or origin. Obviously, most translations are derived from the Masoretic (Hebrew) or Latin Vulgate texts, with the exception of the International Standard Version, which is sometimes useful because it draws primarily from the Dead Sea Scrolls, the Septuagint, and other sources closer to the originals. The ISV translates "sons of God" as "divine beings" in verse 2.

I also read through about a dozen "scholarly" commentaries on Genesis 6:2 to see how the mainstream scholarly community interprets these "sons of God." The more I read, the more appalled I became, as most concluded—apart from a few exceptions—that the "sons of God" were never to be considered divine beings. One exception is *Unger's Commentary on the Old Testament,* which remains among my favorite resources. Dr. Unger explains in excellent detail that the "sons of God" in Genesis 6 were fallen angels.

By contrast, the more notable commentaries I consulted subscribe to what I consider a delusional theory first written by a bishop formally recognized in Roman Catholicism as a "doctor of the church" (there are thirty-seven of these "doctoral saints" in Catholicism today). He is highly accredited for shaping modern Christianity as we know it, and this influence was evident in the scholarly opinions I reviewed, which consistently denied that the "sons of God" were divine beings. Most of these commentaries subscribe to the "Sethite Theory," which originated in ancient Rome and was later widely publicized by the Catholic bishop St. Augustine of Hippo in his book *City of God,* written in the early fifth century.

The "Sethite Theory" maintains that men from the line of Adam through his son Seth intermarried with the daughters of Cain, Adam's other biblically documented son. This view assumes that the line of Adam through Seth was the "godly" line, while the daughters of Cain belonged to a cursed lineage.

My first question is this: If the sons of Seth were truly godly, why does the rest of verse 2 indicate that the daughters of Cain were taken against their will? "They took for themselves wives of all which they chose" speaks of taking women by force and multiplicity. Does it make sense that the godly Sethites would become pillagers and rapists, taking their cousins by force? Doesn't that make them as evil as the Cainites? What would distinguish them as "godly Sethites" if they were characterized as rapists?

My next question is how did the "cousin" genetics from the same origin of Adam and Eve could produce giants (verse 4)? Some Sethite theorists argue that the pure nutritional values of plants and foods in preflood times were so rich that they contributed to great size and strength. But extrapolate that into logical real modern terms: if I were to consume 1,000 grams of protein daily, 1,000 times the recommended daily allowances of vitamins and minerals, and breathe oxygen from a tank all day, would my offspring become giants? Such consumption would be lethal and would have no effect on genetics. Vitamins and protein can enhance physical stature but cannot alter DNA. For a man and woman to produce a giant requires genetic modification, which vitamins alone cannot accomplish. God made certain of this when, in the Days of Creation, it is written: "And God saw that it was good." If God created something and called it good, then the food He created and declared good wouldn't spawn evil giants.

Then there is the question of other giants later in the Old Testament, identified as being identical in nature to the preflood giants (verse 4 connects to Numbers 13:33), having an extra digit on their hands and feet (2 Samuel 21; 1 Chronicles 20). In addition, archaeological finds include multitudes of giants with six fingers and toes, along with an extra row of teeth, many believed to have been buried by the Great Flood.

Among the more amazing discoveries are skeletal remains of six-fingered, double-rowed-teeth giants exceeding twenty feet in height, some even larger. *This points to genetic modification with no dietary influence.* A rooster and a hen eating the richest grains will not produce an ostrich that grows an extra toe on each foot and, upon maturity, becomes evil and eats the rooster and hen. This is totally ridiculous, but that is the Sethite theory in simple terms.

How did something so ridiculous become so widely accepted? Read this comment by Dr. Chuck Missler from www.khouse.org:

Celsus and Julian the Apostate used the traditional "angel" belief to attack Christianity. Julius Africanus resorted to the Sethite interpretation as a more comfortable ground. Cyril of Alexandria also repudiated the orthodox "angel" position with the "line of Seth" interpretation. Augustine also embraced the Sethite theory and thus it prevailed into the Middle Ages. It is still widely taught today among many churches who find the literal "angel" view a bit disturbing. There are many outstanding Bible teachers who still defend this view.[3]

The Sethite theory was solidified during a time when the worship of angels had entered the church in the fifth century AD. The Sethite theory mopped up any ugliness that might have been associated with angels, preserving their divine imagery. Once again, we can thank the Church of Rome for theological confusion that continues to linger in the minds of many scholars even today.

For many students of the Bible, this may feel like beating a dead horse. Yet the truth of the Nephilim origin is becoming more widely accepted within the church. Still, you will encounter some who hold to the Sethite theory, and it is important to be equipped to argue this point with Christians from time to time. I personally know many who refuse to accept the fact that the sons of God in Genesis 6 were fallen angels. So in keeping with 1 Thessalonians 5:21 and Acts 17:11, let's analyze Genesis 6:2 to make sure there were no Sethites behind the woodshed, starting with Strong's Hebrew:

the sons

יְנֵב־ (bə·nê-)

Noun - masculine plural construct

---

3   https://www.khouse.org/personal_update/articles/1997/mischievous-angels-or-sethites

Strong's Hebrew 1121:

1) son, grandson, child, member of a group

1a) son, male child

1b) grandson

1c) children (pl. - male and female)

1d) youth, young men (pl.)

1e) young (of animals)

1f) sons (as characterisation, i.e. sons of injustice [for un- righteous men] ***or sons of God***

[for angels]

1g) people (of a nation) (pl.)

1h) of lifeless things, i.e. sparks, stars, arrows (fig.)

1i) a member of a guild, order, class

of God

הָאֱלֹהִים (hā·'ĕ·lō·hîm)

Article | Noun - masculine plural

Strong's Hebrew 430:

1) (plural)

1a) rulers, judges

1b) divine ones

1c) angels

1d) gods

2) (plural intensive-singular meaning)

2a) god, goddess

2b) godlike one

2c) works or special possessions of God

2d) the (true) God

2e) God

At first glance, this construct in Hebrew seems readily apparent that _bə·nê-hā·'ĕ·lō·hîm_ is a specific reference to sons of God directly and not indirectly by inference. As you continue reading down to "the daughters of men," Strong's translates from the Hebrew accordingly:

<u>the daughters</u>

תֹּונְב (bə·nō·wt)

Noun - feminine plural construct

<u>Strong›s Hebrew 1323:</u> n f

1) daughter

1a) daughter, girl, adopted daughter, daughter-in-law, sister, granddaughters, female child, cousin

1a1) as polite address n pr f

1a2) as designation of women of a particular place 2) young women, women

1a3) as personification

1a4) daughter-villages

1a5) description of character

<u>of men</u>

םָדָאֶה (hā·'ā·dām)

Article | Noun - masculine singular

Strong›s Hebrew 120:

1) man, mankind

1a) man, human being

1b) man, mankind (much more frequently intended sense in OT)

1c) Adam, first ma

1d) city in Jordan valley

Notice that the daughters were of *ha-adam* (*bə·nō·wt-ha-adam*). If the sons of God were truly the sons of Adam, why would the author not have clarified this by stating *bene-ha-adam* rather than *bene-ha-elohim*, which can only be properly interpreted as "sons of God(s)"? And if the daughters were of Cain's lineage, why would the original Hebrew texts not clarify— or worse, confuse the text—by clearly stating "daughters of *ha-adam*" (Adam) in conjunction with *bene-ha-elohim*? This twisting of translations would be the prosecution's strongest case against St. Augustine, for by this interpretation, they cannot be both sons and daughters of Adam when, in the Hebrew, only the daughters are of Adam. The sons are of *ha-Elohim*, not *ha-adam*.

It takes a twisted translator to interpret and extract *ha-adam* from *ha-Elohim*. All translations we have at our disposal today render the phrase as "sons of God" (Elohim directly) or "sons of divine beings" (also Elohim directly). Elohim is never used to refer to Adam or any descendant of Adam. God is God, and man is man. Adam was a son of God, but his descendants were sons and daughters of Adam (Luke 3:38). To twist the translation to mean "sons of Adam," equating Adam with "Elohim," and then to suggest they took the "daughters of Cain" in a violent act of polygamy, is a theological crime that has caused sixteen centuries of confusion in the church.

In addition, if the Sethites were such good people, why was the flood necessary? And why would it be so important to insert into verse 9 that Noah was found "perfect in his generations," meaning his genetic line to Adam remained free of fallen angel DNA? Immediately after the text states that the sons of God took the daughters of men, God proclaims a 120-year curse upon the earth. This marks the time when Noah began building the ark, and 120 years later, the flood came. Following the proclamation of the curse, the daughters of men bore giants in the earth, and the wickedness became so great that God repented of creating mankind (Genesis 6:6).

Why did He repent? *Because there could be no salvation for the sons of God who rebelled against Him.* The plan for man's salvation had already been declared in Genesis 3:15, but for this grave sin of the sons of God (*bene-ha-elohim*), they were destined for elimination by fire (Matthew 25:41). There could be no redemption for the sons of God, and this caused God to grieve and repent for creating man, with whom they sinned so greatly that they guaranteed their own destruction.

I personally need no further convincing, but I know many Christians who hold tightly to the Sethite or "superfood" view. For their sake—and for anyone you may encounter who still embraces this theory—let's keep digging. Even if you're already well ahead on this subject, as I know most "Philadelphia" Christians are, it remains important to argue with facts so that others can be guided toward correcting theological misconceptions. I appreciate your willingness to engage in this academic exercise, which ultimately leads us to a better place, spiritually speaking.

Most of us know the story of Job, but the book of Job contains treasures of information concealed in mystical language. At times, it becomes a baseline for understanding other parts of the Bible. This is especially true when clarifying who the "sons of God" were—and still are. Bear with me as we explore this further.

> *Now there was a day when the sons of God came to present themselves before the Lord, and Satan came also among them.*
>
> *And the Lord said unto Satan, Whence comest thou? Then Satan answered the Lord, and said, From going to and fro in the earth, and from walking up and down in it.*

And the Lord said unto Satan, Hast thou considered
my servant Job, that there is none like him in the earth,
a perfect and an upright man, one that feareth God,
and escheweth evil?

Then Satan answered the Lord, and said, Doth Job fear
God for nought?

Hast not thou made an hedge about him, and about his
house, and about all that he hath on every side? thou
hast blessed the work of his hands, and his substance is
increased in the land.

But put forth thine hand now, and touch all that he
hath, and he will curse thee to thy face.

And the Lord said unto Satan, Behold, all that he hath
is in thy power; only upon himself put not forth thine
hand. So Satan went forth from the presence of the
Lord. (Job 1:6-12 KJV)

In verse 6, the sons of God appear before God, and Satan is with them. This is a court hearing before the throne of God. The fact that God mentions Job first indicates that these "sons of God," who came with Satan, were delivering a list of people aligned with them and opposed to God (this is the time of Nimrod, as I will explain). Then God asks, "Have you considered Job?" Neither the "sons of God" nor Satan mentioned Job—God did—which means they were there to discuss a separate list of human constituencies and had not even considered Job. These are not God's friends; they are His enemies. This is not a friendly meeting of colleagues but a courtroom session to determine who belongs to Satan and who belongs to God.

Obviously, these sons of God are not the sons of Seth appearing with Satan, for by this time after the flood, Job is certainly from the line of Seth, about to be pounced on by the sons of God. How can we interpret the sons of God one way in Genesis 6 and another way in the book of Job if the original Hebrew is precisely the same? Doesn't this make you want to scream? The Sethite theory is a mess!

What does Strong's say about the Hebrew translation of "sons of God" in Job 1?

<u>the sons</u>

יְנֵב (bə·nê)

<u>Strong›s Hebrew 1121:</u>

<u>of God</u>

םיִהֹלֱאָה (hā·'ĕ·lō·hîm)

<u>Strong›s Hebrew 430:</u>

The translation of the sons of God appearing with Satan before the throne of God is exactly the same as the sons of God in Genesis 6:2— *bene-ha-elohim.*

Without going too deeply into the story of Job, chapter 38 reveals God's impatience with Job's manic depression, and the entire chapter serves as His chastisement. In the opening verses, there is another mention of the sons of God, where once again there can be no mistaking them for anything other than angels.

> ***Then the Lord answered Job out of the whirlwind, and said,***
>
> ***Who is this that darkeneth counsel by words without knowledge?***
>
> ***Gird up now thy loins like a man; for I will demand of thee, and answer thou me.***
>
> ***Where wast thou when I laid the foundations of the earth? declare, if thou hast understanding.***

Avoiding rabbit holes that would make this chapter too long, it is important to note something I pointed out in the last book: "in the beginning" cannot refer to the beginning of all things, since the angels were clearly created before the existence of the earth (verse 4). Genesis 1:1 marks the beginning of our story on the earth, not the beginning of everything. See *Unger's Commentary on the Old Testament* for Genesis 1. Dr. Unger's perspective on this was a turning point in my life that brought me closer to God. In the beginning, God reset the clock of the earth by setting it into orbital motion (Genesis 1:14). God has no beginning or end and is not affected by time. "In the beginning" indicates a starting point in time. If God exists outside of time, Genesis 1:1 is a brief narrative of how God reset the earth's clock. "In the beginning" is how our story begins, not God's!

These "sons of God" in Job 38:7 are the same as those in Genesis 6:2. Some of the Genesis 6:2 sons of God may have been among those shouting for joy, since that time precedes the war with God. The sons of God in Genesis 6:2 are among those who fell with Lucifer and attempted to prevent the arrival of the Messiah by contaminating the genetics of mankind. The sons of God in Job 1 also fell with Lucifer, but they were not incarcerated with the Genesis 6 rebels if they were roaming the earth with Satan. Some of the sons of God in the book of Job are still roaming the earth today under their respective spiritual principalities (Ephesians 3:10, 6:12; 1 Peter 3:22; Colossians 1:16, 2:15).

Yet another argument suggests that the sons of God in Genesis 6 cannot be angels because of Matthew 22:30, where Yehshua says our resurrected bodies will be like the angels, who neither marry nor are given in marriage. While this is obviously true because it is spoken by Yehshua, there is evidence that at least some angels, both past and present, have the ability to produce offspring. Remember that there are likely billions of angels of varying rank and power. Some of these were known to have existed in ancient Sumeria and were worshipped as gods. Yehshua is specific when He says "angels in heaven," who, no matter what abilities they have, are obedient to God. The evidence for this can be found in Jude 1:6 (KJV):

> ***And the angels which kept not their first estate, but left their own habitation, he hath reserved in everlasting chains under darkness unto the judgment of the great day.***

Consulting scholarly commentaries on this subject is frustrating because they often defer to the Sethite theory to protect the perceived purity of all angels, even though we know that one-third of heaven rebelled and fell with lucifer. To point out briefly, the word *habitation* in Greek—*oikētērion*—translates as a dwelling or residence, typically assumed to be celestial or heavenly. It also carries a deeper meaning, referring to how the body serves as the abode for the spirit.

<u>STRONGS NT 3613: οἰκητήριον</u>

οἰκητήριον, ὀικητηριου, τό (ὀικητήρ), a dwelling-place, habitation: ***<u>Jude 1:6; of the body as the dwelling-place of the spirit</u>***, 2 Corinthians 5:2 (2 Macc. 11:2; 3Macc. 2:15; (Josephus, contra Apion 1, 20, 7); Euripides, Plutarch, Cebes () tab. 17).

Notice the reference there to 2 Corinthians 5:2 (KJV), where the word is used by Paul as follows:

> ***For in this we groan, earnestly desiring to be clothed upon with our house*** (<u>oikētērion</u>) ***which is from heaven.***

This refers to the body as a dwelling place for the spirit. In my last book, *The Bride, the Wise Virgins and the Last Adam,* I referenced portions of the book of Enoch several times. I know this is risky and refrain from referencing the latter sections, which are more questionable in their authenticity, but I think it is a catastrophic mistake to toss the book out in its entirety, knowing that it was canonized in the Bible used by the apostles. Remember, in chapter 17, verse 1, Enoch states:

> ***And they took me to a place where they were like burning fire, and, when they wished, they made themselves look like men.***

Enoch had been in the company of angels, but these were distinctively different, possessing the ability to morph into a human physical appearance. I believe there is plenty of evidence that fallen angels have interacted with mankind over the millennia in intimate ways, and many of these were the sons of God mentioned in Genesis 6. While they may have experienced some pleasure from their disobedience, I doubt that was the sole purpose of their rebellion. The purpose of the event that led to the hybridized, half-breed giant Nephilim was an act of war in response to Genesis 3:15. To remain ignorant of this fact places crippling limitations on our spirituality and understanding of the supernatural realm, where spiritual entities are still at war with God and all who worship Him.

As an example, I have hypothesized that the entity of Babylon (or the spirit Babalon of the occult) had the ability to morph into both male and female human form for the purpose of deception. In Jonathan Cahn's *Return of the Gods,* he illustrates the intensity with which spiritual warfare and deception have increased in recent history. I am well into my sixties, and my great-grandparents were born during the industrial revolution when society quickly leaped from horses and carriages to automobiles. The electrification of the earth at the end of the nineteenth century introduced technology that seemed otherworldly to my grandparents. They would sit around a radio that picked up signals from far away, hearing a person's voice coming out of a box. Very soon, that person's face could be seen and heard speaking on another box. Then telephones made their way into households across the nation and eventually the world. For six thousand years, only crude options existed for transportation and communication. Suddenly, in the last 125 years, even the poorest people in third-world countries have handheld microwave cellular telephones that also function as computing machines and television screens—devices that only decades ago would have required a 1,000-square-foot building filled with computer equipment and radio transmitters.

This is the return of the gods and their influence on mankind, aimed at man's ultimate destruction. Based on historical evidence, not all these gods are limited to morphing only into men. The Babalon spirit, which pervades the minds of both men and women and causes sexual confusion, is at least one of these so-called gods. Worshippers of this spirit even call her by the same name used in the book of Revelation—the great harlot.

An occult symbol still in use today, which we must be aware of and understand more fully, is the Egyptian obelisk. The obelisk is one of the most obvious symbols used by the Freemasons and has ancient roots tied to its meaning. As with most relics, one of the best ways to uncover their origins is through the etymology of the name itself.

The word *obelisk* comes from the Greek *obelískos*, a diminutive of *obelós*, meaning "pointed shaft." The Egyptian word for the obelisk was *tekhenu*, translated as "to pierce." One of the most difficult tasks in studying history is sorting through the distortions of Egyptology, which often have little to no basis in truth. The most powerful occult secret societies in the world today worship the same gods as the ancient Egyptians. Yet some older studies of history are far more reliable and can be valuable in deciphering modern deceptions to find the real story. One such resource is a book written by John Weisse titled *The Obelisk and Freemasonry*, preserved in the Cornell University Library.

In John Weisse's book, he does not appear overly critical of Freemasonry; rather, he focuses on tracing the history of the secret society. Weisse considers Freemasonry to be far older than is generally assumed, possibly going back to the days of the Sethites and even Seth himself.

Weisse states that Freemasonry was the society of princes and magnates in ancient history, carried forward by covert operatives who continue to guard their ancient secrets and occult rituals under oaths of death or suicide should they be found sharing secrets with the uninitiated. This secret society remains incredibly powerful today, as evidenced by the fact that every powerful influential figure today—including presidents, kings, popes, and corporate executives of global significance—are Freemasons.

The obelisk is an Egyptian artifact with origins attributed by Egyptologists to the earliest dynasties of Egypt, with the oldest examples dating prior to 3200 BC. As I have stated in previous publications, I hold to a literal interpretation of the Bible as the best safeguard against deception. Taken literally, the Bible's well-defined timelines indicate that the predynastic and early dynastic periods of Egypt began shortly after the flood of Noah, not before.

Using the biblical timeline, the flood occurred around 2350 BC. So, who are the Egyptians?

The sons of Ham were Cush, Mizraim, Put, and Canaan. (Genesis 10:6 KJV)

When you see the suffix *-im* in Hebrew, after a word such as "Mizraim," it indicates a plural use of the word. You'll probably screen it as I did for further investigation.

Strong's Exhaustive Concordance

Egypt, Egyptians, Mizraim

Dual of <u>matsowr</u>; Mitsrajim, i.e. Upper and Lower Egypt -- Egypt, Egyptians, Mizraim.

*<u>**Word Origin**</u>: Derived from the name of a son of Ham, מִצְרַיִם (Mitsrayim), who is traditionally considered the ancestor of the Egyptians.*

Well, that's interesting. Ham was Mizraim's father. In the 1960 Reina Valera Spanish version of the King James, I found it interesting that *Ham* is translated as "Cam." Even more interesting is an investigation into Ham.

International Standard Bible Encyclopedia

HAM (1)

ham (cham; Cham):

2. Ham as a Nationality:

The name given, in <u>Psalm 105:23, 17</u>; <u>Psalm 106:22</u>
(compare 78:51), to Egypt as a descendant of Ham,
son of Noah. As Shem means «dusky,» or the like, and
Japheth «fair,» it has been supposed that Ham meant,
as is not improbable, «black.» This is supported by
the evidence of Hebrew and Arabic, in which the word
chamam means «to be hot» and «to be black,» the latter
signification being derived from the former.

3. Meaning of the Word:

That Ham is connected with the native name of Egypt,
Kem, or, in full pa ta› en Kem, «the land of Egypt,» in
Bashmurian Coptic Kheme, is unlikely, as this form
is probably of a much later date than the composition
of Genesis, and, moreover, as the Arabic shows, the
guttural is not a true kh, but the hard breathing h, which
are both represented by the Hebrew cheth.

I thank God for great resources like the *International Standard Bible Encyclopedia*. It seems the Egyptologists tripped on something biblical and never knew it, or perhaps they knew and chose to hide it? Ham is

Khem, the father of Mizraim (the Egyptians). Egyptologists identify the earliest Egyptians as the Khemites, yet they fail to associate Khem with Ham of the Bible. For those who know their Bible, this connection makes perfect sense. This fact also places the existence of the earliest Egyptians after the birth of Mizraim, which was obviously after the flood. The earliest Egyptian dynasties could not have existed prior to the flood if the first Egyptians were born after the flood and named after a descendant of Noah.

I believe this deception is one of many designed to hide the existence of the sons of God and their offspring, who provoked the catastrophic deluge. The pyramids were built by superhuman Nephilim hybrids before the flood, not by slaves wielding copper hammers and chisels—that explanation makes no sense. The critical thinker in me ("those who are led by the Spirit of God") questions most of the claims of Egyptology, especially those concerning architecture and technology in ancient Egypt, which appear far superior when the earth was sparsely populated by first-generation flood survivors. Did Noah carry high-tech laser stone-shaping equipment on the ark? The idea is ludicrous.

The more modern, post-flood obelisks are made of sandstone, and although sandstone is much easier to cut and shape, the details found in these obelisks are far less impressive than those carved from the much older syenite stone. Syenite, a type of granite absent of quartz, takes its name from the region of Syene in Egypt, where it was quarried. Syenite is incredibly hard to cut and engrave, yet the detail in the older syenite engravings is far superior to the later sandstone obelisks. In addition, magnification reveals that the cutting tools used on these syenite obelisks scarcely find comparison even today, in an age that has sent highly polished glass optical telescopes into outer space with jet propulsion. I find this amazing, yet Egyptologists too easily dismiss it, offering explanations that made metals softer than syenite were the tools employed. I was born at night, but not last night—the explanations of Egyptologists are not logical.

What does make sense is that many of these obelisks, and also the pyramids, were constructed before the flood of Noah with the help of the "gods" (sons of God or fallen angels) prior to their imprisonment. These were the *bene-ha-elohim*, the sons of God of Genesis 6. While their hybridized human offspring likely performed the heavy lifting, the masterminds behind Egyptian architecture and artifacts were not of human origin.

John Weisse alludes to this in his book, stating that the obelisks were intended to honor the gods. Honor them how? As is often the case, the name itself provides a clue. *Tekhen*, meaning "to pierce," points in the right direction, though it is not the complete answer.

A Bible researcher named Dr. Cathy Burns, whose degree is in Bible Philosophy, published *Masonic and Occult Symbols Illustrated* (1998). Dr. Burns wrote a variety of controversial books, and I am certain the one I just mentioned is among them. In it, Dr. Burns points out that the obelisk is a phallic symbol in Freemasonry, and that fertility symbols are common within Freemasonry, even the square and compass, which she argues is in reality a diagram of sexual nature referencing the "generative principle." This generative principle is something holy to Freemasons and is found throughout Masonic architecture.

The symbol of the *tekhen* (obelisk) commemorated the event described by Enoch in chapter 6, verses 4–6, as follows:

> *"Let us all swear an oath, and all bind ourselves by*
> *mutual imprecations not to abandon this plan but to*
> *do this thing." Then sware they all together and bound*
> *themselves by mutual imprecations upon it. And they*
> *were in all two hundred; who descended [in the days] of*
> ***Jared*** *on the summit of Mount Hermon, and they called*
> *it Mount Hermon, because they had sworn and bound*
> *themselves by mutual imprecations upon it.*

The "days of Jared" were the days of Enoch's father, Jared (Genesis 5:18). Mount Hermon is where the rebellion escalated, when the "sons of God took for themselves wives of all which they chose" (Genesis 6:2). It was during the time of Enoch's father Jared that this Genesis 6:2 event occurred. After the flood, Nimrod built a monument to these fallen angels right there on the same Mount Hermon, which has since become a tourist attraction.

The obelisk was the phallic symbol that commemorated the rebellion, when these fallen angels transformed themselves into men, took wives of all whom they chose, and illegally spawned the hybrid angel-human Nephilim giants of Genesis 6:4. Though later obelisks were dedicated to Ra the sun god, Osiris, and or other deities, their origin lay in honoring the "sons of God" of Genesis chapter 6. They believed that by abandoning their first habitation, as mentioned by Jude and Peter, they had won the battle against God and that there could be no Messiah as a result of their act of defiance. Yet there was one who was perfect in his generations—dear God, thank You for Noah (Genesis 6:9)!

The Genesis 6 sons of God committed atrocities for which they have no hope of salvation and are eternally condemned. This is why God repented of having created man (Genesis 6:6). Man's salvation was planned before the foundations of the world (Ephesians 1:4), but the fallen angels were irrevocably condemned to everlasting fire (Matthew 25:41). It seems possible that whatever caused the fall of Lucifer might not have immediately condemned those who followed him, until this event and the escalation of war. In any case, they gave up their first estate and left their own habitation. All that was rightfully theirs as the "sons of God" was lost.

And the angels which kept not their first estate, but left their own habitation, he hath reserved in everlasting chains under darkness unto the judgment of the great day. (Jude 1:6 KJV)

I believe the angels abandoning their estates and leaving their habitations (sons of God bodies) were two separate events. Departing from their heavenly bodies compromised their legal rights to their heavenly estates. By leaving their habitations and becoming as men, taking wives of their choosing from among the daughters of men, they believed they could defeat God's Messianic plan and retain a legal claim to their heavenly estates by winning the war through this strategy.

The Egyptian obelisk is the most obvious symbol of the Freemasons, a monument honoring the rebellion in which the sons of God left their own habitation, took wives of all whom they chose, and corrupted human DNA. The Freemasons know precisely what the obelisk represents; they are not ignorant of their own symbolic relics. When you see an obelisk, it is a signpost placed to honor fallen gods in their rebellion against the Most-High. It has no other meaning or purpose. It is a marker dedicating structures or entire cities to the fallen angels. An obelisk signifies a physical location where spiritual warfare follows, serving as a territorial marker consecrated to the fallen sons of God.

The Roman Catholic Church took extreme measures to transport an obelisk from Heliopolis to Rome, placing it before St. Peter's dome. The dome represents an impregnated Semiramis, mother and wife of Nimrod. The obelisk later became the phallic symbol of Nimrod, who was believed to be eternally incarnated in the sun. These are post-flood representations whose origins trace back to Mount Hermon in the days of Jared. According to the Freemasons, who claim lineage reaching back to Cain, at least thirteen Egyptian obelisks stand in Rome, each marking something once dedicated to "the gods," whom we know as the Genesis 6:2 "sons of God." While their meaning may have shifted in post-flood times, their origins began with the Genesis 6 event.

The Washington Monument obelisk stands before the Capitol building with the same symbology, positioned in front of the dome representing the impregnated Semiramis. Beneath the monument are additional generative principle symbols associated with its design.

I highly recommend a book by the late pastor Tom Horn titled *Zeitgeist 2025* as a fascinating and intensely informative research material on this subject. If you are interested in further edification, Tom Horn's research is truly amazing.

The twin obelisks known as Cleopatra's Needles were transported from Heliopolis, Egypt, to New York and London. The obelisk of Theodosius was shipped from Karnak, Egypt, to Istanbul, where it was placed over the remains of the hippodrome in Sultanahmet Square, at the center of the former Constantinople. The Luxor obelisk in Paris was taken from the Temple Aman-Ra in the city of Luxor, Egypt. In the 1830s, one of the two obelisks at the temple was gifted to Paris, France, by the viceroy of Egypt at the time.

I could go on with this, but I want to make an important point about these obelisks. The most important Egyptian obelisks of religious significance—most originating from Heliopolis—have been transported to major cities across the world. Every major city has an obelisk placed in a strategically important location, and the most notable of these came directly from Egypt. Many obelisks are not of Egyptian origin and were made at later dates, but their spiritual significance remains unchanged. They serve as territorial markers for spiritual principalities. The Freemasons are behind this and know exactly what they have done and continue to do. These phallic symbols honor the sons of God who took wives of all whom they chose in rebellion against God, and they mark cities and governments as dedicated to the fallen sons of God. Every city and government that allows these symbols to remain has legally subjected itself to fallen angel influence and authority under Satan—the principalities described in Ephesians 6. Pastor Tom Horn explains this better than I do in his book *Zeitgeist 2025*.

What does God say about obelisks?

You are not to make worthless idols, images, or pillars
for yourselves, nor set up for yourselves carved images
to bow down to them in the land, because I am the Lord
your God. (Leviticus 26:1 ISV)

If this was written for the benefit of the Hebrews who spent four hundred years in Egypt, might these pillars have been obelisks? Many scholars and translators insist that the word *obelisk* does not appear in the Masoretic texts. Well, that makes perfect sense, since *obelisk* is not a Hebrew word. Even I can understand that without a PhD. So what is it, then, that translates from Hebrew as a "sacred pillar"? Here are various translations from 2 Kings 10:26:

> *And they brought forth the images out of the house of*
> *Baal, and burned them. (KJV)*
>
> *They brought out the memorial stones of the house of*
> *Baal and burned them. (NASB)*
>
> *From which they brought out the sacred pillars and*
> *burned them. (ISV)*
>
> *They brought out the sacred pillars (obelisks) of the*
> *house of Baal and burned them. (AMP)*

How grateful I am for the AMP translation. How did the Amplified Bible translators arrive at *obelisk*, a Greek word and not Hebrew? Because that is what the sacred pillars were—obelisks. The *sacred pillars* (ISV) were *memorial stones* (NASB), figures of *images* (KJV), iconic phallic symbols of fallen angels in the house, the temple of Baal, that God despises the sight of—and so should we! The Israelites were instructed to destroy them!

Now remember: the obelisk at St. Peter's Basilica was shipped from Heliopolis, Egypt. My goodness! You can't make this up! Read Jeremiah 43:13 in the various translations:

> *He shall break also the images of Bethshemesh, that is*
> *in the land of Egypt; and the houses of the gods of the*
> *Egyptians shall he burn with fire. (KJV)*
>
> *He will also smash to pieces the obelisks of **Heliopolis**,*
> *which is in the land of Egypt; and the temples of the*
> *gods of Egypt he will burn with fire. (NASB)*
>
> *He will shatter the pillars of **Heliopolis** in the land of*
> *Egypt and will burn the temples of the gods of Egypt*
> *with fire. (ISV)*

The sacred pillars—obelisks transported around the world from *Heliopolis*—are phallic symbols (images in the KJV), stone memorials honoring the sons of God all the way back to Genesis 6, long before the flood. The sacred pillars not destroyed by Nebuchadnezzar or the Israelites will be destroyed by God, or perhaps this will be one of the tasks of the two witnesses of Revelation 11. These territorial markers are an abomination to God and will soon be destroyed into pieces and, according to the Bible, incinerated. In case you might be wondering, syenite begins to melt at around 2,500°F. I'm not sure when God plans to fulfill His promise to burn these temples, but I am sure I don't want to be present when He does.

It is by knowing the truth of history—free from deception—that we identify the true enemies of God. History records many fallen empires that collapsed because they failed to recognize their adversaries. The Freemasons are God's enemies, Satan's operatives on earth, striving to undermine the Bride and her destiny by any means possible. Is this what Revelation 3:11 (KJV) refers to?

The gods of Egypt were the same gods of Sumeria, Babylon and the deities of Rome. Through Rome they were dispersed around the world. Some of these were the sons of God who swore an oath against God on Mount Hermon according to Enoch, vowing to take the daughters of men as wives—all of whom they chose. The sons of God in Genesis 6 sealed their destiny to eternal fire (Matthew 25:41) and forfeited their first estate (Jude 1:6). That estate now lies in limbo, awaiting the manifestation of their replacements—the sons of God led by the Spirit of God—to be revealed (Romans 8:19).

Not all the fallen angels were responsible for the Genesis 6 catastrophe, and not all are bound in chains. Some still operate under Lucifer's authority as the princes of darkness in the spiritual realms Paul describes in Ephesians 6. The sons of God who committed the atrocities of Genesis 6, along with others involved in similar acts after the flood, are bound in chains. Yet those who continue to operate in the spiritual realm today are the ones mentioned in Job 1 and elsewhere. It is against these sons of God that we remain at war. The obelisk stands as a monument to their fallen counterparts, still celebrated as heroes within the Freemason hierarchy, as well as the Vatican. I believe one of the objectives of the CERN project in Europe is to open a portal that could release these fallen angels from wherever they have been imprisoned. I also believe this was Nimrod's objective with the Tower of Babel. Nimrod was the builder, not the architect. The Egyptian pre-flood pyramids likely shared the same architects as the Tower of Babel.

I often wonder if it is possible to know God as intimately as we desire without also knowing His enemies? If we choose to be ignorant of God's adversaries, we fail to understand that they are also our adversaries. In doing so, we operate within a false paradigm, lacking true spirituality and leaving ourselves completely vulnerable to the schemes of the enemy. I hope this first chapter has answered that question for you. Not all of God's enemies have been imprisoned; many continue to fight against us today, as Paul reminds us in Ephesians 6.

CHAPTER 2

Who Are the Sons of God Today?

Put on the whole armour of God, that ye may be able to stand against the wiles of the devil.

For we wrestle not against flesh and blood, but against principalities, against powers, against the rulers of the darkness of this world, against spiritual wickedness in high places.

—Ephesians 6:11-12 (KJV)

Most people assume that verse 12 refers entirely to the demonic realm. In my previous book, I explained that demons came into existence illegally as the cursed offspring of an act of defiance against God. The angels who left their own habitations (Jude 1:6) and are bound in chains (2 Peter 2:4) were the fathers of the demons that still roam the earth today. Though once powerful entities and regarded as gods in the ancient world, they are now locked away, awaiting their final judgment (Matthew 25:41). According to the account of Enoch, only two hundred angels agreed together to rebel against God by contaminating the human genome. Other groups of fallen angels were not part of that illegal act and were not imprisoned. They remain enemies of God, but those not bound in chains continue to operate under Lucifer's authority, as seen in the book of Job long after the Genesis 6 event. If all had been bound, there could be no princes commanding principalities in the spiritual realm.

The book of Job serves as a post-flood documentary. The angels who corrupted the DNA of mankind and caused the flood are those bound in chains, as Peter describes in 2 Peter 2:4. I have many reasons for believing that demons cannot be princes. Not all fallen angels have been imprisoned—only those who crossed the line by committing the illegal acts of creating confusion between species. Their objective is to influence mankind to condemn himself and fall under Satan's authority by opposing God. Those who follow Satan become the sons of disobedience, destined to die with the prince of death.

Several cases can be made for what I am suggesting, and perhaps the strongest case is found in Daniel 10, during the third appearance of an angel to Daniel. Beginning with verse 10:

> *Then behold, a hand touched me and shook me on my hands and knees. And he said to me, "Daniel, you who are treasured, understand the words that I am about to tell you and stand at your place, for I have now been sent to you." And when he had spoken this word to me, I stood up trembling. Then he said to me, "Do not be afraid, Daniel, for from the first day that you set your heart on understanding this and on humbling yourself before your God, your words were heard, and I have come in response to your words. But the prince of the kingdom of Persia was standing in my way for twenty-one days; then behold, Michael, one of the chief princes, came to help me, for I had been left there with the kings of Persia. Now I have come to explain to you what will happen to your people in the latter days, because the vision pertains to the days still future."*

> *When he had spoken to me according to these words, I turned my face toward the ground and became speechless. And behold, one who resembled a human was touching my lips. Then I opened my mouth and spoke and said to him who was standing before me, "My lord, due to the vision anguish has come upon me, and I have retained no strength. For how can such a*

*servant of my lord talk with such as my lord? As for
me, there remains just now no strength in me, nor has
any breath been left in me."*

*Then this one with human appearance touched me
again and strengthened me. And he said, "You who
are treasured, do not be afraid. Peace be to you; take
courage and be courageous!" Now as soon as he spoke
to me, I felt strengthened and said, "May my lord
speak, for you have strengthened me." Then he said,
"Do you understand why I came to you? But I shall
now return to fight against the prince of Persia; so I
am leaving, and behold, the prince of Greece is about
to come. However, I will tell you what is recorded in the
writing of truth. Yet there is no one who stands firmly
with me against these forces except Michael your
prince.*

Daniel was praying and fasting over a dream for twenty-one days
when the angel finally appeared and stated that he had been detained by the
"prince of Persia." The "prince Michael" had to come and help open the
way for the angel to visit Daniel. It is assumed that this angel was Gabriel.
Whether or not it was Gabriel, his appearance was at first terrifying—
his face like lightning and his eyes like fire—possibly indicating that he
had arrived directly from the throne of God, still radiating from God's
presence.

If indeed it was Gabriel, we know he is a powerful angel. So how
powerful must the prince of Persia have been to detain such a warrior for
three weeks, until Michael himself intervened? The prince of Persia, with
that kind of authority, cannot possibly be a disembodied human-hybrid
Nephilim demon. In fact, based on this passage alone, I do not believe it
is possible—or even legal—for a demon to hold the title of "prince." *That
title is reserved for the sons of God, not their illegal hybrid offspring!*

Also note in verse 20 that the angel states he himself is fighting against the prince of Persia, not only Michael. This indicates that he is a high-ranking angel from the armies of God. Yet the prince of Persia proved more powerful than this warring angel without Michael's help. And because the angel was returning to fight, another fallen angel—the "prince of Greece"—was coming to assist the prince of Persia. There are princes under God's authority, such as Gabriel and Michael, and princes under Satan's authority, such as the princes of Persia and Greece. Satan's princes are fallen angels. Demons cannot be princes. What demon could withstand the divine power of Gabriel? None. The princes of darkness are the fallen sons of God who followed Lucifer but are not bound in chains.

Notice something equally important to understand in verse 21: "I will tell you what is recorded in the writing of truth." This is not referring to the Word of God in the canonized Bible that Daniel may have had access to at the time. Rather, this is referring to a written decree issued from the throne of God concerning the Jewish people—Daniel's dream that drove him to prayer and fasting. This prophetic vision would cover the time of the Greek Empire under Antiochus of Epiphanes, the Maccabean revolt, and all the way to the end times and the period of Jacob's Trouble (tribulation). The spiritual warfare between the evil princes of Persia and Greece and the warring princes of God was due to an attempt to prevent Daniel's dream from being documented as official prophecy. Yet what God decrees in heaven will come to pass on earth (Matthew 18:18). This is a royal chain of custody: from the throne of God, to Daniel the servant, and finally into the canonized Word of God on earth—the Holy Bible. If the princes could have prevented Daniel's vision from being written, they might have legally prevented it from occurring, since it specifically relates to their own demise!

Obviously, the princes (fallen angels) at war with Gabriel and Michael were not in chains. They are still at war with God until His final judgment sends them into the everlasting fire. These dark "princes" are also the "sons of God" not bound in chains, revealed in Scripture as adversaries striving against God throughout human history, attempting to alter His plan. Tireless in their work, they labor to secure our demise. The flood of

Noah marks a general dividing line between those sons of God who are bound in chains, and those sons of God found here in Daniel, Job, and elsewhere.

The fallen angel sons of God who "saw the daughters of men were fair, and took for themselves wives all of which they chose," thereby fathering the Nephilim race of giants and provoking God to destroy the earth by flood, are *those now bound in chains*. Not all are bound, but all are condemned as adversaries of God and mankind.

How many are there, and where are they now? The account of Nimrod and the Tower of Babel contains a multitude of mysteries. One of these mysteries concerns the identity of the Sumerian and Babylonian gods. They were fallen angels, sons of God, though not the same ones who rebelled in Genesis 6. However, some of them, I believe, were imprisoned after the flood for similar transgressions. I strongly suspect that the four angels bound beneath the Euphrates (Revelation 9:14) were princes over four of the five cities of the Jordan plain—Sodom, Gomorrah, Admah, and Zeboim—while Zoar was spared.

In fact, I have compiled a study connecting these angels beneath the Euphrates to the events in Sodom and Gomorrah. I will return to this subject and share that connection in detail.

The point I wanted to make is there are seventy nations after the descendants of Noah listed in Genesis 10. In verses 5, 20, and 31, each conclude with the phrase "and these are the sons of (Shem, Japeth, Ham)... after their tongues, families and nations." Each branch of Noah's three sons produced its own languages and nations—seventy in total. Chapter 11, verse 1 states "And the earth was of one language and one speech." This suggests that chapters 10 and 11 are intentionally reversed chronologically to emphasize the events caused by Nimrod, who came from the line of Ham.

Chapter 10 becomes clearer when we understand that the division of nations and languages occurred after the Tower of Babel. When God destroyed the tower and scattered the peoples, He divided them according to the genealogies recorded in Genesis 10, through the three sons of Noah. The final count was seventy nations, corresponding to the living heirs of

Noah at that time. For example, Genesis 10:22 names Elam as a son of Shem, receiving his respective nation and language. Likewise, Genesis 10:2 names Javan as a son of Japeth, also receiving his nation and language.

Here is Javan from Biblegateway.com:

> *JAVAN jă' vən (יָוָן, LXX Ἰωυαν, meaning uncertain). Fourth son of Japheth, father of Elishah, Tarshish, Kittim and Rodanim (KJV Dodanim) (Gen 10:2, 4; 1 Chron 1:5, 7).*
>
> *1. The name corresponds etymologically to Ionia (old Gr. Ἰαλων). As such it is used in the prophets to denote the descendants of Javan in Ionia proper (W coast of Asia Minor) but also in **Greece and Macedonia**.*

> ***Elam from the Topical Encyclopedia:***
>
> ***Biblical References:***
>
> *1. Genesis 10:22 · Elam is first mentioned in the Table of Nations as one of the sons of Shem, making the Elamites Semitic people. «The sons of Shem: Elam, Asshur, Arphaxad, Lud, and Aram.»*
>
> *The Multitude of Elam refers to the people and descendants of Elam, a significant ancient civilization located in what is now southwestern **Iran**. Elam is frequently mentioned in the Bible, often in the context of prophecy and judgment. The Elamites were known for their influence and interactions with the Israelites and other neighboring nations.*

Elam equals Persia, which is Iran today. By the time of Daniel, the nation of the Elamites had fallen and was integrated into the Persian Empire. Returning to Daniel 10, we see that the princes of Persia and Greece were assigned by Satan to the nations of Elam and Javan, descendants of Noah listed in Genesis 10. If there were seventy nations under Noah and his sons, then there were at least seventy princes (sons of God or fallen angels) appointed over each of those descendants and their respective nations, constantly fighting with God's army of angels for control. Yet all of this unfolds under God's total and ultimate sovereignty.

In fact, I believe God allows this conflict to prove His sovereignty. These fallen "princes" have no hope of success against God, but this silliness proves His ruling authority to every angel throughout the universe. Where the Bible references "princes," I believe we can understand them in military terms—as generals commanding vast ranks of spiritual officers and soldiers. This is how we should perceive spiritual warfare: in military terms, with God as the Judge and Mediator, placing limits on spiritual combat much like the Geneva Convention or international tribunals place limits on earthly war. Just as war criminals are imprisoned under internationally agreed limitations and guidelines, I believe this is similar to what happened to many of the fallen angels that are "bound in chains" and the reason they exchanged an oath between themselves on Mount Hermon. It would take all of them by their calculations (or miscalculations) to succeed in contaminating the human genome pool, thus preventing the arrival of the Messiah.

The angels Gabriel and Michael are both princes—or generals for the good team. Notice that Gabriel (or the angel in Daniel 10) spoke of "prince" in the singular, not plural. This suggests that there is one prince, one general, assigned over each of the seventy nations and tongues.

On that basis, I want to go back to the incredible and amazing book of Job (KJV), beginning with chapters 1 and 2, and make some important observations that still apply today.

> *There was a man in the land of Uz, whose name was Job; and that man was perfect and upright, and one that feared God, and eschewed evil.*
>
> *And there were born unto him seven sons and three daughters.*

Nearly every Christian knows the story of Job—or should. When the struggles of life hit us like a train wreck, there is always someone ready to remind us of Job, insisting that testing our faith is necessary. There is always a loving Christian around to tell us all the things we do not want to hear when we're in a state of depression and enduring harsh circumstances. I don't want to bore you with another sermon you've already heard on multiple occasions. I merely want to point out a few things we might have missed from the spiritually dead pulpits of the modern church.

Chapter 1 begins by describing Job's blessings. He is the wealthiest man "in the east." Then the narrative shifts to a vision of the throne room of God, where He reigns as the sole sovereign authority over everything, including Satan. The sons of God (*bene-ha-elohim*) arrive with Satan. These are fallen angels under Satan's authority. The chapter continues:

> *And the Lord said unto Satan, Hast thou considered*
> *my servant Job, that there is none like him in the earth,*
> *a perfect and an upright man, one that feareth God,*
> *and escheweth evil?*
>
> *Then Satan answered the Lord, and said, Doth Job fear*
> *God for nought?*
>
> *Hast not thou made an hedge about him, and about his*
> *house, and about all that he hath on every side? thou*
> *hast blessed the work of his hands, and his substance is*
> *increased in the land.*
>
> *But put forth thine hand now, and touch all that he*
> *hath, and he will curse thee to thy face.*
>
> *And the Lord said unto Satan, Behold, all that he hath*
> *is in thy power; only upon himself put not forth thine*
> *hand. So Satan went forth from the presence of the*
> *Lord.*

God Himself brings Satan's attention to Job, stating that Job is perfect, upright, loves God, and shuns evil—"there is none like him in the earth." This is an incredible statement. Satan replies by stating that Job isn't perfect, rather just overwhelmingly blessed. He argues that if Job is subjected to harsher circumstances, he would curse God.

So God allows this testing of Job to begin, and all hell breaks loose on Job:

> *And there was a day when his sons and his daughters*
> *were eating and drinking wine in their eldest brother›s*
> *house:*

And there came a messenger unto Job, and said, The oxen were plowing, and the asses feeding beside them:

And the Sabeans fell upon them, and took them away; yea, they have slain the servants with the edge of the sword; and I only am escaped alone to tell thee.

While he was yet speaking, there came also another, and said, The fire of God is fallen from heaven, and hath burned up the sheep, and the servants, and consumed them; and I only am escaped alone to tell thee.

While he was yet speaking, there came also another, and said, The Chaldeans made out three bands, and fell upon the camels, and have carried them away, yea, and slain the servants with the edge of the sword; and I only am escaped alone to tell thee.

In this passage, when the attacks on Job begin, the tribes of Sabeans and Chaldeans are the first to appear to do Satan's dirty work. There is much speculation about the book of Job—the period in which it was written, and whether it is allegory or a literal account—largely because of the rare poetic eloquence of its authorship. I believe that the Sabeans in verse 15 can clarify that the book is not only a literal account but also pinpoints the timing of Job's life in the time of Nimrod.

Most if those who have studied the book of Job assume that the land of Uz was in southern Arabia and that the Sabeans came from Sheba, also in Arabia. Even my esteemed mentor Chuck Missler held this view. I want to point out a few things you may find a bit boring, but I want to cover them while we're discussing the sons of God in the book of Job and how they continue to operate today. To do this, I need to break this down into smaller bites for clearer spiritual understanding, and I hope you find this as interesting as I did.

Let's start with a chart of the Table of Nations from Genesis 10:

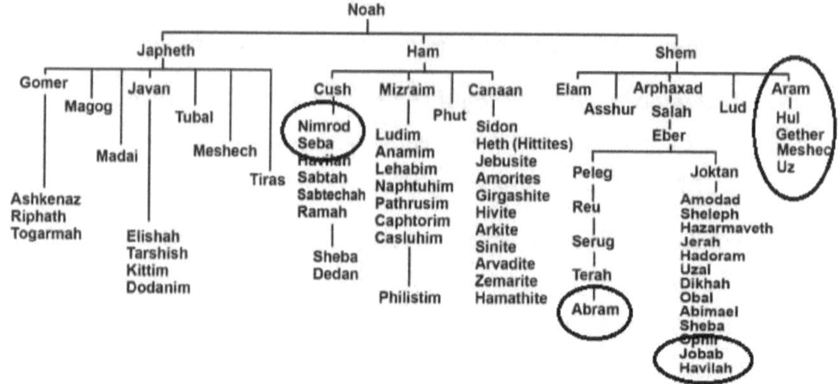

On the top right of the chart we find Uz, a son of Aram and grandson of Shem. The earth was divided among the three sons of Noah, and their seventy descendants populated it, each "after their families, after their tongues, in their lands, after their nations." Wherever the "land of Uz" was located, it lay within the territory of his father Aram's inheritance as a son of Shem.

I cannot overstate the importance of names in the Bible or the significance God places on them. In the case of Aram, the name proves to be foundational in the Bible. Here is what the *Encyclopedia of the Bible* has to say about Aram:

ARAM-NAHARAIM âr' əm nā' ə rā' əm (מְנַהֲרַיִם אֲרַם;
LXX Μεσοποταμίαν Συρίας, Aram of the two rivers;
occurs as Aram-naharaim in the title of <u>Psalm 60</u> and
as Mesopotamia in <u>Genesis 24:10</u>; <u>Deuteronomy 23:4</u>;
<u>Judges 3:8</u>, <u>10</u>; <u>1 Chronicles 19:6</u> in both KJV and
RSV. The area bounded by the upper Euphrates on
the W and the River Habur on the E and including the
city Haran where Terah settled after leaving Ur (<u>Gen</u>
<u>11:31</u>). It is the same area as Paddan-aram. It was the
place to which Abraham's servant went in search of a
wife for Isaac (<u>24:10</u>) and the home of Balaam the son
of Beor (<u>Deut 23:4</u>). After the death of Joshua, Israel
was delivered into the hands of Aram-naharaim for

*eight years (<u>Judg 3:8-10</u>) and the Ammonites later hired
horsemen and chariots from Aram-naharaim against
David (<u>1 Chron 19:6</u>; cf. title of <u>Ps 60</u>).*

Bibliography R. T. O'Callaghan, *Aram Naharaim*
(1948); in modern Heb., A. Malamat, *The Aramaeans in
Aram Naharaim and the Rise of Their States* (1952); M.
F. Unger, *Israel and the Aramaeans of Damascus* (1957).

The land of Aram encompasses all the territory between the Tigris
and Euphrates rivers. I find *The Book of Jubilees* a treasured resource,
and it saddens me that it is not more frequently referenced by renowned
scholars and Bible researchers. Take a look at what we can find plainly
spelled out in chapter 9:

> *And for Aram there came forth the fourth portion, all
> the land of Mesopotamia between the Tigris and the
> Euphrates to the north of the Chaldees to the border of
> the mountains of Asshur and the land of 'Arârâ.*[4]

This is what the inheritance of Aram looks like on the map:

---

4   The Book of Jubilees, chapter 9, trans. R. H. Charles. London [1917]

Map shared from Biblestudy.org

Everything within the green shaded line is within the territory allotted to Shem. Notice the placement of the Armenians. The Armenians are believed to have no direct relationship to the Arameans, but I find that difficult to accept, considering they carry the name of what may be their patriarchal father at the edge of his inheritance as declared by Noah. If traced far back in history, I am certain a distinct connection can be discovered.

The Land of Uz must have been situated within the territory allotted to him by his father Aram, not in southern Arabia. Refer to the Table of Nations chart again, if Jobab, the son of Joktan, is indeed Job from the book of Job, then Uz would have been Job's uncle. This interpretation makes far more sense, though it conflicts with later historical regions that, I believe, were shaped less by Noah's original divisions and more by wars and disputes over previously designated territories.

Here is another map from *Aramnahrin.org* that helps illustrate the point I wish to make regarding the Sabean-Chaldean connection:

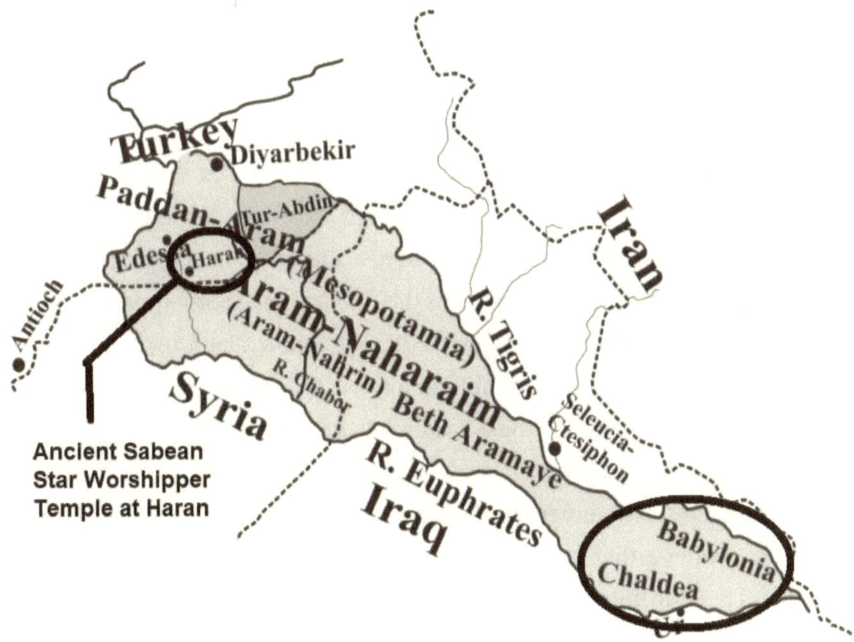

Refer again to the Table of Nations and note that Seba and Nimrod are brothers, both sons of Cush. All evil in the post-flood history of the world can be traced to this line of descendants from Ham and Cush. The post-flood Nephilim tribes, such as the Rephaim and others, are direct descendants of their lineages. I do not believe that the Sabeans who attacked Job in chapter 1, verse 15, were of the tribe of Sheba, a grandson of Cush. The Sheba tribe appears to have respected their inherited territory in Arabia, migrating southward from the north. History records them as a generally peaceful tribe of traders, making it difficult to associate them with anything graphically violent. The confusion regarding the Sabeans in Job 1:15 arises from the fact that the tribe of Sheba was also called "Sabeans."

If Jobab, son of Joktan, is indeed Job from the book of Job, he would have lived during the same period as Abraham. By this time, the kingdom of Babylon was thriving under Nimrod. To the northwest of Aram, between the Tigris and Euphrates, lies Haran, the place where Abraham departed with his father from Ur (Chaldea). I discovered something very interesting near Haran that connects the Sabeans from the tribe of Seba, brother of Nimrod, to this region near Haran.

A great article posted on the blog site Uncharted Ruins[5] shares a number of photos and information about the Sabian Star Worshipper Temples of Haran, located at Sogmatar about forty-five kilometers east. While I am reluctant to reproduce the author's images due to possible copyright concerns, I highly recommend reading through his very informative article and review the photos. Other archaeological studies conducted at the Sogmatar temples of the Sabian Star Worshippers suggest that the temples predate the flood and were reoccupied later by the Sabians. There is no archaeological or biblical evidence connecting these Sabians of Sogmatar near Haran to the Sabeans of the tribe of Sheba in southern Arabia. Likewise, the land of Uz would not have been in Arabia if Uz's father was Aram, who inherited the land between the Tigris and Euphrates. I strongly believe that these Sabians of Sogmatar are the same Sabeans of Job 1:15, from the tribe of Seba, brother of Nimrod and son of Cush, illegally occupying the land of Aram in its northern region.

The Sabeans and the Chaldeans were also present in the land of Uz, where Job lived. Judging by the vast numbers of livestock he owned, Job could have legally operated most or all of this land of Aram. The Chaldeans were essentially synonymous with the Babylonians, and both the Sabeans (from the tribe of Seba, Nimrod's brother) and the Chaldeans were within the kingdom of Nimrod. When God removed the hedge of angels from around Job's vast estate, the sons of God manipulated the minds of the Sabeans and Chaldeans to turn against Job. Some of the Sabeans likely traded in Babylon, a center of commerce in the land of Shinar, and shared much in common with the Chaldeans, being from a tribe whose father was Nimrod's brother. It stands to reason that Job, if indeed Jobab son of Joktan, probably lived somewhere between Babylon and Haran, between the two rivers in the land of Aram, father of Uz.

---

5   http://unchartedruins.blogspot.com/2012/08/the-hall-of-records-temple-of-seven.html

This is classic spiritual warfare that materially manifests though human actors. Let's take a leap forward into the New Testament in Matthew 16:16–23 (KJV):

He saith unto them, But whom say ye that I am?

And Simon Peter answered and said, Thou art the Christ, the Son of the living God.

And Jesus answered and said unto him, Blessed art thou, Simon Barjona: for flesh and blood hath not revealed it unto thee, but my Father which is in heaven.

And I say also unto thee, That thou art Peter, and upon this rock I will build my church; and the gates of hell shall not prevail against it.

And I will give unto thee the keys of the kingdom of heaven: and whatsoever thou shalt bind on earth shall be bound in heaven: and whatsoever thou shalt loose on earth shall be loosed in heaven.

Then charged he his disciples that they should tell no man that he was Jesus the Christ.

From that time forth began Jesus to shew unto his disciples, how that he must go unto Jerusalem, and suffer many things of the elders and chief priests and scribes, and be killed, and be raised again the third day.

Then Peter took him, and began to rebuke him, saying, Be it far from thee, Lord: this shall not be unto thee.

But he turned, and said unto Peter, Get thee behind me, Satan: thou art an offence unto me: for thou savourest not the things that be of God, but those that be of men.

Yehshua first blesses Peter, stating that his insight into who Yehshua truly is did not come from flesh and blood but from the Spirit of God

Himself. Then in the same passage, verses 22–23, Yehshua rebukes Peter and calls him Satan. On both occasions, Peter was speaking from spirits rather than his own thoughts. First, he spoke words of the Father, followed by the words of Satan—both coming from Peter's mouth, yet neither case originating from Peter himself. This is, at first, terrifying, but it explains Paul's detailed outline in Ephesians 6 regarding spiritual warfare. In this case, the helmet of salvation protects against Satan's manipulations, preventing them from entering our minds.

This is one example of the many powers the fallen sons of God use against us, and it is precisely how they attacked Job by influencing their own subjects. The Sabeans and Chaldeans were worshippers of false gods (sons of God/fallen angels) and could be manipulated through dreams or thoughts. The sons of God left the throne room of God with Satan, and the attacks began with the Sabeans and Chaldeans, operatives of Satan under Nimrod's fallen-angel-worshipping empire. But it doesn't end there.

In chapter 2, the attacks continue, and Job is stricken with boils from head to toe. His wife and friends beg him to curse God and die. The thoughts of everyone around Job are manipulated by the fallen sons of God, just as they had influenced the Sabeans and Chaldeans. How does this process begin? It began in the throne room of God with Satan's accusations: if God removed Job's blessings, Job would curse Him. Satan alleged that if everything were taken from Job, he would curse God. Instead, Job fell on his face and worshipped God. After failing in the first attempt, Satan formulated new accusations—that if Job's body were afflicted, he would surely curse God. Yet Job's response, though confused, was again to worship God.

A word study of the names *Satan* and *devil* quickly reflects what happened in the throne room when Satan accused Job. According to the *Online Etymology Dictionary*[6]:

Satan (n.)

____

6   www.etymonline.com

proper name of the supreme evil spirit and great adversary of humanity in Christianity, Old English Satan, from Late Latin Satan (in Vulgate in the Old Testament only), from Greek Satanas, from Hebrew satan "adversary, one who plots against another," from satan "to show enmity to, oppose, plot against," from root s-t-n "one who opposes, obstructs, or acts as an adversary."

In the Septuagint usually translated into Greek as diabolos "slanderer," literally "one who throws (something) across" the path of another (see <u>devil</u> (n.)), though epiboulos "plotter" is once used.

devil (n.)

The Late Latin word is from Ecclesiastical Greek diabolos, which in Jewish and Christian use was "the Devil, Satan," and which in general use meant **<u>"accuser, slanderer" (thus it was a scriptural loan-translation of Hebrew satan; see Satan). It is an agent noun from Greek diaballein "to slander, attack,"</u>** *literally "to throw across," from dia "across, through" (see <u>dia-</u>) + ballein "to throw" (from PIE root <u>*gwele-</u> "to throw, reach").*

In these lessons on spiritual warfare, the most important truth we can learn is that an enemy works against us day and night, accusing and slandering—the "accuser of the brethren" in Revelation 12:10—sometimes gaining permission from God to test his accusations. However, I also believe the story of Job is an exception rather than the rule. I believe that the rule is that as long as we remain obedient, Satan has no legal right except his false accusations. Unlike Job, we have access to the greatest legal defense attorney in the universe! Yehshua stands at the right side of the throne to defend us!

Who is he that condemneth? It is Christ that died, yea rather, that is risen again, who is even at the right hand of God, who also maketh intercession for us. (Romans 8:34 KJV)

Now of the things which we have spoken this is the sum: We have such an high priest, who is set on the right hand of the throne of the Majesty in the heavens. (Hebrews 8:1 KJV)

The Lord said unto my Lord, Sit thou at my right hand, until I make thine enemies thy footstool. (Psalm 110:1 KJV)

Therefore being by the right hand of God exalted, and having received of the Father the promise of the Holy Ghost, he hath shed forth this, which ye now see and hear.

For David is not ascended into the heavens: but he saith himself, The Lord said unto my Lord, Sit thou on my right hand. (Acts 2:33-34 KJV)

We have an intercessor and a powerful legal defense counsel in Yehshua. He stands at the right hand of God and defends us against Satan, the accuser of the brethren. However, I believe there are times, or certain situations, when God must increase the intensity of a trial because of a higher calling, testing whether our faith can endure. This passage in Luke 22 is the best example:

And the Lord said, Simon, Simon, behold, Satan hath desired to have you, that he may sift you as wheat:

But I have prayed for thee, that thy faith fail not: and when thou art converted, strengthen thy brethren. (Luke 22:31-32 KJV)

I believe this is precisely the scene we see here in the throne room, with Satan and the sons of God accusing Job and asking permission that he be sifted like wheat. This is likely always going to be because of a greater plan that God may have for the person being tested.

On the Table of Nations chart, I have circled the names of Jobab and Abraham. I believe Jobab must be Job, since no other Jobab or Job is mentioned in the Bible. Jobab lived at the same time as Abraham, and they were cousins in the line of Eber (father of the Hebrews). If Jobab is Job and occupied the land of Uz as a portion of the land of Aram in Mesopotamia, they were both within a reasonable proximity to each other geographically. When God called Abraham out of Ur, he went to Haran, which lay in the land of Uz under Aram's inheritance. Job was likewise in the land of Uz under Aram, uncle to their grandfather Eber.

I believe God chose Abraham to be the patriarch of Israel, but Abraham's cousin Job also drew His attention through his unwavering obedience and burnt offerings, even on behalf of his children. For a moment, it seems possible that God considered Job for the patriarchal role, given his "perfect" status in His eyes. Both Abraham and Job were Shemites in the line of Eber (possible origin of the term *Hebrew*), assuming Jobab is indeed Job. For a brief moment, Job may have been screened for the position of patriarch of Israel. The test begins in verse 8:

> ***And the Lord said unto Satan, Hast thou considered***
> ***my servant Job, that there is none like him in the earth,***
> ***a <u>perfect and an upright man</u>, one that feareth God,***
> ***and escheweth evil?***

Knowing that God is merciful and loving, He must have been considering a great responsibility for Job to bear. Assuming this occurred at the same time as Abraham—as evidenced by the Sabeans of Haran and the Chaldeans under Nimrod—I believe it is highly possible that Job was tested to determine whether he was qualified for one of the most important roles in the Old Testament. Whatever God was considering for Job's future was extraordinary, as shown by the severity of the trials he endured. The merciful God I have come to know does not torture as an experiment of faith; rather, everything unfolds according to a well-defined purpose in His will.

It is worth considering that Job may have been a candidate for the patriarchal position of the nation of Israel. Extra-biblical rabbinical accounts suggest that Abraham was chosen at birth and raised by Noah and Shem—timelines that can be biblically proven to have overlapped. Perhaps, Job was also being considered: "Have you considered my servant Job…… an upright man" (Job 1:8 NASB). Satan was then given the opportunity to sift him like wheat. God is merciful, and I believe Job was being considered for a greater position in the line of Shem, possibly compared to his cousin Abraham should a backup patriarch have been required.

This is, of course, conjecture, but it offers food for thought that may comfort us in understanding why God permitted such suffering. A high calling may have been considered for Job, one that ultimately became a profound lesson in spiritual warfare.

Before I move on from the subject, notice that the events began when the fallen sons of God and Satan gained permission to attack Job. He went from living a peaceful and prosperous life to having the hedge removed, and the following occurred:

- Oxen and donkeys were stolen and servants were killed.
- Lightning struck, killing all his sheep and more servants.
- His camels were stolen and more servants were killed.
- A strong wind destroyed what was likely a stone house and killed his children.
- His body was covered in sores and boils.
- His wife and friends believed he must have offended God and urged him to curse God and die.
- In all of this, Job worshipped God and his greatest concern was that he had somehow isolated himself from God. Though extremely harsh and painful, Job passed the test.

Murder, death, theft, destruction, weather events, and plagues of health are all tools of the fallen sons of God—princes of darkness—that can and will be used against us. These dark princes are still at work today, behind the scenes, targeting God's people through their nation's leaders, working against them day and night. Think of demons as soldiers of ranks similar to our military structure, where sergeant major is the highest enlisted rank, but the fallen angel sons of God serve as commissioned officers. Few lieutenants or captains make history, and even fewer sergeants, yet princes—whether of darkness or of light—are the highest ranking among God's or Satan's armies. They wield power over weather, life, and death, though always under God's ultimate sovereignty.

Through Yehshua, who stands at the right hand of God interceding for us, we have authority over these princes of darkness. Under Yehshua's authority, we hold the power to rebuke storms, heal the sick, and even raise the dead.

Behold, I give unto you power to tread on serpents and scorpions, and over all the power of the enemy: and nothing shall by any means hurt you. (Luke 10:19 KJV)

Serpents are princes of darkness, the fallen sons of God. Scorpions are demons, and through Yehshua's authority, we have power over both—if we know how to use it. That authority begins with obedience, living by God's rules rather than the ways of the lost world under Satan's rule. It begins with resisting the lures of this world (James 4:7) and avoiding entrapment by the wiles of the devil (Ephesians 6:11).

By the way, there is another point worth noting for those who may not recognize that the event of Genesis 6 marked an escalation in the war against God. Verse 12 (KJV) says:

The fallen angels and their offspring corrupted not only the genetics of mankind but also of animals. "For all flesh had corrupted His way upon the earth" extends beyond the genetics of mankind. The chimeras depicted on the walls of the pyramids were not the idle creations of artists leaving fanciful images for future generations to admire. Rather, the Egyptian depictions tell stories of how life was before the flood. Half-human and half-beast images were not something imagined but were the result of genetic tampering by these so-called "gods" of antiquity—the fallen angel sons of God. This was a direct assault on all of God's creation, carried out under what they believed to be Lucifer's authority after Adam forfeited his position as royalty over the earth.

All of these "abominations" are now confined to Hades, awaiting release at the fourth seal of the tribulation (Rev 6:8), as discussed in my previous book *The Bride, the Wise Virgins, and the Last Adam*. The sons of God who rebelled against God may be powerful, but there is One far greater, and their fate has already been sealed. Fear Him and no other.

Then shall he say also unto them on the left hand, Depart from me, ye cursed, into everlasting fire, prepared for the devil and his angels. (Matthew 25:41 KJV)

The mountains quake at him [kings and princes] and the hills melt [nations], and the earth is burned at his presence, yea, the world, and all that dwell therein. (Nahum 1:5 KJV)

CHAPTER 3

The Good Guys

For he shall give his angels charge over thee, to keep thee in all thy ways.

—Psalm 91:11 (KJV)

If you were not disgusted by the truth of obelisks, hybridized superhuman Nephilim, and Egyptian chimeras, I have already prayed for you. Meanwhile, let us turn to something far more pleasant: the good sons of God.

The first mention of angels who may be considered "sons of God" on the side of good appears in Genesis 3:24 (KJV):

So he drove out the man; and he placed at the east of the garden of Eden Cherubims, and a flaming sword which turned every way, to keep the way of the tree of life.

There is no way to know how many cherubim there are, but these were among the faithful guardians of the Garden of God, where the Tree of Life stood, and apparently no one dares to cross them. Whatever this flaming sword may be, even the sons of God respect its lethality. This was a direct result of the fall, and I doubt that God feared Adam might steal the Tree of Life. In terms of warfare, the fall of Adam was a coup d'état, plain and simple, and his authority over the earth was handed over to Satan. To keep the fallen sons of God from getting any ideas, the cherubim guarded the way to the Tree of Life. The cherubim appear to hold the highest rank among angels, entrusted with guarding the divine presence of God.

I say this because according to Ezekiel, Satan was a cherub, and I assume the cherubim are the highest-ranking order of angels. Among them, Satan held the highest position. Ezekiel 28:14–16 (KJV) reads:

> *Thou art the anointed cherub that covereth; and I have set thee so: thou wast upon the holy mountain of God; thou hast walked up and down in the midst of the stones of fire.*
>
> *Thou wast perfect in thy ways from the day that thou wast created, till iniquity was found in thee.*
>
> *By the multitude of thy merchandise they have filled the midst of thee with violence, and thou hast sinned: therefore I will cast thee as profane out of the mountain of God: and I will destroy thee, O covering cherub, from the midst of the stones of fire.*

This term *covering cherub* indicates authority not only over the cherubim but also over all angels of lower rank beneath them. This is why Satan remains the highest-ranking angel under his authority today. Yet Yehshua, the one true Son of God—not a creation of God—outranks them all, both on the side of good and evil. Yehshua is God, yet born of a woman on earth, and became the perfect Lamb without blemish sacrificed for our atonement. Through Him, our legal authority is raised above that of all angels, under Yehshua's God-given authority.

> *For HE HAS PUT ALL THINGS IN SUBJECTION UNDER HIS FEET. But when He says, "All things are put in subjection," it is clear that this excludes the Father who put all things in subjection to Him. (1 Corinthians 15:27 NASB)*

"You have put everything in subjection under his feet."

*For in subjecting all things to him, He left nothing
that is not subject to him. But now we do not yet see all
things subjected to him. (Hebrews 2:8 NASB)*

The description of the cherubim is awe-inspiring, as detailed by Ezekiel and later by John in Revelation. Ezekiel describes them in chapter 10:

*And each one had four faces. The first face was the
face of a cherub, the second face was the face of a
human, the third, the face of a lion, and the fourth, the
face of an eagle. (Ezekiel 10:14 NASB)*

*And before the throne there was something like a sea
of glass, like crystal; and in the center and around
the throne, four living creatures full of eyes in front
and behind. The first living creature was like a lion,
the second creature like a calf, the third creature had
a face like that of a man, and the fourth creature was
like a flying eagle. And the four living creatures, each
one of them having six wings, are full of eyes around
and within; and day and night they do not cease to say,*

*"Holy, holy, holy is the Lord God, the Almighty, who
was and who is and who is to come." (Revelation 4:6-8
NASB)*

In 2 Chronicles 3:11, we find the account of the construction of Solomon's Temple, where the cherubim were placed over the Mercy Seat of the Ark of the Covenant. The Holman Standard Christian Bible provides the conversion from cubits to feet:

I suggest that the reason these instructions were given to Solomon by his father, David, is that this thirty-foot wingspan of the cherubim represents the actual size of a living cherub. I don't believe it was scaled down, but rather replicated in full.

Satan was a covering cherub, entrusted with vast authority in the universe, but he fell away from God. My view is that Satan was the only cherub to fall within his particular realm of authority. Since cherubim are closely associated with guarding the throne of God, it would be wise to remain on their good side. And remember: no matter what authority Satan once held, he never outranked Yehshua. Satan was a created being—not the rebellious sibling that Mormonism teaches. Lucifer was never Yehshua's brother; that is an obscene lie.

*Thou wast perfect in thy ways from the day that thou
wast created, till iniquity was found in thee. (Ezekiel
28:15 KJV)*

Below the cherubim, I believe the next powerful order of angels are the seraphim. The only direct biblical account of Seraphim appears in Isaiah 6, where God calls Isaiah into His throne room and anoints him for prophetic ministry. These prophecies are remarkable, even foretelling Yehshua's coming more than seven centuries before His birth.

Here is the passage from Isaiah 6:

*In the year that king Uzziah died I saw also the Lord
sitting upon a throne, high and lifted up, and his train
filled the temple.*

Above it stood the seraphims: each one had six wings; with twain he covered his face, and with twain he covered his feet, and with twain he did fly.

And one cried unto another, and said, Holy, holy, holy, is the Lord of hosts: the whole earth is full of his glory.

And the posts of the door moved at the voice of him that cried, and the house was filled with smoke.

Then said I, Woe is me! for I am undone; because I am a man of unclean lips, and I dwell in the midst of a people of unclean lips: for mine eyes have seen the King, the Lord of hosts.

Then flew one of the seraphims unto me, having a live coal in his hand, which he had taken with the tongs from off the altar:

And he laid it upon my mouth, and said, Lo, this hath touched thy lips; and thine iniquity is taken away, and thy sin purged.

Also I heard the voice of the Lord, saying, Whom shall I send, and who will go for us? Then said I, Here am I; send me. (Isaiah 6:1-8 KJV)

This amazing account from Isaiah gives us another peek into the throne room of God where the seraphim, in his account, are serving God directly in His throne room. This is what the *Topical Encyclopedia* has to say about seraphim:

<u>Topical Encyclopedia</u>

The Seraphim are celestial beings mentioned in the Bible, primarily in the book of Isaiah. They are often associated with the worship and service of God, depicted as attendants in His heavenly court. The term "seraphim" is derived from the Hebrew word "śārāph,"

*which means "burning ones," indicating their fiery
nature and purity.*

Hopefully, if you're reading this book, you also read my last book, where I discussed a very important discrepancy in the translation of *saraph*. Remember: I shared something from *Strong's Concordance* that helps explain who the serpent was in the Garden of Eden:

◀ 8314. saraph ▶

Strong's Concordance

saraph: serpent

Original Word: שָׂרָף
Part of Speech: Noun Masculine
Transliteration: saraph
Phonetic Spelling: (saw-rawf')
Definition: fiery serpent

And I also shared what Enoch saw when these "shining ones" (ISV) could take on the appearance of men anytime they wanted.

**And they took me to a place where they (angels) were
like burning fire, and, when they wished, they made
themselves look like men. Enoch 17 verse 1[7]**

In researching word etymologies, the trail inevitably leads to Latin or Greek, which are relatively young compared to the Semitic languages or ancient Sanskrit. One of the things I examine in the names of landmarks, words, or people is their phonetic comparison to Hebrew. In ancient Sanskrit, the word for serpent was *sarpa*. Imagine that. I often receive pushback on this because for some reason, we're all determined to place a

---

7   Enoch 1 by RH Charles

fallen cherub named Satan in the garden as the deceiver of Eve, whereas I believe it was a seraph angel under Satan's authority.

Something that complicates this concept is the serpent and dragon of Revelation 12:9 (KJV):

> *And the great dragon was cast out, that old serpent,*
> *called the Devil, and Satan, which deceiveth the whole*
> *world: he was cast out into the earth, and his angels*
> *were cast out with him.*

> *And I saw an angel come down from heaven, having*
> *the key of the bottomless pit and a great chain in his*
> *hand. And he laid hold on the dragon, that old serpent,*
> *which is the Devil, and Satan, and bound him a*
> *thousand years. (Revelation 20:1-2 KJV)*

According to the book of Revelation, Satan was definitely a serpent or seraph. And according to Ezekiel, Satan was a "covering cherub":

> *Thou art the anointed cherub that covereth; and I*
> *have set thee so: thou wast upon the holy mountain of*
> *God; thou hast walked up and down in the midst of the*
> *stones of fire. (Ezekiel 28:14 KJV)*

If Satan was both serpent (seraph) and cherub, this would indicate that "the anointed cherub that covereth" was a higher rank more than a separate species of angel. Perhaps he was a seraph elevated to the rank of covering cherub, then demoted back to seraph after being cast out. Ezekiel's description of cherubim differs from Isaiah's description of seraphim, yet Lucifer—Satan—is biblically described as being both.

No matter who was in the garden, I believe at least several seraphim fell with Lucifer and were among the "sons of God" mentioned in Genesis

6, Job 1 and 2, and Job 38. Thankfully, Isaiah 6 shows that at least some seraphim were assigned to serve God in the throne room, many centuries after the Genesis 6 event. I feel as though I'm treading on thin ice with this subject, so that's enough about the seraphim for now. Admittedly, I'm attempting to understand something far above my pay grade as a lowly, non-pedigreed human.

Then there are the rest of the angelic orders that come and go as commanded by God. The *Topical Encyclopedia* defines them in this way:

> ### Topical Encyclopedia: Angels
>
> ### Definition and Nature:
>
> *Angels are spiritual beings created by God to serve as His messengers and to carry out His will. They are often depicted as having great power and wisdom, yet they remain subordinate to God. The term "angel" is derived from the Greek word "angelos," meaning "messenger." In the Hebrew Bible, the equivalent term is "mal'akh."*
>
> ### Biblical Descriptions and Roles:
>
> *Angels appear throughout the Bible, fulfilling various roles and functions. They are often seen delivering messages from God, executing divine judgment, providing guidance, and offering protection to God's people.*

After Genesis chapter 6, the next encounter with angels would be with Abraham in Genesis 18:

> **Now the Lord appeared to Abraham by the oaks of Mamre, while he was sitting at the tent door in the heat of the day. When he raised his eyes and looked, behold, three men were standing opposite him; and when he saw them, he ran from the tent door to meet them and**

*bowed down to the ground, and said, "My Lord, if now
I have found favor in Your sight, please do not pass
Your servant by. Please let a little water be brought and
wash your feet, and make yourselves comfortable under
the tree; and I will bring a piece of bread, so that you
may refresh yourselves; after that you may go on, since
you have visited your servant." And they said, "So do
as you have said." So Abraham hurried into the tent to
Sarah, and said, "Quickly, prepare three measures of
fine flour, knead it, and make bread cakes." Abraham
also ran to the herd, and took a tender and choice calf
and gave it to the servant, and he hurried to prepare
it. He took curds and milk and the calf which he had
prepared, and set it before them; and he was standing
by them under the tree as they ate. (Genesis 18:1-8
NASB)*

A few important takeaways from this passage. The "Lord appeared to Abraham" is how the chapter begins. I believe this is very significant in context. In verse 2, Abraham raises his eyes and suddenly sees three "men," but Abraham immediately identifies them as angels. He runs from his tent and bows before them, which explains why verse 1 uses the singular "Lord" rather than the plural "men." Since it is prohibited to bow to angels, one of these figures was not merely an angel. Was Abraham bowing to the Word, who was with God and who was God in the beginning (John 1:1)? Was Abraham bowing to Yehshua, who appeared to him as recognizably angelic? There were two other angels with Yehshua, who we can assume to be warring angels, since Yehshua is the commander of God's army (Revelation 19:11, also see Joshua 5:14).

In chapter 17, Abraham and Ishmael are circumcised at the end of the chapter. Then chapter 18 begins with the birth of the nation of Israel, when the "Lord" tells Sarah she will have a child. The "Oaks of Mamre" serve as the site chosen for this encounter between angels and Abraham. Mamre was an Amorite (Genesis 14:13) who sided with Abraham in the battle of the nine kings at the Valley of Siddim (modern-day Dead Sea). There are no wasted words in the Word of God; every detail carries weight.

Scholarly commentators often claim that chapter 14 offers no benefit beyond historical reference. In fact, I recently read a commentary that stated exactly that. The conventional account places the location of the Oaks of Mamre in the West Bank of Gaza, but biblically this cannot be accurate. This is a biblical reference from *Bibleatlas.org*:

Oaks of Mamre (Kenath) and surrounding area

Occurrences

Genesis 14:13 One who had escaped came and told Abram, the Hebrew. Now he lived by the oaks of Mamre, the Amorite, brother of Eshcol, and brother of Aner; and these were allies of Abram.

Encyclopedia

KENATH

ke'-nath (qenath; Kaath kaanath, in Septuagint, Codex Alexandrinus): A city in Bashan, taken along with its "daughters," i.e. "villages" from the Amorites by Nobah who gave it his own name (Numbers 32:42).

Bashan is located at the foot of Mount Hermon, a region loaded with pagan history. Mount Hermon, of course, is where the fallen angel incursion began. This makes it the most likely place for the appearance of the "Lord" to declare that Sarah would bear a child, who would become the father of Israel (Jacob).

I will not go into all the details of chapter 14 here, but one very important matter is often overlooked in verse 1:

And it came to pass in the days of Amraphel king of Shinar, Arioch king of Ellasar, Chedorlaomer king of Elam, and Tidal king of nations. (Genesis 14:1 KJV)

An Assyriologist named Eberhard Schrader, in his book *Cuneiforms and the Old Testament,* suggested that Amraphel was Hammurabi, the sixth king of the Babylonian dynasty and the first Amorite king of Babylon. The problem I have with this is that Hammurabi's timeline does not align with the biblical timeline of Abraham, which places Abraham roughly three centuries earlier. In addition, it is very difficult to extrapolate Hammurabi from Amraphel. Yet there is another king whose timeline corresponds perfectly with Abraham's, and whose name aligns seamlessly. Take a look at Strong's Hebrew entry for *Amraphel*:

Strong's Lexicon: Amraphel

לְאַמְרָפֶל (*'am·rā·p̄el*)

Noun - proper - masculine singula

Strong›s Hebrew 569: Amraphel = ‹sayer of darkness: fall of the sayer› 1) the king of Shinar (Babylon)

Strong's notes that Amraphel may have been Hammurabi, with the date given as 2100 BC. That's a bit confusing, since that could not have been the time of the sixth Babylonian dynasty, and Hammurabi's birth has been identified by other Assyriologists as 1810 BC. Why, then, did Strong's include this? Because it reflects the approximated biblical timeline for the event at the Valley of Siddim. In fact, fewer than ten years separate the destruction of the Tower of Babel from Abraham's departure from Haran and his arrival in Egypt. The rebellion led by King Amraphel at the Valley of Siddim falls directly in between.

According to the biblical timeline, this Babylonian king Amraphel must have been Nimrod. And according to Jewish rabbinical history, King Amraphel—the fallen sayer (soothsayer) of darkness—was indeed Nimrod.

Jewish Encyclopedia

Amraphel—In Rabbinical Literature:

This makes more sense since Kenath (Mamre) was an Amorite and would not have been allied with Abraham against an Amorite king (Hammurabi).

All of that point out that this "Oaks of Mamre" is a significant landmark for this event where Yehshua and two angels appear to Abraham to warn him of an upcoming event: the destruction of Sodom and Gomorrah.

> **And the Lord said, Because the cry of Sodom and
> Gomorrah is great, and because their sin is very
> grievous;**
>
> **I will go down now, and see whether they have done
> altogether according to the cry of it, which is come
> unto me; and if not, I will know.**
>
> **And the men turned their faces from thence, and went
> toward Sodom: but Abraham stood yet before the Lord.
> (Genesis 18:20-22 KJV)**

There were aspects of this passage that perplexed me. The Lord is with His angels, who can be anywhere at any time and know everything, including our thoughts (Psalm 139:1–2; 1 John 3:20; Romans 8:27–29, among many others). I struggled with this passage to the point of frustration until it struck me that the events at Sodom and Gomorrah were not human-inspired. Sodom, Gomorrah, and the other two cities of the plain that were destroyed were, in fact, a repeat of what happened on Mount Hermon. There were four cities, and I believe four angels—princes over them—were attempting to reinsert the Nephilim hybrid offspring back into the earth in their war against the Genesis 3:15 seed of the woman. For this reason, Genesis 6:4 (KJV) states:

> ***There were giants in the earth in those days; and also after that, when the sons of God came in unto the daughters of men, and they bare children to them, the same became mighty men which were of old, men of renown.***

"And also after that" the same event occurred in which the "sons of God took for themselves wives of all which they chose." I believe the first time may have been more benevolent, with the sons of God perhaps falling in love with some of these human women. But the second time was more violent, aggressive, and torturous. This is conjecture, drawn from connecting the dots that leave gaps in our respective theologies and theories. Stay with me while I get to a more important point that appears in Revelation, which I believe makes a connection here to the four cities of the plains.

The Lord remains with Abraham while he pleads that Sodom not be destroyed if ten righteous people can be found there. Abraham knows his nephew Lot and Lot's family are in Sodom, and though the number is not specified, it may have been ten in total. The Lord agrees, and the story continues. I find it interesting that God rescued one righteous man from the flood and allowed him to bring the other seven members of his family.

But Sodom and Gomorrah would be burned with fire unless ten righteous could be found.

Then two angels appear to Lot, and again he is allowed to bow to them, which I do not fully understand. In Roland Buck's book *Angels on Assignment*, the author discusses a conversation with an angel who claimed to be the one who appeared to Joshua in chapter 5. In that passage, the angel calls himself a captain of the armies of the Lord (verse 14). Joshua was not prevented from bowing to this angel.

I had always assumed this was Yehshua Himself, but I believe Pastor Buck spoke truth in his book. He was a Spirit-filled pastor, and I cannot imagine him risking such a grave lie in print for a small profit, knowing the consequences would be severe. Books are rarely profitable ventures, as I have certainly discovered.

I have said the same of Ron Wyatt, who discovered the Ark of the Covenant in 1980. Many insisted he only claimed to have found it to validate himself and profit from the discovery. Yet a person who spends his life serving God does not take a lie to the grave, especially for what I assume was very little money and little fame. We should be cautious, but we must not disregard God's messengers or servants who are sincere. Pray for the gift of discernment.

So perhaps one of the angels with Lot was a captain—I cannot say for certain—but Lot was not prevented from bowing, and neither of these figures was the Lord, who remained behind to speak with Abraham. Let's continue with chapter 19 (KJV):

> *The two angels arrived at Sodom in the evening, and Lot was sitting in the gateway of the city. When he saw them, he got up to meet them and bowed down with his face to the ground. "My lords," he said, "please turn aside to your servant's house. You can wash your feet and spend the night and then go on your way early in the morning."*

"No," they answered, "we will spend the night in the square."

But he insisted so strongly that they did go with him and entered his house. He prepared a meal for them, baking bread without yeast, and they ate. Before they had gone to bed, all the men from every part of the city of Sodom—both young and old—surrounded the house. They called to Lot, "Where are the men who came to you tonight? Bring them out to us so that we can have sex with them."

Lot went outside to meet them and shut the door behind him and said, "No, my friends. Don't do this wicked thing. Look, I have two daughters who have never slept with a man. Let me bring them out to you, and you can do what you like with them. But don't do anything to these men, for they have come under the protection of my roof."

"Get out of our way," they replied. "This fellow came here as a foreigner, and now he wants to play the judge! We'll treat you worse than them." They kept bringing pressure on Lot and moved forward to break down the door.

But the men inside reached out and pulled Lot back into the house and shut the door. 11 Then they struck the men who were at the door of the house, young and old, with blindness so that they could not find the door.

The two men said to Lot, "Do you have anyone else here—sons-in-law, sons or daughters, or anyone else in the city who belongs to you? Get them out of here, because we are going to destroy this place. The outcry to the Lord against its people is so great that he has sent us to destroy it."

So Lot went out and spoke to his sons-in-law, who were pledged to marry his daughters. He said, "Hurry and get out of this place, because the Lord is about to destroy the city!" But his sons-in-law thought he was joking.

With the coming of dawn, the angels urged Lot, saying, "Hurry! Take your wife and your two daughters who are here, or you will be swept away when the city is punished."

When he hesitated, the men grasped his hand and the hands of his wife and of his two daughters and led them safely out of the city, for the Lord was merciful to them. As soon as they had brought them out, one of them said, "Flee for your lives! Don't look back, and don't stop anywhere in the plain! Flee to the mountains or you will be swept away!"

But Lot said to them, "No, my lords, please! Your servant has found favor in your eyes, and you have shown great kindness to me in sparing my life. But I can't flee to the mountains; this disaster will overtake me, and I'll die. Look, here is a town near enough to run to, and it is small. Let me flee to it—it is very small, isn't it? Then my life will be spared."

He said to him, "Very well, I will grant this request too; I will not overthrow the town you speak of. But flee there quickly, because I cannot do anything until you reach it." (That is why the town was called Zoar.)

By the time Lot reached Zoar, the sun had risen over the land. Then the Lord rained down burning sulfur on Sodom and Gomorrah—from the Lord out of the heavens. Thus he overthrew those cities and the entire plain, destroying all those living in the cities—and also

A mob appears at Lot's house (both young and old, as verse 10 indicates) and demands that he send the angels out to them for sexual purposes. At that point, it becomes clear that judgment has been declared. These two angels are in communication with God, since there is no further mention of investigating "the cries of it" as in chapter 18. The final verse, 29, confirms that Abraham had pleaded for the city to be spared if ten righteous people could be found, hoping that Lot would be included.

But why did they need to physically enter the city to make this decision? That question perplexed me until one day, this verse in Revelation struck me as oddly placed, with no prior reference:

*Saying to the sixth angel which had the trumpet, Loose
the four angels which are bound in the great river
Euphrates.*

*And the four angels were loosed, which were prepared
for an hour, and a day, and a month, and a year, for to
slay the third part of men. (Revelation 9:14-15 KJV)*

This is the Sixth Trumpet Judgment. The trumpet judgments precede the bowl judgments during the seven-year tribulation, each revealing an incrementally worse disaster. But these four angels bound at the Euphrates appear suddenly out of nowhere. Who are they, and why are they locked up there?

The first clue comes from an analysis of brimstone taken from the ancient city of Sodom. Here is a sample analysis of the brimstone found at Sodom, which I believe I found on Ron Wyatt's website:

```
SPECTRACHEM ANALYTICAL
SRS 303-AS
*** Semi Quantitative Analysis of undiluted
Sample: $ssq                               Mea

     H-Be       B         C         N         O
      %         %         %         %         %
      0.0       0.0       0.0       0.0       0.0

     Si         P         S         Cl        K
      %         %         %         %         %
     0.127     0.000    (98.400)   0.311     0.025    0

     Cr        Mn        Fe        Co        Ni
      %         %         %         %         %
```

The purity of the sulfur found at Sodom is unlike that of naturally occurring sulfur. Sulfur needs to be refined to reach this level of purity, unless…

The article I wanted to share on this subject is copyrighted, so I can only share the highlights. Along tectonic plates are what are known as "subduction zones," where the plates collide and one plate is driven beneath the adjacent plate. Between the plates and the magma zone lie the sub arc zones, where oxidized minerals from the earth's surface work their way do the bottom of the tectonic plate and are subjected to extreme heat and pressure in a "reducing environment" (without oxygen). Under these conditions, minerals in the sub arc subduction zone revert to their pure, unoxidized forms under heat and pressure. You can learn more about it here: https://phys.org/news/2014-03-subduction-zones-reveal-sulphur-mineral.html.

Here is a map from another site that shows the collision lines where the subduction zones are located at the Euphrates River:

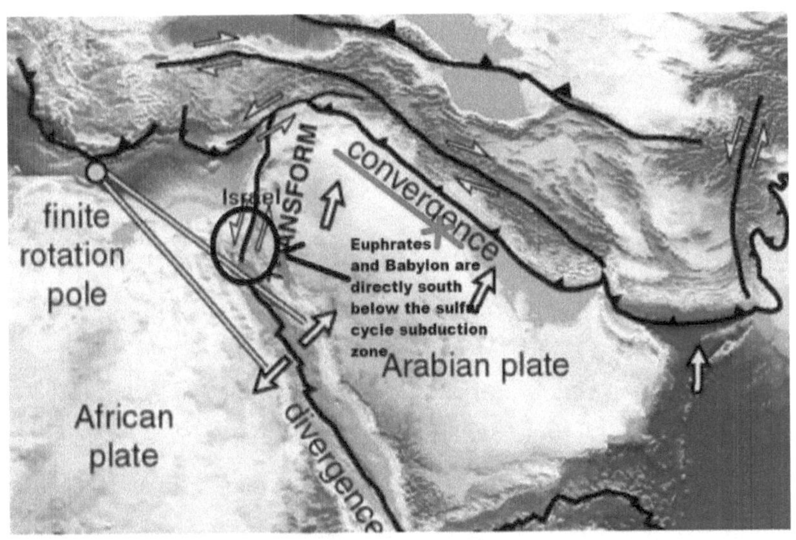

http://www.kjvbible.org/geology_prophecy.html

Can you see where I am going with this? At sixty kilometers beneath the earth's surface, between the African and Eurasian tectonic plates, lies a subduction zone precisely at the Euphrates River. According to the source I just quoted above, this convergence zone between the plates is a sulfur cycle subduction zone, where, at the bottom of this zone, sulfur can be found in the purity, such as that which exists in the samples taken from Sodom.

The earth serves as a prison for fallen angels (sons of God), demons, and their earthly followers. Some are in Hades, while others may be elsewhere. Yet I am certain that four of them are bound beneath the Euphrates sulfur cycle subduction zone, the very place where I believe God opened the earth to collect brimstone to rain down on Sodom, Gomorrah, Admah, and Zeboiim. Then the four angels responsible for the crimes committed in the four cities of the Valley of Siddim (the Dead Sea) were locked away sixty kilometers below the tectonic plates, in the same location from which the brimstone sulfur used to destroy those cities originated.

This is, of course, conjecture for consideration, but I believe it connects to the Genesis 6:4 reference to "and also after that." God shut it down, burning deep into the limestone structures, as can be seen on Ron Wyatt's website. Whatever Nephilim had already been propagated from this event, God permitted the Israelites to eliminate after four hundred years of captivity in Egypt. But the Sodom Nephilim factory was destroyed, and the fallen angels responsible remain bound beneath the Euphrates.

Notice one more point before I leave this topic. This is Genesis 14:2–3 (NASB):

> ***They made war with Bera king of Sodom, and with Birsha king of Gomorrah, Shinab king of Admah, and Shemeber king of Zeboiim, and the king of Bela (that is, Zoar). All these came as allies to the valley of Siddim (that is, the Salt Sea).***

Lot left for Zoar with his daughters, while the rest of these cities were reduced to ashes. Although Abraham had joined forces with them to pursue the other four kings, including Nimrod (Amraphel) a few chapters earlier, they were neither friends of God nor of Abraham:

> ***And the king of Sodom said unto Abram, Give me the persons, and take the goods to thyself.***
>
> ***And Abram said to the king of Sodom, I have lift up mine hand unto the Lord, the most high God, the possessor of heaven and earth,***
>
> ***<u>That I will not take from a thread even to a shoelatchet, and that I will not take any thing that is thine, lest thou shouldest say, I have made Abram rich:</u>***

Although not mentioned directly, Abraham harbored no love for King Bera of Sodom. There is something in the narrative that remains unclear: why would Nimrod travel all the way from Babylon, some 1,500 miles distant, to confront these lesser-developed kingdoms, only to be defeated? Nimrod must have obviously feared a formidable force coming out of the Valley of Siddim and sought to destroy those lesser-developed cities. To me, this suggests the presence of a Nephilim force being developed there, which Nimrod perceived as a threat to his regional authority.

Whatever transpired in Sodom, we know that the land of Canaan was overrun with Nephilim centuries later when Israel returned from Egypt. What remains uncertain is how they became so populated there, except that Genesis 6:4 states "and also after that," implying a similar origin, i.e., by the fallen sons of God.

One more point worth noting is what happened with Lot's daughters. In Genesis 19:8, Lot offers his daughters to the mob:

> *Look, I have two daughters who have never slept with a man. Let me bring them out to you, and you can do what you like with them. But don't do anything to these men, for they have come under the protection of my roof.*

Though the cities were destroyed, the nature of spiritual warfare endured. Lot inadvertently spoke a curse over his daughters when he offered them to the demon-possessed pagan mob at his door. The images drawn from this narrative portray Abraham as fearlessly courageous, even pursuing Nimrod, "a mighty hunter before the Lord" (Genesis 10:9), to recover his nephew. Lot, on the other hand, appears more as a politician, attempting to exchange a lesser sin for a greater one, when God's way is zero tolerance for any of it. And what was the result?

> *Now Lot went up from Zoar with his two daughters and stayed in the mountains, because he was afraid to stay in Zoar; and he stayed in a cave, he and his two daughters. Then the firstborn said to the younger, "Our father is old, and there is not a man on earth to have relations with us according to the custom of all the earth. Come, let's make our father drink wine, and let's sleep with him so that we may keep our family alive*

Lot would be the last member of his immediate family to believe in the one true God. His daughters gave birth to two nations that would remain forever opposed to Israel. I believe this was the consequence of Lot offering them up to the demonic mob instead of the angels; he lost his authority over his daughters, and they became subjects of Satan.

Yet God, in His mercy and forgiveness, and out of His deep love for Abraham, brought forth a future Moabite from Lot's line who would become the great matriarch of Israel. She became the first type and model of the Gentile bride, who, through a kinsman redeemer, would be the great-grandmother of Israel's first anointed king. Her name was Ruth, the Moabite.

What drew my attention and led me down these rabbit holes was the fact that two angels had to walk into Sodom to confirm whether what they suspected was truly happening. This suggests some kind of veil over the cities that obscured God's view, which might only have been possible through technology accessible to the sons of God. The God of our Bible knows everything, even our thoughts, and this account seems inconsistent without the presence of a high-tech veil that concealed their actions below. I don't know how to reconcile this with the rest of the bible. In my opinion, fallen angels must have been present in the four cities destroyed by brimstone, ensuring that nothing they had corrupted could survive. This was Genesis 6:4 revisited—2.0—and it explains the recurrence of Nephilim after the flood.

It is not my intention to deviate from the sin of homosexuality as the cause for Sodom and Gomorrah's total annihilation. Yet if that were the sole reason, why do America, Amsterdam, or other places where homosexuality has proliferated not burn today? Ancient Rome and Babylon both embraced homosexuality, yet no brimstone fell there. Homosexual Christians—though technically an oxymoron—are quick to point out that Ezekiel 16:49–50 makes no mention of homosexuality as the cause of Sodom's destruction. That is correct, as the entire chapter is dedicated to Israel's total embrace of idolatry, comparing Israel to a prostitute. In scripture, the church is portrayed as a woman or bride, while a prostitute represents a false religion honoring a false god. What are false gods? Fallen angels, the sons of God.

I am only sharing my research on this subject, which perplexed me for two major reasons. First, why would an omnipresent God need to send angels on foot into a place to investigate corruption? Second, where did the 98.4 percent pure sulfur come from? This led me to the four angels bound at the Euphrates River.

Speaking of burning, I have already consumed too much time presenting that conjecture. There are more angels to discuss, including another important angel who appeared to the mother of Abraham's first son. Most of us know the story of Sarah, who laughed at the Lord's comment that she would bear a child in her old age in Genesis 18. In Genesis 16, out of desperation, she offered her Egyptian servant to Abraham to bear him a son. The servant's name was Hagar, and Abraham was eighty-six years old when their son Ishmael was born (Genesis 16:16).

It would seem this was never God's plan, except that when Hagar, while pregnant with Ishmael, left Abraham because she was tired of

Sarah's harshness toward her. As she made her way through the desert, an angel appeared to her:

> *Now the angel of the Lord found her by a spring of water in the wilderness, by the spring on the way to Shur. He said, "Hagar, Sarai's slave woman, from where have you come, and where are you going?" And she said, "I am fleeing from the presence of my mistress Sarai." So the angel of the Lord said to her, "Return to your mistress, and submit to her authority." The angel of the Lord also said to her, "I will greatly multiply your descendants so that they will be too many to count." The angel of the Lord said to her further,*
>
> *"Behold, you are pregnant,*
>
> *And you will give birth to a son;*
>
> *And you shall name him Ishmael,*
>
> *Because the Lord has heard your affliction.*
>
> *But he will be a wild donkey of a man;*
>
> *His hand will be against everyone,*
>
> *And everyone's hand will be against him;*
>
> *And he will live in defiance of all his brothers."*
>
> *Then she called the name of the Lord who spoke to her, "You are a God who sees me"; for she said, "Have I even seen Him here and lived after He saw me?" Therefore the well was called Beer-lahai-roi; behold, it is between Kadesh and Bered.*
>
> *So Hagar bore a son to Abram; and Abram named his son, to whom Hagar gave birth, Ishmael. (Genesis 16:7-15 NASB)*

It was God's will that Hagar bear a son to Abraham, for otherwise the angel would not have appeared to her with such a prophecy. This son's descendants would become the arch nemesis of Israel—the "wild donkey." Nothing is tougher or more stubborn than a donkey, but a wild donkey? Who were his descendants?

Now these are the generations of Ishmael, Abraham's son, whom Hagar the Egyptian, Sarah's handmaid, bore to Abraham:

> *And these are the names of the sons of Ishmael,*
> *by their names, according to their generations: the*
> *firstborn of Ishmael, Nebajoth; and Kedar, and Adbeel,*
> *and Mibsam,*
>
> *And Mishma, and Dumah, and Massa,*
>
> *Hadar, and Tema, Jetur, Naphish, and Kedemah:*
>
> *These are the sons of Ishmael, and these are their*
> *names, by their towns, and by their castles; twelve*
> *princes according to their nations.*
>
> *And these are the years of the life of Ishmael, an*
> *hundred and thirty and seven years: and he gave up the*
> *ghost and died; and was gathered unto his people.*
>
> *And they dwelt from Havilah unto Shur, that is before*
> *Egypt, as thou goest toward Assyria: and he died in the*
> *presence of all his brethren. (Genesis 25:12-18 KJV)*

This is basically the entire Arabian Peninsula. Muhammad the prophet believed himself to be a descendant of Ishmael, which is very likely true. What is interesting today is that while Islam has spread across the Middle East, most of Ishmael's descendants can be traced specifically to the Arab nations of the south. After Sarah's death, Abraham had more sons with a concubine named Keturah. I believe the entire Middle East has been populated by the sons of Abraham through three women—Hagar,

Sarah, and Keturah—and that the sons of Hagar and Keturah (1 Chronicles 1:32–33) remain as enemies of the son of Sarah even today.

There is also the dispute between Isaac's sons Jacob and Esau. Esau's descendants (Edomites can be traced to Palestinians and other nations) continue to oppose Israel today. Only one line from Abraham, through Isaac and Jacob, became the nation of Israel; all other descendants of Abraham have been at war with Israel.

The angel appeared again to Hagar in Genesis 21:17 (NASB):

> ***God heard the boy crying; and the angel of God called to Hagar from heaven and said to her, "What is the matter with you, Hagar? Do not fear, for God has heard the voice of the boy where he is.***

It was always God's plan that the descendants of Abraham's surrogates would stand in opposition to Israel. It was likewise His plan that Isaac's twin sons, Jacob and Esau, would contend with one another, making Israel the extreme underdog in the Middle East and throughout the world. There is much more to this, but the focus remains on the faithful ones—the sons of God who serve as messengers (angels) for Him. They surround us in even greater numbers today, anticipating the close of this age and the arrival of the Bridegroom, the King and Commander of heaven's armies (Revelation 19).

The story of Jacob is fascinating, but "Jacob's Ladder" is extraordinary. We read these accounts and often assume such events were isolated to ancient times, yet the good angels— "sons of God"—continue their work today just as they have for millennia. The difference is that we do not fully receive the truth of their existence or recognize their assertive role on our behalf. Make no mistake: they are always near.

> ***Then Jacob departed from Beersheba and went toward Haran. And he happened upon a particular place and spent the night there, because the sun had set; and***

*he took one of the stones of the place and made it a
support for his head, and lay down in that place. And
he had a dream, and behold, a ladder was set up on the
earth with its top reaching to heaven; and behold, the
angels of God were ascending and descending on it.
Then behold, the Lord was standing above it and said,
"I am the Lord, the God of your father Abraham and
the God of Isaac; the land on which you lie I will give
to you and to your descendants. Your descendants will
also be like the dust of the earth, and you will spread
out to the west and to the east, and to the north and to
the south; and in you and in your descendants shall all
the families of the earth be blessed. Behold, I am with
you and will keep you wherever you go, and will bring
you back to this land; for I will not leave you until I
have done what I have promised you." Then Jacob
awoke from his sleep and said, "The Lord is certainly
in this place, and I did not know it!" And he was afraid
and said, "How awesome is this place! This is none
other than the house of God, and this is the gate of
heaven!" (Genesis 28:10-17 NASB)*

I believe an entire book could be written on this event, and in fact,
I am certain of it for many reasons. How many of us have had dreams
or visions so astonishing that they left us in awe, yet we went on with
our lives without grasping their significance? If we believe the Bible and
that God remains the sovereign God of the universe, orchestrating global
events to fulfill His will and prophecies, we should discipline ourselves to
take notes when He speaks. Do you know where Jacob had this vision? It
is highly disputed by highly educated people who, unfortunately, do not
know God.

*So Jacob got up early in the morning, and took the
stone that he had placed as a support for his head, and*

*set it up as a memorial stone, and poured oil on its
top. Then he named that place Bethel; but previously
the name of the city had been Luz. Jacob also made
a vow, saying, "If God will be with me and will keep
me on this journey that I take, and give me food to
eat and garments to wear, and I return to my father's
house in safety, then the Lord will be my God. And this
stone, which I have set up as a memorial stone, will
be God's house, and of everything that You give me I
will assuredly give a tenth to You." (Genesis 28:18-22
NASB)*

*Then God said to Jacob, "Arise, go up to Bethel
and live there, and make an altar there to God, who
appeared to you when you fled from your brother
Esau." (Genesis 35:1 NASB)*

If you ask an academic or consult a map, you will find a town named Bethel about eleven miles north of Jerusalem. This site holds far less significance when compared to Jerusalem. During Israel's four hundred years of captivity in Egypt, the place where Jacob had his dream was buried by an earthquake, as a fault line runs east to west beneath the Mount of Olives, aligning slightly south of the Temple Mount. This fault line has been highly active and has caused significant damage in the region for thousands of years.

According to Genesis 28, 35, and other passages, Jacob's Ladder vision occurred at Bethel. Academics will agree that it is the town of Bethel. But the true location of Bethel was the future site of the "House of God," as Jacob declared in verse 22. This was Mount Moriah—the place where Abraham was stopped from sacrificing his son Isaac, where Solomon's Temple would later be built according to David's specifications, and where the Son of God would ultimately be crucified.

Mt. Moriah is a gateway to heaven, just as Jacob declared in Genesis 28:17. This "gateway" is at least one portal on the earth through which the sons of God travel to and from heaven.

> *Nathanael answered and saith unto him, Rabbi, thou art the Son of God; thou art the King of Israel.*
>
> *Jesus answered and said unto him, Because I said unto thee, I saw thee under the fig tree, believest thou? thou shalt see greater things than these.*
>
> *And he saith unto him, Verily, verily, I say unto you, Hereafter ye shall see heaven open, and the angels of God ascending and descending upon the Son of man. (John 1:50-51 KJV)*

God weaves history like fine thread through a golden needle, concealing truth so that only those led by the Spirit will discover His perfect linen—truth that time and educated academics often misjudge as flawed. Yet God is perfect, and His will is perfect. Abraham was spared the sacrifice of his son, while God Himself would sacrifice His own Son on the threshing floor of David, called Mt. Moriah (2 Samuel 24:18–25).

The next major event unfolds in the Exodus from Egypt, led by Moses, when he is drawn to the thunder and lights upon Mt. Sinai above the camp.

> *And the angel of the LORD appeared unto him in a flame of fire out of the midst of a bush: and he looked,*

and, behold, the bush burned with fire, and the bush
was not consumed. (Exodus 3:2 KJV)

For most of my life I assumed this was God the Father appearing to Moses, just as the Jewish people believe. Yet the verse identifies the figure as an angel, and in verse 5 Moses is commanded to remove his sandals because the ground is holy. For millennia, the Jewish people have not recognized that this was Yehshua, the second person of the Trinity.

This is the same "angel of the Lord" who would accompany the Israelites through the wilderness. Yehshua was with them—His first love—from the very beginning. They witnessed countless amazing miracles but were vexed with the pagan customs of Egypt and their acquired knowledge from the fallen sons of God. I can only imagine the vast multitude of "sons of God" that traveled with the Israelites from Egypt to Cannan beside the commander of heaven's armies, Yehshua.

Then there is something even more extraordinary than anything already mentioned so far, a mystery that has perplexed academics for ages, found in Numbers 21.

And the people spake against God, and against Moses,
Wherefore have ye brought us up out of Egypt to die in
the wilderness? for there is no bread, neither is there
any water; and our soul loatheth this light bread.

And the Lord sent fiery serpents among the people, and
they bit the people; and much people of Israel died.

Therefore the people came to Moses, and said, We
have sinned, for we have spoken against the Lord, and
against thee; pray unto the Lord, that he take away the
serpents from us. And Moses prayed for the people.

And the Lord said unto Moses, Make thee a fiery
serpent, and set it upon a pole: and it shall come to
pass, that every one that is bitten, when he looketh
upon it, shall live.

***And Moses made a serpent of brass, and put it upon a
pole, and it came to pass, that if a serpent had bitten
any man, when he beheld the serpent of brass, he lived.
(Numbers 21:5-9 KJV)***

Until now, any form of graven image worship or idolatry had been
strictly forbidden. This passage perplexed me from the first time I read it,
even leading me to research possible conspiracy theories, wondering if it
had been inserted as a deception. How could looking at the brass serpent
heal the bites of serpents? This is one of those rabbit-hole passages of the
Bible that confuses us when we fail to understand Genesis more clearly.

Strong's Lexicon for verse 6, where the "fiery serpents" appear,
defines the words as follows:

Strong›s Lexicon

saraph: Seraph, fiery serpent

*Word Origin: From the root verb שָׂרַף (saraph), meaning
«to burn» or «to set on fire.»*

*Usage: The term «saraph» is used in the Hebrew Bible
to describe both fiery serpents and celestial beings
known as seraphim. In the context of fiery serpents, it
refers to venomous snakes that inflicted the Israelites
in the wilderness (Numbers 21:6). As celestial beings,
seraphim are depicted as fiery, angelic creatures who
serve in the presence of God, as seen in Isaiah›s vision
(Isaiah 6:2–6).*

The fiery serpents share the same name as the seraphim angels.
Another fiery serpent appears in the Garden of Eden—the ISV translates it
as "shining one," while other translations use "divine beings" or "luminous
ones." In the garden, the seraph brought death. In the wilderness, the
seraphim also brought death. When the Israelites stepped outside God's
covering, the fiery serpents inflicted mortal wounds.

A deeper comparison can be made to another fiery serpent in Isaiah chapters 14 and 30:

> *Do not rejoice, Philistia, all of you, Because the rod that struck you is broken; For from the serpent's root a viper will come out, And its fruit will be a winged serpent. (Isaiah 14:29 KJV)*

> *The burden of the beasts of the south: into the land of trouble and anguish, from whence come the young and old lion, the viper and fiery flying serpent, they will carry their riches upon the shoulders of young asses, and their treasures upon the bunches of camels, to a people that shall not profit them. (Isaiah 30:6 KJV)*

In both instances, these fiery flying serpents are identified as *seraphim* in Hebrew. They are also depicted on the walls of the pyramids in Egypt. In some historical accounts, these seraphim had the ability to confuse telepathically and pursued humans over other prey. These are quite different from the seraphim of the throne room of God described by Isaiah in chapter 6. I am then reminded of the curse pronounced on the *saraph* that deceived Eve in the Garden. Once again, we return to the original war criminal in Eden:

> *The Lord God told the Shining One,*
>
> *"Because you have done this,*
>
> *you are more cursed than all the livestock,*
>
> *and more than all the earth's animals,*
>
> *You'll crawl on your belly*
>
> *and eat dust*
>
> *as long as you live.*
>
> *"I'll place hostility between you and the woman,*
>
> *between your offspring and her offspring.*

He'll strike you on the head,

and you'll strike him on the heel." (Genesis 3:14-15
ISV)

There is a connection between the curse on the saraph in Genesis 3:14, which brought death upon mankind, and the fiery serpents of the wilderness called by the same name. Both brought death. My mistake was attempting to compare Yehshua on the cross to the serpent on the pole, rather than Yehshua hanging on the pole to reverse the curse of the saraph.

And as Moses lifted up the serpent in the wilderness,
even so must the Son of man be lifted up: That
whosoever believeth in him should not perish, but have
eternal life. (John 3:14-15 KJV)

The fiery serpents, called by the same name in Hebrew as the saraph in the garden—seraphim (plural)—brought sin and death. The brass serpent on the pole was prophetic of the cross, reversing the curse placed on mankind when Yehshua was lifted up on the pole. The saraph that deceived Eve was condemned on that same pole where Yehshua was lifted up, and the curse of death reversed.

John 3:14–15 leads to the most well-known verse of the Bible:

For God so loved the world, that he gave his only
begotten Son, that whosoever believeth in him should
not perish, but have everlasting life. (John 3:16 KJV)

Thus the fate of the saraph and his friends was sealed on the pole:

Then shall he say also unto them on the left hand,
Depart from me, ye cursed, into everlasting fire,

prepared for the devil and his angels. (Matthew 25:41 KJV)

Blotting out the handwriting of ordinances that was against us, which was contrary to us, and took it out of the way, nailing it to his cross;

And having spoiled principalities and powers, he made a shew of them openly, triumphing over them in it. (Colossians 2:14-15 KJV)

God standeth in the congregation of the mighty; he judgeth among the gods. (Psalm 82:1 KJV)

What gods? The fallen angels that God is at war with, one of whom Moses symbolized as a serpent (saraph) on a pole. The crucifixion stripped death of its authority, the fiery serpent, a fallen seraphim angel.

Then cometh the end, when he shall have delivered up the kingdom to God, even the Father; when he shall have put down all rule and all authority and power. (1 Corinthians 15:24 KJV)

Which he wrought in Christ, when he raised him from the dead, and set him at his own right hand in the heavenly places,

Far above all principality, and power, and might, and dominion, and every name that is named, not only in this world, but also in that which is to come:

And hath put all things under his feet, and gave him to be the head over all things to the church,

Which is his body, the fulness of him that filleth all in all. (Ephesians 1:20-23 KJV)

Paul makes distinctive connections in his letters between the crucifixion and the end of the authority of principalities and powers of darkness. Sin and death were crucified with Yehshua; this was the symbolism of the seraph on the pole.

> *Forasmuch then as the children are partakers of flesh and blood, he also himself likewise took part of the same; that through death he might destroy him that had the power of death, that is, the devil. (Hebrews 2:14 KJV)*

Meanwhile, there are numerous accounts of the "sons of God," the A Team, appearing either in person or in dreams and to guide God's people in the direction of His will. Another of those is the account of the angel appearing to Joshua in chapter 5:

> *And it came to pass, when Joshua was by Jericho, that he lifted up his eyes and looked, and, behold, there stood a man over against him with his sword drawn in his hand: and Joshua went unto him, and said unto him, Art thou for us, or for our adversaries?*
>
> *And he said, Nay; but as captain of the host of the Lord am I now come. And Joshua fell on his face to the earth, and did worship, and said unto him, What saith my Lord unto his servant?*
>
> *And the captain of the Lord›s host said unto Joshua, Loose thy shoe from off thy foot; for the place whereon thou standest is holy. And Joshua did so. (Joshua 5:13-15 KJV)*

There is a wonderful book titled *Angels on Assignment* by pastor Roland Buck, published in the late 1970s, that has often been criticized for being too far-fetched, which I think is a tragedy. Such accounts are difficult to accept only for those of little faith. Pastors and people who share extraordinary accounts of angelic encounters can be measured by their degree of sincerity. If pastors live lavishly, flying jets from continent to continent, that alone doesn't discredit them. But it seems the humblest pastors are the ones that gain the deepest supernatural insight. Derek Prince, for example, was internationally known for his supernatural experiences, yet lived a humble, even quaint lifestyle. This was also the case with Pastor Buck. When I see a person that truly knows the Word of God and has it engraved on his heart, I cannot believe he would use that knowledge for deception or profit. While some may, the Holy Spirit grants discernment through the Word of God. I believe Pastor Buck saw what he claimed to have seen.

In his book *Angels on Assignment*, Pastor Roland Buck recounts an encounter with an angel named Chroni, who arrived at his home alongside the angel Gabriel. Chroni gave Pastor Buck several opportunities to ask questions, and at one point the pastor asked about Jericho—and if Jesus was who appeared to Joshua in chapter 5. I had always believed this must have been Yehshua, since the angel instructed Joshua to remove his sandals, declaring the ground "Holy". But Chroni responded that it was not Jesus but rather himself, the angel of the Lord sent to help Joshua. Unfortunately, he never answered the question as to why Joshua was required to remove his shoes while Pastor Buck was not. I am left to assume that Chroni carried a special anointing from Yehshua, or perhaps, having just come from His presence, was required to honor the ground on which he stood. I suppose it is difficult to imagine asking every necessary question when standing before an ancient son of God.

The angel named Chroni goes on to describe what happened at Jericho: the warring angels with him actually compressed the walls of Jericho into the ground with tremendous force. Once the walls were down, the Israelites quickly overtook Jericho. What is fascinating is that archaeological researchers over the years have been mystified by some of the remains at the site. Some have noted that while many walls appear to have collapsed, others remain completely intact. The implication is that the walls were pressed straight into the ground, just as the angel Chroni told Pastor Buck.

This is a book I highly recommend every Christian reader acquire and digest. It is a short read that will strengthen the foundations of your faith. Of course, there are always naysayers who insist that people claiming to have seen angels have merely hallucinated these experiences. Was Abraham hallucinating? Was Isaiah hallucinating? Was Daniel hallucinating? Was Ezekiel hallucinating? What about Peter being released from prison by an angel? Many men and women of God are called to certain tasks in which God allows the veil to be lifted between our physical dimension and theirs—or, in some cases, even transported to heaven or the throne room of God (Isaiah 6). For a pastor who clearly knows the Word of God to make false claims regarding angels, knowing the consequences would be severe judgment by God, would be insanity. I do not believe Pastor Buck was insane. I believe God called him to a special purpose, and I wish more people knew his story and could embrace the supernatural presence of the A Team working on our behalf.

The same angel (Angel of the Lord) who was at Jericho appears again in the book of Judges, following the book of Joshua. In Judges 2, the angel states:

And an angel of the LORD came up from Gilgal to Bochim, and said, I made you to go up out of Egypt, and have brought you unto the land which I sware unto your fathers; and I said, I will never break my covenant with you.

And ye shall make no league with the inhabitants of this land; ye shall throw down their altars: but ye have not obeyed my voice: why have ye done this?

Wherefore I also said, I will not drive them out from before you; but they shall be as thorns in your sides, and their gods shall be a snare unto you.

This time the angel appears not only to Joshua but to the entire camp of the Israelites, delivering a stern warning. It is again believed that this was likely Yehshua, since He speaks as one with Yahweh. Yet if Pastor Buck's account of Chroni's presence with Joshua at Jericho is accurate, this angel bore a divine message from the throne, speaking with the authority of the Most High God.

The fact that angels worked so closely with Israel—as with no other people–demonstrates their purpose on earth as God's representatives. In the case of Abraham, angels included him in the decision-making process for the destruction of Sodom and Gomorrah. In Joshua's story, warring angels stood beside him in the battle of Jericho. Part of the reason angels were permitted in this battle was that Jericho was a Nephilim stronghold and likely harbored fallen angels as well. God allowed His warring angels to engage to ensure Israel's victory over His enemies. These are lessons that still apply today, though we are seldom permitted to see through the veil.

In Judges 6, we find the story of Gideon, when the Israelites persisted in idolatry and Baal worship. This account, I believe, continues the work of the same warring "angel of the Lord" guiding the Israelites.

Did not the Lord bring us up from Egypt? but now the Lord hath forsaken us, and delivered us into the hands of the Midianites.

And the Lord looked upon him, and said, Go in this thy might, and thou shalt save Israel from the hand of the Midianites: have not I sent thee?

And he said unto him, Oh my Lord, wherewith shall I save Israel? behold, my family is poor in Manasseh, and I am the least in my father›s house.

And the Lord said unto him, Surely I will be with thee, and thou shalt smite the Midianites as one man.

And he said unto him, If now I have found grace in thy sight, then shew me a sign that thou talkest with me.

Depart not hence, I pray thee, until I come unto thee, and bring forth my present, and set it before thee. And he said, I will tarry until thou come again.

And Gideon went in, and made ready a kid, and unleavened cakes of an ephah of flour: the flesh he put in a basket, and he put the broth in a pot, and brought it out unto him under the oak, and presented it.

And the angel of God said unto him, Take the flesh and the unleavened cakes, and lay them upon this rock, and pour out the broth. And he did so.

Then the angel of the Lord put forth the end of the staff that was in his hand, and touched the flesh and the unleavened cakes; and there rose up fire out of the rock, and consumed the flesh and the unleavened cakes. Then the angel of the Lord departed out of his sight.

And when Gideon perceived that he was an angel of the Lord, Gideon said, Alas, O Lord God! for because I have seen an angel of the Lord face to face.

And the Lord said unto him, Peace be unto thee; fear
not: thou shalt not die.

Then Gideon built an altar there unto the Lord, and
called it Jehovahshalom: unto this day it is yet in
Ophrah of the Abiezrites. (Judges 6:12-24 KJV)

The story of Gideon is a great story of how God will sometimes choose and empower a single individual to lead a multitude out of condemnation. While the story of Gideon is less known than the stories of Daniel, Isaiah, Jeremiah, or David, they each share a denominator: unwavering faith in God as the source of their strength.

Something very important to share here is in verse 25 of chapter 6:

And it came to pass the same night, that the LORD
said unto him, Take thy father›s young bullock, even
the second bullock of seven years old, and throw down
the altar of Baal that thy father hath, and cut down the
grove that is by it: (Judges 25:6 KJV)

What were the "groves" frequently mentioned in the Old Testament with regard to pagan worship? Judges 3:7 (KJV) explains:

So the sons of Israel did what was evil in the sight of
the LORD, and they forgot the LORD their God and
served the Baals and the <u>Asheroth</u>.

The word "Asheroth" appears forty times in the Old Testament. On thirty-three occasions, it is mentioned in conjunction with the "groves" or "Asheroth poles" that accompanied Baal worship, as a separate deity. The *Topical Encyclopedia* defines it as follows:

<u>*Topical Encyclopedia*</u>

Asherah poles and idols are significant elements in the study of ancient Israelite religion and its interactions with surrounding cultures. These objects are frequently mentioned in the Old Testament as symbols of idolatry and apostasy, representing a departure from the worship of Yahweh, the God of Israel.

Historical and Cultural Context

Asherah was a prominent goddess in the ancient Near Eastern pantheon, often associated with fertility, motherhood, and the sea. She was worshiped by various cultures, including the Canaanites, who inhabited the land before the Israelites. Asherah was considered the consort of El, the chief deity in the Canaanite religion, and sometimes associated with Baal, another major Canaanite god.

The worship of Asherah often involved the use of wooden poles or carved images, known as Asherah poles, which were erected in high places, under green trees, or near altars. These poles served as symbols of the goddess and were central to the rituals and ceremonies conducted in her honor.

Biblical References

The Bible frequently condemns the worship of Asherah and the erection of Asherah poles, viewing them as abominations and direct violations of the covenant between God and Israel. The Israelites were repeatedly warned against adopting the religious practices of the surrounding nations, including the worship of Asherah.

In <u>Deuteronomy 16:21</u>, the Israelites are explicitly instructed: "Do not set up any wooden Asherah pole beside the altar you build to the LORD your God." This command underscores the incompatibility of Asherah worship with the exclusive worship of Yahweh.

The Book of Judges records instances where the Israelites fell into idolatry, including the worship of Asherah. <u>Judges 3:7</u> states, "And the Israelites did evil in the sight of the LORD. They forgot the LORD their God and served the Baals and the Asherahs."

During the reigns of various kings, efforts were made to eradicate the worship of Asherah. King Hezekiah, known for his religious reforms, «removed the high places, shattered the sacred stones, and cut down the Asherah poles» (<u>2 Kings 18:4</u>). Similarly, King Josiah›s reforms included the destruction of Asherah poles and other idolatrous objects (<u>2 Kings 23:6</u>).

Theological Significance

The presence of Asherah poles and idols in Israelite society represents a recurring theme of spiritual infidelity and the struggle to maintain covenantal faithfulness. The prophets frequently denounced the worship of Asherah, calling the people to repentance and a return to the exclusive worship of Yahweh.

The worship of Asherah and the use of Asherah poles are seen as manifestations of syncretism, where the Israelites attempted to blend the worship of Yahweh with the religious practices of their neighbors. This syncretism

Archaeological Evidence

Archaeological discoveries have provided additional insights into the worship of Asherah. Excavations in ancient Israelite sites have uncovered artifacts and inscriptions that reference Asherah, suggesting that her worship was more widespread than the biblical texts alone might indicate. These findings highlight the cultural and religious influences that the Israelites encountered and sometimes adopted.

Do you notice a modern-day connection to this deity? "Mother earth, fertility, and the sea" practically define the global leftist political agenda to remove God from all religions and cultures. As Jonathan Cahn points out in his book *Return of the Gods*, Asheroth—also known as Ashterah, Inana, Ishtar, Easter, and Semiramis, wife and mother of Nimrod—is still deified today. We teach our children to search for colored eggs laid by mythical rabbits instead of learning the history and mysteries of Passover. Asheroth not only never left Cannan but is still worshipped today as "Gaia" and "Mother Earth." If you think I am stretching the truth, look at who gazes back at you from your cup of latte, crowned and all. Gaia from Greek mythology is a Canaanite extension of the same deity, Asheroth. On your latte from the world's largest coffeehouse, notice the twin serpent tails on each side of the crowned goddess—tails that, according to mythology, came from a curse on the deity. Somehow, I am reminded of Genesis 3:14.

Make no mistake: all cultures around the world have been subtly subjected to the same idolatry that plagued Israel. I believe there is a distinct spiritual connection between this deity and the great harlot "Mystery Babylon." Asheroth is Babylon, the great harlot, worshipped as such by a cult with its own church. Remember, when you hold a latte while watching your children hunt colored eggs on this day dedicated to

Asheroth, on a day ordained by the Council of Nicaea in AD 325, just know that Easter can never fall on the same day as Passover. Passover is fourteen days from the new moon of Nisan, on a full moon. Easter is the first Sunday after the first full moon following the spring equinox. Passover will never coincide with Ishtar Sunday. The AD 325 Council of Nicaea under Constantine determined this intentionally, so that the sun worship day of Ishtar would never be celebrated on the Jewish Passover. Constantine accepted Christianity but still despised the Jews, and this date has been upheld as the official "Pacha date" for 1,700 years.

> *And after these things I saw another angel come down from heaven, having great power; and the earth was lightened with his glory.*
>
> *And he cried mightily with a strong voice, saying, Babylon the great is fallen, is fallen, and is become the habitation of devils, and the hold of every foul spirit, and a cage of every unclean and hateful bird.*
>
> *For all nations have drunk of the wine of the wrath of her fornication, and the kings of the earth have committed fornication with her, and the merchants of the earth are waxed rich through the abundance of her delicacies.*
>
> *And I heard another voice from heaven, saying, Come out of her, my people, that ye be not partakers of her sins, and that ye receive not of her plagues.*
>
> *For her sins have reached unto heaven, and God hath remembered her iniquities. (Revelation 18:1-4 KJV)*

But I digress. To continue with another great story about the influence of angels in biblical accounts, we turn to the story of Samson, found in the book of Judges.

And the children of Israel did evil again in the sight of the Lord; and the Lord delivered them into the hand of the Philistines forty years.

And there was a certain man of Zorah, of the family of the Danites, whose name was Manoah; and his wife was barren, and bare not.

And the angel of the Lord appeared unto the woman, and said unto her, Behold now, thou art barren, and bearest not: but thou shalt conceive, and bear a son.

Now therefore beware, I pray thee, and drink not wine nor strong drink, and eat not any unclean thing:

For, lo, thou shalt conceive, and bear a son; and no razor shall come on his head: for the child shall be a Nazarite unto God from the womb: and he shall begin to deliver Israel out of the hand of the Philistines.

Then the woman came and told her husband, saying, A man of God came unto me, and his countenance was like the countenance of an angel of God, very terrible: but I asked him not whence he was, neither told he me his name:

But he said unto me, Behold, thou shalt conceive, and bear a son; and now drink no wine nor strong drink, neither eat any unclean thing: for the child shall be a Nazarite to God from the womb to the day of his death.

Then Manoah intreated the Lord, and said, O my Lord, let the man of God which thou didst send come again unto us, and teach us what we shall do unto the child that shall be born.

And God hearkened to the voice of Manoah; and the angel of God came again unto the woman as she sat in the field: but Manoah her husband was not with her.

And the woman made haste, and ran, and shewed her husband, and said unto him, Behold, the man hath appeared unto me, that came unto me the other day.

And Manoah arose, and went after his wife, and came to the man, and said unto him, Art thou the man that spakest unto the woman? And he said, I am.

And Manoah said, Now let thy words come to pass. How shall we order the child, and how shall we do unto him?

And the angel of the Lord said unto Manoah, Of all that I said unto the woman let her beware.

She may not eat of any thing that cometh of the vine, neither let her drink wine or strong drink, nor eat any unclean thing: all that I commanded her let her observe.

And Manoah said unto the angel of the Lord, I pray thee, let us detain thee, until we shall have made ready a kid for thee.

And the angel of the Lord said unto Manoah, Though thou detain me, I will not eat of thy bread: and if thou wilt offer a burnt offering, thou must offer it unto the Lord. For Manoah knew not that he was an angel of the Lord.

And Manoah said unto the angel of the Lord, What is thy name, that when thy sayings come to pass we may do thee honour?

And the angel of the Lord said unto him, Why askest thou thus after my name, seeing it is secret?

So Manoah took a kid with a meat offering, and offered it upon a rock unto the Lord: and the angel did wonderously; and Manoah and his wife looked on.

*For it came to pass, when the flame went up toward
heaven from off the altar, that the angel of the Lord
ascended in the flame of the altar. And Manoah and his
wife looked on it, and fell on their faces to the ground.*

*But the angel of the Lord did no more appear to
Manoah and to his wife. Then Manoah knew that he
was an angel of the Lord.*

*And Manoah said unto his wife, We shall surely die,
because we have seen God.*

*But his wife said unto him, If the Lord were pleased
to kill us, he would not have received a burnt offering
and a meat offering at our hands, neither would he
have shewed us all these things, nor would as at this
time have told us such things as these. (Judges 13:1-23
KJV)*

And from there, we know the amazing story of Samson that could fill its own book.

In the book of 2 Kings is a fascinating account of where, once again, an angel does Israel's dirty work.

*And it came to pass that night, that the angel of
the LORD went out, and smote in the camp of the
Assyrians an hundred fourscore and five thousand:
and when they arose early in the morning, behold, they
were all dead corpses. (2 Kings 19:35 KJV)*

In chapter 18 prior to this event, King Hezekiah, after hearing a report of the advancing Assyrian army, tore his clothes and covered himself in sackcloth before going "into the house of the Lord" in prayer for Israel. The result? Hezekiah's obedience and fear of God rendered an official judgment on the Assyrian army, killing 185,000 of them in their sleep.

*Indeed, he who watches over Israel will neither
slumber nor sleep.*

*The Lord watches over you—the Lord is your shade at
your right hand. (Psalm 121:4-5 KJV)*

This divine protection over Israel was not restricted to Old Testament history. In the 1967 Six-Day War between Israel and its neighboring enemies, as well as the Yom Kippur War of 1973, numerous miraculous events occurred that defy natural explanation. In one instance, the Syrian army held every advantage over the Israeli forces yet inexplicably retreated from what appeared to be an inferior force. After his capture, the Syrian commander reported seeing a huge angel over the Israeli force, warning him not to advance.

Another account describes the Israeli army maneuvering through a minefield to gain a superior strategic position against the Syrians during the same Six-Day War. Suddenly, a strong wind arose from nowhere, uncovering the mines and granting the Israelis a tactical advantage. Prime Minister Netanyahu has publicly stated that miracles account for a major part of Israeli military strategy. Aware that they are outnumbered, they rely on miracles and angels to support their forces.

In 2 Kings 6 is an amazing account of Elisha's experience with angelic forces:

*And when the servant of the man of God was risen
early, and gone forth, behold, an host compassed the
city both with horses and chariots. And his servant said
unto him, Alas, my master! how shall we do?*

*And he answered, Fear not: for they that be with us are
more than they that be with them.*

*And Elisha prayed, and said, Lord, I pray thee, open
his eyes, that he may see. And the Lord opened the
eyes of the young man; and he saw: and, behold, the*

mountain was full of horses and chariots of fire round
about Elisha. (2 Kings 6:15-17 KJV)

They that are with us are far more than those who are with our enemies—not to mention that simple demons are spiritual misfits compared to the sons of God who stand for us! Be with God and be encouraged!

There are over one hundred accounts in the Bible of angelic interactions with people, many involving the Israelites or Jews of the New Testament. In Acts 12, we find the account of Peter being released from prison by an angel. At first, he thought he was dreaming, but later, when the angel departed, he realized it was not a dream:

Now about that time Herod the king stretched forth his
hands to vex certain of the church.

And he killed James the brother of John with the
sword.

And because he saw it pleased the Jews, he proceeded
further to take Peter also. (Then were the days of
unleavened bread.)

And when he had apprehended him, he put him in
prison, and delivered him to four quaternions of
soldiers to keep him; intending after Easter to bring
him forth to the people.

Peter therefore was kept in prison: but prayer was
made without ceasing of the church unto God for him.

And when Herod would have brought him forth, the
same night Peter was sleeping between two soldiers,
bound with two chains: and the keepers before the door
kept the prison.

And, behold, the angel of the Lord came upon him, and
a light shined in the prison: and he smote Peter on the

side, and raised him up, saying, Arise up quickly. And his chains fell off from his hands.

And the angel said unto him, Gird thyself, and bind on thy sandals. And so he did. And he saith unto him, Cast thy garment about thee, and follow me. (Acts 12:1-8 KJV)

Names are often confusing in the Bible when several people share the same name. Such is the case with both Herod and James at the beginning of this chapter. This particular Herod was the son of Herod the Great, who had all the firstborn sons of Judea killed in an attempt to eliminate the threat of the Messiah identified by the wise men (Matthew 2; Luke 2). He was known as Herod II, or Herod Agrippa. The James whom Herod ordered executed was the brother of St. John, author of four books of the New Testament. This was not James, the brother of Yehshua, who was not converted until after Yehshua's death.

After ordering James's beheading, Herod sent for Peter, but Peter had already been released from prison by an angel and escaped death. In Acts 9, Saul was converted on the road to Damascus when he was struck blind by Yehshua Himself. While this was Yehshua and not an angel, it is noteworthy that blindness is one of the weapons—or tools—used by angels. This blindness can be metaphorical, as in spiritual blindness, or physical, as in the case of the angels inflicting blindness on the Sodomites (Genesis 19), Elisha's prayer in 2 Kings 6:18–20, and Paul's experience three chapters before Peter's release from prison.

In all these accounts of angels in the Bible, the "sons of God" carry out God's orders on behalf of mankind. These physical manifestations of the sons of God were not limited to the Bible but continue even today, as told by Pastor Roland Buck and multitudes of other individuals. I have shared my own account of an angelic visitation. I believe their physical appearances either precede or accompany greater moves of God on earth.

There is another exclusive group of these sons of God, distinct in identity and surrounded by great mystique, called the "Morning Stars."

Job 38:7 (KJV) identifies the "sons of God" and "Morning Stars" as being together yet distinct from one another:

> ***When the morning stars sang together, and all the sons***
> ***of God shouted for joy?***

Thankfully, we have this one obscure verse from Job to guide us into a deeper spiritual journey, which I reveal in a subsequent chapter.

CHAPTER 4

Who Will Be Among the Sons of God in the Future?

For as many as are led by the Spirit of God, they are the sons of God.

—Romans 8:14 (KJV)

If you are like me, you may have read that verse many times without considering the full depth of the meaning intended by Paul. One day it struck me like a bolt of lightning: the entire context of the Bible—from the curse on the Seraph in the Garden to the Melchizedek priesthood under the last Adam, Yehshua—connects to this one verse. Paul had divine insight, inspired by the Holy Spirit, and he shared it with us in a way that only those led by the Spirit can or will understand. This is where translations matter.

If you read only the NIV, for example, you will miss the significance of what Paul intended to communicate in Romans 8. The NIV reads as follows:

For those who are led by the Spirit of God are the
<u>children</u> of God. Romans 8:14 (NIV)

You might say, "What's the difference? Children or sons, it's all the same!" That may be true in modern Western cultures, but a first-century Jew would have understood why Paul specifically said "sons" and not "children," since the term refers to a legal right to an *inheritance*. To understand this point Paul makes, we must look into the original language. Here is the Greek from Strong's:

◀ 5207. huios ▶

<u>Strong›s Lexicon</u>

huios: Son

Original Word: υἱός

Part of Speech: Noun, Masculine

Transliteration: huios

***<u>Corresponding Greek / Hebrew Entries:</u>** - H1121 - בֵּן* *(ben): Often translated as «son,» this Hebrew word shares a similar range of meanings, including literal and figurative uses.*

*- **H1248** - רַב (bar): Another Hebrew term for «son,» used in poetic and Aramaic contexts.*

Usage: The Greek word «huios» primarily means «son» and is used in the New Testament to denote a male offspring. It is also employed metaphorically to describe a relationship of kinship or association, such as «sons of God» or «sons of light.» In a broader sense, it can refer to descendants or followers who share a particular characteristic or identity.

*Cultural and Historical Background: In the ancient Greco-Roman world, the concept of «sonship» carried significant social and legal implications. **Sons were often seen as heirs and bearers of the family name and legacy. In Jewish culture, being a «son» also implied a covenantal relationship with God**, as seen in the designation of Israel as God›s «firstborn son» (Exodus 4:22). **<u>The New Testament expands this concept to include all believers as «sons of God» through faith</u>***

To be a "son" implies a legal right to an inheritance. With that concept in mind, let's return to Romans 8 for a full context:

There is therefore now no condemnation to them which are in Christ Jesus, who walk not after the flesh, but after the Spirit.

For the law of the Spirit of life in Christ Jesus hath made me free from the law of sin and death.

For what the law could not do, in that it was weak through the flesh, God sending his own Son in the likeness of sinful flesh, and for sin, condemned sin in the flesh:

That the righteousness of the law might be fulfilled in us, who walk not after the flesh, but after the Spirit.

For they that are after the flesh do mind the things of the flesh; but they that are after the Spirit the things of the Spirit.

For to be carnally minded is death; but to be spiritually minded is life and peace.

Because the carnal mind is enmity against God: for it is not subject to the law of God, neither indeed can be.

So then they that are in the flesh cannot please God.

But ye are not in the flesh, but in the Spirit, if so be that the Spirit of God dwell in you. Now if any man have not the Spirit of Christ, he is none of his.

And if Christ be in you, the body is dead because of sin; but the Spirit is life because of righteousness.

But if the Spirit of him that raised up Jesus from the dead dwell in you, he that raised up Christ from the dead shall also quicken your mortal bodies by his Spirit that dwelleth in you.

Therefore, brethren, we are debtors, not to the flesh, to live after the flesh.

For if ye live after the flesh, ye shall die: but if ye through the Spirit do mortify the deeds of the body, ye shall live.

<u>For as many as are led by the Spirit of God, they are the sons of God.</u>

For ye have not received the spirit of bondage again to fear; <u>but ye have received the Spirit of adoption, whereby we cry, Abba, Father.</u>

The Spirit itself beareth witness with our spirit, that we are the children of God:

And if children, then heirs; heirs of God, and joint-heirs with Christ; if so be that we suffer with him, that we may be also glorified together.

For I reckon that the sufferings of this present time are not worthy to be compared with the glory which shall be revealed in us.

For the earnest expectation of the creature waiteth for the manifestation of the sons of God.

For the creature was made subject to vanity, not willingly, but by reason of him who hath subjected the same in hope,

Because the creature itself also shall be delivered from the bondage of corruption into the glorious liberty of the children of God.

For we know that the whole creation groaneth and travaileth in pain together until now.

And not only they, but ourselves also, which have the firstfruits of the Spirit, even we ourselves groan within ourselves, waiting for the adoption, to wit, the redemption of our body.

For we are saved by hope: but hope that is seen is not hope: for what a man seeth, why doth he yet hope for?

But if we hope for that we see not, then do we with patience wait for it.

Likewise the Spirit also helpeth our infirmities: for we know not what we should pray for as we ought: but the Spirit itself maketh intercession for us with groanings which cannot be uttered.

And he that searcheth the hearts knoweth what is the mind of the Spirit, because he maketh intercession for the saints according to the will of God.

*And we know that all things work together for good
to them that love God, to them who are the called
according to his purpose.*

*For whom he did foreknow, he also did predestinate to
be conformed to the image of his Son, that he might be
the firstborn among many brethren.*

*Moreover whom he did predestinate, them he also
called: and whom he called, them he also justified: and
whom he justified, them he also glorified.*

*What shall we then say to these things? If God be for
us, who can be against us?*

*He that spared not his own Son, but delivered him up
for us all, how shall he not with him also freely give us
all things?*

*Who shall lay any thing to the charge of God›s elect? It
is God that justifieth.*

*Who is he that condemneth? It is Christ that died, yea
rather, that is risen again, who is even at the right hand
of God, who also maketh intercession for us.*

*Who shall separate us from the love of Christ? shall
tribulation, or distress, or persecution, or famine, or
nakedness, or peril, or sword?*

*As it is written, For thy sake we are killed all the day
long; we are accounted as sheep for the slaughter.*

*Nay, in all these things we are more than conquerors
through him that loved us.*

*For I am persuaded, that neither death, nor life, nor
angels, nor principalities, nor powers, nor things
present, nor things to come,*

The gospel hinges on this promise: we who are led by the Spirit are entitled as joint heirs with Christ, no longer condemned by the law of the flesh but saved by the Spirit. For the Spirit Himself bears witness that we are adopted children of the Father. As adopted children, a legal inheritance is our portion along with Christ, God's only begotten Son. No power, present or future, can separate us from this inheritance offered out of love. Even nature anxiously awaits the manifestation of the sons of God to be revealed, when the curse over the earth is reversed and restored as it was in Eden.

Interestingly, Paul shifts between "sons" and "children," where the relevance changes from legal status to general family status. In the distant future beyond Paul's time, this seems to prefigure the statement in Galatians 3:28: there is no Jew or Gentile, male or female, only one family under Christ. Yet the word "sons" must be used interchangeably to denote both legal and spiritual identity as an heir, or "joint heir."

In Genesis 3:18, we see that the entire earth was punished for Adam's disobedience. Remember that Adam was a son of God. I have stated before that Adam was created separately from "male and female created He them, and commanded them to replenish the earth" on Day 6 of Creation (Genesis 1:26 KJV). If Adam was created on Day 6 along with females, why did God say it was not good for man to be alone (Genesis 2:18)? Adam in Eden was, by definition, the first Melchizedek—king and priest of the earth. When Adam fell, his authority over the earth defaulted to Lucifer. That was the beginning of thorns, thistles, sickness, and death.

I live in a desert where, at times, deer are forced to eat cactus to survive. Their mouths and tongues are filled with thorns during seasons when cactus is the only food source available. The creature anxiously awaits the manifestation of the sons of God to be revealed (verse 19), when the curse of the first Adam is reversed by the last Adam.

The first Adam was the only man to be called a son of God until the birth of Yehshua. At the crucifixion, Yehshua reversed the curse on mankind under His authority, so that all who are led by the Spirit are sons of God with Him—joint heirs together with the last Adam, King and Priest (Hebrews 4:14–16, 7:17). Hallelujah!

Therefore, according to Romans 8, those who are led by the Spirit are the future sons of God and joint heirs with Christ. Heirs to what? What is the inheritance? I cannot recall anyone asking this question, since we often assume that salvation is the inheritance we share with Christ in heaven. But doesn't Paul teach that salvation is by grace through faith, a gift from God?

> *For by grace are ye saved through faith; and that not of yourselves: it is the gift of God:*
>
> *Not of works, lest any man should boast. (Ephesians 2:8-9 KJV)*

Paul taught that faith itself is a gift of the Holy Spirit, and that by faith we are saved. Salvation is an opportunity offered to everyone. This is the gift of God (see Romans 8:16 again).

> *For I say, through the grace given unto me, to every man that is among you, not to think of himself more highly than he ought to think; but to think soberly, according as <u>God hath dealt to every man the measure of faith.</u> (Romans 12:3 KJV)*
>
> *So then faith cometh by hearing, and hearing by the word of God. (Romans 10:17 KJV)*
>
> <u>*To another [wonder-working] faith [is given] by the same [Holy] Spirit,*</u> *and to another the [extraordinary]*

We are saved by Grace through faith, and this is a gift of God to those who are led by the Spirit. Yet this is not necessarily the inheritance granted to us as joint heirs with Christ. Something distinctly different is implied: one thing is offered as a gift, while another will be inherited later. Some—but perhaps not all—who receive the gift of faith and salvation will be led by the Holy Spirit to an eventual inheritance. These are the future sons of God, joint heirs with Christ. Who are they, and what is their inheritance?

I believe the answer to the first part of that question can be found in the book of Revelation. Highlights of each church, in order of their appearance, are as follows:

(1) <u>Ephesus</u> (<u>Revelation 2:1–7</u>) - the church that had forsaken its first love (2:4).

(2) <u>Smyrna</u> (<u>Revelation 2:8–11</u>) - the church that would suffer persecution (2:10).

(3) <u>Pergamum</u> (<u>Revelation 2:12–17</u>) - the church that needed to repent (2:16).

(4) <u>Thyatira</u> (<u>Revelation 2:18–29</u>) - the church that had a false prophetess (2:20).

(5) <u>Sardis</u> (<u>Revelation 3:1–6</u>) - the church that had fallen asleep (3:2).

(6) <u>Philadelphia</u> (<u>Revelation 3:7–13</u>) - the church that had endured patiently (3:10).

(7) <u>Laodicea</u> (<u>Revelation 3:14–22</u>) - the church with the lukewarm faith (3:16).

All seven are Christian churches, and we can expect that most of their members had received the gift of salvation, though possibly compromised. Five of the seven churches receive negative reports, while two received good reports. Only one of those two churches is promised something special; that differentiates this church from the rest:

> *And to the angel of the church in Philadelphia write;*
> *These things saith he that is holy, he that is true, he*
> *that hath the key of David, he that openeth, and no*
> *man shutteth; and shutteth, and no man openeth;*
>
> *I know thy works: behold, I have set before thee an*
> *open door, and no man can shut it: for thou hast a little*
> *strength, and hast kept my word, and hast not denied*
> *my name.*
>
> *Behold, I will make them of the synagogue of Satan,*
> *which say they are Jews, and are not, but do lie;*
> *behold, I will make them to come and worship before*
> *thy feet, and to know that I have loved thee.*
>
> *Because thou hast kept the word of my patience, I also*
> *will keep thee from the hour of temptation, which shall*
> *come upon all the world, to try them that dwell upon*
> *the earth.*
>
> *Behold, I come quickly: hold that fast which thou hast,*
> *that no man take thy crown.*
>
> *Him that overcometh will I make a pillar in the temple*
> *of my God, and he shall go no more out: and I will*
> *write upon him the name of my God, and the name*
> *of the city of my God, which is new Jerusalem, which*
> *cometh down out of heaven from my God: and I will*
> *write upon him my new name.*
>
> *He that hath an ear, let him hear what the Spirit saith*
> *unto the churches. (Revelation 3:7-13 KJV)*

In my last book titled *The Bride, the Wise Virgins, and the Last Adam*, I pointed out that this church must be the bride of Christ—the great "mystery of the church" that Paul speaks of in Ephesians 5:32. Compare to passage above:

- Verse 9 is clearly speaking of the Gentile bride before whom many will bow.
- Verse 10 is a promise to escape the Great Tribulation (the "hour of temptation").
- Verse 11 is a promise of a crown if she (the bride church) defends it.
- Verse 12 is a promise to become pillars (perhaps represented by the twenty-four elders in Revelation 4:4) in the temple of God, reigning with Christ. This can only be the bride.
- The New Jerusalem is the bride's gift (Revelation 21:10–27), and this church receives the name of God and Yehshua's new name. This new name, though unknown for now, signifies a transformational shift in universal authority that will be shared with the bride.
- The church of Philadelphia is the bride. She will reign with Yehshua from this new temple of God (Revelation 3:21).
- The other six churches are offered the opportunity to repent and reign with Him, joining Philadelphia as the bride. The overcomers that join Philadelphia will not share in the second death.

References to the saints—the bride—ruling with their King are numerous and can even be found in the Old Testament.

> *And the kingdom and dominion, and the greatness of*
> *the kingdom under the whole heaven, shall be given*
> *to the people of the saints of the most High, whose*
> *kingdom is an everlasting kingdom, and all dominions*
> *shall serve and obey him. (Daniel 7:27 KJV)*

In my last book, I also shared this passage from Jude that comes from Enoch, preceding the Old Testament version we have in our possession:

And Enoch also, the seventh from Adam, prophesied of these, saying, Behold, the Lord cometh with ten thousands of his saints,

To execute judgment upon all, and to convince all that are ungodly among them of all their ungodly deeds which they have ungodly committed, and of all their hard speeches which ungodly sinners have spoken against him. (Jude 14-15 KJV)

If saints are executing judgment, are they not in a position of authority? Of course they are. This is part of reigning with Christ:

If we suffer, we shall also reign with him: if we deny him, he also will deny us. (2 Timothy 2:12 KJV)

Do ye not know that the saints shall judge the world? and if the world shall be judged by you, are ye unworthy to judge the smallest matters?

Know ye not that we shall judge angels? how much more things that pertain to this life? (1 Corinthians 6:2-3 KJV)

Blessed and holy is he that hath part in the first resurrection: on such the second death hath no power, but they shall be priests of God and of Christ, and <u>shall reign with him a thousand years. (</u>Revelation 20:6 KJV)

The Church of Philadelphia perfectly fits this profile and must be the bride of Christ, reigning with Him from the temple of God. Notice something in 1 Corinthians 6:3: if you substitute the word *angels* for *sons of God*, the meaning remains completely applicable under Yehshua's authority. Which angels or sons of God? Obviously, those who placed themselves into the predicament of requiring judgment.

A primary point I intended to make in my last book, *The Bride, the Wise Virgins, and the Last Adam,* was that understanding the appointed times of God is critical. If there were only one final harvest of saints, too many would not be gathered in. Of the seven biblical feasts, three are directly correlated to the agricultural harvests of grains and fruits. The barley was the first harvest, related to the Old Testament saints, and fulfilled at Passover. The wheat is the second harvest, representing the church born on the Day of Pentecost, and is still in the theological field. I do not believe Pentecost can be considered a completely fulfilled feast if the church is the wheat and the Church Age has not come to a close.

The main wheat harvest will be the rapture ahead of the tribulation that closes the age. The gleaning of the wheat will be those Christians who remain after the rapture but refuse the mark of the beast and/or are killed for their steadfastness in Christ.

> *And I saw thrones, and they sat upon them, and judgment was given unto them: and I saw the souls of them that were beheaded for the witness of Jesus, and for the word of God, and which had not worshipped the beast, neither his image, neither had received his mark upon their foreheads, or in their hands; and they lived and reigned with Christ a thousand years. (Revelation 20:4 KJV)*

In my last book, I revealed that the Church of Philadelphia can only be the bride of Christ. It is the wheat that will be raptured to close the Church Age and completely fulfill Pentecost. The Church of Smyrna was the only other of the seven churches to receive a good report and, in my opinion, represents the wise virgins who will be raptured with the bride. The remaining five churches are Christian churches but received negative reports and will be subjected to the fire. Some of these will join the bride, but most will take the mark because they were "not led by the Spirit."

If faith comes by hearing the Word and is a gift of the Spirit, then those who either did not receive the gift or rejected it (Ephesians 2:8–9;

Romans 12:3, 10:17; 1 Corinthians 12:9) will be among the tares cast into the fire (Matthew 13:36–43). If the wheat is the church, the tares must be removed from it and burned. These are those within the church who were "led by the Spirit" but did not obey. Some will not be revealed as the sons of God, falling for lies and deceptions without a solid foundation in the Word of God. I fear that multitudes of Christians will fall into this category. Too many churches today function as social clubs, dressed nicely for sermons that lack spiritual fire or desire. Worse still are churches that condone "abominations," such as the self-identified "lesbian" pastor who lectured the newly inaugurated President Trump concerning the fears of homosexuals. If they truly knew the Word of God, President Trump would be the least of their concerns.

The bride, then, is the Church of Philadelphia during the Church Age. The churches of Philadelphia (the bride) and Smyrna (possibly the wise virgins of Matthew 25) will be raptured to close the Church Age. These will be transfigured at the time of the rapture (1 Corinthians 15:52—sons of God revealed Romans 8:18–19). The other five churches that received negative reports will be subjected to the tribulation. Those who prevail out of the tribulation will join the rest of the wheat harvest.

Revelation chapters 2 and 3 describe the collective churches that proclaim to be Christian. Only two of the seven receive good reports. Chapter 4 begins with a raptured church. The twenty-four elders at the throne in verse 4 represent a larger community of saints—the main harvest at the close of the Church Age. Yet martyred Christians appear again in chapter 7, following the sealing of the 144,000 and the sixth Seal Judgment. This could be the gleaning of the wheat, in keeping with ancient Jewish harvest traditions. The book of Ruth, in fact, is synonymous with the Gentile bride story.

Something I only recently considered is that there is only one seal judgment after the last seal judgment in Revelation 6, which occurs in Revelation 8:1. In Revelation 7, we see the martyred saints who died in the tribulation (verse 14). Then the seventh seal in chapter 8 is a short pause before the trumpet judgments begin. After the trumpet judgments, Yehshua appears on Mount Zion in Revelation 14, and in verses 14–15,

He concludes the harvests before the Bowl Judgments and the final wrath of God is poured out. I did not include this in the last book, but it now seems more likely that the saints of chapter 7 were not raptured but rather, harvested as martyred souls, just as the passage states. The final gleaning of the wheat does not come until Revelation 14:15, ahead of the Bowl Judgments. I know of no alternative view that reconciles the sequence of events in Revelation with the three feast harvests. More on that later.

The bride-church, the wheat of Pentecost, and the "sons of God who are led by the Spirit" are one and the same. Not all wheat is raptured with the Church of Philadelphia.

I need to detour for a paragraph or two to explain something important about Yehshua standing on Mount Zion:

> ***And I looked, and, lo, a Lamb stood on the mount Sion,***
> ***and with him an hundred forty and four thousand,***
> ***having his Father›s name written in their foreheads.***
> ***(Revelation 14:1 KJV)***

I was confounded by this verse because it is technically a second coming that does not occur on the Mount of Olives. I was unable to find any scholarly commentary that addressed my concern, but I did come across a study by Chuck Missler on this chapter. He was teaching through chapter 13, and when he reached chapter 14, he merely stated, "If you think the second coming is on the Mount of Olives, then you have a problem with this verse." Beyond that he offered only conjecture, so it remains a mystery.

My point in sharing this is to illustrate that none of us have all the answers, and we should not be overly dogmatic about one view or another. Some of us may be right; most of us will be wrong.

But the verse clearly states that Yehshua stands on Mount Zion as He makes the final harvest—or gleaning, if you will. After this, the only rare survivors of the Bowl Judgments are the remnant in the wilderness (Revelation 12:6). Why does He stand on Mount Zion for this final harvest event?

And the king and his men went to Jerusalem unto the Jebusites, the inhabitants of the land: which spake unto David, saying, Except thou take away the blind and the lame, thou shalt not come in hither: thinking, David cannot come in hither.

Nevertheless David took the strong hold of Zion: the same is the city of David. (2 Samuel 5:6-7 KJV)

Then Solomon assembled the elders of Israel, and all the heads of the tribes, the chief of the fathers of the children of Israel, unto king Solomon in Jerusalem, that they might bring up the ark of the covenant of the Lord out of the city of David, which is Zion. (1 Kings 8:1 KJV)

These two verses demonstrate that the tourist site called Mount Zion in Jerusalem today is not the biblical location. At present, Mount Zion is believed to be the highest point on the western ridge of the Central Valley. Some also claim it is the Temple Mount, which would be true except that the Temple Mount revered as a holy site today is not the City of David. The City of David and the original temple were destroyed, just as Yehshua prophesied in Matthew 24:2–4. What was not destroyed was the Roman fortress known as Fort Antonia, which is the modern-day Temple Mount—not the original temple location. I am certain that rabbinical leadership, as well as the Israeli government, knows this fact and conceals the true location.

Research on this subject is rather obscure. Many researchers believe that Mount Zion was the location of the temple, at the City of David, not the modern-day Temple Mount. A great work was done by Bible researcher Bob Cornuke, as well as others such as Pastor Ken Klein's production titled *Lost Temple of the Jews,* both of which can be found on YouTube.

So why is Yehshua standing on Mount Zion—the City of David—at this final harvest?

For ye are not come unto the mount that might be touched, and that burned with fire, nor unto blackness, and darkness, and tempest,

And the sound of a trumpet, and the voice of words; which voice they that heard intreated that the word should not be spoken to them any more:

(For they could not endure that which was commanded, And if so much as a beast touch the mountain, it shall be stoned, or thrust through with a dart:

And so terrible was the sight, that Moses said, I exceedingly fear and quake:)

But ye are come unto mount Sion, and unto the city of the living God, the heavenly Jerusalem, and to an innumerable company of angels,

To the general assembly and church of the firstborn, which are written in heaven, and to God the Judge of all, and to the spirits of just men made perfect,

And to Jesus the mediator of the new covenant, and to the blood of sprinkling, that speaketh better things than that of Abel.

See that ye refuse not him that speaketh. For if they escaped not who refused him that spake on earth, much more shall not we escape, if we turn away from him that speaketh from heaven:

Whose voice then shook the earth: but now he hath promised, saying, Yet once more I shake not the earth only, but also heaven.

And this word, Yet once more, signifieth the removing of those things that are shaken, as of things that are made, that those things which cannot be shaken may remain.

Wherefore we receiving a kingdom which cannot be moved, let us have grace, whereby we may serve God acceptably with reverence and godly fear:

For our God is a consuming fire. (Hebrews 12:18-29 KJV)

You may want to read the AMP version for clarity. Mount Sinai was of the Old Testament covenant of the law and untouchable—even Moses "feared and quaked." The gospel's New Covenant has a new mediator on Mount Zion, where we approach the living God in Christ's righteousness and not our own: "To the general assembly and church of the firstborn, which are written in heaven, and to God the Judge of all, and to the spirits of just men made perfect…"

Revelation 14:1 and the appearance of Yehshua on Mount Zion for the final harvest are symbolic of His leadership over the "general assembly and church of the firstborn." This gathering completes the harvests of the church, including all who were chosen out of the other five churches of chapters 2 and 3 that received bad marks. Those who understood God's Word and refused to take the mark are the final harvest, and the general assembly of the church of the firstborn is completed on Mount Zion (verse 15).

To be clear, I do not believe that the churches of Philadelphia and Smyrna are separated into bride and bridesmaids. I use this comparison figuratively, drawing from the parable of the ten virgins in Matthew 25. But in theory, there is only the bride raptured and those rejected, as far as the church is concerned. The collective bride comprises the first two grain harvests and their crop gleanings. The last is the olive harvest—the woman in the wilderness (Revelation 12:6)—but she is not the church. She is Israel, not the bride. The olive harvest is separate from the bride church harvests. I covered this in the last book.

So, the sons of God are joint heirs with Christ in an eternal inheritance, and the Bible gives many examples of what this inheritance shall be. Here is a short list of direct references:

To an <u>inheritance</u> incorruptible, and undefiled, and that fadeth not away, reserved in heaven for you. (1 Peter 1:4 KJV)

In whom also we have obtained an inheritance, being predestinated according to the purpose of him who worketh all things after the counsel of his own will. (Ephesians 1:11 KJV)

In whom ye also trusted, after that ye heard the word of truth, the gospel of your salvation: in whom also after that ye believed, ye were sealed with that holy Spirit of promise,

Which is the earnest of <u>our inheritance</u> until the redemption of the purchased possession, unto the praise of his glory. (Ephesians 1:13-14 KJV)

Ephesians 1:14 is very important to understand. Being sealed with the Holy Spirit is, in a sense, a legally binding contract—a down payment, or earnest, on our inheritance until the final redemption.

No one puts it more eloquently than David:

The Lord is the portion of my inheritance and my cup; You support my lot.

The measuring lines have fallen for me in pleasant places; Indeed, my inheritance is beautiful to me. (Psalm 16:5-6 NASB)

In a word, heaven is our inheritance. But the earth will also be our inheritance. In fact, all that has been given to Christ by the Father will be our inheritance. Nothing in the known universe is excluded. We cannot comprehend what God has prepared for us.

But as it is written, Eye hath not seen, nor ear heard, neither have entered into the heart of man, the things

*which God hath prepared for them that love him. (1
Corinthians 2:9 KJV)*

(See also Isaiah 64:4, from which Paul is assumed to have quoted this passage in Psalm 16.)

God is possessor of all heaven and earth (Genesis 14:19) and, by implication, reserves the right to distribute all that is at His disposal according to His will. What belongs to the Father also belongs to the Son. God's sovereign authority is Yehshua's sovereign authority.

*And Jesus came and spake unto them, saying, All
power is given unto me in heaven and in earth.
(Matthew 28:18 KJV)*

*That the God of our Lord Jesus Christ, the Father
of glory, may give unto you the spirit of wisdom and
revelation in the knowledge of him:*

*The eyes of your understanding being enlightened; that
ye may know what is the hope of his calling, and what
the riches of the glory of his inheritance in the saints,*

*And what is the exceeding greatness of his power to
us-ward who believe, according to the working of his
mighty power,*

*Which he wrought in Christ, when he raised him from
the dead, and set him at his own right hand in the
heavenly places,*

*<u>Far above all principality, and power, and might, and
dominion, and every name that is named, not only in
this world, but also in that which is to come:</u>*

*<u>And hath put all things under his feet, and gave him to
be the head over all things to the church. (Ephesians</u>
1:17-22 KJV)*

Notice verse 21 states *"far above all principality..."* It's not even close. The sons of God to be revealed are the bride—the Church of Philadelphia—the *mystery of the church* (Ephesians 5:32). The bride, the sons of God to be revealed, are joint heirs with Christ, sharing authority over all that has been placed under His feet. All power in heaven and on earth has been given to Him. The sons of God will reign with Him over all that is under His authority.

This is the inheritance that the sons of God, who are led by the Spirit, will receive when they are revealed. Until that revelation, they are the bride, and all creation awaits this great unveiling to manifest and be delivered from the curse that consumes the earth.

The sons of God of the future are the bride of today. This is the church—not to be confused by the masculine term *sons*. *Sons* refers to legal status and how we will be changed upon our transfiguration. There is no male or female. The bride and the sons of God are the theological wheat in the field, before and after.

How does Paul define the bride?

> ***There is neither Jew nor Greek, there is neither bond***
> ***nor free, there is neither male nor female: for ye are all***
> ***one in Christ Jesus. (Galatians 3:28 KJV)***

The bride is the church. And of course, thank God for John's anointing of insight and wisdom:

> ***Beloved, now are we the <u>sons of God</u>, and it doth not***
> ***yet appear what we shall be: but we know that, when he***
> ***shall appear, we shall be like him; for we shall see him***
> ***as he is.***
>
> ***And every man that hath this hope in him purifieth***
> ***himself, even as he is pure. (1 John 3:2-3 KJV)***

Hallelujah! No matter what we face on this earth, we have the hope of not only seeing Eden restored as it was before the fall of Adam and the transfer of his authority to Lucifer, but also of receiving everything else that is under Yehshua's authority as part of our joint inheritance with Him.

Recall that one-third of heaven fell with Lucifer. Heaven and earth are not merely two fixed points in space with a straight line between them. There are multitudes of multidimensional realms that were once under Lucifer's authority but have since been stripped from him. I believe these regions of authority were shared with fallen angels, now referred to as "princes"—the other "sons of God" who are at war with God. This is why they were associated with stars and planets in ancient times, when they arrived from space. There is no other explanation for the advanced astronomical knowledge demonstrated by ancient cultures. The ancients possessed a vast understanding of the stars, their names, and their locations, going as far back as Nimrod and Abraham in ancient Sumeria. The stars were associated with the gods of ancient times, many of whom bore their names. These "gods" were fallen angels, "sons of God" such as those responsible for the rebellion in Genesis 6.

With that in mind, many of the biblical references to stars are, I believe, references to the sons of God who rebelled with Lucifer. Here is an example where a star is an angel in Revelation 9:

> *And the fifth angel sounded, and I saw a star fall from heaven unto the earth: and to him was given the key of the bottomless pit. (Revelation 9:1 KJV)*

A star fell from heaven and was given a key to open the abyssal? This is one example of why I believe that stars were associated with "gods," i.e., fallen angels in ancient times. Continue reading through verse 11:

> *And they had a king over them, which is the angel of the bottomless pit, whose name in the Hebrew tongue is Abaddon, but in the Greek tongue hath his name Apollyon. (Revelation 9:11 KJV)*

There are a few ways you can interpret this, but I believe the star that fell from heaven was released from another prison somewhere in space. It was given a key to the abyss and authority over the demonic forces imprisoned there. I intend to cover more on this in another chapter, drawing from the book of Jubilees.

Here is another example:

> *And the stars of heaven fell unto the earth, even as a fig tree casteth her untimely figs, when she is shaken of a mighty wind.*
>
> *And the heaven departed as a scroll when it is rolled together; and every mountain and island were moved out of their places. (Revelation 6:13-14 KJV)*

Many have surmised that these are nuclear missiles falling from the sky. While this is certainly possible, it is not my view. I believe that the Gog and Magog War of Ezekiel 38 begins slightly before the tribulation and is a nuclear war imposed on Israel, setting the tribulation prophecies in motion. This war triggers a peace agreement mediated by the antichrist, which will establish the seven-year timeline.

The timing of verse 13 is at the sixth seal and before the third trumpet event of "wormwood" in Revelation 8, which marks the midpoint of the tribulation. While it is possible that these stars are nuclear missiles, the following verse (Revelation 6:14) indicates an intergalactic phenomenon that our current understanding of astrophysics cannot accommodate. There is a cosmic shift in our galaxy, and everything in the visible sky is shaken from its place.

We know that when Lucifer fell, a multitude of angels under his authority fell with him, and many were eventually imprisoned. We do not know for certain which ones are imprisoned and which are allowed to operate as "princes" under Lucifer's authority. We do know that Lucifer is not currently in prison and does not operate alone. Demons are the disembodied spirits of the Nephilim and do not possess the astrophysical or multidimensional powers of fallen angels.

There are at least seventy "princes," or fallen angels, operating with Lucifer under God's sovereignty, as we covered in a previous chapter. Yet many fallen angels are still bound in chains, as mentioned in Jude 1:6 and 2 Peter 2:4. I noticed something different in 2 Peter 2:4 that is a slight variation from Jude's comment:

> *For if God did not spare angels when they sinned, but threw them into the lowest hell and imprisoned them in chains of deepest darkness, holding them for judgment. (2 Peter 2:4 ISV)*

The ISV renders "chains of deepest darkness" as miscellaneous pits. The Amplified Bible gives a similar rendition:

> *For if God spared not angels when they sinned, but cast them down to hell, and committed them to pits of darkness, to be reserved unto judgment. (2 Peter 2:4 AMP)*

This is the King James version:

> *For if God spared not the angels that sinned, but cast them down to hell, and delivered them into chains of darkness, to be reserved unto judgment. (2 Peter 2:4 KJV)*

It becomes obvious that each translation interprets "chains of darkness" as something apart from hell. I believe that black holes could be the chains of darkness—prisons in space—and that the stars falling from heaven are fallen angels reserved for that great day of judgment, the "Day of the Lord." The heavens open like a scroll, black holes burst and release their energy, and fallen angels are released from the black holes and cast down to the earth.

That's a lot of conjecture and is sure to draw a great deal of criticism, but let's continue. Read this comment from www.astronomy.com:

> *But even the black holes will one day die. And when they do, these monsters won't go gently into the night. A burst of fireworks will light up the universe in the final moments of each black hole, heralding the end of the era.*

> **And the heaven departed as a scroll when it is rolled together; and every mountain and island were moved out of their places. (Revelation 6:14 KJV)**

This is a time when geniuses like Stephen Hawkings will have their opportunity to witness a "big bang," but nothing they think they know will apply or even matter. None of their intelligence or wealth will buy them an extra second to call for help.

In Revelation 1:20, the angels of the seven churches are called stars:

> **The mystery of the seven stars which thou sawest in my right hand, and the seven golden candlesticks. The <u>seven stars are the angels of the seven churches</u>: and the seven candlesticks which thou sawest are the seven churches. (Revelation 1:20 KJV)**

"Stars" in the Bible are *angels*, both the good and the bad. I believe it is possible that even the star "wormwood" in Revelation 8:10–11 is an orbiting prison chamber with an angel locked up inside an asteroid that will be cast to the earth. The tribulation *"day of the Lord"* is also their time of judgment which occurs on the earth where their rebellion began!

> **He telleth the number of the stars; he calleth them all by their names. (Psalm 147:4 KJV)**

I personally do not know any astrophysicists, but obviously, it would be necessary to name every point in the universe in order to traverse it with reference points, like a map. But could it also be possible that stars bear the names of their assigned angels? Or is it that angels bear the names of their assigned stars?

Notice this comment in Strong's for the word "star":

Strong's Exhaustive Concordance

star, stargazer

Probably from the same as Kabbown (in the sense of rolling) or kavah (in the sense of blazing); a star (as round or as shining); **figuratively, a prince** -- star((-gazer)).

Princes are fallen angels and can also be related to stars by definition. With stars in mind as angels or fallen angels, think about what the following verse from Isaiah might be implying. When I first read it, I could not comprehend its intended meaning, but over time, in the context of sons of God being synonymous with stars, it became clearer:

> _And I have put my words in thy mouth, and I have covered thee in the shadow of mine hand, that **I may plant the heavens**, and lay the foundations of the earth, and say unto Zion, Thou art my people. (Isaiah 53:16 KJV)_

"That I may plant the heavens"? Isaiah chapters 50–53 contain some of the most powerful prophecies of the Messiah and of the final days. This verse is generally accepted as one of those prophetic passages in which God promises to restore everything as it was before the curse of death and suffering entered the earth. Planting and laying foundations are the first steps toward something greater. We plant what we intend to grow and possibly harvest later, and we lay foundations for what we intend to build.

Most commentators agree that this passage looks forward to the restoration of the earth and the heavens upon Yehshua's return. I believe that is true, but what if it is more literal and less metaphorical with a reference to something else on a scale incomprehensible to us?

The book of Jude is perhaps the richest book of the Bible, given the depth of information contained in so few words. From Jude I derive the central point of this book: the joints heirs of Christ, the sons of God led by the Holy Spirit.

In about the middle of the book we read the verse:

Raging waves of the sea, foaming out their own shame; <u>wandering stars, to whom is reserved the blackness of darkness for ever. (Jude 1:13 KJV)</u>

Yet another reference to stars trapped in darkness forever. These are fallen angels, the sons of God who rebelled against Him. Then I noticed verse 15 of Isaiah 51, just one verse prior to verse 16:

But I am the Lord thy God, that divided the sea, whose waves roared: The Lord of hosts is his name. (Isaiah 51:15 KJV)

Raging waves foaming in shame? He divided the seas whose waves roared? Hold that thought.....

Did you know that the term "Lord of Hosts" appears at least two hundred times in the Bible? The word *hosts* in Hebrew is Sabaoth and directly translates as "armies."

◄ 4519. sabaóth ►

Strong›s Lexicon

sabaóth: Hosts, Armies

When Yehshua returns to execute judgment upon the nations, He comes as the Commander of heaven's armies:

> *And I saw heaven opened, and behold, a white horse, and He who sat on it is called Faithful and True, and in righteousness He judges and wages war. His eyes are a flame of fire, and on His head are many crowns; and He has a name written on Him which no one knows except Himself. He is clothed with a robe dipped in blood, and His name is called The Word of God. And the armies which are in heaven, clothed in fine linen, white and clean, were following Him on white horses. From His mouth comes a sharp sword, so that with it He may strike down the nations, and He will rule them with a rod of iron; and He treads the wine press of the fierce wrath of God, the Almighty. And on His robe and on His thigh He has a name written: "KING OF KINGS, AND LORD OF LORDS." (Revelation 19:11-16 NASB)*

I believe that throughout the Bible, where we see "Lord of Hosts" more than two hundred times, it is Yehshua as the commander of heaven's armies. Compare Amos 4:13 and Mark 4:41 to illustrate this observation:

> *For, lo, he that formeth the mountains, and createth the wind, and declareth unto man what is his thought, that maketh the morning darkness, and treadeth upon the high places of the earth, <u>The Lord, The God of hosts, is his name</u>. (Amos 4:13 KJV)*

> *And they feared exceedingly, and said one to another, What manner of man is this, that even the wind and the sea obey him? (Mark 4:41 KJV)*

This passage in Mark is a direct reference to the Old Testament verse in Amos 4, just as Jude 1:13 is a direct reference to Isaiah 51:15. Yehshua is the Lord of hosts who goes to war against the stars wandering in darkness—raging waves of the sea foaming in their own shame. The entire context of the book of Jude revolves around two themes: fallen angels and saints (the bride church).

> *And Enoch also, the seventh from Adam, prophesied of these, saying, Behold, the Lord cometh with ten thousands of his saints,*
>
> *To execute judgment upon all, and to convince all that are ungodly among them of all their ungodly deeds which they have ungodly committed, and of all their hard speeches which ungodly sinners have spoken against him.*
>
> *These are murmurers, complainers, walking after their own lusts; and their mouth speaketh great swelling words, having men›s persons in admiration because of advantage.*
>
> *But, beloved, remember ye the words which were spoken before of the apostles of our Lord Jesus Christ;*
>
> *How that they told you there should be mockers in the last time, who should walk after their own ungodly lusts.*
>
> *These be they who separate themselves, sensual, <u>having not the Spirit</u>. (Jude 1:14-19 KJV)*

Jude 1:14 is the same group of "saints" from Romans 8:14, the "sons of God" led by the Holy Spirit.

Jude 1:19 is the same group as Colossians 3:6, the "sons of disobedience."

The sons of God are the saints of Jude 1:14, joining the armies of heaven in Revelation 19:14. These are the joint heirs with Christ, whose reward is in heaven. And heaven implies our eternal place with Yehshua and the Father.

In my Father›s house are many mansions: if it were not so, I would have told you. I go to prepare a place for you.

And if I go and prepare a place for you, I will come again, and receive you unto myself; that where I am, there ye may be also. (John 14:2-3 KJV)

The Father's house is the abode of the Father, and within it are a myriad of abodes. The King James Version translates these as "mansions," though the direct Hebrew is generally "dwelling places." Whether mansions or dwelling places, it is assumed that they are located where the Father is, and there we will always be with Yehshua.

However, Isaiah 51:16 leads us to a broader degree of speculation. Could these "mansions" be spread throughout the heavens, rather than confined to one specific place in "heaven" singular?

Then there is the problem with the phrase "plant the heavens," which I believe indicates a parallel to Genesis 1 on the sixth day of Creation:

So God created man in his own image, in the image of God created he him; male and female created he them.

And God blessed them, and God said unto them, Be fruitful, and multiply, and replenish the earth, and subdue it: and have dominion over the fish of the sea,

*and over the fowl of the air, and over every living thing
that moveth upon the earth.*

*And God saw every thing that he had made, and,
behold, it was very good. And the evening and the
morning were the sixth day. (Genesis 1:27-28, 31 KJV)*

You would not plant something in empty space. Solid, fertile ground—like the earth—is required for planting. The earth itself is a point in space, one among millions of other points in the heavens. "That I may plant the heavens" sounds a great deal like Genesis 1:28, when the earth was being "planted."

When Lucifer fell and took with him one-third of the angels, a great void was left in heaven. I believe that much of the war on earth relates to that void, left in the heavens when they fell in their rebellion against God. There are parts of the universe currently rudderless, except for God's total sovereignty over them, until this situation is resolved in Revelation 19. All creation groans, anxiously awaiting the moment when the manifest sons of God will be revealed. The armies of heaven follow Him whose eyes are like flames of fire and on whose head are many crowns: the King of kings and Lord of lords, who comes to conquer and execute judgment with them.

As Jude makes these extremely relevant connections, notice a crucial point we often overlook:

*And the angels which kept not their first estate, but left
their own habitation, he hath reserved in everlasting
chains under darkness unto the judgment of the great
day. (Jude 1:6 KJV)*

The Amplified Bible, NASB, and other translations render "habitation" as "proper dwelling place." This word for dwelling place comes from the Greek οἰκητήριον (*oikétérion*) and also appears in 2 Corinthians 5:2, referring to a spiritual dwelling place:

*For indeed, in this tent we groan, longing to be clothed
with our dwelling from heaven. (2 Corinthians 5:2
NASB)*

In this context, Paul is referring to our resurrected, glorified bodies.
In Jude 1:6, the fallen angels gave up their glorified bodies and assumed
human flesh and bone for the purpose of corrupting mankind in the Genesis
6 narrative. But when connecting other dots—such as "stars" being angels
and *"planting the heavens,"* where this void continues until we receive
our glorified bodies—I believe that *the future sons of God of Romans 8:14
will inherit the estates forfeited by the fallen sons of God throughout the
heavens when they rebelled.*

These abandoned estates may correspond to the many metaphorical
mansions in the Father's house that Yehshua has been preparing for us
over the past two thousand years. It makes no sense that the earth was
recreated out of chaos in six days by the same Creator (the Word of John
1) who has taken two millennia to construct a dwelling place for the bride
in heaven.

Whatever the inheritance may be, it is something the human mind
cannot conceive (1 Corinthians 2:9). The fact that my mind has imagined
it likely negates the possibility; however, I don't think I am too far off the
path in connecting Isaiah 51:16 to the fallen angel sons of God—"stars"—
and their former estates. When they assumed human form *"and took wives
for themselves, whomever they chose,"* they lowered themselves to man's
level and forfeited their proper dwelling places. Their former estates are
our future inheritance.

When the future sons of God, led by the Spirit, are revealed in their
glorified bodies, death will be swallowed up (1 Corinthians 15:52–54). We
will see Yehshua as He is, because we will be like Him (1 John 3:2). We
will be elevated to receive those forfeited dwelling places as joint heirs
with Christ. Where one fell lower, giving up his estate, another was raised
to receive it. Their reward is eternal darkness; our reward is the eternal
light they forfeited.

It is impossible to understand who the future sons of God will be without understanding what happened in Genesis 6 that brought about the flood. The sons of God—"stars"—who fell with Lucifer and rebelled against God lost their estates with no hope of salvation. *What was theirs is our inheritance as joint heirs with Christ.*

Is it any mystery why they despise us to such an extent? Why they work feverishly, day and night, to destroy us and separate us from God? They once had paradise. They had godlike powers. They were free to travel the universe. They had everything—and lost it—and are now reserved for eternal judgment.

Their loss is our reward. But it isn't free. Where much is given, much is required.

CHAPTER 5

The Harvesters

He that gathereth in summer is a wise son: but he that sleepeth
in harvest is a son that causeth shame.

—Proverbs 10:5 (KJV)

To every thing there is a season, and a time to every purpose
under the heaven:

A time to be born, and a time to die; a time to plant, and a time to
pluck up that which is planted;

—Ecclesiastes 3:1-2 (KJV)

Solomon, son of David, was the second wisest man to have ever lived, next to Yehshua. His words have inspired me to not become a son who brings shame to my Father. In God's wisdom, the wheat grains of the church were both harvested and planted (John 12:24) on the day of Pentecost, fifty days after the Passover crucifixion of the Perfect Lamb without blemish. You and I, as the "sons of God" led by the Spirit were chosen for the final harvest.

- The close of the Church Age is right here upon us. We have only a few days left to gather the wheat from the field before the shaking of the olive tree begins (Isaiah 24:13). Israel is our prophetic clock, and the "end times" of the Church Age were set in motion on May 14, 1948, when Isaiah's prophecy in chapter 66, verse 8, was fulfilled, along with Isaiah 11:11 and prophecies from Ezekiel, Jeremiah, Amos, and others.

- Less than a year earlier, in late 1947, a Bedouin shepherd named Muhammad ed-Dib discovered the Dead Sea Scrolls in a cave at Qumran while searching for a lost goat. Although credit is given to the Essene priests of Qumran for the scrolls, I believe it is possible that John the Baptist lived in this area and may have hidden the scrolls there to protect them from destruction by the Romans, who were persecuting Christians. In any event, who placed the scrolls in the caves is less important than the fact that they remained hidden for nineteen centuries until roughly nine months before Israel was officially reborn as a nation in a single day, fulfilling Isaiah's prophecy. This is no coincidence. It is the hand of God preparing for the return of Yehshua to earth and exposing truth in time for the harvests. Much of that truth has been concealed by the Vatican, but enough has escaped that we know where we are on the prophetic clock with accuracy.

- Forty years after Israel was reborn as a nation, the earth began to shake beneath the Dead Sea, and suddenly sinkholes released fresh water into its depths, fulfilling more prophecy. Here is a headline from the *Times of Israel* in 2017:

As the Dead Sea dries, its collapsing shores force a return to nature

The rapid appearance of more than 6,000 sinkholes is compelling locals, who rely heavily on tourism, to come up with creative solutions to stay afloat.

Since the time of Abraham and the destruction of Sodom and Gomorrah on the shores of the Dead Sea, nothing had survived there—until now. In recent years, flowers once thought extinct have blossomed along its shores, and freshwater fish have appeared in the pools formed by the sinkholes. These sinkholes emerge when fresh running water beneath the Dead Sea dissolves the salt. The salinity has been diluted to the point that the specific gravity of the water has decreased.

The Dead Sea itself was formed by the destruction of Sodom and Gomorrah. As we read in Genesis 13:10, this was once a well-watered valley, as rich as the "Garden of the Lord" (Garden of Eden).

> *And Lot lifted up his eyes, and beheld all the plain of*
> *Jordan, that it was well watered every where, before*
> *the Lord destroyed Sodom and Gomorrah, even as*
> *the garden of the Lord, like the land of Egypt, as thou*
> *comest unto Zoar. (Genesis 13:10 KJV)*

In the destruction of Sodom and Gomorrah, everything was mineralized into salt, including Lot's wife when she disobediently turned her eyes back toward Sodom:

> *But Lot's wife, from behind him, looked back, and she*
> *became a pillar of salt. (Genesis 19:26 KJV)*

This passage indicates that she stayed behind, looking back toward the cities, placing herself in the path of destruction. That Lot's wife became a pillar of salt was not unique; everything in the path of destruction was mineralized. This was not the original condition of the Dead Sea. Its original state was a well-watered valley, even as the Garden of the Lord. Becoming the Dead Sea was a curse upon the entire area, everything blotted out of history except the evidence of salt and pure sulfur balls still burned into the limestone—until now:

> *Then said he unto me, These waters issue out toward*
> *the east country, and go down into the desert, and go*
> *into the sea: which being brought forth into the sea, the*
> *waters shall be healed.*
>
> *And it shall come to pass, that every thing that liveth,*
> *which moveth, whithersoever the rivers shall come,*
> *shall live: and there shall be a very great multitude of*
> *fish, because these waters shall come thither: for they*

shall be healed; and every thing shall live whither the
river cometh. (Ezekiel 47:8-9 KJV)

That the waters need "healing" in verse 8 indicates that the current condition of the Dead Sea is not its natural created state when God declared, *"and it was good"* (Genesis 1:31). Healing is restoration, and anything requiring restoration is not in its original *"good"* state.

And it shall be in that day, that living waters shall go
out from Jerusalem; half of them toward the former
sea, and half of them toward the hinder sea: in summer
and in winter shall it be. (Zechariah 14:8 KJV)

This verse from Zechariah refers to "living waters" as the gospel flowing east and west from Jerusalem, metaphorically spreading throughout the land. It follows Yehshua standing on the Mount of Olives, when the mountain splits east and west, setting the course for the thousand-year reign. I believe this passage is a prophecy of total restoration, not only at Jerusalem but also the Dead Sea, where fresh water full of life will once again flow to and from it, as it did before the curse of destruction. This restoration of Jerusalem will sustain life exactly as it did before the curse of Sodom and Gomorrah, when, as Ezekiel prophesied, the waters *"shall be healed."* In the context of this chapter from Zechariah, we're at the end of the tribulation, yet the healing process at the Dead Sea began years ago.

I share this to indicate where we are on Israel's prophetic clock. We began counting the "last days" in 1948, now we're counting minutes and seconds until the remaining harvests are fulfilled. Reluctantly, I must point out that falling asleep on pews during boring sermons isn't an anointed calling for the urgency of these times. The clock is ticking, lest we bring shame to the Father. Find your calling and pursue it diligently. Your 401(k) will be worthless when Israel's clock strikes the "zero" hour.

Beyond these less subtle signs are the more obvious ones we see daily in the news. Iran launched an attack on Israel for the first time in history on October 1, 2024. The Psalm 83 war will precede the Gog and Magog war of Ezekiel 38, and both are in alignment today and could begin at any time. The Psalm 83 war confederacy looks like this:

> *Keep not thou silence, O God: hold not thy peace, and be not still, O God.*
>
> *For, lo, thine enemies make a tumult: and they that hate thee have lifted up the head.*
>
> *They have taken crafty counsel against thy people, and consulted against thy hidden ones.*
>
> *They have said, Come, and let us cut them off from being a nation; that the name of Israel may be no more in remembrance.*
>
> *For they have consulted together with one consent: they are confederate against thee:*
>
> *The tabernacles of Edom, and the Ishmaelites; of Moab, and the Hagarenes;*
>
> *Gebal, and Ammon, and Amalek; the Philistines with the inhabitants of Tyre;*
>
> *Assur also is joined with them: they have holpen the children of Lot. Selah. (Psalm 83:1-8 KJV)*

This is a basic lineup in modern terms:

- Edom: Southern Jordanian refugees
- Ishmaelites: Arab nations—currently represented by radical factions such as the Houthis of Yemen to the south, financed by Iran (Persia), a major constituent of the Gog and Magog war. This is significant and should not be overlooked, as the Psalm 83 war involves the same key players as Gog-Magog operating in the background.
- Moab: Central and Southern Jordanians
- Hagarenes: These are generally believed to be Egypt, but in brief anthropological research, this is very difficult to prove. They are

believed to be related to the Ishmaelites/Arabs and are recorded in 1 Chronicles 5:10 and 1 Chronicles 5:18–20 at war with Saul, east of Palestine. Their history has become obscured, and they likely assimilated into other cultures. What is interesting is that various researchers believe they are of a region named after Hagar, Abraham, and Sarah's Egyptian handmaid, though not necessarily Hagar herself, and that they occupied territory around modern Kuwait. Interestingly, Kuwait today has no diplomatic relations with Israel and refused to sign President Trump's Abraham Accords, stating they would be the last to do so.[8] Kuwait has maintained an anti-Israel position in favor of Gaza, in fact stating it "strongly denounces Israel's genocide in Gaza."[9] The Kuwait Ministry of Foreign Affairs also strongly denounced Israel's attack on Iran.[10]

In short, the Hagarenes were a nomadic tribe, possibly descendants of Hagar—but not necessarily and probably not Egyptians at all. I think we should keep an open mind while watching Kuwait in line with prophecy and consider that the Hagarenes may not be Egyptians at all. Since thousands of years and hundreds of wars have shifted tribes and nations on the map, we should keep an open mind in following possible alternatives in these prophetic events. ISIS, Hamas, Hezbollah, Fatah, and the PLO are the most outspoken enemies of Israel and will be connected to one or all of this ten-member war confederacy outlined in Psalm 83.

- Gebal: Northern Lebanon/Syria
- Ammon: Northern Jordan
- Amalek: The Amalekites were descendants of Esau (Genesis 36:12). By the time of Judges 12:15, they had inhabited an area

---

8   https://www.timesofisrael.com/kuwaiti-officials-reject-israel-normalization-reaffirm-support-for-palestinians/

9   https://www.arabtimesonline.com/news/kuwait-condemns-israeli-aggression-calls-for-unsc-action/

10   https://timeskuwait.com/kuwait-strongly-denounces-israeli-occupation-attack-on-iran/

known as Ephraim, which is within the borders of Israel a few miles north of Jerusalem. This makes it difficult to determine who they are today. However, according to most modern rabbis, Hamas is believed to be the seed of the Amalekites. In an article published in the *Jewish Journal* by Morton Shapiro, he connects Deuteronomy 25:19 to the fact that Hamas and the Amalekites were considered the eternal enemies of Israel. Many scholars and researchers see the Amalekites as Egypt (Sinai Peninsula), but I have been unable to make that connection in my own research.

- Philistines and Tyre: Gaza (Hamas) and S.Lebanon (Hezbollah)
- Assur/Assyria: The region of Assyrian control during King David's time. If we're using the timeline when Psalm 83 was written, it would not specifically include modern Syria, since that was an Aramean nation conquered by David before Psalm 83 was written. The Assyrian Empire in David's era would be a region that borders modern-day Iran and Southeastern Turkey, within what is now Iraq. With Hezbollah controlling much of present-day Syria, the radical Islamic factions within Iraq are more appropriate for identifying the Assur of the Psalm 83 war confederacy. If we consider the base of operations for ISIS (Islamic State in Iraq and Syria) and their extreme hostility toward Israel, they fall precisely within the ancient empire of Assur (Assyria) during David's time. This is the group to keep an eye on. In addition, ISIS has received state backing from various nations, including Iran.

I know of very few people who connect what is happening now in the Middle East to the Psalm 83 war because Egypt is missing from this engagement against Israel. This is because the Hagarenes are believed to represent Egypt, though my research has not revealed an obvious connection between them beyond Sarah's handmaid, "Hagar" having come from Egypt. If we consider radical militant separatist groups operating within sovereign Islamic nations—funded by those same nations and strongly opposed to Israel's response to the Hamas attack on October 7, 2023—I believe we have witnessed the Psalm 83 war covertly unfolding before our eyes while trying to make all the modern biblical connections that are misaligned to ancient biblical tribes and regions. A pragmatic approach might be to ignore the noise of academia arguing over who, why, when, and where and assume that perhaps the Psalm 83 war is currently ongoing (or passed by the time of this publication). We don't want to be caught by surprise in all the noise and confusion and realize too late that we missed a pivotal event in prophecy!

Something else I covered in the last book are the identifying characteristics of the final Antichrist globalist leader. To review briefly, he will arise from the Roman Empire (Daniel chapters 2 and 9). He will be an Assyrian which became part of the Roman Empire, and I believe specifically from Istanbul due to its religious and political significance, though he could emerge from any area of Turkey or Iraq (Micah 5:5; Isaiah 10:5–6). He will have a crippled right arm and right eye (Zechariah 11:17). In the Psalm 83 war, all of Israel's enemies are Islamic nations. In the Gog and Magog war, the entire world turns against Israel, but Psalm 83 sets the stage with a strictly Islamic alliance. The final Antichrist global leader will likely be of Muslim origin. He will attempt to unite all religions the same way as Pope Francis and the papacy had, except with emphasis on Islam, and "Allah" being the predominant deity above all others, especially Jesus. We'll cover this in another chapter.

Let us not forget that many of the weapons being used by some of these radical factions were donated by the US military. We are bombarded by sound bites of information that cloud our short-term memories. Under former President Biden's leadership, we abandoned $83 billion USD in weapons and military equipment in Afghanistan. Much of that equipment made its way to combatants fighting against Israel. God's memory isn't as short as ours. We'll soon know the limits of His patience and mercy.

What do we all overlook in this Psalm 83 confederacy? There are ten fallen angel or sons of God "princes" operating behind the scenes, driving this Islamic confederacy and their desire to annihilate Israel. Wars on earth are the physical manifestation of spiritual conflict.

The next war to unfold after the geopolitical alignment of the Psalm 83 war is the Gog and Magog war in Ezekiel 38.

And the word of the Lord came unto me, saying,

Son of man, set thy face against Gog, the land of Magog, the chief prince of Meshech and Tubal, and prophesy against him,

And say, Thus saith the Lord God; Behold, I am against thee, O Gog, the chief prince of Meshech and Tubal:

And I will turn thee back, and put hooks into thy jaws, and I will bring thee forth, and all thine army, horses and horsemen, all of them clothed with all sorts of armour, even a great company with bucklers and shields, all of them handling swords:

Persia, Ethiopia, and Libya with them; all of them with shield and helmet:

Gomer, and all his bands; the house of Togarmah of the north quarters, and all his bands: and many people with thee. (Ezekiel 38:1-6 KJV)

The chapter begins by addressing Gog as a chief prince. I would like to reiterate that I do not believe demons can hold the titles of "prince," which is reserved for the "sons of God." In this case, Gog is identified as a prince over the region of Turkey (Meshech and Tubal). In my last book, I noted that Gog was regarded as a lesser deity within the ancient Akkadian polytheistic arrangement of gods, serving as a messenger to higher-ranking gods or fallen angels, particularly to the god of "Saturn." The name is pronounced *Gaag-a* with a long "a," and I have speculated that this is who the entertainer known as "Lady Gaga" intends to identify with, for reasons we probably never want to imagine. Many illicit allegations have been made regarding her involvement with certain secret societies. Satan's world is strange and bizarre, indeed.

The nations listed are as follows:

- Meshech and Tubal, Gomer and Togarmah: The more reliable Bible atlases, such as Zondervan's, HarperCollins, Holman's, consolidate these in the Asia Minor region, where modern *Turkey* is located. I'll explain below why that makes the most sense if the war were to unfold today. Some commentators have these nations spread out from Germany to Russia, which is possible. I do not believe Germany is in this war for the simple reason they have no nuclear weapon capabilities, and this will be a nuclear war.

- Persia: Iran
- Ethiopia: (Map below)
- Libya: In *The New Unger's Bible Dictionary*, Dr. Unger defines "Magog": *"It is clear that Lydia [Turkey] is meant, and that by 'Magog,' we must understand, 'the land of Gog.'"*

In some translations, the name "Rosh" appears in chapters 38 and 39, leading many to believe this refers to Russia. "Rosh" simply means "chief" or "head" in Hebrew, as in chief prince or head prince (*Rosh Hashanah* = head of the year, for example). We assume Russia is the modern correlation but keep an open mind. If *Rosh* means "chief" or "head," it could imply that other princes preside over the nations involved and are mentioned for this reason. Gog is chief among them, which is why God declares war on him and drags him out by "setting a hook in his jaw" (see Ezekiel 38:4). God is dragging Gog into this war, not the other way around. If Gog is the deity *Gaag-a* and serves as a messenger, then God intends to send His own message—whether Gog wants it or not. This war will demonstrate to the world that He alone is the God of Israel and that there are no other gods before Him (see Psalm 82). It will be nuclear, and Israel will be defended miraculously. Russia, already a nuclear supplier to Israel's enemies, should be considered an important part of this alliance.

Let's assume that the first four nations on the list are accurately located in modern Turkey. This placement makes the most sense for the chief prince, Gog, to be located at the center of the former Roman Empire (Constantinople/Istanbul) and the subsequent Byzantine Empire, which endured for another thousand years on the eastern leg after the fall of Rome. Over the last thirty years, Turkey has shifted from a previously secular, neutral state into an entirely Muslim nation. In a recent interview,

Prime Minister Netanyahu was asked what nation he feared the most, thinking the obvious answer was Iran. His response was chilling when he replied, "Turkey is who we fear the most, without a doubt."

One nation that stands out as an oddball on this list is Ethiopia—that is, until we look at a map from the time period of Ezekiel and notice a nation is missing that appears today and is in the news daily:

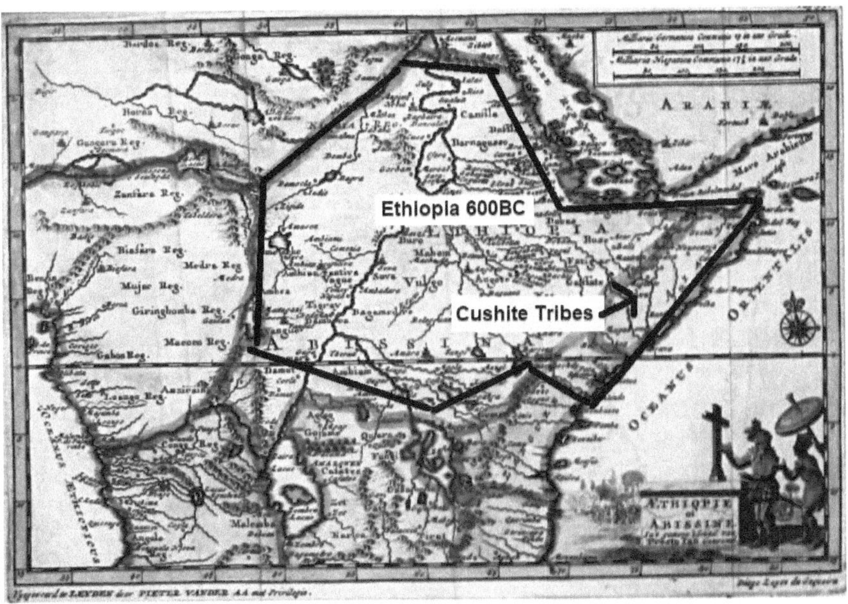

At the time of Ezekiel in the early fifth century BC, the eastern region of Ethiopia was occupied by the Cushite tribes under various names. I'll give you one guess what country is there today.

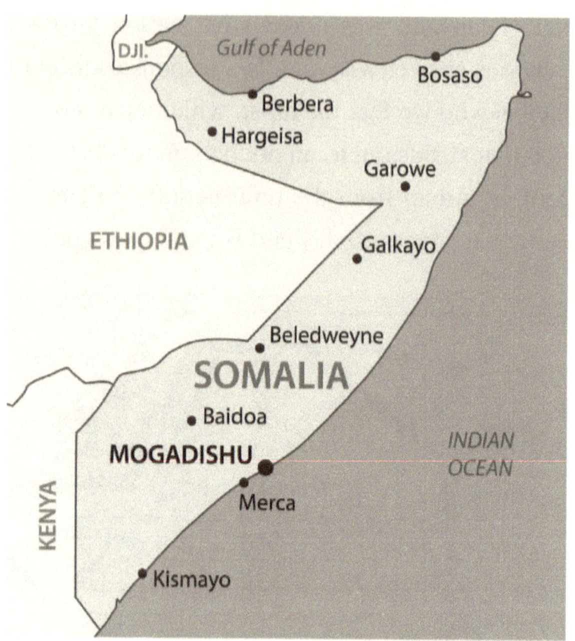

I find it fascinating that the land of the ancient Cushites includes the same piece of land we know today as Somalia. As you know, I like to research name etymology for clues:

Etymology and Meaning of Somalia (Etymology online)

Somalia (Somali: Soomaaliya, Arabic: الصومال, romanized: Aṣ-Ṣūmāl) is the name of a country located in the Horn of Africa. The etymology of the name «Somalia» can be traced back to the ancient Egyptian language.

Arabic Influence

«Al-Suwad» (Arabic: السواد): The Arabs, who traded with the Somalis, referred to the region as «Al-Suwad,» meaning «the Black Land,» likely due to the dark complexion of its inhabitants.

«Aṣ-Ṣūmāl» (Arabic: الصومال)*:* Over time, «Al-Suwad» was corrupted into the Arabic form «Aṣ-Ṣūmāl,» which was later adopted as the name of the country.

We discussed that Ham was Khem, father of the Khemites, who were the Egyptians. The name *Khem* meant "burnt," and in tracing the etymology, we find that "Somalia" has an Egyptian origin with a name applied due to their dark complexion. Cush was the son of Ham/Khem, so it makes perfect sense that the name would be Egyptian and Arabic, meaning "dark complected," just as the Khemites shared the same DNA as the Cushites, some of whom are now the Somalis, located in the land of Cush (divisions of the earth, Genesis 10 and *Jubilees* 9).

Ezekiel's Ethiopia doesn't seem out of place when we consider that radical Jew-hating Islamists are the majority in Somalia, while Ethiopian Orthodox Christians make up 68 percent of the population in modern Ethiopia. I may not be fully up to date on current events in that region, but I would be more confident in Somalia playing a role in attacking Israel than Ethiopia. Making the connection to the Cushites sheds new light on the Somalis— a spotlight!

While Somalia may seem too insignificant to be involved in a nuclear confrontation, consider the alliances of the Psalm 83 war and how they are supported by larger nations. Iran supports Hamas, Hezbollah, and groups like the Houthis. Could this be where Russia or maybe even Turkey enters the picture—not engaged in direct conflict, but supporting radical Islamic proxies like some of the Somali terror groups? And let's not forget that here in the United States, a radical Islamist, born in Mogadishu, Somalia, was duly elected to Congress to represent the Fifth District of Minnesota. Anything can happen, my friends. Don't look for the obvious, or you'll be caught by surprise and unprepared.

In fact, being from Texas and limiting my domestic travels to the southern portions of the US, I only know of the radical leftist Somalis who make the news daily. We tend to think of Somalis as pirates at sea, looting maritime cargo or trafficking contraband on the high seas. Let me enlighten you with a little-known fact about the extent to which the "Cushites" of

Somalia have crusaded to the West. Take a look at this list from Wikipedia of Somali Americans in politics:

- Asha Ahmed Abdalla, politician; member of the Transitional Federal Parliament
- Raqiya Haji Dualeh Abdalla, sociologist and politician; president of the Somali Family Care Network
- Mana Abdi, member of the Maine House of Representatives
- Hussein Sheikh Abdirahman, politician and judge; former minister of defense of Somalia
- Munira Abdullahi, member of the Ohio House of Representatives
- Nimco Ahmed, political activist
- Ayaan Hirsi Ali, writer, political activist, and former legislator
- Abukar Arman, political analyst, writer, and diplomat; former special envoy of Somalia to the US
- Abdirizak Bihi, social activist
- Deqa Dhalac, member of the Maine House of Representatives
- Omar Fateh, member of the Minnesota Senate
- Anisa Hajimumin, politician, social activist and writer; minister of Women & Family Affairs of Puntland
- Ahmed M. Hassan, entrepreneur and politician; member of the Clarkston City Council
- Hodan Hassan, member of the Minnesota House of Representatives
- Samakab Hussein, member of the Minnesota House of Representatives
- Ismail Ali Ismail, writer and former diplomat
- Kayse Jama, majority leader of the Oregon State Senate
- Fatima Jibrell, environmental activist; cofounder of Adeso
- Safiya Khalid, former member of the Lewiston, Maine, City Council
- Hassan Ali Mire, politician; former minister of education of Somalia
- Anquam Mahamoud, member-elect of the Minnesota House of Representatives

- Abdinur Sheikh Mohamed, educator and politician; former minister of education of Somalia
- Ismail Mohamed (Ohio politician), member of the Ohio House of Representatives
- Mohamed Abdullahi Mohamed, diplomat, professor, and politician; former president of Somalia
- Nadia Mohamed, Minnesota municipal politician; mayor of St. Louis Park
- Zaynab Mohamed, member of the Minnesota Senate
- Mohamud Noor, member of the Minnesota House of Representatives
- Ilhan Omar, US representative for Minnesota's fifth congressional district
- Jamal Osman, member of the Minneapolis City Council
- Mohamed Abshir Waldo, journalist, activist, and former politician
- Abdi Warsame, politician; former member of the Minneapolis City Council
- Yusuf Yusuf, politician; member of the Maine House of Representatives

Isn't this interesting? Have you ever heard of SAEON?

"Somali Elected Officials Network". Here is the mission statement from their website, www.saeon.org: "Our Mission is to create a National

Network of all Somali Americans Elected to Political Office in the United States. SAEON hosts community engagement events and acts as a central resource for political engagement with Somali Elected Officials nationwide."

Meanwhile, as we remain more interested in NFL or college football games, the Cushites have established a formidable political presence in the US, with an organization that coordinates their own political agenda networks nationwide. The sons of disobedience have done a marvelous job of blindfolding the uninformed voters of this once-great nation. Actually, uninformed is not accurate. *Misinformed* is more accurate, as we are lied to nonstop by corporate media propaganda outlets. But I digress.

Turkey will have the backing of other nations in this war, as they are not as well equipped with nuclear weapons as Israel. Russia seems to fit this role well, as Turkey considers Russia as its closest ally. By looking at a map of the region, it is obvious that Hamas in the south, Hezbollah and Iran in the north, rogue agents from Somalia in the east, and Turkey from the north and the Mediterranean, can easily have Israel surrounded within proximity of missile range.

If we're looking at Israel to see what time it is, the Psalm 83 war seems to be fulfilled, and the Gog and Magog war is pre-aligned with prophecy as no other time in world history. Gog and Magog could commence theoretically at any moment without notice. For this reason, I wanted to share this information in relation to the primary responsibility of those who are led by the Spirit, future sons of God, to expand every effort to assist in increasing the harvest. There is no time. I regret having wasted my life in factories around the world, ignorant of the urgency of the times in which we were chosen to live.

Regarding the Gog and Magog war, there is a verse from Ezekiel 38 in the context of this war that seems to be inconsistent with prophecy, if we look at modern circumstances:

> ***And thou shalt say, I will go up to the land of unwalled villages; I will go to them that are at rest, that dwell***

safely, all of them dwelling without walls, and having neither bars nor gates. (Ezekiel 38:11 KJV)

The only explanation seems to be that a peace treaty must be in place after the Psalm 83 war that creates a false sense of security. But I do not believe we can be overly dogmatic about any particular view, except that since the birth of Israel, there has never been a sense of peaceful security for the nation. President Trump's plan to develop the Gaza Strip certainly seems to be the missing piece of this puzzle? If so, it needs to happen quickly because the Gog Magog War is perfectly aligned except for this one verse in chapter 38.

Beyond these last day's signs of the times, recall the anomalies surrounding Hurricane Harvey that I mentioned in my last book. There have been blood moons timed with prophetic events in Israel. There have been eclipses marking an *X* over the USA that have only occurred several times in history, exactly like what happened in Ninevah during the time of Jonah—the Jubilee repeat year of the 1973 Yom Kippur War when Hamas attacked Israel on October 7, 2023. It seems the warning signs of the last hours of the last days have been nonstop for the last ten years or more for anyone paying attention. But if you believe that any of this is subjective or coincidental, there is one verse that should connect the dots for the doubters.

Matthew 24 is a description of the end times and a prophecy of how the last days unfold. Yehshua makes this statement in verse 37–38:

But as the days of Noah were, so shall also the coming of the Son of man be.

For as in the days that were before the flood they were eating and drinking, marrying and giving in marriage, until the day that Noe entered into the ark. (Matthew 24:37-38 KJV)

The close of the Church Age will catch most people by surprise. The signs will be everywhere, but people will live normally—blissfully ignorant of the flood of wrath that will come upon the world. It was not until rain fell from the sky for the first time since Creation that the people of Noah's day knew something was wrong. That is exactly how the timing of the wrath of the Lamb and of God will unfold this time. When will this happen? Verses 32–34 give us a clue in this same passage (KJV):

> *Now learn a parable of the fig tree; When his branch is yet tender, and putteth forth leaves, ye know that summer is nigh:*
>
> *So likewise ye, when ye shall see all these things, know that it is near, even at the doors.*
>
> *Verily I say unto you, This generation shall not pass, till all these things be fulfilled.*

The fig tree began budding forth leaves in 1948. That was our first major sign. The growth and prosperity of Israel putting forth new leaves after 1948 was a perfectly fulfilled prophecy. This generation of Jews who saw the rebirth, regathering, and rise of Israel to global power will still be alive when the flood of God's wrath consumes the earth, as it did in the days of Noah.

On May 14, 2025, Israel was seventy-seven years old. Some of the generation of Jews born on or before May 14, 1948, will be alive to witness the wrath of God ahead of Yehshua's return to the Mount of Olives at the end of it (Zechariah 14:4). If the "Day of the Lord" were to begin today, any Jew born on or before May 14, 1948, would be eighty-three to eighty-four years old by the end of the tribulation.

Do you see why I feel this sense of urgency and why I feel I may have missed my destiny while writing these books far too late?

Another point I want to reiterate is God's appointed times regarding the birth of Yehshua, crucifixion, and return, in keeping with the fifty-year jubilee and seven-year Shemitah cycles. It is difficult to determine exactly what year Yehshua was born. We know it had to be before Herod the Great died because Yehshua could have been close to two years old when the Magi kings arrived in Jerusalem and Herod sent a decree to kill all firstborn males two years or less of age. The Magi had been traveling with this star leading the way for almost two years. This account is found in Matthew 2. This star was an angel leading them to the Messiah, which is obvious from verses 9 and 10.

Joseph took Mary and Yehshua to Egypt to escape persecution. While there, Joseph had a dream in which he was told that Herod had died and it was safe to return to Jerusalem. No details are given about the nature of Herod's death, but the context suggests it occurred shortly after Joseph's arrival in Egypt. According to the Gospel of Luke, chapter 2, Yehshua was born around the time of "the first census" ordered by Augustus Caesar that would later be used by Quirinius as governor of Syria, placing his birth between 6 and 4 BC.

The consensus among scholars is that Herod died in 4 BC. However, the discovery of his sarcophagus in 2007, along with the artifacts it contained, suggests his death may have occurred a few years later, around 1 BC on the Gregorian calendar.

Yehshua's ministry began in the fifteenth year of Tiberius Caesar's reign, following His baptism in Luke, chapter 3. Most academics place the date of Tiberius's reign beginning in AD 14, which means Yehshua's ministry began in AD 29. Based on the timing of Herod's death at 4BC-5BC, Yehshua would have been thirty-three or thirty-four years old when His ministry began. From there, we know it lasted three and a half years until He was crucified.

By that timeline, Passover of AD 33 was the most likely date of the crucifixion.

I have numerous difficulties in reconciling these dates, because they do not match up with the assumption that Yehshua was thirty years old—the earliest age to become a rabbi—and the fact that there should be some symbology connected with King David, who became king at thirty (2 Samuel 5:4). This is a bit of a moving target because history is so subjective due to the confusing calendar changes between Hebrew, Julian Roman, and Gregorian Roman. I am in no way considering any of this to be perfectly accurate. Do your own search for dates, and a long list of frustrating possibilities will begin to pile up.

The number forty appears repeatedly in the Bible, often associated with testing, leadership, discipline, etc. The deluge of Noah lasted forty days, Moses remained on Mount Sinai for forty days, the Israelites wandered the wilderness for forty years, and Yehshua fasted forty days, among other examples. By these figures, forty jubilees from the beginning of Yehshua's ministry would fall in 2029 (40 x 50), and forty jubilees from his death would fall in 2033.

On the Hebrew calendar, the year beginning Nisan 1, 5786 on the biblical Hebrew calendar, (not the Talmudic Rosh Hashanah that places the new year in the fall), is also a shemitah year. In God's perfect timing, nothing of significance occurs outside a shemitah or jubilee year (this is March 19, 2026 on our calendar). Because we are approaching exactly forty jubilees from Yehshua's ministry and crucifixion, we should be prepared for major global events between now and 2033. Theoretically, the tribulation could begin forty jubilees from Yehshua's baptism. While we have no precise way of knowing when that occurred, it is generally assumed to have been around the fall feasts. I believe the forty-day fast in the wilderness after His baptism represented forty days of atonement leading up to Yom Kippur. If so, August 20, 2028, could mark forty jubilees from the date of His baptism, preceding Passover, March 31, 2029.

The years from 2026 to 2033 align well with the Hebrew calendar, shemitah, and jubilee cycles, making the period after 2029 the most probable marker of forty jubilees from the beginning of Yehshua's ministry. In addition, two asteroids large enough to extinguish vast regions of the earth are orbiting toward the planet earth during these shemitah cycles, either of which could fulfill the wormwood prophecy of Revelation 8:10–11.

If all of this seems impossible to imagine, do you think Israel could last another fifty years until the next jubilee cycle? Of course not. Not to mention the improbability of Jews living to beyond 135yrs of age to fulfill Matthew 24 and Luke 21 (*this generation shall not pass*).

This is all very confusing and difficult to decipher, so here is a recap:

- Nisan 1 of the Hebrew calendar year 5786 begins at sundown March 18, thru sunset March 19, 2026.

- In Exodus 12:2, God declared the new year to be Nisan 1. I do not believe we should use the Talmudic new year of Rosh Hashanah in calculating years, shemitahs, and jubilees on the Hebrew calendar. You may calculate whatever you want, but God told Moses that Nisan 1 would begin the year. I believe Rosh Hashanah confuses the calendar and appointed times, and I prefer to do what God says.

- The year 2029 is not a jubilee year on the calendar, but it marks forty jubilees from the beginning of Yehshua's ministry, calculated from the fifteenth year of Tiberius's reign (Luke 3:1). This could also be as early as 2028.

- The year 2029 falls in the middle of the current shemitah cycle, making AD 29 more likely as the beginning of His ministry, so that the crucifixion would occur on a shemitah year, three and a half years later, and one 7 year shemitah from a jubilee year.

- The assumption is that Yehshua was baptized in the spring, and after forty days in the wilderness His ministry began. I don't want to make an entire chapter of this timeline, but most historians agree that Yehshua attended three Passovers during His ministry, which would not include the Last Supper, and that His ministry lasted three and a half years. It is more likely that His baptism occurred forty days prior to Yom Kippur, the Day of Atonement, and that His ministry began after the forty-day fast leading up to the feast. By this reckoning, He would have been baptized in the month of Elul in AD 25, if we follow the chronology of the gospels.

- This places the crucifixion at Passover in AD 33.

- The calendar changes are terribly confusing, given the differences between Hebrew and the Roman calendars (Julian and Gregorian), as well as the shift from BC to AD. So, we can also use the prophecy of Daniel chapter 9 and the seventy weeks and sixty-nine weeks of years, which was fulfilled to the very day.

- In Daniel 9, Gabriel's message to Daniel stated that the time from the decree of the temple to the crucifixion of the Messiah would be 483 years.

- This decree was given by Artaxerxes of Persia in 444 BC. The numbers do not seem to align until we account for calendar conversions: 360-day Jewish years to 364-day Roman years, then the transition from BC to AD. With these adjustments, the calculation yields 476 Roman years; or 483 Jewish years, and places the crucifixion date again in AD 33. Nehemiah 2:1-8 confirms this 444BC date for the temple decree.

- By these separate dating methods, it appears that 2029 will mark forty jubilees from the beginning of Yehshua's ministry, and 2033 will mark forty jubilees from His crucifixion. The year 2040 will correspond to Hebrew year 5800. The last shemitah before the end of the current jubilee begins in 2033, or 5793 on the Hebrew calendar. It is highly likely that this period represents the "Time of Jacob's Trouble" (Jeremiah 30:7).

- Keep in mind that the Hebrew calendar begins with the chronology of the creation of Adam, not creation in general. Many people are expecting the Church Age to end at the Hebrew year 6000, when the sabbatical millennium begins. I believe there are four jubilees of years not accounted for on the Hebrew calendar, marking the time when creation—or the re-creation of the earth out of chaos—began, and when humanity was created on day six long before Adam. The Hebrew calendar begins with Adam. This would explain whom Cain feared after killing his brother; it could not have been his mother and father, the only other two family members recorded by the time Genesis chapter 4 unfolds.

- There is no possible way the Gog and Magog war could be postponed for another two hundred years, though many people believe more in the calendar than in prophetic events. I'll leave this for you to decide.

I point all this out to demonstrate a closing window of time, just as in the days of Noah, when all but eight people were caught off guard by the deluge. How many are watching the signs today? Wherever you attend church, does your pastor express the same sense of urgency I am suggesting? Does your pastor recognize that the days of Noah are upon us? If not, pray that the Holy Spirit will enlighten him because, my friends, we are here. The days of Noah are now. We are calmly eating, drinking, and planning wedding ceremonies, unaware of the impending deluge of wrath.

Now consider this prophecy from Hosea 6:

Come, and let us return unto the Lord: for he hath torn, and he will heal us; he hath smitten, and he will bind us up.

After two days will he revive us: in the third day he will raise us up, and we shall live in his sight. (Hosea 6:1-2 KJV)

This prophecy can only refer to one time: the end of the time of Jacob's Trouble, which concludes Daniel's seventy-week prophecy. Two prophetic days equal two thousand years, and at the beginning of the third prophetic day the sabbatical millennium will begin, when "they shall live in His sight."

The prophecy from Hosea serves as further confirmation that something monumental is about to happen between the forty jubilees from the beginning of Yehshua's ministry in 2029 and the forty jubilees from His crucifixion in 2033. Let's not be like the Jewish people who failed to recognize the time of His coming (Luke 19:41). Yehshua rode into Jerusalem at the end of Daniel's sixty-ninth week. The Jews should have been awaiting His arrival, but they did not know Him, and He wept over Jerusalem. Let's not disappoint Him a second time by failing to anticipate the signs of His imminent return. The Church Age is closing, and the wheat is about to be harvested from the field.

Think of the harvest in this way: you are a wheat farmer, and your wheat is ripe. Clouds gather on the horizon in a season when storms are likely, and your instincts warn of a severe storm approaching. Would you sit idly by and risk losing most or all of your harvest? Or would you gather as much help as possible to save the crop before the storm, like the "wise son" of Proverbs 10:5?

What do we do? I'll answer that with another question: what are we called to do?

> *And he said unto them, Go ye into all the world, and preach the gospel to every creature. (Mark 16:15 KJV)*

The harvest is what those who are led by the Spirit are called to do. In Mark 16:15, Yehshua gives a direct command after His resurrection. Sounds easy, right? If you're like me, it is difficult living in this world where even so-called believers hardly resemble anything from the early church. When I try to discuss these subjects with most Christians, especially Catholics, I quickly find myself sitting alone in the room.

Remember the two verses that follow verse 15?

> *And these signs shall follow them that believe; In my name shall they cast out devils; they shall speak with new tongues;*
>
> *They shall take up serpents; and if they drink any deadly thing, it shall not hurt them; they shall lay hands on the sick, and they shall recover. (Mark 16:17-18 KJV)*

Who are they who believe in Him? The church over which Yehshua is the head.

> *And He put all things [in every realm] in subjection under Christ's feet, and appointed Him as [supreme and authoritative] head over all things in the church. (Ephesians 1:22 AMP)*

The reason verses 17–18 follow verse 15 is that Yehshua knew five of the seven churches that would not understand (Revelation 2–3). The true church, as He intended, would resemble the church of Acts, exercising authority over princes, principalities, serpents, scorpions, and forces of darkness in the spiritual realm. Unfortunately, very few Christian churches today bear any resemblance to the church of Acts. Some of the largest congregations in America applaud entertainers on a stage who calls themselves pastors or reverends, yet show no likeness to the Mark 16 believer. Our job is to harvest these people ahead of the tribulation, though many will be saved through it—if books like this one are not burned by the Antichrist system before they find a copy.

I began this in-depth research in 2017, after Hurricane Harvey, because I thought I might die of cancer before understanding the Bible. I had often said that too much of it didn't make sense to me and seemed more like story telling than literal truth. I spent my career understanding technical aspects of a complicated process in the field of metallurgy, where problems could not be solved with hope or random luck until they were fully understood. I dismissed much of the Bible because I could not make sense of it, beginning with lonely Adam in Genesis 2, when chapter 1 clearly states that male and female were created on the same day. Yet, if you ask your pastor who was the first man was, he will insist that the Bible clearly says Adam, without a concise reconciliation of the differences between the two chapters.

Through a diligent and painstaking mission, guided by the studies of the late Chuck Missler and research materials such as Dr. Merrill Unger's *Commentary on the Old Testament,* my eyes were opened, and I began to see the life breathing in and out of God's living word. In fact, the term "living word" is perfectly appropriate. It was as though the characters of Abraham, Moses, Elijah, and others became so real to me that I felt they had become my friends. I don't know how else to explain it.

So, what happened? How did we derail so far off track that the Bible now seems reserved for a small, select echelon group of scholars to understand? Were those who spread the gospel in the book of Acts biblical scholars? Of course not. They were average, everyday working people like the rest of us.

When I am researching and reading scholarly commentaries on verses and chapters of the Bible, I often feel as though I need a translator for my own language. Scholars throw words at us as if everyone should know what they mean. Here is a short list, just to name a few:

- **<u>Dispensationalism</u>** – *A doctrine prevalent in some forms of Protestant Christianity that divides history into distinct periods, each marked by a different dispensation or relationship between God and humanity. Dispensationalism further holds that Christian believers will be transported to heaven without warning and that soon thereafter, there will be a period of tribulation, followed by the Second Coming.*

- **<u>Eschatology</u>** – *(1) The branch of theology that is concerned with the end of the world or of humankind. (2) A belief or a doctrine concerning the ultimate or final things, such as death, the destiny of humanity, the Second Coming, or the Last Judgment. (3) The doctrine of the last or final things, such as death, judgment, and the events therewith connected.*

- **<u>Apologetics</u>** (has nothing to do with apologizing) - *The branch of theology that is concerned with defending or proving the truth of Christian doctrines.*

- **<u>Beatitudes</u>** – *(1) Supreme blessedness or happiness. (2) Any of the declarations of blessedness made by Jesus in the Sermon on the Mount.*

- **<u>Hermeneutics</u>** – *(1) The theory and methodology of interpretation, especially of scriptural text. (2) The science of interpretation and explanation; exegesis; esp., that branch of theology which defines the laws whereby the meaning of the scriptures is to be ascertained.*

- **<u>Diaspora</u>** – *Jews dispersed outside of the land of Israel*

When researching the Bible and reading scholarly commentaries, you'll need both a dictionary and a thesaurus. This is what I admired about Dr. Missler—his ability to take a complicated subject and teach it in simple terms that average people like me could understand. In the final years of my career, my successes as a technical consultant depended on my ability to take engineering-level knowledge and communicate it to the hourly wage workers on the plant floor. The success of the organization depended on the engineers and technicians who could simplify complicated matters into palatable terms for the less educated who perform the work.

The result of this over-complication of the living Word of God has led us to leave the work to pastors or scholars, only to return to life as usual on Monday morning, much as it was in the days of Noah. In our confusion of having the living Word fed to us on Sunday like baby food, then having PhD-level terminology sprinkled into that baby food—we have become somewhat blindfolded. We are not following the direct command given by the resurrected Yehshua in Mark 16:15. In these final days and hours before the harvest, this must change. We will be held accountable for our ignorance of the living Word. So here is an idea: *K.I.S.S. (Keep it simple @#$%!!).*

> **The gospel is so simple that simple children can**
> **understand it, and it is so profound that studies by**
> **the wisest theologians will never exhaust its riches.**
> **(Charles Hodge)**

We are commanded to share the gospel around the globe. But what is the gospel? The gospel is, quite literally, the good news. Good news about what? That we are no longer subject to death. Under our first king and priest, Adam, mankind was placed under the authority of Lucifer when Adam forfeited his royal position through disobedience to God. This was a legal property rights transfer from Adam to Lucifer, and we are the property.

But of the tree of the knowledge of good and evil, thou
shalt not eat of it: for in the day that thou eatest thereof
thou shalt surely die. (Genesis 2:17 KJV)

Adam was cast from God's presence and placed under Satan's authority because of this. By the nature of a merciful God, there is more to the story than we may ever know. I gave up trying to satisfy my curiosity as to what kind of tree would cause a six-thousand-year death curse. What kind of tree could impart knowledge of good and evil simply by eating its fruit? All we need to know for now is that Yehshua redeemed us—purchased from death with His death—out from beneath Satan's authority. Yehshua is the last Adam, and those who believe in Him belong to Him through this repurchasing of property rights accomplished by His crucifixion. We were bought back on terms that are not negotiable, forfeited only by our own choosing.

In whom we have redemption through his blood, the
forgiveness of sins, according to the riches of his grace.
(Ephesians 1:7 KJV)

The reward for obedience to God is eternal life and love in His presence. The reward for obedience to Satan is the same as his reward:

Then shall he say also unto them on the left hand,
Depart from me, ye cursed, into everlasting fire,
prepared for the devil and his angels. (Matthew 25:41
KJV)

There is a heaven and there is a hell. *The gospel is a story of life and the conquer of death.* Yehshua is the authority that separates life from death.

Forasmuch then as the children are partakers of flesh
and blood, he also himself likewise took part of the

same; that through death he might destroy him that had the power of death, that is, the devil. (Hebrews 2:14 (KJV)

The first step to salvation is understanding the need for salvation. We are all condemned to death according to the curse of Adam and the transfer of authority to Satan, the prince of the kingdom of death. Abel, the son of Adam, demonstrated the only acceptable sacrifice before God when he presented the best of his flock (Genesis 4). Under the Law of Moses, the sacrificial lamb became the acceptable method of atonement for the Hebrews and Israel as a nation.

For the life of the flesh is in the blood: and I have given it to you upon the altar to make an atonement for your souls: for it is the blood that maketh an atonement for the soul. (Leviticus 17:11 KJV)

(It is the soul that is atoned by blood. This is so profound that we speed right past it without noticing the significance that it is the soul that is redeemed by blood. Souls are eternal, and bodies are not. Next chapter!)

By faith, we believe and know in our hearts that the only Lamb worthy of the eternal atonement of mankind was Yehshua. *The crucifixion transcended the dimension of time, redeeming souls past, present, and future.* By grace, we are exempt from the sacrificial law of having to kill a lamb every time we are disobedient to God's requirements. From the crucifixion forward, the only acceptable blood offering for atonement is that of Yehshua's. His blood covered all sins, past and future, for all that come to Him by faith.

By faith Abel offered unto God a more excellent sacrifice than Cain, by which he obtained witness that he was righteous, God testifying of his gifts: and by it he being dead yet speaketh. (Hebrews 11:4 KJV)

> *But without faith it is impossible to please him: for*
> *he that cometh to God must believe that he is, and*
> *that he is a rewarder of them that diligently seek him.*
> *(Hebrews 11:6 KJV)*

> *For Christ also suffered for sins <u>once for all time</u>,*
> *the just for the unjust, so that He might bring us to*
> *God, having been put to death in the flesh, but made*
> *alive in the spirit; in which He also went and made*
> *proclamation to the spirits in prison, who once were*
> *disobedient when the patience of God kept waiting in*
> *the days of Noah, during the construction of the ark, in*
> *which a few, that is, eight persons, were brought safely*
> *through the water. (1 Peter 3:18-20 NASB)*

Our only escape from death is through Yehshua, God in the flesh, who came as a man and died as a redemptive purchase for all who believe in Him.

> *He that believeth on him is not condemned: but he that*
> *believeth not is condemned already, because he hath*
> *not believed in the name of the only begotten Son of*
> *God. (John 3:18 KJV)*

The bad news is that Satan gained authority over mankind when Adam lost it. Under Satan, all are condemned to death because of the transfer of authority that took place in the Garden of Eden. *The gospel—the "good news"—is that we have been purchased by Yehshua, blood for blood. This blood purchase nullifies Satan's authority for those who choose life with Yehshua. The good news is that believing He came for this purpose cancels the authority of death through the redemptive power of blood for blood. This is the basic concept of salvation, simple enough for all to understand.*

Yet a vast majority of Christians remain unclear as to why Yehshua's sacrifice was necessary. Each of us must make the choice between the kingdom of heaven—life through Yehshua—and the kingdom of Satan—death. We are born into Satan's kingdom, and the only door to heaven is through Yehshua.

> *Since all have sinned and continually fall short of the glory of God, and are being justified [declared free of the guilt of sin, made acceptable to God, and granted eternal life] as a gift by His [precious, undeserved] grace, through the redemption [the payment for our sin] which is [provided] in Christ Jesus, whom God displayed publicly [before the eyes of the world] as a [life-giving] sacrifice of atonement and reconciliation (propitiation) by His blood [to be received] through faith. This was to demonstrate His righteousness [which demands punishment for sin], because in His forbearance [His deliberate restraint] He passed over the sins previously committed [before Jesus' crucifixion]. It was to demonstrate His righteousness at the present time, so that He would be just and the One who justifies those who have faith in Jesus [and rely confidently on Him as Savior]. (Romans 3:23-26 AMP)*

Why a lamb? The *Topical Encyclopedia* provides the best overview for the answer to this question:

Topical Encyclopedia (biblehub.com)

> *The symbolism of the lamb in the Bible is rich and multifaceted, deeply rooted in the religious and cultural context of ancient Israel and carried through to the New Testament. The lamb is emblematic of innocence, sacrifice, and redemption, serving as a profound symbol of Christ and His atoning work.*

Old Testament Foundations

The lamb first emerges as a significant symbol in the Old Testament, particularly in the context of sacrifice. In <u>Genesis 22</u>, God commands Abraham to offer his son Isaac as a burnt offering. At the last moment, God provides a ram as a substitute, prefiguring the sacrificial system that would be central to Israelite worship. The Passover lamb, as described in <u>Exodus 12</u>, is perhaps the most prominent Old Testament symbol. The Israelites were instructed to slaughter a lamb without blemish and apply its blood to their doorposts, so the angel of death would pass over their homes. This act of deliverance is commemorated annually in the Passover feast, highlighting the themes of redemption and divine protection.

The sacrificial system outlined in Leviticus further underscores the lamb's role in atonement. <u>Leviticus 4:32-35</u> describes the offering of a lamb as a sin offering, emphasizing the necessity of a spotless sacrifice to atone for sin. The lamb's innocence and purity make it an apt symbol for the removal of guilt and the restoration of fellowship with God.

Prophetic Imagery

The prophetic literature of the Old Testament also employs the lamb as a symbol of the coming Messiah. <u>Isaiah 53:7</u> portrays the Suffering Servant as a lamb led to the slaughter, silent before its shearers. This imagery conveys the themes of submission and sacrifice, foreshadowing the redemptive work of Christ. The prophet Jeremiah similarly uses the lamb to describe his own experience of persecution, likening himself to "a gentle lamb led to the slaughter" (<u>Jeremiah 11:19</u>).

New Testament Fulfillment

In the New Testament, the symbolism of the lamb reaches its fulfillment in the person and work of Jesus Christ. John the Baptist identifies Jesus as "the Lamb of God, who takes away the sin of the world" (John 1:29). This declaration encapsulates the essence of Christ's mission: to serve as the ultimate sacrificial lamb, providing atonement for humanity's sin.

The book of Revelation further develops this symbolism, presenting the Lamb as both a sacrificial victim and a triumphant conqueror. Revelation 5:6 describes a Lamb standing as though it had been slain, possessing seven horns and seven eyes, symbolizing perfect power and knowledge. The Lamb is worthy to open the scroll and execute God's judgment, underscoring His divine authority and redemptive power. Revelation 7:17 promises that "the Lamb in the center of the throne will be their shepherd," highlighting the dual role of Christ as both sacrificial lamb and shepherd of His people.

Theological Significance

The symbolism of the lamb is central to Christian theology, encapsulating the doctrines of atonement, redemption, and divine love. The lamb's innocence and purity make it an ideal representation of Christ's sinless nature and His willingness to bear the sins of the world. The sacrificial aspect of the lamb underscores the necessity of a perfect offering to satisfy divine justice and reconcile humanity to God.

In Christian worship and art, the lamb continues to be a powerful symbol of Christ's sacrificial love and victory over sin and death. The imagery of the lamb invites believers to reflect on the profound mystery of redemption and the transformative power of Christ's atoning work.

The gospel consists of three critical components (paraphrasing the late Chuck Missler):

- Yehshua was the Son of God and died for us, as prophesied and according to Scripture.
- He was buried and secured in a tomb, ensuring that His death was undeniable.
- His body resurrected after three full days, fulfilling prophecy. Because He was raised from the dead, we are guaranteed to also raise from the dead if we believe in Him.

This is the gospel—the "good news" message. If any component is removed, there is no gospel. Our first priority, as those led by the Spirit, is to plant this basic message in the minds of the lost.

That is the harvest in a nutshell—but there is more.

For by grace are ye saved through faith; and that not of yourselves: it is the gift of God. (Ephesians 2:8 KJV)

We are saved by faith when we believe in the Son of God and the three basic components of the gospel. Faith is a gift of the Spirit. Where does faith come from?

So faith comes from hearing [what is told], and what is heard comes by the [preaching of the] message concerning Christ. (Romans 10:17 AMP)

I used the Amplified Bible translation for that verse because it perfectly connects to the command Yehshua gives in Mark 16:15.

The last two pages present the K.I.S.S. method of evangelizing, and I have even better news for you. The best way to communicate this is by living the example. If we radiate peace and joy in all circumstances, guard our tongues, stop gossiping and backstabbing, and demonstrate compassion for others, people will desire what we have. This opens the door to ask the simple question, "Have you chosen life?"

You will certainly get a peculiar look before having the opportunity to make the next statement: "It's an individual choice. I can't make it for you, but I can help you decide for yourself." From there, you can lay out the K.I.S.S. method of salvation. The pressure is off because we are only called to spread the gospel—we cannot make choices for others. The gift of faith is not ours to give, only the sharing of the gospel message.

We are each personally responsible for this choice. Our job is to plant seeds of faith and keep our noses clean. If we're caught up in a scandal or caught cheating on a spouse or whatever, it reflects poorly on Christians in general and turns people away. This is one of the problems in the church today, and I have experienced this far too often. I have a close friend who once told me, "When someone says they want to pray for me over a business deal, I know I'm about to lose money." The sons of God are above this. We must remain conscious of how our actions can persuade others away from salvation, for the judgment will be harsh for this.

> *For if we go on willfully and deliberately sinning after receiving the knowledge of the truth, there no longer remains a sacrifice [to atone] for our sins [that is, no further offering to anticipate], but a kind of awful and terrifying expectation of [divine] judgment and the fury of a fire and burning wrath which will consume the adversaries [those who put themselves in opposition to God]. (Romans 10:26-27 AMP)*

Yikes!! Most of this book, as well as the last, is dedicated to helping Christians gain a deeper knowledge of the Word and a sense of urgency for the times we have been chosen to live in. I see the clock ticking and time running out, even as we continue to live as in the days of Noah. For those called and led by the Spirit, a deeper knowledge of the Word is required of us. Consider this: *if faith is a gift of God that comes by hearing the Word, how vital is the calling and anointing of those led by the Spirit? If the sons of God are called to help impart the gift of faith to others—faith that comes by hearing the Word—can there be a higher calling than this?*

Faith is the seed that, when planted, becomes a harvest. Without the seed of faith, there is no harvest, and faith comes by hearing the Word. The ultimate task of those led by the Spirit, who will be revealed as the sons of God, is to share the gospel, whereby faith makes the grace of salvation possible for all who hear. Yehshua has placed the responsibility for the harvest in our hands. The bride is the church, led by the Spirit to become the sons of God and joint heirs with Christ. The sons of God have been tasked with planting for the harvest.

And with that last paragraph, I will close this chapter with the same scriptures I opened it with:

> **He that gathereth in summer is a wise son: but he**
> **that sleepeth in harvest is a son that causeth shame.**
> **(Proverbs 10:5 KJV)**

> **To every thing there is a season, and a time to every**
> **purpose under the heaven:**
>
> **A time to be born, and a time to die; a time to plant, and**
> **a time to pluck up that which is planted. (Ecclesiastes**
> **3:1-2 KJV)**

Soon is the time to pluck up that which was planted. I often wonder how accountable I will be before God for having not planted enough to harvest.

> **Those born once will die twice and those born twice**
> **will die once. (Chuck Missler)**

CHAPTER 6

Let No One Take Your Crown

Most of us struggle with the panoramic view of metaphors in the book of Revelation. Perhaps the reason we struggle is that the language is graphic yet not completely metaphorical. It presents vivid imagery projected through a window of time, looking ahead to the pouring out of the wrath of the Lamb (Revelation 6) and the wrath of God (Revelation 16)—"the time of Jacob's trouble" during the final week of Daniel's prophecy (Daniel 9:24–27). Honestly, I do not know what stands out as the most profound revelation in the book of Revelation. Certainly, these verses rank very high on my list:

> *Because thou hast kept the word of my patience, <u>I also will keep thee from the hour of temptation</u>, which shall come upon all the world, to try them that dwell upon the earth.*
>
> *Behold, I come quickly: hold that fast which thou hast, that <u>no man take thy crown</u>. (Revelation 3:10-11 KJV)*

This is a promise to keep a select group of people from the tribulation reserved for "earth dwellers", is accompanied by a warning. The warning is not to compromise their future royal status and reign with King Yehshua. This refers to the Church of Philadelphia in chapter 3, which can be none other than the bride of Christ, as mentioned earlier. The question remains: who is trying to take the crown, and how would they take it?

See to it that no one takes you captive through philosophy and empty deception [pseudo-intellectual babble], according to the tradition [and musings] of mere men, following the elementary principles of this world, rather than following [the truth—the teachings of] Christ. (Colossians 2:8 AMP)

I love the AMP translation of this verse! How often have you fallen asleep while listening to pseudo-intellectual babble of mere men? This AMP translation is priceless!

Deception is the most formidable enemy of those who are led by the Spirit. If we are led by the Spirit, we are inspired to know the living Word of God and, thus, not deceived.

Let no one deceive you with empty arguments [that encourage you to sin], for because of these things the wrath of God comes upon the sons of disobedience [those who habitually sin]. (Ephesians 5:6 AMP)

Ephesians 5:6 illustrates the stark contrast between those who are led by the Spirit (future sons of God to be revealed Romans 8:19) and the "sons of disobedience." The sons of disobedience are led by another spirit that is not the Holy Spirit. It is by this false spirit of darkness imitating light that the sons of disobedience are deceived and pursue the destruction of the future sons of God. The sons of God must guard against this persistent deception.

Do not be deceived: "Bad company corrupts good morals." (1 Corinthians 15:33 NASB)

This is the nature of spiritual warfare: the manipulation of soul and spirit to lead the body into condemnation, driven by opposing spiritual forces. The sons of disobedience follow a lying spirit, while the sons of

God follow the Holy Spirit. John gives us a macro description of the dark spirit who seeks to take—or rather steal—the crown of the bride:

> *The thief cometh not, but for to steal, and to kill, and to destroy: I am come that they might have life, and that they might have it more abundantly. (John 10:10 KJV)*

Paul asks us to do the following to avoid falling into deception:

> *Wherefore come out from among them, and be ye separate, saith the Lord, and touch not the unclean thing; and I will receive you. (2 Corinthians 6:17 KJV)*

We are called to separate ourselves from the sons of disobedience. While the "unclean thing" in Leviticus 5 refers to the ceremonial law, in a modern context we can assume it as idolatry. Idolatry comes in a multitude of forms.

A basic definition of idolatry would be anything or anyone exalted higher in our lives than God. In this age of technology, it is easy to fall into idolatry without realizing we have stepped into the trap. Perhaps, one of the most dangerous forms in our social media culture is the exaltation of self, and self-indulgence. Walk into any public place and you will see people of all ages taking photos of themselves to post online. This is not necessarily a form of idolatry, unless it becomes an obsession. In fact, any obsession that is not of God could possibly be a "deception" intended to steal our crown by becoming idolatrous.

It is difficult in these times not to be subjected to influences that can take the place of God. The best way to avoid this is to become better managers of our time and make time for God. I believe God had this in mind when He set aside the seventh day of rest. The Sabbath was made for man, not man for the Sabbath (Mark 2:27). By the Sabbath principle, it would be wise not only to dedicate one day in seven to drawing near to God, but also to allocate one-seventh of our time in general. By this metric, we would spend roughly two hours each day divided between prayer and reading the living Word of God. If we disciplined ourselves to devote that time to Yehshua and the Father, it would be difficult to fall victim to idolatrous deceptions. Keep in mind that our modern, nonbiblical seventh day—Sunday—is mostly dedicated to football games, golf, or other "bread and circuses" distractions, which can certainly become forms of idolatry if not kept in balance.

We live in a secular world that is virtually void of any real knowledge of God. Sadly, this is true even in most churches. We live in the superficial "feels good, do it" age of the scoffers that Peter warned about (2 Peter 3:3–4).

Within human nature lies a desire to achieve financial freedom. I spent my entire working life pursuing financial wealth, only to end up with none. Worse still, I nearly lost both wealth and God after wasting forty years chasing financial success. We strive to get our children in the best neighborhoods, near the best schools, hoping they will be accepted into the best universities, acquire the best jobs, or even become successful entrepreneurs. Meanwhile, life races past until more of it lies in the past than in the future. And for what? Why do we work so hard and dedicate so much to something that does not transcend this life? Quite simply, we are deceived, and through that deception, we inadvertently serve the wrong god. This is what Paul meant when he said, "Touch not the unclean thing"—and we're all at least a little guilty.

The Amplified Bible offers the best translation of Yehshua's comment in Matthew 6:24:

> *No one can serve two masters; for either he will hate*
> *the one and love the other, or he will be devoted to*
> *the one and despise the other. You cannot serve God*
> *and mammon [money, possessions, fame, status, or*
> *whatever is valued more than the Lord]. (Matthew 6:24*
> *AMP)*

There is indeed a difference between living a prosperous life in the promised blessing of Abraham and living *for* prosperity. How do we do this? For most Americans, and for many people around the world, we have been subjected to systems that enslave populations through abusive laws and taxation. We're considered poor if we aren't making large monthly installments on an automobile, and then judged by others according to the type of car we drive. We pay more in mandatory insurance premiums than we give to charities. We all fear becoming either poor and destitute, or worse, rejected by the Joneses. Looking around at the growing pandemic of homelessness in what is supposed to be the wealthiest nation in the world, we realize there is a fine line between where we are and where they are. No one wants to be poor and homeless, begging on the streets—or worse, falling into prostitution or selling illegal narcotics to survive in a hopeless society to avoid homelessness.

There is only one thing that separates the hopeless from the rest of us: His name is Yehshua, the Son of God, born of a human woman, who came specifically to save the world from the authority of chaos, destruction, and death—Satan. When we are called to be separate, it is not only from the sons of disobedience. We are also called to be separate from the "unclean thing," the other half of 1 Corinthians 6:17.

Behind every "unclean thing" is a demon whose goal is to separate the sons of God, as described in Romans 8:19, from God Himself. No matter how subtle these unclean things may seem, we must separate ourselves from them as those who are led by the Spirit. Demons use unclean things to weaken us through our natural senses. We are manipulated through taste, touch, hearing, smell, and sight. If it tastes good, feels good, sounds good, smells good, or looks good, we must proceed with biblical wisdom. There are five specific areas of the brain that manage the senses, and through them we can easily be provoked to disobedience.

For the first time in the history of the world, there is a global epidemic of obesity, with the United States leading in this category. Another area where America leads is in pornography, as the USA is the world's largest exporter of it. The problem with pornography is it appeals to more than one of the senses and overwhelms the brain. We become consumed by something that opens multitudes of demonic pathways into our lives. We are called to be separate from "unclean things" of any nature. When something unclean becomes idolatrous, it closes the door to the throne and opens the door to Satan's control.

The mind is the battlefield of spiritual warfare. It is through the mind that demons enter our lives. If by the gift of faith we came to know Yehshua, then by that same gift of faith we will overcome all that comes against us through Him. But we must first separate ourselves from the unclean things that can replace God and become forms of idolatry in our lives.

By the terminology of "unclean things," certainly any addiction can be idolatrous. Addictions begin with the mind's desire for something that affects one or more of the senses. In spiritual warfare, learning to discipline the mind results in a body free of sinful scars. Addictions can manifest in many ways, and we must be vigilant in guarding ourselves with the "breastplate of righteousness" and the "helmet of salvation" from Ephesians 6. The "sword," or Word of God, is the tool that brings us to separation from the world. Imagine that as you put the living Word of God into your mind, it forces out the unclean, idolatrous garbage. Addictions are powerful, but not so powerful as to overcome the Word of God engraved on our hearts and minds. By disciplining the mind to consume the Word, all else is forced out, no matter how strong the addiction.

We think of addictions as drug abuse in general, but think of addiction as being any behavioral pattern that you cannot control. The *American Heritage Dictionary* defines "addiction" as follows:

> *A condition involving use of a substance, such as a drug or alcohol, or engagement in a behavior, such as gambling, in which a person has strong cravings, is unable to stop or limit the activity, continues the activity despite harmful consequences, and experiences distress upon discontinuance.*

Meanwhile, Wikipedia defines it as follows:

> *Addiction is a neuropsychological disorder characterized by a persistent and intense urge to use*

I generally avoid Wikipedia but, in this instance, I used it for their description of addiction as being a "neuropsychological disorder." They continue as follows:

Classic signs of addiction include compulsive engagement in rewarding stimuli, preoccupation with substances or behavior, and continued use despite negative consequences. Habits and patterns associated with addiction are typically characterized by immediate gratification (short-term reward), coupled with delayed deleterious effects (long-term costs).

Addiction is tied to the five senses and originates in the brain. The brain then drives the body to "engage in rewarding stimuli." Behind every addiction is a demon that can be driven out and replaced by the Word of God! The demon-induced idolatry of addiction is one of the unclean things from which we are called to be separate.

We've all had our share of demons while living on this fallen planet under Satan's rule. In the next chapter, I will cover something very deep on the metaphysical operation of demons upon the soul, and how the soul serves as an interface between spirit and body that can either condemn or bless the body. I've had my share of struggles with demons, often without comprehending the forces behind the behavior. One example is how easily we convince ourselves that we "deserve a drink." Through subliminal messaging, we have been conditioned to believe we should constantly reward ourselves for achievements or "decompress" from stressful situations. By this deceptive reward system, we gratify the senses. Short-term decisions bring long-term consequences, and we can go too far, opening demonic pathways into our lives. Soon one beer leads to twelve, and one tequila shot leads to waking up in a strange room with no memory of how we arrived there.

Anything that rewards the senses becomes a doorway to addiction and to hosts of demons waiting to seize the opportunity to exercise curses upon us and our families. If we are led by the Spirit and separate ourselves from unclean things, we cannot become the "sons of disobedience." Our destiny is not of this world if we are led by the Holy Spirit. The future sons of God are called to be separate from the sons of disobedience. Any appeal to the senses can lead to the unclean if not kept in conformity with the living Word of God while being led by the Spirit of God.

If addictions were the only nemesis of those led by the Spirit, the journey would be far easier. Yet deceptions lie crouching at every door, like wolves stalking unsuspecting prey. Just before writing this chapter, I watched an interview between Tucker Carlson and an investigative reporter discussing one of the motives behind the open-border policy of the Biden administration. One of the greatest pandemics of our time is human trafficking, and far worse is child trafficking. Smugglers have been bringing children into America by simply walking across the border with minors from countries around the world, mostly from Latin America. These children are sometimes drugged and almost always threatened that if they do not lie to arresting agents, they will die. A large percentage of them never live to see adulthood. They are exploited for sex, and even President Trump has stated that most will probably never be found.

Tucker made a very insightful comment about pedophilia during this interview. He said, "This is spiritual. Once a child is a victim of pedophilia, his or her spirit is never the same, and is damaged for life."

Tucker was correct: pedophilia is demonic. At this precise moment, as we watch intensely for prophetic events unfolding in the Middle East concerning Israel, we also live in an age where the worst atrocities since the days of Noah are occurring in the shadows. What is worse is that elected leaders are involved in perpetrating these atrocities. Some of the most bizarre and unthinkable "unclean things" are becoming mainstream with the support of those in power. In the same interview, Tucker Carlson mentioned what is now public knowledge—that the First Lady of France is not a woman, but rather a transvestite. This person is much older than his husband and was a so-called "groomer" who fell in love with and married his subject. This is open pedophilia in the highest places of aristocracy and society.

In addition, it is no secret that a former US president was suspected of being a pedophile, along with numerous others in high-ranking government positions bearing household names familiar to all. It is no mystery why the "Epstein List" is considered top secret, or why he supposedly committed suicide while a guard slept and the cameras were turned off.

Beyond these daily horrors that cause us to shrink into a ball in disgust, there is an active campaign to depopulate the earth. COVID and everything related are the most obvious examples, *but as those led by the Spirit, we must train ourselves to be aware of any deception that threatens to steal our crown.* We must question the motives behind everything, especially if it is promoted by corporate media or government funded. Is it a coincidence that unprecedented numbers of senior deaths from the flu virus coincide with the widespread practice of annual flu shots? Is it a coincidence that trillions of dollars spent fighting "climate change" over the last twenty years have resulted in the worst droughts and floods in recorded history? How is the money being spent? Many obvious ways, such as cloud seeding and geoengineering, have made climate conditions worse by design. Meanwhile, subjugation of the planet through mandatory insurance regulations and abusive taxation to sponsor criminal enterprises operated by elected officials runs amuck.

I do not wish to turn this book into a conspiracy theory novel, but come on! As the senator from Louisiana so wisely stated, "conspiracy theorists are up 37-0"! Learn to become a critical thinker, one filled with the Word of God. If we are truly in the last hours of the last days, shouldn't we be expecting the heightened deceptive activity of the princes of darkness? Learn to identify the "sons of disobedience" by comparing their actions to the Word of God. Almost no one in positions of high-ranking political leadership is currently led by the Holy Spirit. They are the sons of disobedience, subjects of every "unclean thing," and are being led by dark spirits attempting to steal the crown from the Church of Philadelphia.

This is war, and it begins in the mind with "unclean things" that appeal to the senses.

> *Or do you not know that the unrighteous will not inherit the kingdom of God? Do not be deceived; neither the sexually immoral, nor idolaters, nor adulterers, nor homosexuals, nor thieves, nor the greedy, nor those habitually drunk, nor verbal abusers, nor swindlers, will inherit the kingdom of God. (1 Corinthians 6:9-10 NASB)*

Rest assured, God is watching all of this and His patience will expire.

> *Now I will shortly pour out My wrath on you and expend My anger against you; I will judge you according to your ways and bring on you all your abominations. (Ezekiel 7:8 NASB)*

If we understand the book of Revelation, we see that the promise in the book of Ezekiel was not isolated to Israel. However angry you might be at the individuals behind the atrocities of human trafficking, pedophilia, or even the mass global deception of false pandemics that have made several evil billionaires even wealthier while making us sick, disrupting weather patterns, and poisoning our planet, we can rest assured that God knows every secret and keeps His promises.

> *Do not be deceived, God is not mocked; for whatever a person sows, this he will also reap. (Galatians 6:7 NASB)*

Those who are led by the Spirit will separate themselves from the "unclean things."

Those who are led by the Spirit are called not only to be separate from the sons of disobedience but also to harvest. How can we do both? How can we separate ourselves from those in need of salvation?

The more we understand spiritual warfare, the more it resembles a formidable military strategy. There is strategic command, deployment, and execution, just as in any military campaign. The difference is that the troops responsible for the offensive campaign, are supported by an enormous force. This is a macro view of the image I wish to convey:

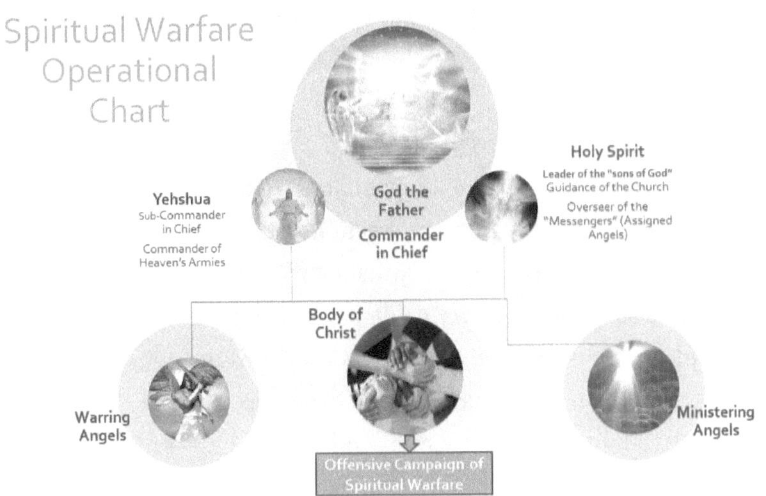

This is a basic representation of how spiritual warfare should operate for the church. God the Father is the ultimate authority—the CEO and sole shareholder of the universe—under whose command all decisions flow.

Spiritual warfare, however, begins with the church, the sons of God led by the Spirit of God. The church is responsible for launching offensive campaigns through prayer and fasting against the princes of darkness and their minions. Spiritual warfare begins with the church, or at least it should. When a group of righteous followers of Yehshua unite in prayer and fasting against a principality or demonic stronghold, Yehshua dispatches as many troops—warring angels—as necessary. Yehshua is the Lord of Hosts (armies).

The Psalm of David in chapter 91 was not only appropriate in David's time but also prophetic, pointing forward to the authority we would be given in the name of Yehshua.

> *For he shall give his angels charge over thee, to keep thee in all thy ways. (Psalm 91:11 KJV)*

> *And whatsoever ye shall ask in my name, that will I do, that the Father may be glorified in the Son. If ye shall ask any thing in my name, I will do it. (John 14:13-14 KJV)*

I have heard prosperity preachers take this verse out of context, turning it into what I call the "Santa Claus verse." Think positively, pray in Jesus's name, and receive your dream house, fine automobile, or private jet. That interpretation is tragically distant from the true context. In chapter 14, Yehshua is preparing His disciples for His departure, and this is a command of offensive spiritual warfare given to the church. Yehshua did not spend His life teaching people how to acquire dream vacations through prayer. He fought invisible enemies and taught the church how to combat those same invisible forces and glorify the Father. These verses are an assurance of His authority over what they would encounter in spiritual warfare. And to confirm that their prayers would be heard and acted upon, He immediately followed with this command:

> *If ye love me, keep my commandments. (John 14:15 KJV)*

Why would Yehshua say this immediately after the promise "Ask anything in my name and I will do it"? Because our righteousness is through

Him alone. We are justified by His righteousness, through forgiveness of sin by His blood sacrifice for us.

Much more then, being now justified by his blood, we shall be saved from wrath through him. (Romans 5:9 KJV)

Most of us make the mistake of thinking this forgiveness is a one-time, once-and-for-all transaction, and that grace will extend into the shadows where we continue certain disobedient behaviors. Yet we commit acts of disobedience daily that require atonement. It is impossible for human nature on this planet to live perfectly free of sin. Each time we catch ourselves gossiping, manipulating a situation through even the slightest deception, or lusting in our minds over anything, we must atone for it. If we fear anything more than God, we must atone for it and stop fearing anything except God. These are legal strongholds that block our prayers and render them ineffective.

I know some will disagree with me on this, so I offer a list of verses for review. I cannot overstate the importance of understanding that we are called to conform to the image of Christ as His church. To behave in any manner not becoming of the bride of Christ will impact our standing in righteousness, and our prayers will likely fall on deaf ears. Our righteousness is in Yehshua, but righteousness comes by forgiveness, forgiveness by atonement, and atonement by confession.

The Lord is far from the wicked: but <u>he heareth the prayer of the righteous</u>. (Proverbs 15:19 KJV)

Confess your faults one to another, and pray one for another, that ye may be healed. The effectual fervent prayer of a righteous man availeth much. (James 5:16 KJV)

*Now we know that God heareth not sinners: but if any
man be a worshipper of God, and doeth his will, <u>him he
heareth</u>. (John 9:31 KJV)*

*For the eyes of the Lord are over the righteous, and
<u>his ears are open</u> unto their prayers: but the face of the
Lord is against them that do evil. (1 Peter 3:12 KJV)*

*The eyes of the Lord are upon the righteous, and his
ears are open unto their cry. (Psalm 34:15 KJV)*

*But your iniquities have separated between you and
your God, and your sins have hid his face from you,
that <u>he will not hear</u>. (Isaiah 59:2 KJV)*

If we love Him and follow His commandments, we have confidence in knowing our prayers will be heard, and greater things than Yehshua did shall we do until His return.

*Verily, verily, I say unto you, He that believeth on me,
the works that I do shall he do also; and greater works
than these shall he do; because I go unto my Father.
(John 14:12 KJV)*

The sons of God, led by the Spirit of God, are obligated to cast out demons, heal the sick, raise the dead (Mark chapter 16), and even greater works than these, while Yehshua is with the Father. This is the Church of Philadelphia, for whom every door Yehshua has opened remains open, and every door He has shut remains shut. These doors are supernatural pathways of spiritual warfare that connect us to the throne of God through Yehshua. No prince or demon can close a door to the throne that Yehshua has opened, nor can they open a door to hell that He has shut. This promise, nearly 2000 years old, is still valid if we comprehend the living Word of God.

Miracles should be more common than they currently are. *Evil should be on the run, not on the rise.* The church has been compromised by a lack of understanding, much of which begins in the pulpits and commentaries from scholars.

Recently, I received a call from someone who had just joined a new church and was pleased with the atmosphere and culture of the congregation. However, the pastor occasionally made comments that seemed contrary to this person's understanding of Scripture: "My new pastor says that the time of miracles was restricted to the time of Jesus and miracles are no longer possible. In addition, the pastor said that if we heard any other teachings from any other churches to discuss it with him before sharing with the congregation."

I replied, "Find a new church immediately and pray for this pastor that his eyes be opened by the Holy Spirit to know the purpose of the church." Not knowing the word is how captain kool-aid of Guyana convinced a crowd to commit mass suicide. The bride is the fulfilment of Christ on earth in His absence, under the guidance and direction of the Holy Spirit. If we love Yehshua and keep His commandments, we will do greater works than He did as His bride. Yet very few truly believe this today. Meanwhile, a few great spiritual warriors, such as Jonathan Cahn and others, lead a powerful minority steering God's will on earth. I shudder to think where we would be without them.

This must change in the few short days that remain before His imminent arrival to take up His fragile little bride. Oh, we of little strength—the Church of Philadelphia.

I know thy works: behold, I have set before thee an open door, and no man can shut it: for thou <u>hast a little strength</u>, and hast kept my word, and hast not denied my name. (Revelation 3:8 KJV)

We separate ourselves from the unclean things, we love Yehshua and keep His commandments, and greater works shall we do in His name. The gospel must go forth to the sons of disobedience, even though we are called to be separate from them. We pursue righteousness and separation from the unclean, yet we must also engage with the sons of disobedience. Salvation is an unharvested field, awaiting the arrival of the harvesters. Nothing will be gathered into the Father's barn without them (Matthew 13:30). It is because of the harvesters that the tares are separated from the wheat.

> *Another parable put he forth unto them, saying, The kingdom of heaven is likened unto a man which sowed good seed in his field:*
>
> *But while men slept, his enemy came and sowed tares among the wheat, and went his way.*
>
> *But when the blade was sprung up, and brought forth fruit, then appeared the tares also.*
>
> *So the servants of the householder came and said unto him, Sir, didst not thou sow good seed in thy field? from whence then hath it tares?*
>
> *He said unto them, An enemy hath done this. The servants said unto him, Wilt thou then that we go and gather them up?*
>
> *But he said, Nay; lest while ye gather up the tares, ye root up also the wheat with them.*
>
> *Let both grow together until the harvest: and in the time of harvest I will say to the reapers, Gather ye together first the tares, and bind them in bundles to burn them: but gather the wheat into my barn. (Matthew 13:24-30 KJV)*

The gospel of Christ is the "good seed." Without planting, there can be no harvest (Mark 16:15). Deception is the tares—the sons of disobedience. Just as tares grow among the wheat, so will the sons of disobedience exist among the sons of God. Yet the sons of God have a responsibility not only to sow but also to harvest.

While sowing the good seed, there will be spiritual warfare. This is an inevitable fact. As we love Yehshua and keep His commandments, we will not lose our crown of righteousness. Though we are of little strength, He has gone before us and opened a doorway to the throne, where we must present ourselves clothed in Yehshua's righteousness. Our strength is not our own. The gates of hell will not prevail against us, for He is our strength (Matthew 16:18, Philippians 4:13).

Referring to the spiritual warfare chart: above us stands the Commander in Chief, God the Father, under whose command all decisions are executed. On one side is Yehshua, God the Son, Sub-commander and Commander of Heaven's Armies (Revelation 19:11–20). On the other side is the Holy Spirit, leading the sons of God (Romans 8:19). At the center is the Church of Philadelphia—the bride—launching offensive assaults against the princes and powers of darkness, flanked by ministering angels on one side and warring angels on the other.

Nothing is more powerful than the fervent prayer of the righteous bride (James 5:16). Through Yehshua, the highest authority above all, angels are commanded concerning us. And through Him, greater things than these shall we do until He returns.

And Jesus came and spake unto them, saying, All power is given unto me in heaven and in earth. (Matthew 28:18 KJV)

Far above all principality, and power, and might, and dominion, and every name that is named, not only in this world, but also in that which is to come. (Ephesians 1:21 KJV)

*Wherefore God also hath highly exalted him, and
given him a name which is above every name: That
at the name of Jesus every knee should bow, of things
in heaven, and things in earth, and things under the
earth; And that every tongue should confess that
Jesus Christ is Lord, to the glory of God the Father.
(Philippians 2:9-11 KJV)*

*Then he called his twelve disciples together, and gave
them power and authority over all devils, and to cure
diseases. (Luke 9:1 KJV)*

*And when he had called unto him his twelve disciples,
he gave them power against unclean spirits, to cast
them out, and to heal all manner of sickness and all
manner of disease. (Matthew 10:1 KJV)*

*And the seventy returned again with joy, saying, Lord,
even the devils are subject unto us through thy name.
(Luke 10:17 KJV)*

*Behold, I give unto you power to tread on serpents
and scorpions, and over all the power of the enemy:
and nothing shall by any means hurt you. (Luke 10:19
KJV)*

*And I say also unto thee, That thou art Peter, and upon
this rock I will build my church; and the gates of hell
shall not prevail against it.*

*And I will give unto thee the keys of the kingdom of
heaven: and whatsoever thou shalt bind on earth shall*

*be bound in heaven: and whatsoever thou shalt loose
on earth shall be loosed in heaven. (Matthew 16:18-19
KJV)*

*Who is gone into heaven, and is on the right hand of
God; angels and authorities and powers being made
subject unto him. (1 Peter 3:22 KJV)*

*Who will transform the body of our lowly condition
into conformity with His glorious body, by the exertion
of the power that He has even to subject all things to
Himself. (Philippians 3:21 NASB)*

*And whatsoever ye do in word or deed, do all in the
name of the Lord Jesus, giving thanks to God and the
Father by him. (Colossians 3:17 KJV)*

*Truly, truly I say to you, the one who believes in Me,
the works that I do, he will do also; and greater works
than these he will do; because I am going to the
Father. (John 14:12 NASB)*

Yehshua came for all generations—past, present, and future. God's
Grace and mercy are not constrained by the dimension of time. Mark 16
applies to all generations since the time of Yehshua's ministry on earth:

*Later He appeared to the eleven disciples themselves as
they were reclining at the table; and He reprimanded
them for their unbelief and hardness of heart, because
they had not believed those who had seen Him after
He had risen from the dead. And He said to them,
"Go into all the world and preach the gospel to all*

creation. The one who has believed and has been
baptized will be saved; but the one who has not believed
will be condemned. These signs will accompany those
who have believed: in My name they will cast out
demons, they will speak with new tongues; they will
pick up serpents, and if they drink any deadly poison, it
will not harm them; they will lay hands on the sick, and
they will recover."

So then, when the Lord Jesus had spoken to them,
He was received up into heaven and sat down at the
right hand of God. And they went out and preached
everywhere, while the Lord worked with them, and
confirmed the word by the signs that followed. (Mark
16:14-20 NASB)

This passage comes after the resurrection, and the language is not very subtle. It carries a rather harsh tone. "The one who has not believed will be condemned" precedes the signs that will accompany believers: "These signs will accompany those who have believed: in My name they will cast out demons, they will speak with new tongues; they will pick up serpents, and if they drink any deadly poison, it will not harm them; they will lay hands on the sick, and they will recover."

Do you know anyone today who is truly accompanied by these signs? By this measure, the Church of Philadelphia is a very small group of Christians. I have known a few, but they are rare. One of the greatest Christian warriors I've known in my lifetime was my feisty great-aunt, a sister to my grandmother. At the drop of hat, she would break out into speaking tongues and praying, laying on hands anywhere and at any time for any multitude of reasons.

One day, a beggar held out his hand asking for change. I'll never forget her response: "What's your name?" she asked. He replied and she proceeded with "I'm going to lay hands on you and pray for you that from this day forward, you will be delivered from the demon of rejection and poverty and be free in the name of Jesus, no longer begging for change on the street corner, okay?"

Unfortunately, the beggar took off running, and my aunt never had the opportunity to lay hands on him. Yet I assure you she prayed for him, and it wouldn't surprise me to learn that his life was changed that day. I wish I knew what happened to him.

My aunt was led by the Spirit—a son of God to be revealed. Her reward will be great. She set a high bar for me, one I have yet to reach. She did not run away from the beggar. Instead, she attempted to separate him from the unclean things and bring him to salvation. This is the task at hand for the sons of God led by the Spirit.

We can only separate ourselves to the extent that our own salvation is compromised by the unclean things of the sons of disobedience. Beyond that, we must engage with them—for where else is there to sow the good seed? They are the unplanted field; we are the farmers.

We only get one chance to get this right before we depart. There is no guarantee of success, wealth, or even where we will be tomorrow. The only guarantee is the first death, upon which time our chances for reward in heaven are sealed.

Let no one steal your crown. Be not deceived in this age of deception. Sow the good seed. The harvest is coming—and for all we know, it could be today.

I have no doubt the world stands because of the prayers of Christians. (Aristides of Athens)

CHAPTER 7

A Blameless Spirit, Soul, and Body

And the very God of peace sanctify you wholly; and I pray God your whole spirit and soul and body be preserved blameless unto the coming of our Lord Jesus Christ.

—1 Thessalonians 5:23 (KJV)

In him was life; and the life was the light of men.

And the light shineth in darkness; and the darkness comprehended it not.

There was a man sent from God, whose name was John.

The same came for a witness, to bear witness of the Light, that all men through him might believe.

He was not that Light, but was sent to bear witness of that Light.

That was the true Light, which lighteth every man that cometh into the world.

—John 1:4-9 (KJV)

What in the world is Paul talking about? How can a soul or spirit carry blame for something the body does? Is there a connection between a blameless spirit, soul, and body and the Light of men that John refers to?

I had many reservations about sharing this chapter. What I am about to share is very difficult to understand and even more difficult to explain. Before you read further, I would like to plant a thought in your mind:

We know that many animals in nature can hear sound frequencies outside the human range of perceptions. Elephants have been known to communicate across entire continents with other elephants. Many animals can detect fear in a human even when fear is not outwardly expressed. A dog may dislike one person for no reason and love another without explanation. Some dogs can even detect cancer in individuals. Do cancer cells emit an odor that can be sensed beneath skin and tissue? Or do cancer cells vibrate at a different frequency than normal cells, allowing the dog to detect them?

Elephants are perhaps my favorite mammal. On several travel adventures in Southeast Asia, I visited many elephant camps and could never get enough of these fascinating creatures. Once, while in Bangkok enjoying a fabulous meal at an outdoor restaurant with a large group of locals and friends, I suddenly felt someone tapping on my shoulder. When I turned, I was surprised to see an elephant right behind me. Of course, I didn't expect to see an elephant standing there and was very surprised. The young elephant extended his trunk, and someone at the table said, "Don't feed him! He's a street bum looking for handouts!" Well, street bum or not, I wasn't passing up this opportunity. I looked around the table for anything he might eat, handed him what I had, and he quickly inhaled it before stretching his trunk out again. I was in trouble, though, because I couldn't find anything else on the table that he might like.

The restaurant owner came out and shooed the poor elephant down the street. That was when I learned that a few homeless orphan elephants beg on the streets for food, and I was heartbroken. The group laughed at the elephant choosing me to beg from, and someone said, "He picked the biggest sucker at the table! Haha!" Everyone at the table laughed at my expense.

Fortunately, an older Thai man at the table spoke up and said, "No, the elephant sees the heart of the man."

When I began this study on body, soul, and spirit, I recalled many times in my life when animals seemed to know people better than people know each other. There were several other amazing events involving elephants in Southeast Asia, but I won't bore you with all of them. One occasion that was especially memorable was when a baby elephant walked right up to me, wrapped me in his trunk, and held me tightly. The mother was close by, and one of the trainers came running toward me, afraid that the mother might become protective of her calf. She watched but never moved from her place. The trainer commented that the baby had made an instant friendly connection with me, one that usually takes some time to establish trust.

I have walked right up to dogs considered dangerous and vicious even by their owners, only to be greeted as though they had always known me. As a teenager, I was once trapped in an alley of a cattle auction barn with a 2,500-pound angry Brahma bull. He charged within a few feet of me and could have injured or killed me, but instead he only looked at me and walked away after hurting several other people in the barn. Birds have flown up to me and stared as if wanting to say something but couldn't.

Some of these events may have been angelic protection, but others seem related to something spiritual that cannot be seen. I do not understand this, but I believe it is possible that many animals can see the soul. Studies by organizations such as the Australian Institute of Parapsychological Research suggest that colorful auras can be detected around the human body and even used to diagnose disease. The human eye is limited in its ability to perceive certain spectrums of light, but most animals are not limited in their visual perception of wider bands of light frequencies.

I have always been fascinated by hummingbirds. I am certain there are many hummingbirds in heaven, as they are simply too beautiful and amazing to be confined to earth. Did you know that hummingbirds have a fourth retinal cone in their eyes, allowing them to see millions more colors than humans? It is believed that they can actually identify and distinguish sugar in water by its light color frequency. In one study I read, a plain water sample was placed near another sample containing sugar. Neither sample had any dyes, just clear water. The hummingbirds quickly congregated around the sugary water, showing no interest in the plain water. They never even tasted the plain water.

Other animals have been known to perceive angels and demons invisible to humans. Many people believe angels are present when certain species of birds appear, while others associate birds such as owls or crows with demons. I challenge you to find a Hollywood movie that features beautiful songbirds singing in the background. Nearly every outdoor scene in Hollywood films is filled with crows cawing in the background, never the pleasant melodies of songbirds. If Hollywood productions are generally demonically inspired, it stands to reason that their work would not align with the Light of men. It seems clear that film producers prefer the obnoxious sounds of the "unclean bird" over the more pleasant voices of songbirds. If you were from another galaxy and intercepted a Hollywood movie, you might conclude that the only birds on earth were cawing crows.

For anyone familiar with horses, you know how quickly they can detect fear or aggression in a person. I once knew a horseshoer who was very rough and aggressive with horses. Whenever he approached a new horse, the animal's eyes would widen and its breathing would quicken at the mere sight of him. If a fearful person climbs onto a horse, it is almost certain that the horse will throw them off. Horses can see right through people. Or perhaps they perceive something within a person that is invisible to humans?

In Numbers chapter 22 is the account of Balaam, whose donkey stopped in front of an angel that Balaam himself could not see. Much of what I have shared on this subject comes from my own opinions and research, but the story of Balaam's donkey that could see the angel and spoke to Balaam through the angel is biblical. Perhaps animals have something to teach us about the soul.

So Balaam arose in the morning, saddled his donkey,
and went with the leaders of Moab. The Angel and
Balaam But God was angry that he was going, and
the angel of the Lord took his stand in the road as
an adversary against him. Now he was riding on his
donkey, and his two servants were with him. When
the donkey saw the angel of the Lord standing in the
road with his sword drawn in his hand, the donkey
turned off from the road and went into the field; and

Balaam struck the donkey to guide her back onto the road. Then the angel of the Lord stood in a narrow path of the vineyards, with a stone wall on this side and on that side. When the donkey saw the angel of the Lord, she pressed herself against the wall and pressed Balaam's foot against the wall, so he struck her again. Then the angel of the Lord went farther, and stood in a narrow place where there was no way to turn to the right or to the left. When the donkey saw the angel of the Lord, she lay down under Balaam; so Balaam was angry and struck the donkey with his staff. Then the Lord opened the mouth of the donkey, and she said to Balaam, "What have I done to you, that you have struck me these three times?" And Balaam said to the donkey, "It is because you have made a mockery of me! If only there had been a sword in my hand! For I would have killed you by now!" But the donkey said to Balaam, "Am I not your donkey on which you have ridden all your life to this day? Have I ever been in the habit of doing such a thing to you?" And he said, "No."

Then the Lord opened Balaam's eyes, and he saw the angel of the Lord standing in the way with his sword drawn in his hand; and he bowed all the way to the ground. Then the angel of the Lord said to him, "Why have you struck your donkey these three times? Behold, I have come out as an adversary, because your way was reckless and contrary to me. But the donkey saw me and turned away from me these three times. If she had not turned away from me, I certainly would have killed you just now, and let her live." So Balaam said to the angel of the Lord, "I have sinned, for I did not

know that you were standing in the way against me.
Now then, if it is displeasing to you, I will turn back."
But the angel of the Lord said to Balaam, "Go with
the men, but you shall speak only the word that I tell
you." So Balaam went along with the representatives of
Balak. (Numbers 22:21-35 NASB)

In the last chapter, I mentioned the power of the living Word of God. Many have argued that the author of the book of Hebrews is unknown and may not have been Paul. Yet I will argue that no one else speaks of the three parts of our design except Paul (see 1 Thessalonians 5:23). In reading this verse from Hebrews, I believe it could only have been written by Paul:

For the word of God is living and active, and sharper
than any two-edged sword, even penetrating as far
as the division of <u>soul and spirit</u>, of both joints and
marrow, and able to judge the thoughts and intentions
of the heart. (Hebrews 4:12 NASB)

This subject of the soul and spirit being divided within the human body seems to have been common knowledge among many of the authors of the Bible. Perhaps this is another translation problem, where more accurate words do not exist in most languages to provide more accurate interpretations. We'll look at some of those and see where the dots connect. This is a complex subject that once again requires faith to comprehend the metaphysical characteristics of something invisible to humans.

In this research, I was reminded of my sophomore year in high school when I had a lackadaisical algebra teacher. We never realized how far behind we were until we were introduced to a better teacher. When we realized we had fallen behind, it seemed we had to return to eighth-grade math before we could catch up to the junior level in high school algebra. This study of body, soul, and spirit has reminded me of that time in my life. It isn't until we seek knowledge that we become aware of our lack of it. The more we learn, the more we realize there is yet to know.

Many people focus only on the New Testament, neglecting the Old Testament prophecies and foundational biblical knowledge. This is like trying to learn algebra without first mastering basic math skills. If you read Revelation without understanding Genesis, you will never truly comprehend it.

When we try to steer conversations toward the Bible and God, how often do the people you're trying to help begin by responding with, "Well, in my opinion…"? When a response begins that way, you can be certain of a few things:

- They haven't studied the subject.
- They don't really care what you have to say about it.
- You're not going to change what they already believe, no matter what you say.

The beauty of this study is that I don't think you'll encounter anyone who can claim to have an opinion on what I am about to share. This is some mind-blowing stuff. If you are like me, you will find yourself sitting alone after trying to share it. No one will have an opinion on something they've never heard of, and rather than becoming intrigued, most people simply walk away.

As with everything, it is best to start at the beginning. Genesis chapter 2 contains something important regarding the soul.

And the Lord God formed man of the dust of the ground, and breathed into his nostrils the breath of life; and man became a living soul. (Genesis 2:7 KJV)

When the Bible says Elohim created man in His image, the spirit is required to complete that image. It is this "breath of life" from the living

God that sets man apart from the rest of creation. It is the soul and spirit of man that complete his image of God.

Unfortunately, that doesn't help me understand it any better, except to recognize that the soul has an origin that gives the body life and, in context, is distinct from the spirit—the "breathe of life." In some way I cannot fully comprehend, the soul contributes to the life of the body. Interestingly, the word for life in Hebrew comes from the same word for water. Maybe we'll come back to that later. James makes this comment:

For just as the body without the spirit is dead, so also faith without works is dead. (James 2:26 NASB)

This is great insight from James, helping us understand that the spirit—or soul, in this case—is what gives life to the body. The word for spirit in this verse comes from the Greek *pneuma,* meaning "breath" or "wind", as described in Genesis 2:7. Yet Paul says there are three parts: spirit, soul, and body. Are spirit and soul not the same? Not according to Paul. Going back to Hebrews 4:12, I noticed something different using Strong's:

◄ *5590. psuché* ►

<u>Strong's Lexicon</u>

<u>psuché:</u> *Soul, life, self, inner being*

This peculiar word *"psuché"* caught my attention. It is where we get the root word "psyche" for psychology.

psychology (n.)

1650s, "the study of the soul," from Modern Latin psychologia, probably coined mid-16c. in Germany by Melanchthon from Latinized form of Greek psykhē "breath, spirit, soul" (see <u>psyche</u>) + logia "study

of" (see -logy). The meaning "science or study of the phenomena of the mind" is attested by 1748, in reference to Christian Wolff's "Psychologia empirica" (1732).
The modern behavioral sciences sense is from the early 1890s.[11]

No wonder Paul understood this so clearly, while we continue to struggle with such a complex metaphysical concept. Psychology and the soul are one and the same, distinct from both spirit and body. Hmmm.

This feels like a missing link in something I have been researching for years, hidden under my nose the entire time. If you already know what I am about to share, I will be surprised. I don't believe many people are aware of this connection between acoustical physics and the spiritual realm. Could there be a mystery concealed in John 1 that relates to this metaphysical phenomenon?

> **In the beginning was the Word, and the Word was with God, and the Word was God.**
>
> **The same was in the beginning with God.**
>
> **All things were made by him; and without him was not any thing made that was made.**
>
> **In him was life; and the life was the light of men.**
>
> **And the light shineth in darkness; and the darkness comprehended it not.**
>
> **(John 1:1-5 KJV)**

Through the first ten verses of John chapter 1, the Holy Spirit opened my eyes to a journey that has yet to conclude. I continue to uncover new portals of ancient mysteries revealed in the Bible through this passage from John. One example is the term *Elohim* from Genesis. In Hebrew, the

---

11   https://www.etymonline.com/word/psychology

-im ending makes the word plural, meaning "gods," not God singular. In his opening chapter, John reveals that at least one other Creator in Genesis was Yehshua Himself. Nothing was created without Him, and in Him was life, and that life was the light of men. In the context of John 1, Yehshua was one of the *Elohim* in Genesis 1.

Already, at least half a dozen mysteries are solved in the first five verses of John! Yehshua was with God, was God, and is inseparably connected to Creation, the Word, and the Light. Nothing in Creation exists apart from Him. The life in Yehshua is the light of mankind. The term *Word* in the Greek translation of John chapter 1 is "logos."

◀ *3056. logos* ▶

Strong's Lexicon

logos: Word, speech, message, account, reason, doctrine

Usage*: The term "logos" is a multifaceted Greek word that encompasses a range of meanings including "word," "speech," "reason," "doctrine," and "account." In the New Testament, "logos" is used to denote the spoken or written word, the message of the Gospel, and, most profoundly, as a title for Jesus Christ, emphasizing His role as the divine Word of God incarnate. Theologically, "logos" signifies the communication of God's will and truth to humanity.*

Cultural and Historical Background*: In ancient Greek philosophy, "logos" referred to the principle of order and knowledge. Philosophers like Heraclitus used it to describe the rational principle governing the cosmos. In the Hellenistic Jewish context, "logos" was associated with divine wisdom and the intermediary between God and the world. The Apostle John, in his Gospel, appropriates this term to articulate the preexistence and divinity of Christ, presenting Jesus as the ultimate revelation of God.*

The terminology John chose for this passage was by divine inspiration. "Logos" encompasses speech, doctrine, wisdom, and knowledge in one word. Yehshua was the divine wisdom between God and the world, and John understood this deep concept when he wrote chapter 1. But how does this equate to Creation and Light? By knowledge and wisdom? The simple answer is yes, but only to an extent we are incapable of comprehending in our present finite state of mind. I'm going to take you down the same trail of clues the Holy Spirit led me on, beginning with "hallelujah."

The *Topical Encyclopedia* explains that *hallelujah* means "praise the Lord" in Hebrew. That is the way most of us have come to understand the meaning of *hallelujah*. The word itself is derived from the verb *halal*. Here is what Strong's has to say:

Strong's Lexicon

Hallelujah

הַלְלוּ (hal·lū)

Verb - Piel - Imperative - masculine plural

Strong‹s Hebrew 1984: 1) to shine 1a) (Qal) to shine (fig. of God‹s favour) 1b) (Hiphil) to flash forth light 2) to praise, boast, be boastful

The primitive root for the word *halal* or *hallu* means "to shine" or "to project light, to flash forth light." A lesser use of the word is connected to "praise." Would it surprise you to know that flashing forth light and praising God are the same?

The seven chords of music—A, B, C, D, E, F, and G—are sound frequencies that, when increased by forty octaves, become light-band frequencies corresponding exactly to the seven colors of the rainbow. These are represented in what is known as the "Scriabin Circle," and can be outlined as follows:

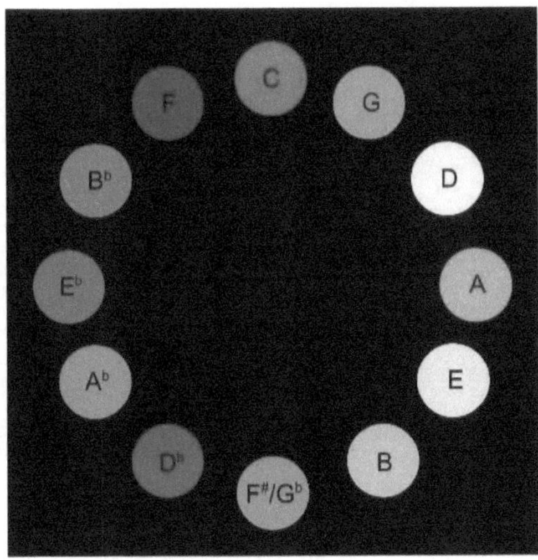

A more comprehensive view, including the chord transitions forty octaves lower from the light-band frequencies associated with each chord transition, looks like this:

	0	1	2	3	4	5	6	7	8
C	16.35	32.7	65.41	130.81	261.63	523.25	1046.5	2093	4186
C#	17.32	34.65	69.3	138.59	277.18	554.37	1108.73	2217.46	4434.92
D	18.35	36.71	73.42	146.83	293.66	587.33	1174.66	2349.32	4698.63
D#	19.45	38.89	77.78	155.56	311.13	622.25	1244.51	2489	4978
E	20.6	41.2	82.41	164.81	329.63	659.25	1318.51	2637	5274
F	21.83	43.65	87.31	174.61	349.23	698.46	1396.91	2793.83	5587.65
F#	23.12	46.25	92.5	185	369.99	739.99	1479.98	2959.96	5919.91
G	24.5	49	98	196	392	783.99	1567.98	3135.96	6271.93
G#	25.96	51.91	103.83	207.65	415.3	830.61	1661.22	3322.44	6644.88
A	27.5	55	110	220	440	880	1760	3520	7040
A#	29.14	58.27	116.54	233.08	466.16	932.33	1864.66	3729.31	7458.62
B	30.87	61.74	123.47	246.94	493.88	987.77	1975.53	3951	7902.13

(Interactive chart with sound is provided on https://muted.io/note-frequencies/)

Color	Frequency	Wavelength
violet	668–789 THz	380–450 nm
blue	631–668 THz	450–475 nm
cyan	606–630 THz	476–495 nm
green	526–606 THz	495–570 nm
yellow	508–526 THz	570–590 nm
orange	484–508 THz	590–620 nm
red	400–484 THz	620–750 nm

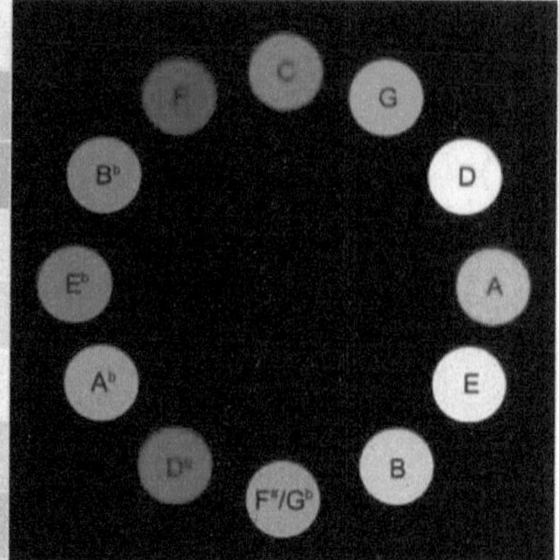

Since the word *hallelujah* was understood as shouting praises and song to the Father (Yah), it was translated as "praise" rather than "flashing forth of light." But if you were a Hebrew during the time of Moses, you would have known the true meaning of *hallelujah*. By understanding that sound is light, forty octaves lower, "flashing forth of light" back to the Father by singing and praising is perfectly accurate. Thanks to modern technology, we now know what the ancient Hebrews knew 3,500 years ago.

Hallelujah is literally "flashing forth light to Yah," accomplished by singing and praising in sound frequencies that translate into light forty octaves higher. "In Him was the light of men" begins to make perfect sense. In fact, even human DNA vibrates at frequencies that, through a series of shorter and shorter wavelengths, begin as sound frequencies and end in a burst of light at the end of the DNA strand. Everything in creation vibrates at sound frequencies forty octaves below their corresponding frequencies of light, in harmony with musical chords. The seven chords of music correspond to the seven colors of light in the rainbow, separated by forty octaves of frequency. Since the speed of light is known, these light frequencies can be calculated from their corresponding sound frequencies with mathematical precision.

Even the earth resonates at a low frequency of 7.83 Hz +/-. As we move down the scale from light to sound, then lower to 60 Hz, these lower-frequency wavelengths become electrical and radio frequencies.

The Schumann Resonance was discovered mathematically in 1952, and early "Apollo" astronauts discovered the physiological effects of being deprived of the 7.83 Hz frequency during space travel. To counter this, a Schumann Resonator was developed to help astronauts avoid the physical and psychological deterioration associated with the absence of the earth's vibrational frequency. These resonators have since been developed as economical household devices designed to protect against harmful EMF frequencies that interfere with the body's natural, healthy frequencies.

Sound is light and light is sound, depending on the scale of each frequency. The Word was the light of men! Yehshua exists at both ends of the electromagnetic spectrum of wave frequencies. If you're getting older, like me, you may have to stretch your mind beyond its limits to comprehend this.

In our daily struggles and spiritual battles, there is nothing more comforting than absorbing the Word of God through the voice of King David in the Psalms. We should take time each day to bathe in the Psalms, allowing their inherent peace to penetrate our troubled minds and soothe our troubled hearts. The wisdom of God permeates our soul through the Psalms of David, harmonizing our frequencies with His.

If none of that blew your mind, congratulations! But there is something else you may not have known: there are twenty-two Hebrew letters in the Hebrew alphabet, and each letter corresponds directly to a note on the musical scale of David's harp. The famous harp of David had twenty-two strings, each of which corresponds directly to a Hebrew letter, making every letter of the Hebrew language a specific musical note on his harp's scale.

Remember that Hebrew was the first language, and for reasons just described, I believe it came directly from "the Word, who was with God and who was God." The Word of God is light, and now we understand that sound is light, forty octaves lower. To "sing a joyful noise" (Psalm 98:4) is, quite literally, to project light back to the Father from our limited physical dimension forty octaves lower.

Psalm 98:4 is the definition of *hallelujah*! In a brief search for "sing a joyful noise to the Lord," I found over one hundred verses in the Bible emphasizing its importance—most of which are found in the Psalms of David. Singing praise is a direct connection to the throne of God through this "Word" phenomenon of sound and light. Singing praise purifies the soul as it connects directly to the light of the Father. Sound is light. The Word is the light of men!

If *hallelujah* means "flashing forth light to God," then singing praise is *hallelujah*. If singing praise can bless and purify the soul, the next question is: what does the opposite do to our souls? If what we speak flows from the soul and can be translated to light, can our words (or music) also carry darkness?

Here are two instances where Solomon associates the power of the mouth with the springs of life on the higher spectrum and with violence and evil on the lower spectrum. Words are powerful because they come from the soul and resonate with the spiritual realm in a range of frequencies. Flashing forth light to the Father (*hallelujah*) comes from the mouth, and so does violence and evil. Both begin in the soul before they are expressed as words or actions.

Yehshua was confronted by the Pharisee priests on a Sabbath while plucking grain for Himself and the disciples. The priests strongly condemned Him for doing this on a Sabbath. Then read His response:

> *You brood of vipers, how can you speak good things when you are evil? For the mouth speaks out of that which fills the heart. (Matthew 12:34 AMP)*

Read another proverb in this context:

> *If you [claim ignorance and] say, "See, we did not know this,"*
>
> *Does He not consider it who weighs and examines the hearts and their motives?*
>
> *And does He not know it who guards your life and keeps your soul?*
>
> *And will He not repay [you and] every man according to his works?*
>
> *(Proverbs 24:12 AMP)*

When we speak of the "heart," we are referring to the soul. Motives begin in the soul and manifest in the body. Here is a great verse from the book of Psalms:

> *The [spiritually ignorant] fool has said in his heart, "There is no God."*
>
> *They are corrupt, they have committed repulsive and unspeakable deeds;*
>
> *There is no one who does good. (Psalm 14:1 AMP)*

How does the heart speak? It is the soul that speaks. The soul is the well from which the springs of life flow. It is from the soul that we either praise God or say in our heart, "There is no God." The soul is where spiritual warfare occurs. The actions of the body are the physical manifestations of darkness or light that begin in the soul.

One night I was watching *Sid Roth's It's Supernatural*, where he interviewed a pastor who caught a demon on camera. The demon was cast out of a man who had given himself to Christ at an evening service. When it left the man's body, it exited through (you guessed it) the mouth. For a split second, it was visible through the camera lens.

About fifteen years ago, I met a pastor from Oregon named Ken Klein, who published an amazing documentary in which demonic figures were captured on camera using a combination of digital night-vision technology and a high-powered infrared beam. We are surrounded by peculiar entities that are sometimes inadvertently caught on camera. Even more remarkable is that some of these same demonic-looking figures seen today have been carved into rocks by indigenous peoples thousands of years ago.

Before I derail on that wild subject, let's return to Paul's reference to "touch not the unclean thing" and idolatry from the previous chapter. It is not the narcotic or the alcohol that defiles us; rather, the induced physical effect is how the flesh becomes defiled. Physical manifestations begin in the soul.

Think of the soul as the operating system software for the body. The body follows commands that originate in the soul. The flesh is defiled by actions of the body that began in the mind. The mind and the soul are directly linked and either bless or defile the body. Is the body to blame? The body is condemned by what began in the soul. By purging the mind with the Word of God, there is no corrupt soul to defile the body. A purified soul blesses the body.

By flashing forth light to the Father, we link the soul to the Spirit, blessing body, soul, and spirit between the frequencies of sound and light. King David may not have understood the physics of this wave phenomenon, but he certainly understood its effect.

The body is subject to the soul in every way. The body can do nothing without the soul. Without the soul, the body is anesthetized. Therefore, if we heal the soul, we heal the body. The soul has the power to either bless or defile the body.

Is the brain part of the soul?

How does the brain work?

The brain sends and receives chemical and electrical signals throughout the body. Different signals control different processes, and your brain interprets each. Some make you feel tired, for example, while others make you feel pain.

Some messages are kept within the brain, while others are relayed through the spine and across the body's vast network of nerves to distant extremities. To do this, the central nervous system relies on billions of neurons (nerve cells).[12]

We're encroaching upon Einstein-level concepts that are difficult for most of us to comprehend. I will not pretend to fully understand this subject. However, I would like to attempt to understand it well enough to comprehend how the body, soul, and spirit can be preserved blameless before the Lord (1 Thessalonians 5:23).

Hopefully, we all have electricity in our homes, but most of us have no idea how it arrives there. Free electrons in motion are collected by electrical generators, while copper or aluminum cables act as pipelines to send electricity downstream from power source. At various points downstream, transformers convert high voltage to low voltage, lighting our homes. This voltage varies worldwide in hertz frequencies from 30 Hz to 60 Hz. Most of the western world operates at 60 Hz, while most of the eastern world uses 50 Hz.

---

12   https://www.hopkinsmedicine.org/health/conditions-and-diseases/anatomy-of-the-brain

In the human body, sodium and potassium ions are exchanged through "voltage-gated ion channels," where neurons utilize either the sodium or potassium ion charge to transmit information across all neurological pathways.

Conventional electricity generated by the motion of free electrons differs in frequency from neurons. Remember we discussed the earth's resonance (Schumann Resonance) at 7.83 Hz, which is the low end of the electromagnetic frequency scale. Neurons, however, resonate at a slightly higher frequency. Studies of the neuronal frequency coding in the body calculate this resonance mathematically at around 200 Hz.

You can go online and find tone generators for a wide range of sound frequencies. If you locate a tone generator for 200 Hz, listen to it for a few seconds and notice the effect it has on your brain. You may immediately feel a strange sense of stimulation, slight dizziness, or momentary disorientation that is too complex for words. All electrical frequencies from 0–200 Hz have correlating sound frequencies, and now we know that all sound waves have corresponding light frequencies forty octaves higher.

By flashing forth light to the Father in praise, we align the sound and electrical frequencies of the body and soul with the higher frequencies of the light (spirit). The spirit is the highest frequency of light, connecting us to the Father and the Holy Spirit. The soul resonates at a lower frequency than the spirit but higher than the body. The soul resonates with electrical and sound frequencies that must remain in harmony with the higher frequency "light of men." The only way this harmony occurs is by keeping the living Word of God in our minds, allowing the atoned soul to guide the body.

In an amazing study conducted by Pastor Henry Wright over more than twenty years, he proved a connection between the manifestation of diseases in the body and underlying spiritual problems. The spirits of fear, unforgiveness, pride, hatred, and violence all have direct links to cancers, diabetes, Alzheimer's, and even the flu. It is important to note that many times we fail to forgive ourselves, which can be just as damaging to the soul as failing to forgive others. If God does not record a forgiven transgression, neither should we (1 Corinthians 13:5). Holding on to it is a waste of time that prevents us from experiencing the high frequency light power of the Spirit.

As I began researching the effects of sound on the soul and how *hallelujah* is light to the Father, I believe I discovered the connection between the body, soul, and spirit as they relate to the specific wave frequencies of electricity, sound, and light. When we are in perfect harmony with Yehshua, the Word, healing flows as our body and soul resonate with His higher frequencies of the Spirit, which is light (the light of men or mankind).

I consider this recommended reading by Pastor Wright. His book is titled *A More Excellent Way: A Teaching on the Spiritual Roots of Disease* and based on 1 Corinthians 12:31:

> **But covet earnestly the best gifts: and yet shew I unto you a more excellent way. (1 Corinthians 12:31 KJV)**

At this point, you might be shaking your head, thinking I'm becoming a Tibetan monk or Buddhist. I am aware that this sound wave theory crosses over into some false religions. It is also part of the modern trend of combining religions based on commonalities so that "we can all just get along." Remember when Pope Francis said, "All religions are a path to God"? I am not sure which god he was referring to, since the God of the Bible strictly prohibits false gods. I am in no way attempting to connect Buddhism or Hinduism with Christianity.

One of my doctors during cancer treatment became a dear friend and once shared his religious beliefs with me: "I am a Christian, Buddhist, and Shamanist. These religions are the same." I cringed before responding that Christianity has nothing in common with any other religion, except that we share the same planet, for now.

I know this sound frequency theory is associated with false religions, but please don't throw the baby out with the bathwater. I believe wave frequencies are directly connected to the soul and spirit within the three-part body-soul-spirit connection. I can't see oxygen, but it obviously exists or we wouldn't be alive. These wave frequencies are a dynamic part of the spiritual realm. Not being able to see or fully comprehend them does not negate their existence.

As I write, I am using a wireless internet connection through Starlink. High-frequency radio waves carry information to and from a satellite orbiting the earth. This is over my head (pun intended), but radio technology has evolved from AM radio electromagnetic wave tuner frequencies, to microwave "cellular," and now to what we call "5G." Just as sound and light are separated by forty octaves of wave frequencies, AM radio and 5G are separated by many gigahertz in their respective frequencies. Information travels faster on 5G because it is a radio wave approaching the speed of light in frequency.

In my last book, I discussed a demonic invasion of my home and my life. This was a physical manifestation of demonic activity, and one of the many bizarre circumstances surrounding this event in my life was how the demon(s) spoke through my cellphone. At the time, I had five different cellphones furnished by five different companies I was consulting for internationally. It sounds strange today, but cell service was costly twenty years ago, and clients would provide a complimentary phone rather than pay for expensive international calls. It was very inconvenient! The voices sounded threatening and horrifying, but I could never understand what they were saying. The person on the other end could never hear them. I would always ask, but they could never hear them—and this occurred on every call, on all five cellphones, with different service providers.

I believe demons use these microwave frequencies to manipulate our thoughts, even planting ideas and images in our minds, in the same way information travels across a wireless internet connection to a computer. Demons operate in these lower-than-light electrical frequencies that affect the soul.

The occurrences of mass deaths among migratory birds around the world have increased dramatically as technology expands across the globe. Reports of wildlife demonstrating abnormal behavior, such as unprovoked attacks on humans, are also rising. I believe technology is at least partly responsible for these unnatural anomalies in animal behavior. Rural areas that only recently gained access to electricity now have wireless internet and cell phones. In the late 1980s and early 1990s, I traveled some of the most beautiful coastline in southern Mexico. Most of that region had no electrical grid yet. Fishing villages relied on dry ice deliveries to preserve their catch, and people were still using kerosene lamps in rural areas just forty years ago. Today, even the poorest people of the humblest circumstances have cellphones and internet. I am inclined to believe we have saturated our atmosphere with dark "dirty" microwave frequencies that are not in harmony with the "light of the world" (John 8:12).

If we heal the soul, we heal the body and "preserve them blameless before the Lord." In Creation we see millions of color combinations, and we know that Yehshua is the light of men. Light and color have corresponding frequencies connected to every physical aspect of Creation. Does it not stand to reason that these frequencies can affect the soul—especially if *hallelujah* is a word that, when literally translated, connects sound to the light of the Father?

In 1 Samuel chapters 14–17, we read of Saul's fall from favor with God and David's rise to become king of Israel in his place. Saul was instructed to destroy the Amalekites, their king Agag, and everything in their possession—including children and animals. (Not to stray from the subject, but this total annihilation was always related to genetic contamination from Nephilim tribes.) In prideful disobedience, Saul spared the king of the Amalekites and kept their possessions as spoils of war. In chapter 15, Saul immediately falls out of favor with God for this prideful act, and the "Spirit of the Lord departs from him." Saul is immediately given over to demonic spirits.

Now the Spirit of the Lord departed from Saul, and
an evil spirit from the Lord tormented and terrified
him. Saul's servants said to him, "Behold, an evil
spirit from God is tormenting you. Let our lord now
command your servants who are here before you to
find a man who plays skillfully on the harp; and when
the evil spirit from God is on you, he shall play the
harp with his hand, and you will be well." So Saul

told his servants, "Find me a man who plays well and bring him to me." One of the young men said, "Behold, I have seen a son of Jesse the Bethlehemite who is a skillful musician, a brave and competent man, a warrior, discerning (prudent, eloquent) in speech, and a handsome man; and the Lord is with him." So Saul sent messengers to Jesse and said, "Send me David your son, who is with the flock." Jesse took a donkey [loaded with] bread and a jug of wine and a young goat, and sent them to Saul with David his son. Then David came to Saul and attended him. Saul loved him greatly and [later] David became his armor bearer. Saul sent word to Jesse, saying, "Please let David be my attendant, for he has found favor in my sight." So it came about that whenever the [evil] spirit from God was on Saul, David took a harp and played it with his hand; so Saul would be refreshed and be well, and the evil spirit would leave him. (1 Samuel 16:14-23 AMP)

I have heard many people ask, "Why were demons only in the New Testament?" Accounts of demons were never restricted to the New Testament, and this passage in 1 Samuel proves that fact. What changed in the New Testament was the arrival of the Word in the flesh, who demonstrated His authority over demons. This doesn't mean they didn't exist in the Old Testament; they have been around since the flood of Noah. Yehshua came so that we would no longer be subject to serpents and scorpions—dark princes and demons.

Pride was the source of Saul's disobedience. Pride was the cause of Lucifer's fall (Isaiah 14:12–17; Ezekiel 28:12–19). Pride is the beginning of all disobedience and the root of all sin in God's eyes. Because of pride, the *"Spirit of the Lord departed from Saul,"* and he was given over to an evil spirit. The Spirit of God is a gift given to every believer by faith (Acts 2:38, 10:45; 1 Corinthians 12). Remember that faith itself is also a gift (Ephesians 2:8). If we lack faith, we compromise the Spirit as well, leaving the soul vulnerable to evil spirits. Pride will expose areas of the soul that need healing. Conquer pride by consuming the Word of God. We can do nothing without the Spirit of God—never forget this.

David would play his harp for Saul, comprised of twenty-two notes that correspond directly to each letter of the Hebrew alphabet. Though "the Word" contained in the musical tones of the Hebrew language, the evil spirits would promptly depart from Saul. The power of the Word is the power of the light of men that expels demons. The Psalms of David were in perfect harmony with the light frequency of God, which was—and still is—painful to demons.

A man named Steve Rees discovered the correlation between the Psalms, Hebrew letters, and musical notes, and went to the painstaking effort of deciphering several of the written Psalms from Hebrew into music. By returning to the original Hebrew texts, Rees converted the letters into their corresponding musical notes and produced some of the most amazing harp music ever heard. Steve has a website where you can purchase and download some of his songs, and I strongly recommend this experience for all Christians.

We know that David's harp, in tune with the twenty-two musical letters of the Hebrew language, could drive out demons. Yet it is also true that demons are attracted to certain sounds and music. In certain African cultures, such as the Yoruba people of Nigeria in West Africa, drums are believed to serve as a bridge between the physical and spiritual realms. Their so-called "talking drums" are used for many purposes, including the conjuring of spirits. This spiritual connection to drums can be found across many African tribes and nations, where drum music—combined with influences such as smoking or drinking—can result in demonic possession. Drum rhythms are used for religious, spiritual, and even medical purposes while summoning spirits.

The practice of using drums to call or drive away spirits was never limited to Africa. Many Asian and Latin cultures also use drums for spiritual purposes. The deeper the bass drum, the greater the spiritual influence over the listener. This practice dates back to the earliest post-flood cultures of ancient Babylon and Sumeria. Recall our discussion of the Sabean tribes that attacked Job in the first chapter? The Sabean temples of Haran were carved from stone in such a way that low-frequency chanting within their cavernous rooms induces mind-altering hallucinations even today.

Many studies have been conducted at the Celestial Temple of Sogmatar, Turkey, about thirty-five miles from Haran, where Abraham lived briefly before departing for Canaan. The construction of these stone structures, known as "archaeoacoustics," continues to amaze scientists and archaeologists today. A hollow, low-frequency chant inside one of the carved stone rooms produces a mind-altering experience that the Sabeans used during Abraham's time for spirit-conjuring purposes. What is even more interesting is that the vibration of the stone, as chants continue over time, results in measurable electromagnetic radiation emitted into the surrounding area, proving direct correlations between low frequency sound and electricity.

Then there is modern heavy metal music, associated not only with rebellion but with direct satanic worship. With names like *Megadeath* or *Black Sabbath*, what else would we expect? Some are worse than others, and listeners can come under a curse whether they realize it or not. The rhythms, sounds, and lyrics of musicians such as Marylin Manson or guitarist Nergal of the band Behemoth can and will curse their listeners with music dedicated to Satan. Nergal's real name is Adam Michał Darski, and he assumed the stage name "Nergal" after a Babylonian god of plague and death. The Babylonian Nergal was likely a fallen angel, known in ancient Babylonian culture as a king of hell who married a queen of hell.

You can be certain that any music written by someone who associates himself with a king of hell is not in harmony with King David's Psalms and will attract demons rather than drive them away. The point I intend to make here is that sound has consequences that affect the soul. Demons can be repelled by sound, as in the case of Saul, or drawn to sound, as in the case of African drums and heavy metal music. The difference between the Psalms and drums or heavy metal is the frequency. There are frequencies harmonically in tune with the Word of God and the Light of men, just as there are frequencies in tune with darkness. The soul can be pulled toward either dark or light frequencies if we are not led by the Spirit.

If we are led by the Spirit, we sense realities in the spiritual realm that our eyes cannot see. At times you may walk into a room and feel your hair stand on end for no obvious reason. When the soul resonates with the light of the Holy Spirit, you will sense things that are not in harmony with that light. You begin to recognize dark spirits when your soul resonates with the light of men. At a higher spirit level, you instinctively know when a politician is lying or when a threat is imminent, even without visible signs. This is part of being led by the Spirit and aligning soul and body in harmony with Him. David's harp was perfectly tuned to light frequencies capable of driving out dark spirits forty octaves lower. The twenty-two letters of the Hebrew alphabet were tuned to the light frequencies of the Word, who is the light of men. I find this incredibly fascinating!

Few pastors or Christians believe that a demon can occupy a Spirit-filled believer. Yet if you study the ministry of Derek Prince, you will discover this is far from the truth. In fact, Derek Prince encountered entire congregations under demonic influence. I believe that when we harbor unatoned sin, we leave doors open to the demonic realm, which can influence us—or worse, overtake our souls so that our bodies become defiled. The late Derek Prince shared numerous accounts of casting demons out of Christians. In some cases, they knew they had a problem but overlooked the possibility of demon possession.

How is this possible? The body-soul-spirit interface is separated by wide gaps between their respective frequencies. Demons operate at the soul level—sound and electrical frequencies—while the Holy Spirit occupies the spirit level, the frequencies of light. Those who are led by the Spirit are the sons of God (Romans 8:19). If body-soul resonance is dark and out of harmony with the light of the Holy Spirit, demons gain access to the soul and manipulate the body, compromising the spirit. Without the soul, the body has no guidance system. Demons can guide the soul in the absence of the Spirit. The body follows neurological commands that originate in the soul. If the soul is not healed, the body cannot be healed. Healing is a physical manifestation of a spiritual condition that begins in the soul when we are reborn in the Spirit.

> *Jesus answered, Verily, verily, I say unto thee, Except a man be born of water and of the Spirit, he cannot enter into the kingdom of God.*
>
> *That which is born of the flesh is flesh; and that which is born of the Spirit is spirit.*
>
> *Marvel not that I said unto thee, Ye must be born again.*
>
> *The wind bloweth where it listeth, and thou hearest the sound thereof, but canst not tell whence it cometh, and whither it goeth: so is every one that is born of the Spirit. (John 3:5-8 KJV)*

The first step in correcting our operational guidance system (soul) is receiving the gift of faith by which we believe in the Son of God. Faith occurs in the mind before manifesting in the body.

> *For by grace you have been saved through faith; and that not of yourselves, it is the gift of God. (Ephesians 2:8 NASB)*

The next step is confession:

> *But what saith it? The word is nigh thee, even in thy mouth, and in thy heart: that is, the word of faith, which we preach;*
>
> *That if thou shalt confess with thy mouth the Lord Jesus, and shalt believe in thine heart that God hath raised him from the dead, thou shalt be saved.*
>
> *For with the heart man believeth unto righteousness; and with the mouth confession is made unto salvation. (Romans 10:8-10 KJV)*

Remember that the mouth is the wellspring of the heart (soul)? We believe in our heart, then we confess with our mouth, then confession is made unto salvation, of course, by faith.

This is Strong's translation and definition of heart:

◀ 2588. kardia ▶

Strong's Lexicon

kardia: Heart

Original Word: καρδία

Part of Speech: Noun, Feminine

Transliteration: kardia

Pronunciation: kar-DEE-ah

Phonetic Spelling: (kar-dee'-ah)

Definition: Heart

Meaning: lit: the heart; mind, character, inner self, will, intention, center.

Word Origin: Derived from a primary root word

Corresponding Greek / Hebrew Entries: - H3820 (בֵל, leb): Heart, inner man, mind, will

- H3824 (בֵבָל, lebab): Heart, understanding, inner part

Usage: *In the New Testament, «kardia» is used metaphorically to refer to the inner self, encompassing the mind, will, emotions, and moral center of a person. It is not limited to the physical organ but represents the core of human identity and spiritual life. The heart is seen as the seat of thought, emotion, and decision-making, reflecting one›s true character and intentions.*

Cultural and Historical Background: *In ancient Greek culture, the heart was considered the center of physical and spiritual life. This understanding was carried*

Though there are two words for *heart* and *soul* in both Greek and Hebrew, they are often used synonymously. I believe the soul is influenced by sound and electrical frequencies that must be in perfect harmony with the light frequency of the Spirit. When we are directly led by the Spirit of God, the body and soul are harmonically balanced with the Light of men.

The heart believes, the mouth confesses, and we are baptized—born into the kingdom of heaven by the Spirit. Without the Spirit, no one will enter the kingdom of heaven. The soul is born with the body. The Spirit is light, and the Word is the light of men. When we believe in our heart (soul) and confess with our mouth, we are born again in the Spirit and begin to resonate in harmony with the Light of men, Yehshua.

How does the body-soul achieve total harmonic resonance with the Spirit (light)?

Love must dwell in the soul and manifest through the body. Love is the perfect frequency, in harmony with the "light of men." Love is what brings body, soul, and spirit into harmony with one another.

Love is patient, love is kind, it is not jealous; love does not brag, it is not arrogant. It does not act disgracefully, it does not seek its own benefit; it is not provoked, does not keep an account of a wrong suffered, it does not rejoice in unrighteousness, but rejoices with the truth; it keeps every confidence, it believes all things, hopes all things, endures all things.

Love never fails; but if there are gifts of prophecy, they will be done away with; if there are tongues, they will cease; if there is knowledge, it will be done away with. (1 Corinthians 13:4-8 NASB)

Therefore, in the soul:

- There can be no impatience.
- There can be no jealousy (tenth commandment).
- There can be no pride or arrogance.
- There can be no disgraceful acts or language.
- There can be no taking advantage of others for personal gain.
- There can be no provocation to anger.
- There can be no harboring of unforgiveness.
- There can be no joy in evil or lies.
- Love cannot fail, even in the absence of the gifts of the Holy Spirit.

Love is the fruit of the Spirit. Love endures all circumstances. If the mouth is the wellspring of the heart, then 1 Corinthians 13:4–8 must be the condition of the soul so that both body and soul may be preserved blameless before the Lord. Where any of these conditions exist, confession by mouth cleanses the soul through the perfect power of the blood of Yehshua.

If these conditions of the soul are not remedied, opportunities arise for demonic manifestation within the soul, which in turn defiles the body and can result in disease or affliction. The soul must resonate in harmony with the love of God—for the love of God is the light of men.

> *He that loveth not knoweth not God; for God is love. (1 John 4:8 KJV)*

John also says this in the same chapter:

> *There is no fear in love; but perfect love casteth out fear: because fear hath torment. He that feareth is not made perfect in love. (1 John 4:18 KJV)*

We can add another condition to the 1 Corinthians 13 description of "love." Fear is not of love and will damage the soul. There can be no fear except the fear of God in love. Fear is not in harmony with the spirit; it damages the soul. Fear separates the soul from the spirit.

First Corinthians 13 begins like this:

> *If I speak with the tongues of mankind and of angels,*
> *but do not have love, I have become a noisy gong or*
> *a clanging cymbal. If I have the gift of prophecy and*
> *know all mysteries and all knowledge, and if I have all*
> *faith so as to remove mountains, but do not have love,*
> *I am nothing. And if I give away all my possessions*
> *to charity, and if I surrender my body so that I may*
> *glory, but do not have love, it does me no good. (1*
> *Corinthians 13:1-3 NASB)*

If God is love, then love is light. Love is the perfect frequency that heals the soul and will manifest in a body healed of all afflictions and diseases. Those who are led by the Spirit will be free of all negative frequencies associated with a damaged soul—therefore preserved blameless in body, soul, and spirit before the Lord. We can consume the Word relentlessly, but in the absence of love, it is all for naught. The fruit of the spirit will manifest fully through a healed soul that resonates with the light of men.

In Ephesians chapter 4, we can find important instructions given by Paul for the devoted Christians ("sons of God led by the Spirit"):

> *Do not let unwholesome [foul, profane, worthless,*
> *vulgar] words ever come out of your mouth, but*
> *only such speech as is good for building up others,*
> *according to the need and the occasion, so that it will*
> *be a blessing to those who hear [you speak]. And do*
> *not grieve the Holy Spirit of God [but seek to please*
> *Him], by whom you were sealed and marked [branded*
> *as God's own] for the day of redemption [the final*
> *deliverance from the consequences of sin]. Let all*
> *bitterness and wrath and anger and clamor [perpetual*

I was a lukewarm Christian with a deeply wounded soul. I became critical and fault-finding, quick to anger, with a plethora of soul wounds over the course of a hard life that made me bitter and cynical. As a child, I had always been fun, witty, with a good sense of humor, and eager to be "good." I wanted to be recognized as a good child and a good student, never rebellious or vulgar. Vulgar language made me cringe. But as I grew older and became jaded by the cruelty of satan's world, my personality changed, and I became someone else.

During the transition from elementary to junior high school, I was bullied and at times beaten by older, larger kids. There was no good reason for this, except that I was the grandson and prodigy of a "Church of Philadelphia" pastor, and some of the kids were manipulated by demons and despised me for no logical reason.

Little by little, I began working out and trying to excel in athletics to better defend myself. I worked hard to gain respect from adults, though I made mistakes along the way that caused some to lose respect. I found it difficult to keep their opinions out of my mind, and I wanted to impress my peers and please my mentors. Over time, I became known as a hard worker and high achiever, ready to confront anyone who stood in the way of those achievements.

The deepest injury to my soul, one that would change me for decades, was my divorce after having three children. The pain of being separated from them was unbearable, and in the early years of the divorce, my ex-wife often used the children to inflict more pain by refusing to honor visitation rights or making visitation periods difficult. Shortly after the divorce, I experienced infidelity for the first time from a partner I thought I loved. It was at that time that I began to struggle in every area of my life.

I became a brutal brawler and drank heavily, at times hoping I would die in my sleep. My physical strength and agility made me dangerous to others when consumed by drunken rage, and I would physically hurt people. I began to date for the wrong reasons and developed an inability to love anyone or anything, totally consumed in myself and my anger towards the world.

Soon, I became a rejected misfit in society, looked down upon as someone to avoid. A spirit of rejection was followed by a spirit of depression that dragged me to new lows. I was broke, and broken, with no visible future, no reason to live, and no will to go on living. I resonated perfectly with the frequencies of darkness, in the total absence of "the light of men." Love had vacated my soul. There was no light in me.

As I mentioned in my last book, I became physically plagued by demons in addition to everything else. If there is one good thing about a demonic encounter, it is that it drives us to search for God. I found my Bible, stored away in a closet for years, and began to read. Immediately, tears flowed as the Holy Spirit began purging the darkness from my soul— the operating system of my body. On that day in July of 2007, a slow healing process began, along with a new direction for my life.

However, certain negative aspects would not depart from me. I continued to have outbursts of anger, remained critical of others, and experienced repeated failures in relationships. In fact, I stopped pursuing relationships altogether because they became predictable "wash-rinse-repeat cycles." Though I was reading and studying the Word, I was slow to apply what I learned—going through the motions without operating from a healed soul. In effect, I was isolating the Holy Spirit from my life through my wounded soul behavior. My operating system was still in harmony with dark frequencies, even though I was consuming the Word. I was saved, but not yet a "son of God led by the Spirit."

In addition to the list above and adding fear to the list of "do nots," there is one more critical command revealed in Ephesians 4: Do not grieve the Holy Spirit!

*And do not grieve the Holy Spirit of God [but seek to
please Him], by whom you were sealed and marked
[branded as God's own] for the day of redemption
[the final deliverance from the consequences of sin].
(Ephesians 4:30 AMP)*

How do we grieve the Holy Spirit? (Ephesians 4:29–31)

- Foul profane vulgarities
- Bitterness
- Wrath and anger
- Clamor (perpetual animosity, resentment, strife, and fault-finding)
- Slander
- Malice (all spitefulness, verbal abuse, malevolence)

Rather: *Be kind and helpful to one another, tender-hearted (compassionate, understanding), forgiving one another (readily and freely), just as God in Christ also forgave you. (Ephesians 4:32 AMP)*

Grieving the Holy Spirit injures our soul and separates us from the light of the Spirit.

In the next chapter, I will go into more detail about the Holy Spirit. But in the context of the three-part body, soul, and spirit, I believe the *spirit* is the spiritual result of our death in Satan's kingdom and our rebirth into the kingdom of God. The spirit is the seal of the Holy Spirit, declaring that we are redeemed—purchased by the work of the cross—and no longer the property of Satan. The spirit is what identifies us as the property of God, purchased by the Son and sealed by the official witness of the Holy Spirit.

Grieving the Holy Spirit not only damages the soul but may also compromise the reborn spirit. We should be more careful not to grieve the Holy Spirit, lest our spirits fail to be preserved blameless before the Lord.

Going back to John 1, let's take a deeper look at this:

*But as many as received him, to them gave he power
to become the sons of God, even to them that believe
on his name: Which were born, not of blood, nor of*

the will of the flesh, nor of the will of man, but of God.
(John 1:12-13 KJV)

In verse 13, the spirit is born of God. The spirit is not born of carnal will or blood, but of God Himself. This is the spirit. Upon believing in Yehshua and being saved, we are given the right to become the "sons of God." The sons of God are led by the Spirit, yet not all who are saved will follow even though they have a reborn spirit from God. There is a special inheritance reserved for those who follow the lead of the Holy Spirit. Nonetheless, all who are saved receive a spirit born of God and not of man. Receiving the spirit born of God is the seal of those who belong to the kingdom of God, with the Holy Spirit as witness.

The sons of God led by the Spirit are completely justified in Christ's righteousness. They live righteously, and when they stumble, they atone through the blood of Yehshua. This is the meaning of justification through Christ. We all fall short of the glory of God, yet we are freely justified by His grace *through the redemption that is in Christ Jesus* (Romans 3:23–24 KJV). If we transgress, we must atone. Where atonement is absent, a demonic doorway is opens to that part of the soul. Grieving the Holy Spirit exposes a spiritual problem that must be rectified at the soul level, retuning the soul in harmony with the Spirit frequency.

Take another look at John chapter 3:

Jesus answered, "Truly, truly, I say to you, unless someone is born of water and the Spirit, he cannot enter the kingdom of God. That which has been born of the flesh is flesh, and that which has been born of the Spirit is spirit. Do not be amazed that I said to you, 'You must be born again.' The wind blows where it wishes, and you hear the sound of it, but you do not know where it is coming from and where it is going; so is everyone who has been born of the Spirit." (John 3:5-8 NASB)

John reiterates that the spirit is born separately from the body, and this birth only occurs through a transformation of the soul and mind.

Yet in Galatians 3:26, Paul says that we are all sons of God, which at first seems to contradict what John says in that they "have the right to become" sons of God.

> *But before faith came, we were kept under the law, shut up unto the faith which should afterwards be revealed.*
>
> *Wherefore the law was our schoolmaster to bring us unto Christ, that we might be justified by faith.*
>
> *But after that faith is come, we are no longer under a schoolmaster.*
>
> <u>*For ye are all the sons of God by faith in Christ Jesus.*</u>
>
> *For as many of you as have been baptized into Christ have put on Christ. (Galatians 3:23-27 KJV)*

In the context of this chapter, Paul delivers a strong reprimand to the Galatians, who were attempting to keep the law while also identifying as Christians. Under Christ, the Mosiac Law was nullified, and by faith, we now live under grace rather than the law (Romans 6:14–23). So, I do not know precisely how to reconcile the difference between John's statement and Paul's statement, except that *faith* is the key word. The Galatians could not compromise their salvation, but they certainly compromised their faith by choosing to live under the law, thereby excluding themselves from grace.

It is through baptism and "putting on Christ" that, by faith and grace apart from the law of Moses, we become sons of God. In the case of the Galatians, they were baptized yet continued to live by the nullified law, and thus could not be led by the Spirit as sons of God. Choosing the nullified law over the blood of Yehshua is a serious crime in Christianity. Paul clarified this to the Galatians.

To clarify: the spirit is born of God by the seal of the Holy Spirit when we proclaim Yehshua Christ as Lord and Savior. The soul is cleansed when we confess our sins. The body must respond to the soul, and together both body and soul are led by the Spirit if they are truly the sons of God. Not all who receive the spirit will become sons of God, but they are guaranteed the *right* to become sons of God by following the Spirit (John 1:12). Wow!

I do not want to be overly dogmatic about this, but it seems there is a distinction between being born of the Spirit at baptism in Christ and becoming sons of God led by the Spirit. The next step—being led by the Spirit—is not necessarily achieved by all who receive Christ and are reborn (receive) of the Spirit by God.

The soul functions as the operating system of the body through the mind. The Spirit is the seal of the Holy Spirit, born of God and not of flesh. If this is true, it would mean that everyone possesses a soul, but not everyone has a spirit until they are reborn of God (Ephesians 4:30). The Spirit is the higher frequency—the light of men—and only those who are born again and baptized are reborn of the Spirit. The soul operates at a lower frequency range of neurons and sound. The sons of God led by the Spirit have energized their souls and bodies to the higher frequency power of light, preserving body, soul, and spirit blameless before the Lord by faith, by grace, and by putting on Christ, the Light of men.

I hope this three-part study of body, soul, and spirit has not left you confused. The metaphysical realm is not easy to understand or articulate. I prefer to analyze until things make sense; I am not one to simply accept and move on without full understanding. I want to understand it well enough to avoid the frustration I once felt in high school algebra. Failing to understand these issues can compromise our faith under certain circumstances, so I break them down until even someone simple like me can comprehend.

One example of this light-soul-body relationship is before us every day: the electromagnetic relationship between the sun and the earth.

I am somewhat reluctant to use this analogy because this "soul" subject is already very deep, but I will attempt to explain without complicating it further.

Among the many deceptions we are taught through secular education is the belief that the sun is some kind of a nuclear reactor that will eventually burn out or explode. I do not believe this at all. I believe that the sun is a type of transformer that receives its energy source from heaven—or from a place designated by God—and redistributes it into our solar system. Everything we claim to know about the sun is theoretical, since no one has ever been there. I believe the sun receives energy from an unknown source, and, like a transformer, redistributes it into our solar system. The planets act as capacitors, receiving and storing the energy transformed by the sun.

Everything that happens on earth results from this electromagnetic relationship between the earth's storage capacity and the sun's infinite supply of light energy. As we observe a rainbow, we see the sun's incredible light divided into seven distinct frequencies, combined as one, as they are sent forth in harmony throughout the solar system. Without the lower-frequency physics of the earth, we would never imagine the extent of the sun's light as a source of higher-frequency power.

I believe the relationship between the sun and the earth is how our body, soul, and spirit interact in a similar way. The Godhead is the light source that when reborn by the Spirit of God, the soul is energized in harmony with a higher frequency. The body's operating system undergoes a dynamic shift when we accept the "light of men's" desire to empower the soul. The soul, as the lower-frequency electromagnetic interface between spirit and body, must remain in harmony with the Light of men, Yehshua. When this dynamic shift occurs in the soul empowered by the light, these are the sons of God who are led by the Spirit of God. The soul must be fully healed (atoned), or it will compromise both body and spirit.

But put on the Lord Jesus Christ, and make no provision for the flesh in regard to its lusts. (Romans 13:14 NASB)

Desires do not begin in the body; they begin in the mind. If neurons in the brain control the body, they are, by default, part of the soul that commands the body. Knowing that neurons resonate at the 200 Hz range on the electromagnetic scale, we can understand the soul itself as a low-frequency operational system of the body, forty octaves lower than that of the spirit (the light of men).

This dynamic "soul-to-spirit" shift has been lacking in the church for centuries, until now. I believe the rise of the sons of God has begun and is about to impact the church (and the nations) in a huge way. There is an awakening occurring, where Christians are becoming more aware of the power of God and are inviting miracles. Jews are converting to Christianity. Even Muslims and members of Hamas are turning to Christ. False doctrines are being challenged in the pulpits, and the spirit of Jezebel is being identified and rebuked in many churches. As the lawless one is revealed in these final hours (2 Thessalonians 2:8), the glory of God will be revealed through the sons of God, just as it was in the days of Moses and Elijah. As this occurs, the tares will be separated from the wheat before the harvest begins. The rise of the sons of God is synonymous with the wheat maturing in the field before the harvest.

Embrace the Holy Spirit and heal your soul, body, and spirit through the power of the light of men, Yehshua. Cleanse your soul, body, and spirit with the healing authority of the Word—the light of men who purchased us with His blood sacrifice on the cross. Yehshua's authority cannot be challenged anywhere in the universe, but we can isolate ourselves from His power by refusing to transform and heal our afflicted souls. Our souls must resonate in harmony with the higher frequencies of the spirit. The fruit of the spirit is total love. Anything not rooted in love can grieve the Holy Spirit and, if left unatoned, wounds the soul. If the soul interface between body and spirit is healed, then the body, soul, and spirit can be preserved as blameless before the Lord! If God is love, then love is light and the highest possible frequency on the healing spectrum.

Pastor and author Katie Souza has published some fantastic books on how to heal the wounded soul. Her insights from the Holy Spirit are truly revolutionary and amazing. Some of her books are out of print, but I strongly urge you to acquire any of her books you can find about soul healing. Two of my favorites are *Healing the Wounded Soul*, which I found on Amazon, and *Soul Decrees*, which is out of print but, I believe, is available in e-book format. Katie Souza shares some extraordinary research, and I believe many people will discover new miracles in their lives by applying her work.

Let's go back to where this chapter started with animals and their perception of a person's inner light or darkness. I have had a few animals that I loved. My first was a bird named "Chief." I was young, maybe ten years old, and this bird went everywhere I went. He was a different breed of parakeet, slightly larger and all white. He would go back and forth from one shoulder to the other and keep his balance no matter what chore I was involved in. He learned many words and phrases. My favorite was "I'm a pretty bird!" One day while I was outdoors, he flew away, completely out of sight, and I was devastated. I broke down into tears and thought I had lost Chief forever. I had no idea where he had flown away to and feared he would probably be eaten by a cat.

Suddenly, something caught my eye–it was Chief, returning to his roost on my shoulder! He was panting and out of breath since he wasn't accustomed to flying much. I was so happy to have my friend back. Then one day, when I went to let him out of his cage, I found him dead on the floor. I wondered if I would see Chief again someday in heaven.

When my favorite dog died in 2018, I had been through so much—first cancer, then shingles on my right eye and scalp. It seemed one affliction after another was plaguing me. But one of the worst days of my life was when my German Shepherd, Rocky, died from a blood infection that had been misdiagnosed by the veterinarian and not treated promptly. Rocky was my closest friend, and I still struggle at times without him. How is it possible that we become so attached to a nonhuman creature without a soul?

Well, hang on, because this is good news!

In Matthew 8, we find some amazing accounts where Yehshua demonstrated His authority over storms and demons. Read below from Matthew 8:28–33 (AMP)

When He arrived at the other side in the country of the Gadarenes, two demon-possessed men coming out of the tombs met Him. They were so extremely fierce and

Two demon-possessed men were living among the tombs of the dead, so violent that people feared to pass by them. They immediately recognized Yehshua and their tone changed. Rather than a violent exchange, as they might have with any other passerby, they begged that if they must be driven out of the men, they be allowed to enter the pigs grazing close by. Yehshua cast the demons out, and they entered the pigs, which then went berserk and rushed off a cliff into the sea.

What we know now is that the soul operates at a frequency far lower than light, with certain soul frequencies resonating either with light or with darkness. From what we know about how demons operate at the soul level, they exist within this range of frequencies that are not in harmony with the light. I believe that what defines the clean and unclean is their frequency of existence. Swine are not kosher and are considered unclean, according to Deuteronomy 14:8 and Leviticus 11:7 (KJV):

Many birds are also specified as unclean. I believe this is due to their ability to interact metaphysically with demons. Take a look at some of these species:

> *These you shall detest among the birds; they are not to be eaten, for they are hated things: the eagle and the vulture and the buzzard, the kite, every kind of falcon, every kind of raven, the ostrich, the nighthawk, the sea gull, every species of hawk, the little owl and the cormorant and the great owl, the white owl, the pelican, the carrion vulture, the stork, all kinds of heron, the hoopoe, and the bat. (Leviticus 11:13-19 AMP)*

In the extra-biblical book of Jubilees, there is an account of Abraham as a youth rebuking flocks of ravens that had been commanded by Mastema (Satan) to eat all the corn planted by the people in the area where Abraham lived. This story, found in chapter 11, if you're interested, underscores the raven as an unclean bird responding to Satan's commands. Is it possible then that inside the ravens bodies were demons driving the ravens at Satan's will? I believe so.

In 1 Kings 17 is the account of the ravens being commanded again—this time by God—to bring Elijah food. This is very interesting given that Leviticus is very clear that the raven is a "hated" bird, yet here is Yahweh ordering them to supply Elijah with food.

> *And the word of the Lord came to him, saying, "Go from here and turn eastward and hide yourself by the brook Cherith, which is east of the Jordan [River]. You shall drink from the brook, and I have commanded the ravens to sustain you there [with food]." So he went and did in accordance with the word of the Lord; he went and lived by the brook Cherith, which is east of the Jordan. And the ravens brought him bread and meat in the morning, and bread and meat*

in the evening; and he would drink from the brook. It
happened after a while that the brook dried up, because
there was no rain in the land.

Here is what I think about that event, though I cannot prove it. This conjecture comes from knowing God and how He creates examples for us in every letter of His Word.

Elijah confronted the king of Israel, Ahab, and his wife, Jezebel, and all the pagan priests of Ba'al. The story of Elijah in 1 Kings is a must read for Christians because Elijah will likely be one of the two witnesses during the tribulation. He was a son of God, led by the Spirit of God, and an example of what we should strive to become.

I believe it is possible to consider that the demons that manipulated Ahab and Jezebel were tasked by God with providing food for Elijah from the king's table through the ravens. Elijah was more deserving of that food than Ahab and Jezebel ever were. I would love to know the truth behind these ravens, but my conjecture is that God used the ravens, charging Ahab's demons to inhabit them and bring food from the king's table to the one person in Israel who stood for God and Israel against Ahab and Jezebel. Therefore, the ravens brought food to Elijah from the king's table. This remains conjecture, but I believe it is possible!

Now consider this from Revelation 18:

And he cried out with a mighty voice, saying, "Fallen,
fallen is Babylon the great! She has become a dwelling
place of demons and a prison of every unclean spirit,
and a prison of every unclean and hateful bird.
(Revelation 18:2 NASB)

Babylon the great harlot (the Vatican) is home to every unclean and hateful bird, resonating on the same dark frequencies as demons. Demons can inhabit these unclean birds, which is what makes them unclean!

After my bout with demons had passed in 2007, I had a strange experience the following year with an owl. I was working on my south

Texas land, and an owl flew up and perched on a tree just a few yards away. It was early afternoon, bright sunlight—an odd time to see an owl. He sat on a mesquite tree limb, just staring at me. As I walked toward him, he looked away, then back at me. When I came within about twenty feet, he flew off. I sensed in my spirit that it was ominous, though I didn't know what to make of it, and I returned to work.

A few minutes later, the owl returned to the same limb, staring at me again. I walked toward him again, and he let me get relatively close before flying away again. This happened several times, and it took me years to understand that this owl was likely being manipulated by a demon that was probably still angry about his friend being cast into the abyss. I shared this story in *The Bride, the Wise Virgins and the Last Adam*, recounting the demons that had overtaken my home in 2006. This owl encounter was likely connected to that group of demons. Owls do not behave this way, especially in Texas. They are among the "unclean and hated birds." I don't even recommend keeping figures of owls around the home.

If demons can inhabit unclean animals and birds, this means they have souls that can be possessed by the demons. If you read the last book, I shared a story about mules or donkeys, whichever they were, cursing my grandfather after leaving the man who was possessed. I do not believe God hates donkeys, but they are considered unclean, according to Leviticus, which means they might be inhabited by demons. How else can a donkey speak except through a demon? Or angel in the case of Balaam (Numbers 22:28–30)?

The Garden of Eden was inhabited by all of God's created animals, so obviously, heaven will be as well. There is a great chance that we will see our beloved pets again in heaven, especially now that we understand animals also possess souls that can be in harmony with love. We know from Revelation that horses will be in heaven because Yehshua arrives on one! If our pets aren't there, I'm not worried about it. I just want to be with Yehshua and get away from the sons of disobedience! Whatever God does for us there cannot compare to this world (1 Corinthians 2:9)!

Something that just occurred to me as I was writing this chapter: even during my darkest years of having departed from the Spirit and walking with a damaged operating system (the soul), my experiences with animals were the same as when I was delivered. The elephants and horses, dogs, and birds, etc., saw a better soul in me than the one that drove my angry and jaded body at the time. So even if a horse or dog can spot the silver beneath a tarnished soul, how much more can Yehshua see us not for who we are but for who we can become? If we bring our body and soul into harmony with the Spirit?

Shout forth light unto the Father with a "hallelujah"! For even the creature anxiously awaits the manifestation of the sons of God to be revealed!

And now I entrust you to God and to the word of His grace, which is able to build you up and to give you the inheritance among all those who are sanctified. (Acts 20:32 NASB, Paul's farewell to the Ephesians)

CHAPTER 8

The Great Comforter

We declare, upon Scriptural authority, that the human will is so desperately set on mischief, so depraved, and so inclined to everything that is evil, and so disinclined to everything that is good, that without the powerful, supernatural, irresistible influence of the Holy Spirit, no human will ever be constrained towards Christ.

—Charles Spurgeon

"If you love Me, you will keep My commandments.

I will ask the Father, and He will give you another Helper, so that He may be with you forever; *the Helper is* **the Spirit of truth, whom the world cannot receive, because it does not see Him or know** *Him; but* **you know Him because He remains with you and will be in you.**

"I will not leave you as orphans; I am coming to you. After a little while, the world no longer *is going to* **see Me, but you** *are going to* **see Me; because I live, you also will live. On that day you will know that I** *am* **in My Father, and you** *are* **in Me, and I in you. The one who has My commandments and keeps them is the one who loves Me; and the one who loves Me will be loved by My Father, and I will love him and will reveal Myself to him."**

—John 14:15-21 (NASB)

If we are vessels of Christ on earth, then the Holy Spirit is the wind in our sails. Without the Holy Spirit, we can do nothing and we are nothing. Just as we discussed, before salvation, we are composed only of body and soul. But upon confessing that Yehshua is Lord (renouncing our citizenship under Satan) and being baptized, we receive the gift of the Spirit and become three complete parts. The soul (*psuché*, from which we derive the words "psyche" and "psychology") encompasses the mind and the heart. It must be kept in check, or the body and spirit will not remain blameless before the Lord (1 Thessalonians 5:23). Without the Holy Spirit, we would wander aimlessly through life, without direction and condemned to the second death. Those who pursue only wealth in this life will miss the real treasures that exist beyond it. Our only real purpose in this life is to reach the next life, rescuing others from satan as we go. This is only possible with the help of the Holy Spirit. If we neglect our Holy Comforter, we lose the wind in our sails and navigate aimlessly into the tidal currents of hell.

In focusing on redemption and the redemptive process, it is imperative that we respect the Holy Spirit's operative power in uniting the "sons of God" (the bride, the church) against the forces of darkness. Even Yehshua, while in human form, was only able to offer Himself as a sacrifice to God through the power of the Holy Spirit. How much more, then, could we possibly do without Him?

> *How much more will the blood of Christ, <u>who through the eternal [Holy] Spirit</u> willingly offered Himself unblemished [that is, without moral or spiritual imperfection as a sacrifice] to God, cleanse your conscience from dead works and lifeless observances to serve the ever living God? (Hebrews 9:14 AMP)*

In addition, the Holy Spirit is the Chief Administrator of the inheritance of the promise as joint heirs with Christ. The verses that follow Hebrews 9:14 allude to this fact:

> *For this reason He (Christ) is the Mediator and Negotiator of a new covenant [that is, an entirely new*

*agreement uniting God and man], so that those who
have been called [by God] may receive [the fulfillment
of] the promised eternal inheritance, since a death has
taken place [as the payment] which redeems them from
the sins committed under the obsolete first covenant.
For where there is a will and testament involved, the
death of the one who made it must be established, for a
will and testament takes effect [only] at death, since it
is never in force as long as the one who made it is alive.
So even the first covenant was not put in force without
[the shedding of] blood. (Hebrews 9:15-18 AMP)*

It is important to understand that though Yehshua gave Himself as the ultimate sacrifice, the redemption process was completed with the Holy Spirit.

*In Him, you also, when you heard the word of truth,
the good news of your salvation, and [as a result]
believed in Him, were stamped with the seal of the
promised Holy Spirit [the One promised by Christ]
as owned and protected [by God]. The Spirit is the
guarantee [the first installment, the pledge, a foretaste]
of our inheritance until the redemption of God's own
[purchased] possession [His believers], to the praise of
His glory. (Ephesians 1:13-14 AMP)*

The Holy Spirit Himself is an installment on our inheritance, a down payment on what is to come that we should freely utilize on earth with Yehshua's authority. We are born with body and soul, and the Spirit is a gift from God—a down payment on our inheritance as joint heirs with Christ. By Yehshua, we have an authority that can only be asserted through the Holy Spirit.

Read this verse from Acts 10:

*How God anointed Jesus of Nazareth with the Holy
Spirit and with great power; and He went around doing
good and healing all who were oppressed by the devil,
because God was with Him. (Acts 10:38 AMP)*

Yehshua's authority over the devil began with the gift of the anointing of the Holy Spirit. Having been anointed by the Holy Spirit, He was also with God. For God to be with us, we must receive the anointing of the Holy Spirit. Only through this anointing can the power of God be made manifest in the redemptive power of Yehshua's blood within us. Through Yehshua, we have authority over the powers of darkness, destruction, and chaos, yet this authority requires *activation* by the anointing of the Holy Spirit. Being redeemed by the blood and anointed by the Holy Spirit activates the power of God through those that wear the seal of the Holy Spirit. This is a gift from God.

*Now it is God who establishes and confirms us [in joint
fellowship] with you in Christ, and who has anointed
us [empowering us with the gifts of the Spirit]; It is
He who has also put His seal on us [that is, He has
appropriated us and certified us as His] and has given
us the [Holy] Spirit in our hearts as a pledge [like a
security deposit to guarantee the fulfillment of His
promise of eternal life]. (2 Corinthians 1:22 AMP)*

*Now He who has made us and prepared us for this
very purpose is God, who gave us the [Holy] Spirit as a
pledge [a guarantee, a down payment on the fulfillment
of His promise]. (2 Corinthians 5:5 AMP)*

It is through the redemptive power of Yehshua's blood that we were purchased from the authority of this earth and death then we are sealed by the Holy Spirit. Both are required to gain access to the Father.

For through him we both have access by one Spirit
unto the Father. (Ephesians 2:18 KJV)

Between Paul and John, it is difficult to choose whose books are the most powerful, but I love this passage in John 14 regarding the "Comforter":

And I will ask the Father, and He will give you another
Helper (Comforter, Advocate, Intercessor—Counselor,
Strengthener, Standby), to be with you forever— the
Spirit of Truth, whom the world cannot receive [and
take to its heart] because it does not see Him or know
Him, but you know Him because He (the Holy Spirit)
remains with you continually and will be in you. "I will
not leave you as orphans [comfortless, bereaved, and
helpless]; I will come [back] to you. (John 14:16-18
AMP)

Many translations use the word *orphans*. The sons of God were never left as orphans, having received the promise of the Holy Spirit. In Luke 24:49, Yehshua reveals the task of the Holy Spirit concerning the sons of God:

Listen carefully: I am sending the Promise of My
Father [the Holy Spirit] upon you; but you are to
remain in the city [of Jerusalem] until you are clothed
(fully equipped) with power from on high. (Luke 24:49
AMP)

"Remain in Jerusalem until you are fully clothed" was in anticipation of the first Pentecost fifty days after Passover when the Holy Spirit would fill the upper room (Acts 2) with His presence and the gift of the Spirit was given (fully clothed). Pentecost was the birth of the church—the "wheat"—and the Holy Spirit would be tasked with uniting the church under His direction. The Holy Spirit would take charge of preparing the bride for Yehshua's return at the final wheat harvest. We must remain glued to the Holy Spirit or risk missing Yehshua's return for His bride. The book of Acts is where this operation begins:

> *While being together and eating with them, He commanded them not to leave Jerusalem, but to wait for what the Father had promised, "Of which," He said, "you have heard Me speak. For John baptized with water, but you will be baptized and empowered and united with the Holy Spirit, not long from now." (Acts 1:4-5 AMP)*

It is very interesting that a condition for the Holy Spirit's arrival to Jerusalem for the Feast of Pentecost was dependent upon Yehshua's departure.

> *"But now I am going to Him who sent Me; and none of you asks Me, 'Where are You going?' But because I have said these things to you, sorrow has filled your hearts [and taken complete possession of them]. But I tell you the truth, it is to your advantage that I go away; for if I do not go away, the Helper (Comforter, Advocate, Intercessor—Counselor, Strengthener, Standby) will not come to you; but if I go, I will send Him (the Holy Spirit) to you [to be in close fellowship with you]. And He, when He comes, will convict the world about [the guilt of] sin [and the need for a Savior], and about righteousness, and about judgment: about sin [and the true nature of it], because they do not believe in Me [and My message]; about righteousness [personal integrity and godly character], because I am going to My Father and you will no longer see Me; about judgment [the certainty of it],*

*because the ruler of this world (Satan) has been judged
and condemned.*

*"I have many more things to say to you, but you cannot
bear [to hear] them now. But when He, the Spirit of
Truth, comes, He will guide you into all the truth [full
and complete truth]. For He will not speak on His own
initiative, but He will speak whatever He hears [from
the Father—the message regarding the Son], and He
will disclose to you what is to come [in the future]. He
will glorify and honor Me, because He (the Holy Spirit)
will take from what is Mine and will disclose it to you.
All things that the Father has are Mine. Because of
this I said that He [the Spirit] will take from what is
Mine and will reveal it to you. (John 16:5-15 AMP)*

It is a bit difficult to understand the omnipresent nature of the Godhead, yet Yehshua cannot be in the same place as the Holy Spirit for now. I believe the reasons are related to both spiritual warfare and the fact that the primary duty of the Holy Spirit is to prepare the bride for the completion of Yehshua's ministry through a united church. Recall the structure outlined in chapter 6 where Yehshua is in command of heaven's armies while the Holy Spirit is in command of ministering angels and the earth's armies (the church). These are two different commands, yet they are dependent upon each other for the success of the bride.

Another factor we lose sight of in our academic analysis is the Galilean wedding tradition where the bride and groom would not see each other until the Father declares that the time for the wedding in His house has arrived. The Holy Spirit is the bride's keeper until the Father of the groom says, "Go get your bride." In this ancient traditional sense, Yehshua and the Holy Spirit are keeping an ancient Galilean tradition. Yehshua is "preparing a place for us" at the Father's house (John 14:13) while the Holy Spirit is the keeper of the bride until the groom returns.

As odd as it may seem to us as Gentiles, remember that Yehshua was a Galilean Nazarene Jew, and I believe He will keep those ancient Galilean traditions until the very end. The Holy Spirit is the keeper of the bride until the return of the Groom. And the bride is the church. The Feast of Pentecost at the wheat harvest, fifty days after the Feast of Passover and the barley harvest, would mark the birthdate of the church. The church continues today ahead of the arrival of the bridegroom. The Holy Spirit is the keeper of the church.

The church is the temple of God under Yehshua's authority by guidance and direction of the Holy Spirit.

> *Do you not know and understand that you [the church]*
> *are the temple of God, and that the Spirit of God dwells*
> *[permanently] in you [collectively and individually]? If*
> *anyone destroys the temple of God [corrupting it with*
> *false doctrine], God will destroy the destroyer; for the*
> *temple of God is holy (sacred), and that is what you*
> *are. (1 Corinthians 3:16-17 AMP)*

The Spirit of God has established His permanent dwelling in the church—or temple—as well as in its constituents. This is not to be taken lightly, as we can see by the staunch warning against false doctrine in verse 17. The Holy Spirit is the keeper of the bride church, which is the body of Christ. The head of the body is Christ.

> *And He put all things [in every realm] in subjection*
> *under Christ's feet, and appointed Him as [supreme*
> *and authoritative] head over all things in the church,*
> *which is His body, the fullness of Him who fills and*
> *completes all things in all [believers]. (Ephesians 1:22-*
> *23 AMP)*

> *And he is the head of the body, the church: who is*
> *the beginning, the firstborn from the dead; that in all*
> *things he might have the preeminence. (1 Corinthians*
> *1:18 KJV)*

Yehshua is the head of the body, the bride, and the Holy Spirit is the bride's keeper until He returns for her. False doctrine churches will be cut out of the body like a cancer (God will destroy the destroyer). The sons of God in the Church of Philadelphia, led by the Spirit, are called to rebuke false doctrines so that people are not deceived and lost (1 Timothy 5:19–20). Be careful not to be caught judging, only rebuking based on the Word and with witnesses. However, Paul called out false doctrine preachers by name!

You are aware of the fact that all who are in Asia turned away from me, among whom are Phygelus and Hermogenes. (2 Timothy 1:15 NASB)

For Demas, having loved this present world, has deserted me and gone to Thessalonica; Crescens has gone to Galatia, Titus to Dalmatia. (2 Timothy 4:10 NASB)

Keeping faith and a good conscience, which some have rejected and suffered shipwreck in regard to their faith. Among these are Hymenaeus and Alexander, whom I have handed over to Satan, so that they will be taught not to blaspheme. (1 Timothy 1:19-20 NASB)

And their talk will spread like gangrene. Among them are Hymenaeus and Philetus. (2 Timothy 2:17 NASB)

Ouch! I am very reluctant to call out anyone by name except the popes of Rome whose crimes are well documented. Still, I hold strong opinions about pastors who, I believe, have turned their churches into industrial cash cows for selfish motivations. There are a prideful few who are focused on money and wealth only. One in particular has a large following here in Texas. I tried listening to a sermon one day to satisfy my curiosity. After nearly ten minutes into it, he never quoted a single scripture, only made reference to biblical accounts to complete a point that was not even biblical. These are the "power of positive thinking" types totally focused on wealth and/or self-improvement seminars and not the mission of the bride-church. But I do not want to be too outspoken about them for this reason:

> *So then, let us [who minister] be regarded as servants of Christ and stewards (trustees, administrators) of the mysteries of God [that He chooses to reveal]. In this case, moreover, it is required [as essential and demanded] of stewards that one be found faithful and trustworthy. But [as for me personally] it matters very little to me that I may be judged by you or any human court [on this point]; in fact, I do not even judge myself. I am aware of nothing against myself and I feel blameless, but I am not by this acquitted [before God]. It is the Lord who judges me. So do not go on passing judgment before the appointed time, but wait until the Lord comes, for He will both bring to light the [secret] things that are hidden in darkness and disclose the motives of the hearts. Then each one's praise will come from God.*

> *Now I have applied these things [that is, the analogies about factions] to myself and Apollos for your benefit, believers, so that you may learn from us not to go beyond what is written [in Scripture], so that none of you will become arrogant and boast in favor of one [minister or teacher] against the other. For who regards you as superior or what sets you apart as special? What do you have that you did not receive [from another]? And if in fact you received it [from God or someone else], why do you boast as if you*

> *had not received it [but had gained it by yourself]? (1
> Corinthians 4:1-7 AMP)*

In 1 and 2 Timothy, we see Paul's reprimands, but in 1 Corinthians 4, we recognize that those reprimands come from a humbled heart. There are occasions when the Holy Spirit will prompt us to rebuke false doctrine. Apply Paul's words in 1 Corinthians 4 before any rebuking remarks and test the spirit. I am not on Paul's level, and I fear being caught in condemnation of judgment where I might have been mistaken. Nevertheless, we tread a thin line because false doctrines must be rebuked, just as Paul did. The sons of God led by the Spirit will know how and when to rebuke in agreement with the Great Comforter of the church.

With that out of the way, here is something I will rebuke. On January 21, 2025, the Service of Prayer for the Nation at the Washington National Cathedral was given by the bishop of the Episcopal Diocese of Washington, Mariann Budde. While there is little argument that most of her fifteen-minute sermon could pass as perfectly "Christian" in theme, there was a part of it that cannot be supported as sound doctrine.

The following is a quote from an article posted by *The Christian Century* two days after the controversial sermon by bishop Budde:

> *Budde, in her sermon, had asked Trump to show mercy*
> *to "the people in our country who are scared now," and*
> *she specifically held up the fears felt by many LGTBQ+*
> *people and immigrants at the start of Trump's second*
> *term.*[13]

I hear this acronym more often than I would prefer and had always assumed its meaning. But to write about this, I had to look it up. Here is a post from a website named *www.them.com*, written by Quispe López on October 28, 2022, that explains the acronym better than I can:

---

13   The Christian Century, Jan 23, 2025

In July 2011, during an interview with a reporter from the *Washingtonian*, Bishop Budde was asked: "You were also a voice against the same-sex marriage ban in Minnesota. What are your thoughts on that now, especially as you move to DC, where same-sex marriage is legal?"

She replied: "I'm very pleased to be moving to Washington, DC, where same-sex marriage is legal. While there is no legal marriage for same-sex couples in Minnesota, I have presided at many sacramental blessings of life-long unions for gay and lesbian couples, among them some of the most loving people and faithful Christians I know. I have the sense that the momentum is slowly building across the country for change on this issue, and that within five years, many more states will legalize same-gender marriage."

If you read the last book, I included a long list of what God calls "abominations, detestable and hated things." I didn't write the Bible, but I can read it and know that this LGBTQ+ movement does not come from the church of Acts, born on the Feast of Pentecost. The Episcopal Church is not the only one that embraces "confusion." Let's review again so I can make a point about the condition of this church:

> *Thou shalt not lie with mankind, as with womankind: it is abomination. (Leviticus 18:22 KJV)*

> *If a man also lie with mankind, as he lieth with a woman, both of them have committed an abomination: they shall surely be put to death; their blood shall be upon them. (Leviticus 20:13 KJV)*

Did the blood sacrifice of Yehshua reverse this specific Levitical law under grace? Not according to Paul:

> *For this cause God gave them up unto vile affections: for even their women did change the natural use into that which is against nature:*

> *And likewise also the men, leaving the natural use of the woman, burned in their lust one toward another; men with men working that which is unseemly, and receiving in themselves that recompence of their error which was meet.*

> *And even as they did not like to retain God in their knowledge, God gave them over to a reprobate mind, to do those things which are not convenient. (Romans 1:26-28 KJV)*

Or do you not know that the unrighteous will not inherit the kingdom of God? Do not be deceived; neither the sexually immoral, nor idolaters, nor adulterers, nor homosexuals, nor thieves, nor the greedy, nor those habitually drunk, nor verbal abusers, nor swindlers, will inherit the kingdom of God. (1 Corinthians 6:9-10 NASB)

How does someone earn the title of "bishop" in any Christian denomination without reading and understanding the New Testament? Paul explains this in verse 28 of Romans chapter 1. If we defy God and resist God and live according to our desires and not according to God's design for creation, He gives us over to a reprobate mind. The reprobate mind can no longer rationalize God's ways and becomes totally self-serving and misguided. The reprobate mind is given to a demonic spirit. Sadly, the reprobate mind now describes a large demographic within global politics. In America, I would estimate the reprobate mind to be between one-fourth and one-third of the population. This was not the case forty years ago. Reprobate minds are spreading like a Fauci-Gates gain-of-function virus. (By the way, I just read that Epstein was involved in that scam as well.)

If you look at the rest of the list in 1 Corinthians 6:9–10, take caution in casting the first stone. However, "sexuality" is mentioned three times out of the first four items on the list (sexually immoral, adulterers, and homosexuals). But also on the list are:
- idolaters
- thieves
- *the* greedy
- the habitually drunk
- verbal abusers
- swindlers

Given the broad array of things that could be considered idolatrous, and knowing I am guilty of more than one, I will rebuke Bishop Budde's embrace of reprobates with caution. I was once sued by an employee for verbal abuse and was also a heavy drinker. Hallelujah, I am atoned and redeemed by the blood of the Lamb after controlling both! But the Bible is clear on this long acronym LGBTQ+: it is a false doctrine.

Budde's position as a "pastor" and religious leader puts her and her church at risk of "destruction" because God will not allow a reprobate mind to proliferate within the church (1 Corinthians 3:17). The Episcopal Church is not alone in supporting false doctrines. Recently, many Methodists have abandoned the United Methodist Church, which embraces the same doctrines supported by Bishop Budde. Read some of these pastor's remarks regarding Budde's sermon: "I encourage you to listen to the whole sermon, which is a reflection on Godly unity, and what it means to be united across disagreement," Arizona Bishop Jennifer Reddall said on Facebook while sharing video of Budde's sermon. "It's a vision of the Kingdom of God, deeply rooted in the Gospel of Jesus Christ." (Cringe…)

Los Angeles Bishop John Harvey Taylor went further in his Facebook post about the sermon, saying Budde had "held Trump accountable to his face for ten years of hate speech."

How did we get here? The reprobate mind has another name: progressivism.

The Christian Century is the organization that published what I shared above. Next to the title heading of their publication website are these words: "Thoughtful – Independent – Progressive."

Progressivism is a political buzzword we've heard often over the last couple of decades, but its roots began with the Industrial Revolution in the late nineteenth century. Many powerful people began to adapt a new view that human ingenuity had surpassed the imaginations of the founding fathers and a new order needed to be created.

This subject is a book of its own, and I want to get to the point of how it permeated the churches. Here is a great overview of progressivism by Pastor and author Bruce Ashford. I do not agree with all his views, but he has done a lot of research on this subject. This is titled *The 9 Sins of Progressivism:*

> ***Propitiationism****: Christianity asks us to do unto others according to their needs, but progressivism replaces*

*needs with wants. It reinforces and enables public
fighting for money, government preference, and social
esteem (e.g. same-sex marriage). If a unwed mother
wants to marry the government instead of a man, the
liberals will always find a way to let her.*

Expropriationism*: This is Robin Hood fallacy in which
we take from some to help others. In this type of politics,
those with power take wealth by force and give it to
whomever they wish. Although it is not inherently wrong
for government to tax, still taxation should only be for
causes such as punishing wrongdoers and commending
right doers (1 Pet 2:13–14).*

Solipsism*: This is the error of thinking that humans
are essentially self-creating beings who belong to
themselves. Historically, not all liberals believed this.
John Locke, for example, roots human dignity in our
creation by God. But others, such as Kant, argue that
each individual is an end in himself.*

Absolutionism*: Political progressivism doesn't want
to blame people for breaking the moral law. Instead,
it wants to give them an excuse. It wants either to say
they can't help it for some reason or to question the
moral law itself. Although often this absolutionism is a
misguided attempt at mercy, in the end it is cruel because
it reinforces sin tendencies and thus encourages people
to circumvent the mercy that comes from God when we
ask his forgiveness.*

Perfectionism*: Progressivism tends to underestimate the
evil embedded in the human heart, and to overestimate
human ability to cure that evil. In response Christianity
declares that we humans sin, we think wrongly, and we
cannot fix ourselves through progressive education or*

progressive social revolutions. "We might as well expect a surgeon to sew his severed hands back on." (11)

Universalism: *Progressives tend to view the divisions among humanity as either unreal or unimportant. They think we all want the same thing, all seek the same God, etc. But the divisions are real.*

Neutralism: *Progressivism promotes a type of tolerance in which we suspend judgment about good and evil. Progressives ask us to avoid having strong convictions, except for the convictions they deem good. In other words, it cannot be practiced consistently. It attempts to absolve itself from responsibility for decisions (e.g. "I am not pro-abortion, I am pro-choice.")*

Collectivism: *Progressives tend to think that a child needs the state more than it needs a family. But there is a reason why, historically, societies have trusted most families to raise their own children. Family is more fundamental than government. Family has a closer harmony of interests among its members than the state does. The state, therefore, should only intervene to restrain abuse or wickedness; it should not try to fulfill the functions of the family.*

Desperate Gestures: *Progressives often commit the fallacy of desperate gestures. Budziszewski writes, "People do wrong, and I have to do something. People are unhappy, and I have to do something. People are foolish, and I have to do something. I will absolve them. I will give them things. I will take their children. At last we come to the ninth and most mysterious moral error of political liberalism: the fallacy of desperate gestures... The desperationist acts to relieve his own: the pain of pity, the pain of impotence, the pain of indignation. He is like a man who beats on a foggy television screen with a*

pipe wrench, not because the wrench will fix the picture
but because it is handy and feels good to use."

Progressivism gave birth to the concept of the US Constitution as a "living document" that needed to evolve to meet cultural changes. Progressivism also spread to the Christian church. While the Bible is a living document, it does not evolve with cultural changes in humanity. Hebrews 13:7–9 reminds us that Jesus is the same yesterday, today, and forever; do not be carried away by strange doctrines. The gospel is the same today as it was two thousand years ago and does not evolve to coddle human corruption. "Progressive Christianity" is a deception and a false doctrine to be avoided.

As I watched the US presidential debate between Trump and Harris, I noticed that at fifteen minutes in, the candidates were still locked in discussion over abortion. The debate mediator wouldn't get off the subject of abortion. At the nineteen-minute mark, they were still debating abortion, and I turned off the television. I was so disgusted that with all the problems facing the world, one-third of the debate was consumed by a single issue that affects less than .001 percent of Americans. This reflects an agenda of the "new order of progressivism" that began more than 120 years ago.

Abortion is one aspect of a progressive ideological order aimed at dismantling the barriers between male and female. Abortion stands on the same level as drag queens being allowed to indoctrinate children in schools and transgender boys being allowed to compete in girls' sports. As we read our daily headlines, morality and the rule of law are being abandoned. In some cities of my own state of Texas, murderers and rapists get out of jail on PR bonds, continuing to rape and murder while awaiting trial. Progressives hate the US Constitution, conventional Christianity, and anything that places human will under the sovereignty of God. The founders of progressivism know our God is real, which is why they support Islam or any other religion that stands opposed to God.

America was founded on Christian principles that proved too strong to be conquered outright. There are two primary roads to a tyrannical communist dictatorship: one by sheer force and conquest, the other by slowly boiling the frog until he's fully cooked. Progressivism is that slow road to tyranny, replacing God with human will. Progressivism has introduced the age of deception, the "great falling away" (2 Thessalonians 2:3). The Industrial Revolution gave rise to the progressive Church of Thyatira as early as 1906, and only now, 120 years later, we are witnessing its full manifestation.

Look at our world today and see if these verses resonate with you:

I know your deeds, and your love and faith, and service and perseverance, and that your deeds of late are greater than at first. But I have this against you, that you tolerate the woman Jezebel, who calls herself a prophetess, and she teaches and leads My bond-servants astray so that they commit sexual immorality and eat things sacrificed to idols. I gave her time to repent, and she does not want to repent of her sexual immorality. Behold, I will throw her on a bed of sickness, and those who commit adultery with her into great tribulation, unless they repent of her deeds. And I will kill her children with plague, and all the churches will know that I am He who searches the minds and hearts; and I will give to each one of you according to your deeds. (Revelation 2:18-23 NASB)

The coming of the [Antichrist, the lawless] one is through the activity of Satan, [attended] with great power [all kinds of counterfeit miracles] and [deceptive] signs and false wonders [all of them lies], and by unlimited seduction to evil and with all the deception of wickedness for those who are perishing, because they did not welcome the love of the truth [of the gospel] so as to be saved [they were spiritually

In Jonathan Cahn's *Return of the Gods*, he illustrates how entities of evil work together as a team. Satan is the head of the fallen realm, the "lawless one" of 2 Thessalonians, but he does not work alone. Jezebel is a key player in their agenda to undermine the bride, working beside the lawless one. In much the same way as we have the Holy Spirit to lead us, those who reject the love of the truth of the gospel are led by fallen spirits. They ignore truth and follow seduction and self-servitude. Where there is sexual immorality, there is Jezebel. Christian progressivism is the Church of Thyatira under Jezebel's spell.

Jezebel is the spirit behind progressivism, promoting every perversion in the church that God hates. She is the enemy of God, the Holy Spirit, and the bride. The Holy Spirit is the keeper of the bride church, and Thyatira under Jezebel is not the bride! However, there is a caveat I will explain shortly. For now, it is worth pondering the connection between Thyatira and Jezebel from the book of 1 Kings. In God's wisdom, we see that Jezebel, the wife of Ahab, was inhabited by a spirit opposed to God. The spirit that inhabited Jezebel in 1 Kings is the same spirit that inhabits the Church of Thyatira in Revelation 2.

This chapter is dedicated to the Great Comforter, the Holy Spirit, who is the keeper of the bride ahead of Yehshua's return. As the bride, we are the wheat of Pentecost and need to know the enemy forces that would sow tares among us.

Let's go back to Matthew 13 because Christian progressivism and the Church of Thyatira are the enemy sowing weeds among the wheat. Yehshua warned us that this would happen and the keeper of the bride will lead us (sons of God led by the Spirit) through to the wheat harvest if we follow.

*his enemy came and sowed weeds [resembling wheat]
among the wheat, and went away. So when the plants
sprouted and formed grain, the weeds appeared also.
The servants of the owner came to him and said, 'Sir,
did you not sow good seed in your field? Then how does
it have weeds in it?' He replied to them, 'An enemy has
done this.' The servants asked him, 'Then do you want
us to go and pull them out?' But he said, 'No; because
as you pull out the weeds, you may uproot the wheat
with them. Let them grow together until the harvest;
and at harvest time I will tell the reapers, "First gather
the weeds and tie them in bundles to be burned; but
gather the wheat into my barn."'" (Matthew 13:24-30
AMP)*

The letters to the seven churches of Revelation are an accounting statement of who is sealed by the keeper of the bride (Holy Spirit) and who is not sealed. In my book *The Bride, the Wise Virgins, and the Last Adam*, I emphasize the fact that the more we understand and apply the appointed times to biblical themes, the more we comprehend the prophetic harvests. Thyatira is a perfect example of how an "enemy" sowed weeds among the tares and choked out some of the wheat, just as weeds do. The enemy sowing weeds in the Church of Thyatira is Jezebel. The sons of God led by the Holy Spirit will recognize and reject the spirit of Jezebel.

I will include more about Jezebel in another chapter. For now, it is important to visualize the connection between the Holy Spirit and who is being led by the Spirit. There are only two churches of the seven churches of Revelation chapters 2 and 3 that have been given a good report by Yehshua. If the Holy Spirit is the keeper of the bride church and redemption can only be signified by the seal of the Holy Spirit, then only two out of the seven churches represent the bride church. The other five churches have issues that keep them in the spiritual "weeds" and are not being led by the Holy Spirit as the sons of God (Romans 8:14).

Now for the caveat: God is merciful. The more I researched the mainstream views of post-tribulation, mid-tribulation, and pre-tribulation rapture theories, the more I could not reconcile a post-tribulation rapture theory with the Scripture. The punishment theology view of the post-tribulation rapture is out of harmony with a merciful God, His prophecy, and His appointed times. His wrath is reserved for the sons of disobedience, not the sons of God led by the Spirit (Colossians 3:6, Ephesians 2:2, Romans 5:9). I covered this in detail in the last book, so I don't want to be overly redundant, except to point out a few things I may have missed before.

In verses 18–21 of Revelation chapter 2 are the charges against Thyatira and the spirit behind the church, which is Jezebel. Then the warning begins in verse 22:

> *Listen carefully, I will throw her on a bed of sickness,*
> *and those who commit adultery with her [I will bring]*
> *into great anguish, unless they repent of her deeds.*
> *And I will kill her children (followers) with pestilence*
> *[thoroughly annihilating them], and all the churches*
> *will know [without any doubt] that I am He who*
> *searches the minds and hearts [the innermost thoughts,*
> *purposes]; and I will give to each one of you [a reward*
> *or punishment] according to your deeds. (Revelation*
> *2:22-23 AMP)*

If Thyatira's bishops are addressing the president of the United States and the nation, then obviously the church has not yet been annihilated as promised. This is a direct reference to being thrown into the tribulation that the Church of Philadelphia has been promised to be spared from (Revelation 3:10). But now take a look at what follows:

> *But to the rest of you in Thyatira, who do not hold this*
> *teaching, who have not explored and known the depths*
> *of Satan, as they call them—I place no other burden*

*on you, except to hold tightly to what you have until
I come. And he who overcomes [the world through
believing that Jesus is the Son of God] and he who
keeps My deeds [doing things that please Me] until
the [very] end, to him I will give authority and power
over the nations; and he shall shepherd and rule them
with a rod of iron, as the earthen pots are broken in
pieces, as I also have received authority [and power to
rule them] from My Father; and I will give him the
Morning Star. He who has an ear, let him hear and
heed what the Spirit says to the churches.' (Revelation
2:24-28 AMP)*

There is only one possibility as to who could be ruling with authority and power over the nations next to Yehshua: the bride church. The warning of annihilation is followed by a promise of being included as the bride church. This group is not being excluded from the tribulation; rather, they are harvested out of it if they choose the Bridegroom. The Church of Thyatira has a fate of destruction that is sealed, but its members have an opportunity given by a merciful God to those who reject Jezebel's teachings and come out of the church. This happens in the fire of the tribulation and not before.

In fact, this is true of all five of the churches that received negative remarks. Even the members of the Church of Pergamum are given the opportunity to be spared if they come out of it.

*He who has an ear, let him hear and heed what the
Spirit says to the churches. To him who overcomes [the
world through believing that Jesus is the Son of God],
to him I will give [the privilege of eating] some of the
hidden manna, and I will give him a white stone with a
new name engraved on the stone which no one knows
except the one who receives it.' (Revelation 2:17 AMP)*

All five of the churches that received negative marks are given the same opportunity to be spared if they come out of their respective church. The following are AMP translations of Revelation 2 and 3:

> ***Ephesus:*** *He who has an ear, let him hear and heed what the Spirit says to the churches. To him who [d] overcomes [the world through believing that Jesus is the Son of God], I will grant [the privilege] to eat [the fruit] from the tree of life, which is in the Paradise of God.'*
>
> ***Smyrna:*** *He who has an ear, let him hear and heed what the Spirit says to the churches. He who overcomes [the world through believing that Jesus is the Son of God] will not be hurt by the second death ([f]the lake of fire).'*
>
> ***Pergamum:*** *He who has an ear, let him hear and heed what the Spirit says to the churches. To him who overcomes [the world through believing that Jesus is the Son of God], to him I will give [the privilege of eating] some of the [m]hidden manna, and I will give him a [n]white stone with a new name engraved on the stone which no one knows except the one who receives it.'*
>
> ***Thyatira:*** *I place no other burden on you, 25 except to hold tightly to what you have until I come. 26 And he who overcomes [the world through believing that Jesus is the Son of God] and he who keeps My deeds [doing things that please Me] until the [very] end, to him I will give authority and power over the nations; 27 and he shall shepherd and rule them with a rod of iron, as the earthen pots are broken in pieces, as I also have received authority [and power to rule them] from My Father; 28 and I will give him the [t]Morning Star. 29 He who has an ear, let him hear and heed what the Spirit says to the churches.'*

***Sardis:** But you [still] have a few people in Sardis who have not soiled their clothes [that is, contaminated their character and personal integrity with sin]; and they will walk with Me [dressed] in white, because they are worthy (righteous). 5 He who overcomes [the world through believing that Jesus is the Son of God] will accordingly be dressed in white clothing; and I will never blot out his name from the Book of Life, and I will confess and openly acknowledge his name before My Father and before His angels [saying that he is one of Mine]. 6 He who has an ear, let him hear and heed what the Spirit says to the churches.'*

***Laodicea:** I counsel you to buy from Me gold that has been heated red hot and refined by fire so that you may become truly rich; and white clothes [representing righteousness] to clothe yourself so that the shame of your nakedness will not be seen; and healing salve to put on your eyes so that you may see. 19 Those whom I [dearly and tenderly] love, I rebuke and discipline [showing them their faults and instructing them]; so be enthusiastic and repent [change your inner self—your old way of thinking, your sinful behavior—seek God's will]. 20 Behold, I stand at the door [of the church] and continually knock. If anyone hears My voice and opens the door, I will come in and eat with him (restore him), and he with Me. 21 He who overcomes [the world through believing that Jesus is the Son of God], I will grant to him [the privilege] to sit beside Me on My throne, as I also overcame and sat down beside My Father on His throne. 22 He who has an ear, let him hear and heed what the Spirit says to the churches.'"*

In five of the seven churches, there is a promise of becoming the bride if they repent and come out of deception. The church of Smyrna is not criticized, per se, but apparently has a few problems that will lead some to be tested, according to the wording of verse 10 in chapter 2. The academic understanding is that this was during the time of persecution by the Caesars. This may well be true, but I do not believe that the seven churches are confined to specific time segments in history, as many scholars suggest. Rather, I see them as grouped according to their spiritual and regional influence throughout history with an end times spiritual consolidation before the tribulation, identifying who will and will not be spared from God's wrath.

The Christian church of the Roman Empire could be predominantly described as the Church of Smyrna, but this church is not necessarily confined to that specific time in history. My opinion is that Smyrna is the bridesmaids to the bride, but both are the bride church, as indicated by a lack of reprimand. Some of Smyrna will be subjected to the tribulation (Rev. 2:10), just as the foolish virgins ran out of oil in their lamps (Matthew 25).

The only church that receives no reprimand and is given a promise is the Church of Philadelphia.

> *I know your deeds. See, I have set before you an*
> *open door which no one is able to shut, for you have*
> *a little power, and have kept My word, and have not*
> *renounced or denied My name. Take note, I will make*
> *those of the synagogue of Satan, who say that they are*
> *Jews and are not, but lie—I will make them come and*
> *bow down at your feet and make them know [without*
> *any doubt] that I have loved you. **Because you have***
> ***kept the word of My endurance [My command to***
> ***persevere], I will keep you [safe] from the hour of***
> ***trial, that hour which is about to come on the whole***
> ***[inhabited] world, to test those who live on the earth.** I*
> *am coming quickly. Hold tight what you have, so*
> *that no one will take your crown [by leading you to*
> *renounce the faith]. He who overcomes [the world*

through believing that Jesus is the Son of God], I will make him a pillar in the temple of My God; he will most certainly never be put out of it, and I will write on him the name of My God, and the name of the city of My God, the new Jerusalem, which descends out of heaven from My God, and My [own] new name. He who has an ear, let him hear and heed what the Spirit says to the churches.

The Church of Philadelphia is the bride church and the closest to Yehshua's heart, given a promise of exclusion from the tribulation with no reprimanding remarks. The Church of Philadelphia is sealed by the Holy Spirit and justified by Yehshua's blood.

Therefore, since we have now been justified [declared free of the guilt of sin] by His blood, [how much more certain is it that] we will be saved from the wrath of God through Him. (Romans 5:9 AMP)

Revelation 3:10 and Romans 5:9 are perfectly synonymous with each other. There is no question in my mind that the Church of Philadelphia will be spared from the tribulation. I do not know another way to reconcile these verses. If not, then God is not only unmerciful but misleading, neither of which could possibly be true in context with the rest of the Bible. The gospel is the good news. It is hard to find good news in a promise to be spared from the wrath in multiple scriptures, to later find out it isn't true. A post-tribulation rapture view is precisely that, bad news for all.

Putting that aside, the real point I wanted to make was a common theme in each letter to each church: *"He who has an ear, let him hear and heed what the Spirit says to the churches."*

Those who hear and heed the Holy Spirit are the sons of God led by the Spirit. They are the joint heirs with Christ who will rule and reign by His side.

Now read this again in the context of the seven churches of Revelation:

*So then, brothers and sisters, we have an obligation,
but not to our flesh [our human nature, our
worldliness, our sinful capacity], to live according
to the [impulses of the] flesh [our nature without the
Holy Spirit]—for if you are living according to the
[impulses of the] flesh, you are going to die. But if [you
are living] by the [power of the Holy] Spirit you are
habitually putting to death the sinful deeds of the body,
you will [really] live forever. <u>For all who are allowing
themselves to be led by the Spirit of God are sons of
God.</u> For you have not received a spirit of slavery
leading again to fear [of God's judgment], but you
have received the Spirit of adoption as sons [the Spirit
producing sonship] by which we [joyfully] cry, "Abba!
Father!" The Spirit Himself testifies and confirms
together with our spirit [assuring us] that we [believers]
are children of God. And if [we are His] children,
[then we are His] heirs also: heirs of God and fellow
heirs with Christ [sharing His spiritual blessing and
inheritance], if indeed we share in His suffering so that
we may also share in His glory.*

*For I consider [from the standpoint of faith] that
the sufferings of the present life are not worthy to be
compared with the glory that is about to be revealed to
us and in us! (Romans 8:12-18 AMP)*

The Church of Philadelphia hears and heeds the voice of the Holy Spirit, but there are sons of God within all seven churches who will be separated from the tares at the wheat harvest. The tares will be burned, but the wheat will be gathered into the barn. The Church of Philadelphia will not face the wrath of God that comes upon the whole world in the tribulation. Some from the Church of Smyrna will join the Church of Philadelphia when the harvest begins, while others will be tested by fire. The remaining five churches of Revelation 2 and 3 will also be tested by fire, but the sons of God who hear and obey the voice of the Holy Spirit will be delivered from it. Those who overcome are promised the privilege of ruling and reigning with Christ as His bride.

The Holy Spirit is the keeper and "comforter" of the bride church until Yehshua returns for her. These are the sons of God led by the Spirit, joint heirs with Christ. We have the assurance of the Great Comforter that this promise will be fulfilled. Therefore, comfort one another with these words (1 Thessalonians 4:18).

What do we do in the meantime while we wait for the bridegroom? Read the book of Acts and apply it. The church born at Pentecost and the Church of Philadelphia are one and the same theologically. In 5 of the other seven churches, the wheat stands shoulder to shoulder with the tares, and the tares must be removed for the sons of God (wheat) to be revealed.

The Holy Spirit is our Keeper and Comforter until Yehshua returns. He did not leave us as orphans; rather, He left us with His best friend. We are to be clothed with power from on high (Luke 24:49) until the return of the bridegroom.

One of the things that can strip us of that clothing of power from the Holy Spirit is grieving the Spirit. In Ephesians 4, Paul describes in very plain language how we should not only live as Christians but also how we can avoid grieving the Holy Spirit. For as long as we reside in Satan's kingdom on earth, we must clothe ourselves in the Spirit daily. Here is how Paul states it:

So this I say, and solemnly affirm together with the Lord [as in His presence], that you must no longer live as the [unbelieving] Gentiles live, in the futility of their minds [and in the foolishness and emptiness of their souls], for their [moral] understanding is darkened and their reasoning is clouded; [they are] alienated and self-banished from the life of God [with no share in it; this is] because of the [willful] ignorance and spiritual blindness that is [deep-seated] within them, because of the hardness and insensitivity of their heart. And they, [the ungodly in their spiritual apathy], having become callous and unfeeling, have given themselves over [as prey] to unbridled sensuality, eagerly craving the practice of every kind of impurity [that their desires may demand]. But you did not learn Christ in this way! If in fact you have [really] heard Him and have been taught by Him, just as truth is in Jesus [revealed in His life and personified in Him], that, regarding your previous way of life, you put off your old self [completely discard your former nature], which is being corrupted through deceitful desires, and be continually renewed in the spirit of your mind [having a fresh, untarnished mental and spiritual attitude], and put on the new self [the regenerated and renewed nature], created in God's image, [godlike] in the righteousness and holiness of the truth [living in a way that expresses to God your gratitude for your salvation].

Therefore, rejecting all falsehood [whether lying, defrauding, telling half-truths, spreading rumors, any such as these], speak truth each one with his neighbor, for we are all parts of one another [and we are all parts of the body of Christ]. Be angry [at sin—at immorality, at injustice, at ungodly behavior], yet do not sin; do not let your anger [cause you shame, nor allow it to] last until the sun goes down. And do not give the devil an opportunity [to lead you into sin by holding a grudge, or nurturing anger, or harboring resentment, or cultivating bitterness]. The thief [who has become a believer] must no longer steal, but instead he must work hard [making an honest living], producing that which is good with his own hands, so that he will have something to share with those in need. Do not let unwholesome [foul, profane, worthless, vulgar] words ever come out of your mouth, but only such

In harmony with the light of men, ("*if you love me, you will keep my commandments*" [*John 14:15NASB*]), we cannot grieve the Holy Spirit. When we clothe ourselves in the Spirit, it looks like this:

- We do not harbor resentment.
- We are quick to forgive just as we have been forgiven.
- We reject falsehoods, deceptions, and manipulative acts rooted in selfish behavior.
- We do not use profane and vulgar language.
- All types of wrath, anger, and bitterness are put away from us.
- We are not critical and fault-finding of others.
- We are helpful, compassionate, tender-hearted, and understanding with others.
- We renew ourselves in the Spirit daily, seeking to please the Holy Spirit.

When I read Ephesians chapter 4, I realize that I need constant atonement. Recently, my pickup truck was in the shop for maintenance, and I was driving a loaner vehicle. I wasn't used to driving it, and it had a number of blind spots on the right and left rear. While backing out from the grocery store parking lot, I almost nicked a woman who was walking up behind me because I simply didn't see her. She immediately went into a rage, very upset that I didn't see her.

I thought about what a terrible day she must have been having, or maybe a terrible life. I just smiled and apologized and kept driving, quickly putting the matter out of my mind. But before this transformation in Christ, attempting to clothe myself in the Spirit daily, I would have blasted her with profanities for foolishly overreacting in the way that she did.

Honestly, though, it is challenging given our vain and profane culture today. The lawless one has been at work for 120 years in the progressive movement, slowly undermining God's end times church. When I was a youth, an R-rated movie was enough to bring you to your knees at the altar at church. These days, the worst profanities that were unheard of even in R-rated movies fifty years ago are now common daily language. If you watch an internet television service like Pluto or some of the others, they will have homosexual advertisements at the commercial breaks. The frog is almost cooked, and we never even felt the water begin warming.

We live in a world of digital psyops, subliminal mass messaging, witchcraft and sorcery on the television screen, a laundry list of things that grieve the Holy Spirit—bioengineered foods, biotech poisoning, geoengineering dumping chemicals over our heads daily, mRNA human-genome vaccine experiments, and more. We live in a spiritual and biological minefield that, without the Holy Spirit, is impossible to navigate without being spiritually or physically annihilated. And that's just in the USA.

As I write, someone is being tortured for being a Christian in a growing number of countries around the world. Christians are being hunted and killed like wild dogs in Syria and Nigeria, imprisoned in China, and tortured in countries like Eritrea, north of Ethiopia on the Red Sea. At the time of this writing, state-sponsored Islamic militant groups in Nigeria are targeting Christians for genocide at a rate of 500,000 per year.

I recently heard how Christians are treated in Eritrea, where they are captured and placed in torture camps for forming Christian prayer and worship groups. Religious prisoners are confined in metal shipping containers that become ovens in the desert heat, given barely enough food and water to survive in unsanitary conditions with nowhere to defecate. They sleep in the containers, stacked like cordwood, in extremely cruel, worse-than-Hitleresque death camp conditions. This is not Christian persecution in ancient Rome under the Caesars; this is the modern-day Horn of Africa, the Middle East, and Asian countries.

We American Christians give a boring prayer at mealtime in our fattened complacency and imagine we are bold for showing up for an Easter-Ishtar Sunday service. Meanwhile, there are Christians being persecuted around the world year-round, giving thanks even for the heat, the inhumane treatment, and the torture, because Paul said to give thanks in all circumstances (1 Thessalonians 5:18). Do not be surprised to see these saints wearing a crown that might have been ours when we arrive at the Father's house.

Despite torturous living conditions, survivors of these death camps testify to many miracles that led to their survival. Many of them escaped their native countries and found a place where they can worship without harassment—at least for now. Yet the window of time is closing fast. Soon it will not be possible for at least five of the seven churches of Revelation 2 and 3 under a global Antichrist leader.

The gates of hell will not prevail (Matthew 16:18) against the Church of Philadelphia, which is promised to be spared from the hour of temptation. This will not be the case for many, as indicated by the scorecards of at least five of the seven churches. However, those led by the Spirit of God—the sons of God—will come out of the tribulation to join the bride church.

Meanwhile, the Holy Spirit is our comforter and guide, the keeper of the bride. We are the temple of the Holy Spirit, both individually and collectively. We must not grieve the One that seals our fate as joint heirs with Christ. The Holy Spirit is the Administrator of our inheritance, a down payment of what is to come in the kingdom of heaven. For those trapped in a progressive church like Thyatira, or the pagan traditions of Pergamum, or any of the others destined to be tested by fire alongside the tares, remember these words: *"He who has an ear, let him hear and heed what the Spirit says to the churches."*

> ***The Helper is the Spirit of truth, whom the world cannot receive, because it does not see Him or know Him; but you know Him because He remains with you and will be in you.***
>
> ***<u>I will not leave you as orphans; I am coming to you.</u> (John 14:17-18 NASB)***

> ***For as many as are led by the Spirit of God, they are the sons of God.***
>
> ***For ye have not received the spirit of bondage again to fear; but ye have received the Spirit of adoption, whereby we cry, Abba, Father.***
>
> ***The Spirit itself beareth witness with our spirit, that we are the children of God:***
>
> ***And if children, then heirs; heirs of God, and joint-heirs with Christ; if so be that we suffer with him, that we may be also glorified together.***
>
> ***For I reckon that the sufferings of this present time are not worthy to be compared with the glory which shall be revealed in us.***
>
> ***For the earnest expectation of the creature waiteth for the***
>
> ***<u>manifestation of the sons of God.</u> (Romans 8:14-19 KJV)***

CHAPTER 9

The Sons of Disobedience

The tragedy of life and of the world is not that men do not know God; the tragedy is that, knowing Him, they still insist on going their own way.

—*William Barclay*

And you were dead in your offenses and sins, 2 in which you previously walked according to the course of this world, according to the prince of the power of the air, of the spirit that is now working in the _sons of disobedience_.

—Ephesians 2:1-2 (NASB)

Therefore, treat the parts of your earthly body as dead *to* sexual immorality, impurity, passion, evil desire, and greed, which amounts to idolatry. 6 *For it is* because of these things that the wrath of God is coming upon the sons of disobedience.

—Colossians 3:5-6 (NASB)

I have occasionally been criticized for not being an educated "academic." If I could recommend only one Bible institute or school, it would be Koinonia House, founded by Chuck and Nancy Missler, or perhaps a Bible institute not tailor-fashioned by any specific religious organization. There are many good Bible schools and institutes, but I would likely avoid any seminary sponsored by a specific denomination for the reasons I've pointed out. Many of them have become too much like the Pharisees, insisting on their own interpretations above all else. They consider my views as "too far outside of their theological guidelines".

I have heard anti-rapture theory pastors rail against the rapture, declaring, "If anyone tells you there will be a rapture it is a lie." Really? Are they so certain that the wrath of the Lamb is aimed at His bride? On this rock I will build my church and the gates of hell will not prevail… until the 4th seal of Revelation when Hades is released onto the earth? (Matthew 16:18; Revelation 6:8). Many scholars still support the Sethite Theory for the Genesis 6 event, which is just one example of what is learned in many seminary schools. If you lived in ancient Jerusalem and attended the synagogues of the Pharisees, you would have missed the Messiah.

In the areas of health, wealth, and spirituality, always exercise prudence and educate yourself as much as possible to avoid falling into the hands of those more indoctrinated than educated. In Dr. Missler's wisdom, he would say, "Don't believe what Chuck Missler tells you; go study the Bible for yourself and prove it out." Amen to that! I never attended seminary school and certainly learned even less by attending churches pastored by some of their students. Except for an acute exposure to the supernatural realm, I might never have learned anything about the Bible at all.

It is also true that I worked as an engineer and technical consultant in twenty-two countries around the world, having never completed a formal degree. I learned by necessity and surpassed most of my colleagues in the field, becoming known for developing various patented processes used by many well-known manufacturers worldwide. In some cases, these were achievements that had previously been considered impossible, even defying the physical properties of metallurgy as we understood them. From the lofty towers of academia, I might never have attempted what was considered impossible. However, I also had great mentors to turn to when confronted by difficult challenges, and my life would have been far different without them. One of the most notable was a physics professor who retired from Case Western University, though there were many others.

This is why I am so grateful for the life of Dr. Chuck Missler. I believe I might still be lost had he never pursued his calling. If the numerous 266 Christian denominations in the USA had a few more mentors like Dr. Missler, the world would be a far better place today, filled with great spiritual leaders as one bride and not 266 wayward sisters. This is why, of the seven churches of Revelation, only one gets a pass—the Church of Philadelphia.

In the late 1990s, I worked under a manager I greatly respected. One day he asked why I had never pursued a master's degree or higher. I said, "Frankly, and no offense intended, but I have made a career out of bailing out the master's and PhDs who get lost in the clouds of academic knowledge, failing in the practical applications of it."

He nodded and said, "You're right. Don't change a thing. The best way to kill the success of a project is to put two pedigreed engineers on it. They'll analyze it to death and never build it."

Many people are full of knowledge, but what we do with knowledge requires wisdom. Pray for wisdom daily above all things in your life, for it is a gift of God.

The fear of the LORD is the beginning of wisdom: and the knowledge of the holy is understanding. (Proverbs 9:10 KJV)

But if any of you lacks wisdom, let him ask of God, who gives to all generously and without reproach, and it will be given to him. (James 1:5 NASB)

Knowledge is knowing a tomato is a fruit; wisdom is not putting it in a fruit salad. (Miles Kington)

Is this what has happened to the church? Have we fallen down a different path by failing to be led by the Spirit? Are we educated or indoctrinated? I do not ask this rhetorically. When I research the enterprises of Christianity, it seems we have derailed from many of our intended missions. According to Pew Research, there are over 217 million Christians in the USA, divided among over 200 denominations. By one estimate, there are 266 Christian denominations in the USA and over 45,000 worldwide. Huh? If all Christians were truly led by the Holy Spirit, there would be one denomination for the body of Christ born in Acts chapter 2. This vast division of the church is a major indicator of a serious spiritual infection.

We are surrounded by evil. In fact, I am convinced it is nearly impossible to be a Spirit-filled Christian in this world and also become a billionaire, an influential corporate executive, or high ranking political leader. You will not be allowed to join the club. (Unfortunately, this also includes some of the leaders of a few of those 266 denominations.) The more I learn about the "sons of disobedience," the more I wish they were not real. The world and its rulers are far more evil than most of us realize, and yet we have all power and authority over them through Yehshua.

What has happened to the bride? Have the sons of God strayed too far from the Spirit of God? We must examine our relationship with the Holy Spirit daily. We have such a short time, yet Satan seems to rule unchallenged. Was this Yehshua's intention? Have we ignored the Spirit while floating on the clouds of academia, spewing out four-syllable theological terminologies to demonstrate our pedigrees from the pulpits before the less educated sitting in the pews? I do not know. I am asking you, the reader, to help me understand why the bride has been pushed toward near obscurity, with no resemblance to the church of Acts, while the sons of disobedience rule the world with hardly any opposition.

Part of the answer to that question is that it is difficult for the sons of God led by the Spirit of God to comprehend who the sons of disobedience are and the extent to which some of them are pure evil. Part of being led by the Spirit is learning to discern the operational realm of the sons of disobedience and pray against them.

I believe the sons of disobedience can be represented by three basic macro groups of people:

1. Those who are trapped by carnal pleasures and make a conscious choice not to change their ways and acknowledge the One True God;

2. Those who follow another god or are blinded from receiving the truth of the Messiah; and

3. Those who know our God yet live in direct defiance to Him. This group worships Satan while knowing he is God's adversary. These are the most evil of all sons of disobedience, and they rule the world.

Group 3 rules the world quietly in the shadows. These are the worst of all the sons of disobedience. They are the organized pedophile rings who perform atrocious sexual and violent acts on animals and children, including child and human sacrifice. People whose faces you see every day in the news, on television, in movies, and in magazine articles—corporate and political leaders around the world—are among these operatives of Satan. They are deeply engaged in a plot to destroy God's plan and take the planet for themselves, based on the most ancient of lies: *"You shall be as gods..."* (Genesis 3:5).

These are the worst of the worst of the sons of disobedience. Some raise and groom their own children for the purpose of becoming sex slaves or, worse, human sacrifices in satanic rituals. Some of the victims have survived and psychologically recovered well enough mentally to become witnesses against these sons of disobedience. Jeffrey Epstein was but one of thousands of willing worshippers of Satan.

I was reluctant to share what I have learned about Group 3 because the truth of their existence is absolutely gut-wrenching. It is horrifying, disgusting, and nauseating to know what the rulers of this world do in secrecy. They are beyond vain and defiled, putrid in their souls, and have destroyed millions of lives in their allegiance to Satan. Their victims learn to live with split personalities to erase memories, while being given powerful drugs to remain subject to the will of their persecutors.

The church has a responsibility to the victims of these satanic cults. To hide from the truth is to enable their captors without opposition. The church has a responsibility to pray on behalf of the victims and petition for their freedom from the sexual servitude and torture enacted by their oppressors. As I began researching this, I thought these were isolated situations, far and removed from society. The truth is far worse than most of us are mentally capable of bearing. The victims need us—the church—to intercede and intervene on their behalf. The bride of Christ cannot bury her head in the sand while children are raped and tortured for Satan all over the world. This must stop now. The bride is the ultimate intercessor for the helpless and destitute captives of these sons of disobedience who serve Satan.

Now, this is not to diminish the fact that Group 1 is also guilty of creating sex slaves and committing horrific crimes around the world. Their actions are equally cruel and horrific, with the distinction that most do not sacrifice children to Satan. I say "most" because Group 1 and Group 3 are merging. In Juarez, Chihuahua, Mexico, across the border from El Paso, Texas, pregnant mothers are being kidnapped and killed so their babies can be removed and sold to the Group 3 satanists. Victims of these traffickers can be seen in every major city, and they too need our prayer and intercession. I do not wish to diminish the need for prayer on their behalf. The difference between Group 1 traffickers and Group 3 satanists is that Group 3 rules the world under the prince of death. Group 3 knows the God of Abraham and despises Him, while the god of Group 1 is money and pleasure. However, that is slowly changing as Group 1 grows more satanic in its pursuit of supernatural power.

One of the most disturbing comments repeated in the testimonies of victims of satanic cults is that they believed "no one cared enough to help them." Gloria Masters was one of these children, groomed to become a sex slave for Satan worshippers. Her father was a deeply evil man, but it was her grandmother who carried out the grooming and preparation. The entire family was steeped in evil, and by no choice of her own Gloria was born into that family and dedicated to Satan and his followers.

Before I continue, we are all tempted to ignore this information due to its repulsiveness. I absolutely hate that this problem even exists. But it does. I am going to share a few brief accounts, and I want you to please be cognizant of the fact that there are literally millions of children who need our help today. Burying our heads in the sand destroys any hope these victims may have for escaping their captors. There are millions of children in hopeless captivity to traffickers and satanists, most of whom will not survive. For the satanists, only the "special ones" are kept as sex slaves and not murdered. Many infants and toddlers are murdered through child sacrifices. If this is too painful for you to acknowledge, you are perfectly normal. Congratulations, you are among the sons of God led by the Spirit of God to become joint heirs with Christ.

However, please do not turn away from these children just because their story hurts your eyes and ears. The bride of Christ is their only hope here on earth. We may not know who these children are, but we can pray against their captors and we can support foundations like the one Gloria Masters has established called Handing Back the Shame.[14] At the end of this chapter, I will name a few charities dedicated to rescuing the victims of child trafficking and satanic pedophiles.

If it were up to me and God gave me the power, I would bring fire down on them as Elijah did on the Moabite captain and his fifty men (2 Kings 1:10–12). One of the pagan customs that made its way into Israel during the time of Elijah was child sacrifice. This tradition of child sacrifice, including rituals involving pedophilia and bestiality, is as old as the sons of Cain—which we will discuss later. The good news is we are at the end of the Church Age and Satan was judged long ago (John 16:11). The bad news is we are at the end of the age, and the bride is ignorant of the grotesque rituals of her adversary. I am certain that God expects more from us than we have done in this matter.

Back to Gloria Masters story. Her earliest memories of being a sex slave began as early as a toddler. By the age of eleven and a half, she was forced to have her first abortion, and by sixteen years old, she lost count of how many abortions she had had, nearly dying as a result. She wanted to die, but didn't. She tried to take her own life at least three times but failed. Gloria is from New Zealand, and her father was involved with a group of powerful New Zealand Freemasons. One of these was a Grand Master

---

14   https://www.handingtheshameback.org/

Mason. They would drug the children and assemble them into satanic geometric formations, subsequently raping both boys and girls. The acts of violent rape were followed by sacrificing some of the children—first torturing them then cutting them into pieces while chanting words she can't remember, while she was forced to watch.

One of Jeffrey Epstein's victims, Virginia Giuffre, became a loud voice for the victims of pedophilia and child sex trafficking. Before her mysterious death, she encouraged many victims to begin speaking out and testifying against their perpetrators. Since Virginia's mysterious death, hundreds of victims have come forward with stories equally as horrifying as Gloria's. Epstein was only one of these many sons of disobedience, and the children he trafficked numbered into thousands. The victims tell of personal encounters with the richest and most powerful men and women in the world. Yes, women. Ghislaine Maxwell might be the woman's name we are the most familiar with, but she is not alone. Queen Elizabeth and the royal family have been exposed as having numerous pedophilia and child sacrifice claims against them.

If you search the web for this information, at least two dozen "fact checkers" debunk the claims without any reference to witnesses and whistleblowers either being incarcerated or mysteriously killed. Do not underestimate the reach of the satanists who control every aspect of public media platforms. I prefer to rely on investigative journalists whose work favors the victims and not the accused, such as this article by Judy Byington, an advocate for abused children:

QUEEN ELIZABETH FOUND GUILTY IN MISSING CHILDREN CASE–WHISTLE BLOWERS INCARCERATED

In the second week of May 2014, British soldier Vivian Cunningham was drugged and institutionalized against his will. Apparently, his "crime" on May 6 was daring to ask superiors about Queen Elizabeth's outstanding arrest warrant.

The order to arrest Queen Elizabeth was issued in 2013 by six judges of the International Common Law Court of Justice in Brussels.

After nearly a year of litigation, Queen Elizabeth and her husband, Prince Phillip, were found guilty in the disappearance of ten native children from the Catholic-run Kamloops residential school in British Columbia. Grieving parents haven't seen their children since they left for a picnic with the Royal couple on Oct. 10 1964.

On May 10th, the International Tribunal into Crimes of Church and State was asking concerned citizens to demand Cunningham's immediate release. The ITCCS successfully prosecuted Queen Elizabeth's kidnapping, along with 50,000 cases of other missing children.

Regiment soldier Cunningham had innocently questioned a senior officer about Queen Elizabeth's arrest warrant, only to be committed to a mental care unit in Stafford England.

He was injected with an atypical anti-psychotic drug olanzapine under orders of Captain Murrell and Doctors Khan and Sema. The soldier was committed for six months to the St. George Hospital Psychiatric Unit with a "diagnosis" of suffering from an acute psychotic episode.

"Queen Elizabeth had direct involvement in the kidnapping and death of aboriginal children" it was reported on the ITCCS website. "Royal Family members also appeared to regularly participate in Ninth Circle Satanic Cult rituals at the Mohawk Indian School in Brantford, Ontario, Canada."

In April, a second international trial began in Brussels on global elite members of the Ninth Circle Satanic Cult.

A court document had been filed indicating that in Jan. 2012 UK Archbishop of Canterbury Justin Welby acted under the direction of Queen Elizabeth to destroy forensic remains of a Ninth Circle Satanic Cult child homicide. Two eyewitnesses have testified that as children they were present during this same murder of a native child.

The satanic rite evidently occurred in a sub basement catacomb under the west wing of the Canadian Branton Ontario Mohawk Indian residential school. The two eyewitnesses alleged that they saw a young girl being bound to an altar.

The five or six year-old child was gagged, repeatedly raped, killed, disemboweled and dismembered. Her blood was consumed by nine red-robed figures that included a member of the British Royal Family.

Unfortunately Cunningham was not alone in his victimization after exposing these Ninth Circle Satanic Cult activities. Several incarcerations and even a death appeared to surround exposures of Queen Elizabeth's kidnapping case.

Former Kamloops School resident William Combes died after a 2010 radio interview where he discussed witnessing Queen Elizabeth and Prince Phillip leave the school with his ten friends and fellow Kamloops residents.

Directly after the interview the healthy Combes was ordered to report for tests at the Vancouver St. Paul's Catholic hospital. There he was given an injection that put him into a coma. Within hours and without consent of his family members, Combes was permanently pulled off life support.

British citizen David Compan was another victim of whistleblowing against Queen Elizabeth. In 2013 he was twice arrested, as was his wife. Compan's "crime" was daring to post Queen Elizabeth's arrest warrant on a Catholic Church.

Compan was never charged, but accosted, drugged and incarcerated in the London Park Royal Mental Health Center. After several days of protests irate citizens secured the couple's release. Compan discussed the incarceration in this video.

Last October in Kitchener Ontario Canada Steve Finney was trying to expose this same Ninth Circle Satanic Cult case on 50,000 missing native children that included Queen Elizabeth's kidnapping charges-conviction. Finney was arrested without cause and held in prison for three days. Protests around the globe organized by the ITCCS appeared effective in Finney's release.

"Like my friends Combes, Compan and Finney, Cunningham is being cruelly drugged and imprisoned against his will because he simply mentioned the existence of a citizens arrest warrant against Queen Elizabeth" stated Kevin Annett of the ITCCS.

"As a British soldier and citizen, Cunningham has now become a Prisoner of Conscience at the hands of the British Crown in an effort to hide proven crimes of the Royal Family."

Annett himself has felt the wrath of Queen Elizabeth. In 2013 when Annett was in London attending a rally for the 50,000 missing children, he was detained, held in jail overnight, then deported – all done without being charged.

In March the ITCCS began a second prosecution on global elite members of the Ninth Circle Satanic Cult.

In my observation, there are multitudes of witnesses whose personal testimonies outweigh the rigged deployment of supposed "fact checkers" who represent the elite superclass. The elite superclass maintains a public persona intended to deceive the lower-class, enslaved subjects of their satanically motivated empires. One of these witnesses is a woman named Anya Wick, formerly Anya Epstein.

Anya Epstein was Jeffrey's niece, fathered and raised by his brother to become a sex slave for their "cult of Baal," one of the many satanic cults. Baal worship is as old as ancient Babylon, and many of the super-elite

---

15   http://cloakedtruth.com

are Baal worshippers. Anya's story is almost identical to Gloria's, having been raised for the purpose of performing in the rituals of the cult. She was groomed by her mother, and when the time came to commit vile and disgusting sexual acts in her toddler years, she was drugged so she could not resist. Over time, the drugs served another purpose: Anya became unable to distinguish the sex-slave events from reality, choosing to believe that they were nightmares instead. This did not explain her subsequent pain or bruises, but she was too confused by the drugs to perceive reality.

According to Anya, Jeffrey Epstein and his family are multigenerational Baal worshippers. The children who become their victims are mere props, many raised and groomed for satanic rituals that include child sex and sacrifice. But who is the Ninth Circle Satanic Cult mentioned in Judy Byington's report?

The Ninth Circle is perhaps the darkest and most powerful of the elite satanic cults, including names that would shock and horrify. In his books, author and investigator Kevin Annett exposes evidence that is painful to confront. According to Annett, every pope has either had direct involvement in, or at the very least, exposure to, Ninth Circle satanic ceremonies. These are the most powerful people in the world, supported by nearly every governmental body. Annett also claims it is not possible to become a Roman Cardinal without participating in a Ninth Circle sacrificial ritual at some point in their clerical career. This includes the current "American" pope, and witnesses have made horrifying statements about all of them.

To determine who might be the most evil of all the popes would be a difficult contest, but in recent history, Joseph Ratzinger would take the blue ribbon:

Pope Benedict XVI

The devil-horn hand signal is one of the easiest giveaways revealing whom they truly serve. By the way, if the body of Christ has one head— Christ Himself—why does no one ask about this second head who calls himself the "Vicar of Christ on earth"? The pope's self-assertion as head of the church should be the first red flag that something is wrong with Catholicism in general.

Pope Benedict XVI had close ties to the Nazis, having worked around death camps such as Auschwitz, where witnesses claimed he regularly extracted people from the camps for torture and sacrifice. This is the pope mentioned by Judy Byington in her article above. By numerous eyewitness accounts and testimonies, Joseph Ratzinger—known as Pope Benedict XVI—was a pedophile, child rapist, and child murderer, and because this was becoming publicly well-known is why he was forced to resign.

We spend billions of tax dollars in the name of justice pursuing drug traffickers. We fill prisons and build new ones for people convicted of victimless crimes in many cases. Prisons are great business for politicians. Meanwhile, the worst of the worst are only asked to "resign," while there is no justice for their victims, who live with multiple personality disorders and PTSD—if they survive at all.

There is at least one major clue as to why the elite superclass participates in satanic cult membership. Yehshua was offered the same opportunity, and He turned it down.

> *Again, the devil taketh him up into an exceeding high mountain, and sheweth him all the kingdoms of the world, and the glory of them;*
>
> *And saith unto him, All these things will I give thee, if thou wilt fall down and worship me. (Matthew 4:8-9 KJV)*

They know this and have taken Satan up on his promise—and what do you know? They are rich and powerful under the authority of the prince of death. They will join him in his kingdom of death. Meanwhile, the church has a responsibility to intercede and intervene for these innocent little ones. For a child to be tortured or raped, raised into sexual servitude for the elite superclass, cannot continue without consequences for the perpetrators. This is a global problem that has gone unpunished and is getting worse. The bride has authority under Yehshua to stop them. Punishment is not our job, but fasting and prayer are our responsibility to these innocent children trapped in satanic cults and sex-trafficking rings.

Look, I didn't want to spend time on this, but the more I researched, the more I found. Much of this is thanks to the Epstein situation and Virginia Giuffre's death, which has emboldened witnesses to come forward. It is disgusting, repulsive, nauseating, and horrifying to know that pedophilia and child sacrifice to a false god is the religion of the elite superclass, who impose tyranny and abusive taxation through their puppet politicians. They rule and reign over us for lack of prayer against them—and for no other reason.

On the earth there are two parallel kingdoms. Satan is the god, or prince, of this world (John 16:11, 14:30). There was a coup in the Garden of Eden when an agent of Satan deceived Eve. Adam chose Eve over God. It was then that life became death on the earth under Satan's reign: "You will surely die" (Genesis 2:17).

We are born into the kingdom of Satan and become heirs of death with him. By faith in the Son of God and baptism by submersion, we are sealed by the Holy Spirit, choosing life in Yehshua's kingdom rather than death in Satan's kingdom. Once baptized, we become citizens of God's kingdom, though we still reside in Satan's realm until the "sons of God" are revealed (Romans 8).

Notice in both verses:

- Satan, the prince of the power of the air, is the spirit at work in the sons of disobedience (Ephesians 2:2).
- Satan has blinded the minds of the unbelieving (2 Corinthians 4:4).

Disobedience is a spirit. The spirit of disobedience causes spiritual blindness.

In Ephesians 2:2, the King James Version uses "children of disobedience," but in most other translations, the word "sons" is used from the original Greek *huios*. As we discussed previously, this denotes the right to an inheritance, whereas "children" in general does not. The sons of disobedience are heirs to the kingdom of Satan—death. The sons of God are joint heirs with Christ in His kingdom.

The kingdom of death inherits death, and the kingdom of life inherits life.

Disobedience is rebelliousness, and rebelliousness stems from pride—the original sin. God hates pride more than any other sin, and disobedience is akin to it. Pride caused Lucifer's demise.

Remember that rebelliousness is as the sin of witchcraft.

> *For rebellion is as the sin of witchcraft, and*
> *stubbornness is as iniquity and idolatry. Because thou*
> *hast rejected the word of the Lord, he hath also rejected*
> *thee from being king. (1 Samuel 15:23 KJV)*

Samuel informs Saul that his rebelliousness is as witchcraft and his stubbornness is as idolatry—both of which are the primary operative devices of demonic spirits. Also recall that Saul was handed over to those same demonic spirits and tormented by them. Disobedience is a spirit of darkness under Satan's authority. Rebelliousness has destroyed kings and nations that depart from God.

The sons of disobedience are joint heirs with Satan in the kingdom of death, just as the sons of God are joint heirs with Christ in the kingdom of life.

In the context of the two kingdoms of life and death, consider Paul's words again in Colossians 3:

> *When Christ, who is our life, is revealed, then you also*
> *will be revealed with Him in glory.*
>
> *Therefore, treat the parts of your earthly body as dead*
> *to sexual immorality, impurity, passion, evil desire, and*
> *greed, which amounts to idolatry. For it is because of*
> *these things that the wrath of God is coming upon the*
> *sons of disobedience. (Colossians 3:4-6 NASB)*

Now compare this to Paul's words in Romans 5:

> *Much more then, being now justified by his blood, we*
> *shall be saved from wrath through him. (Romans 5:9*
> *KJV)*

In 1 Thessalonians 5:9, Paul says that believers are not appointed to wrath—the final tribulation. The two kingdoms are divided between the sons of God and the sons of disobedience. The kingdom of death is destined for the wrath of God, while the kingdom of life is destined for the glory of God. The bride does not share in the wrath that targets the sons of disobedience. Rather, she has a far more glorious destiny with the Prince of Life, reserved for the sons of God led by the Spirit.

Remember that in six of the seven churches of Revelation 2 and 3, members are offered the opportunity to come out of them or else receive the plagues destined for the sons of disobedience. Five of the churches have been blinded by the spirit of disobedience, and unless they open their spiritual eyes, they will receive the inheritance of the prince of death. Not all who identify as Christians will be spared the hour of temptation that shall come upon the whole world. There is a small group not blinded by the spirit of disobedience, called the Church of Philadelphia. A progressive LGBTQ+ Thyatira church, for example, is blinded by the spirit of disobedience and will be appointed to wrath unless they open their spiritual eyes in time to avoid it. They may not be the Group 3 satanists, but they will not be counted worthy to escape these things (Luke 21:36) if they refuse to open their spiritual eyes.

By my estimate, it is likely that at least one billion Christians live in spiritual blindness. They identify as Christians but have little knowledge of the truth of the Bible or of God. Part of the bride's responsibility is to enlighten the five lost churches and assist in healing their spiritual blindness. It is amazing that in Yehshua's vision of Revelation shared with John, Christianity was already fractured and divided into seven segments, only one of which followed Christ in the purest sense. This divided church was established in less than one generation after the crucifixion.

There are 1.4 billion Catholics, a large percentage of whom may actually believe the pope is God on earth, as the papacy and many world leaders claim (see George Bush's interview with Raymond Arroyo, April 11, 2008). But what about the rest of Satan's kingdom? The global population is rapidly approaching nine billion. Many powerful people around the world believe that both God and Satan exist—and have chosen Satan's kingdom of death in blatant opposition to God. How is this possible?

To answer that question, we must go back to Genesis. It is impossible to understand the book of Revelation without first knowing the book of Genesis.

In the account of Cain and Abel and their offerings before God, we see the first example of a "son of disobedience" in Cain when he murdered his brother. Cain was prideful, and his offering was unacceptable, being the work of his own hands. Abel offered the first appropriate sacrifice in the Bible when he presented "the best portions of the firstborn of his flock" (Genesis 4:4). In Hebrews 11:4, Paul says that Abel offered the "more excellent sacrifice."

Cain's response was one of anger and jealousy, characteristic of a son of disobedience. But there is something that perplexes me in a deeper view of this story that appears in 1 John 3:12:

Not as Cain, who was of that wicked one, and slew his brother. And wherefore slew he him? Because his own works were evil, and his brother's righteous. (1 John 3:12 KJV)

What does John mean by "who was of the wicked one"? Was Cain under the influence of the spirit of disobedience? Or is John referring to Cain having a completely different genetic origin? I want to be very careful prefacing this question as interrogative—I simply do not know.

However, I found a bizarre statement in Matthew Poole's *Commentary* that gave me chills:

*And what again, on the other hand, (q.d.) can be more devil-like, than such a temper as Cain's was, whose hatred of his brother brake out into actual murder, upon no other account but because his brother was better than he? Which showed him to be **of that wicked one, of the serpent's seed**: so early was such seed sown, and so ancient the enmity between seed and seed.*

How Matthew Poole makes this suggestion is based on Genesis 3:15:

***And I will put enmity between thee and the woman, and
between thy seed and her seed; it shall bruise thy head,
and thou shalt bruise his heel. (Genesis 3:15 KJV)***

Another question arises based on the Hebrew translations of chapter 4. In verse 1—just three verses prior to the offering of the two offspring of Adam, Eve says, "With the help of the Lord I have brought forth a man." As opposed to what? And why with the help of the Lord? This is all immediately after being expelled from the garden, then comes the man child who is named Cain. Take a look at the name Cain according to Strong's:

◄ 7014. Qayin ►

Strong's Lexicon

Qayin: Cain

Word Origin: *Derived from the root קָנָה (qanah),
meaning «to acquire» or «to possess.»*

It would seem that this definition refers to Eve's statement in verse 1: "I have brought forth," or acquired a "man." However, various commentators seem to prefer that the name *Cain* refers to "possession." If it is possession, then possessed by whom? Adam and Eve? Or God? Or was Cain literally possessed by Satan and therefore the "serpent's seed"? I do not know and will not assume. But to fulfill Genesis 3:15 in its literal interpretation, there must be one seed against another seed. Otherwise, it is allegorical—and I believe allegorical interpretation can lead to deception and misinterpretation. The Bible is to be read and understood literally.

The only reason to dig deeper into this disquieting question is the stark contrast between the names Cain and Abel in their meanings. Here is *Abel* according to Strong's:

◄ 1893. Hebel or Habel ►

Strong›s Lexicon

Hebel or Habel: Abel

Word Origin: Derived from the root verb לָבָה (haval), meaning "to be vain" or "to act emptily."

But this definition used by Strong's is in reality a broader sense of its true definition, which is "breath" or "vapor." Strong's elaborates on this further:

> ***Usage:*** *The name «Hebel» or «Abel» is most prominently known as the second son of Adam and Eve, as recorded in the Book of Genesis. The name is often associated with the concept of **«breath» or «vapor,»** symbolizing transience or fleetingness. In a broader sense, the term «hebel» is used throughout the Hebrew Bible to denote vanity, futility, or something ephemeral.*

When I saw the word *breath*, I was interested to know the comparison between the breath of Abel and the breath of Adam when God breathed the "breath of life into his nostrils" (Genesis 2:7). This is the difference between the two "breaths" in the Hebrew translation:

◄ 5397. neshamah ►

Strong›s Lexicon

neshamah: Breath, spirit, soul

They are not the same. Abel received a breath that was vain and without Spirit. Adam was the only man to be born with the Spirit of God. After Adam, the Spirit would only be given as a gift upon redemption.

Redemption could never have occurred without Yehshua—the seed of the woman who crushed the head of the serpent. If Adam had remained obedient to God rather than follow Eve, Cain would never have been born possessed, and Abel would not have received a vain, transient breath of death.

This is the distinction between the two "breaths." But then there is another verse that throws wrinkles into the entire question of whether Cain was possessed by the serpent or the seed of the serpent. In John 8:44–45, Yehshua makes another profound statement that tends to shock a reader:

This verse identifies Cain and Satan as the same person. Yehshua clearly states that the devil was a murderer from the beginning and the father of lies. If Cain was a murderer from the beginning, who else can we connect this passage to besides Satan? Does this just remain in the archives of mysteries? Was Cain possessed, or was he the seed of the serpent—or both?

I apologize that I cannot reconcile this with confidence, and I do not want to mislead you. The "serpent's seed doctrine" has circulated widely and caused conspiracy theories based on these verses that may or may not be truly understood. I'll leave it to the reader to decide.

That said, the sons of disobedience have a father whose name is Satan, and the spirit of disobedience began with the "possession" of Cain.

Perhaps this is what Yehshua was referring to in this passage. But this doesn't answer the question of seed against seed in Genesis 3:15. Who or what is the seed of the serpent? This remains a mystery, but there are occult societies currently ruling global affairs as Satan's operatives in relative obscurity who believe they are his posterity. At the hierarchy level of these occult groups, some believe they are the descendants of Cain. I don't know anyone who can positively claim whether this is true or false. However, this does not change the fact of their existence and exertion of powerful influence on global politics and world events. These occult societies of "Cain" have been behind every war since the time of Pope St. Innocent in the fifth century as the Roman Empire continued to transition from the Caesars to the Popes.

The Freemasons believe they can trace their roots to Tubal-Cain, grandson of Cain through his son Lamech. We find him named in Genesis 4:

> *And Zillah, she also bare Tubalcain, an instructer*
> *of every artificer in brass and iron: and the sister of*
> *Tubalcain was Naamah. (Genesis 4:22 KJV)*

Unfortunately, this is all we get from the biblical narrative on this person named Tubal-Cain. All we know from this verse is that he was a metalworker and taught metalworking. I researched the Hebrew translations for the names in this passage and came up empty, except for another valuable resource in etymologies. *Abarim Publications* offers a different perspective on the name that makes sense in trying to connect the Freemasons to Tubal-Cain:

> *The name Tubal-cain: Summary*
> *Meaning*
> Global Smith, World-Spear, World Government
> *Etymology*

From (1) the noun לבת (*tebel*), the whole world-
economy, and (2) the noun קין (*qyn*), spear, the symbol of
government, from the verb קין (*qyn*), to fabricate.

My goodness, what a connection indeed! Given the insurmountable amount of evidence of Freemason influence on the world and their "New World Order" agenda, I can see why they would trace their roots to Tubal-Cain based on the etymology of the name.

Before Tubal-Cain, there was another Enoch. This is not the Enoch, son of Jared from the line of Seth, that departed from earth with God. This was Enoch, the son of Cain:

And Cain knew his wife; and she conceived, and bare Enoch: and he builded a city, and called the name of the city, after the name of his son, Enoch. (Genesis 4:17 KJV)

Interesting—a city for one child? Wouldn't a lakeside stone palace with servants be enough? This family is recorded as building cities and forming world governments—for whom? This is yet more evidence to support my belief that Adam was the "chief man" (1 Corinthians 15:45), not the first man.

Let me reiterate something I feel is important before I complete this point on the subject of Cain. On day six, God created male and female, blessed them, and commanded them to repopulate the earth (Genesis 1:27–28). Yet in chapter 2, there is no one to till the garden. If there were only a gap of one day between the garden and mankind, why was there no one to tend it? If Yehshua has delayed nearly two millennia to return, what is a single day to wait for a gardener?

Genesis chapter 2 begins with this:

So the heavens and the earth were completed, and all their hosts (inhabitants). And by the seventh day God completed His work which He had done, and He

We are currently in the Hebrew year 5785 (2025 on the Gregorian calendar), which is calculated from the creation of Adam based on the biblically verified chronological timelines for the patriarchs. Simultaneously, we are within a few years of the Sabbatical Millenium—which will be the 1,000 years of peace (Revelation 20:2–3)—if we assume the prophetic timelines of the Psalm 83 war are being fulfilled now while standing at the precipice of the Gog and Magog War now rapidly unfolding in the Middle East. This indicates that we are at the end of the Church Age and at the doorway of the "Time of Jacob's Trouble" (Jeremiah 30:7).

The second day of Hosea chapter 6 verse 2 (2,000 years) since the beginning of Yehshua's ministry will be complete anytime between Passover 2025 and 2029, depending on the actual year of the crucifixion. I have had to adjust timelines from what I originally understood to align with the Hebrew calendar, shemitahs, and jubilees. I believe Yehshua's ministry began AD 29, and the crucifixion took place in AD 33. Beginning 2,000 years from AD 29 ministry or AD 33 crucifixion could fulfill the prophecy of Hosea 6:2.

The Hebrew year 5800 will begin on Nisan 1, which corresponds to March 15, 2040 on our calendar. That year will complete 116 jubilees from the time of the creation of Adam. Two thousand years before this would be AD 40, or 3800 on the Hebrew calendar. These timelines fit neatly into Hosea's prophecy: if the crucifixion was in AD 33, then Yehshua's ministry would have begun in AD 29, which fits neatly into a vast consensus among scholars. Based on Luke 3:1, Yehshua's ministry began in the fifteenth year of Tiberius Caesar's reign, a chronology that is easier to establish.

Cross-referencing the Hebrew year with Luke 3:1, Yom Kippur of 2029 falls at the midpoint between shemitah seven-year cycle (2026–2033) and one and a half shemitah cycles before the major jubilee year ending in 2040. Hosea's prophecy will be fulfilled in the Hebrew year 5793, which is 2,000 years from the crucifixion and seven years before the close of the jubilee year 5800.

This would mean that between now and the end of the tribulation—possibly ending in the next decade, based on 2033 completing the second day of Hosea's prophecy, plus seven years for the tribulation—we will have completed the sixth millenium and entered the Sabbatical millennium sometime by 2040. This, however, leaves a gap of over two hundred years unaccounted for on the Hebrew calendar that begins with the creation of Adam.

Applying logic from the biblical Adamic timeline, I believe that mankind from Day 6 had 200 years to populate the earth before the creation of Adam, if we triangulate between the timing for Sabbatical Millenium and the current fulfilment of prophecies converging Hosea's prophecy. Adam was created to be the "chief" over mankind—the first Melchizedek, with Yehshua as the last. There was already a subset of Day 6 mankind roaming the earth, over which Adam was created by "Yahweh Elohim" in chapter 2, verse 7, to rule the earth as king and priest (Melchizedek). For this reason, Tubal-Cain was forming world governments and Cain was building cities for a growing population that existed before Adam. How else can we make sense of this? It makes no sense to build a city for one son, but it makes perfect sense to build a city over which that son would rule.

We can argue about this forever, and you'll have your opinion and I'll have mine, but the biblical narrative is illogical according to conventional interpretations. The total population of my family over the last century is only a few hundred people. If a great-uncle built a city for one son, it would take another century before that city had a population worth calling even a small town. Using common sense, I do not believe we have a clear understanding of Genesis chapters 1 and 2.

Adam was created to be the first Melchizedek. The last Adam is the last Melchizedek—Yehshua (Hebrews 7:17). Adam was not created on Day 6, but after all had been created as indicated by verse 1 of Genesis chapter 2. If Adam was a mature, lonely man when Eve was created, then she certainly was not created on the same day. That fact alone excludes Adam from being part of Day 6 mankind.

This is not to mention the question of whom Cain was so afraid would kill him when he was expelled from God's presence.

> ***Behold, You have driven me out this day from the face of the land; and from Your face (presence) I will be hidden, and I will be a fugitive and an [aimless] vagabond on the earth, and whoever finds me will kill me. (Genesis 4:14 AMP)***

As far as we know, Cain only had one brother—and he killed him. There are only two brothers offering sacrifices in chapter 4. So who was Cain so afraid of? The only possible answer is that there was already a growing population on the earth who were not members of the Adamic royal family.

I have derailed too far from the subject, but there are a few more things to cover before leaving Genesis chapter 4. The "mark of Cain" in verse 15 was a sign that identified Cain as untouchable. Whoever had populated the earth by the time of Cain would have known exactly what this "sign" signified. Many secret societies have adopted symbolism believed to be the mark of Cain, but no one really knows what it was, as is evident when researching it.

There are other signs mentioned in the Bible where the same word is used:

> ***And God said, Let there be lights in the firmament of the heaven to divide the day from the night; and let***

*them be for <u>signs</u>, and for seasons, and for days, and
years. (Genesis 1:14 KJV)*

*And God said, This is the <u>token</u> (sign) of the covenant
which I make between me and you and every living
creature that is with you, for perpetual generations.
(Genesis 9:12 KJV)*

*And the blood shall be to you for a <u>token</u> (sign) upon
the houses where ye are: and when I see the blood, I
will pass over you, and the plague shall not be upon
you to destroy you, when I smite the land of Egypt.
(Exodus 12:13 KJV)*

*Therefore the Lord himself shall give you a sign;
Behold, a virgin shall conceive, and bear a son, and
shall call his name Immanuel. (Isaiah 7:14 KJV)*

If anything, these uses of the word "signs" for the mark of Cain further complicate the issue, as none of them really have much in common. The sign of Noah was a rainbow, the sign on the houses in Egypt was blood, and the same word is used for the sign of Cain. Secret societies such as the Illuminati and their Freemason counterparts believe that the mark was a red cross in a circle, possibly placed on Cain's forehead. How this would identify Cain as untouchable remains a mystery.

It is also believed that the descendants of Ham, who populated the regions of ancient Sumeria and Egypt, had knowledge of their preflood ancestors through Noah and knew exactly what the mark was, wearing it for protection. That mark was in a circle but was not a cross within a circle.

Whatever the mark of Cain was—or is—I am certain it is no mystery to the hierarchy of secret societies and the papacy of Rome, i.e., the "sons of disobedience." For years, I believed that the mark of the beast and the mark of Cain were one and the same. However, there is a distinction between the two marks if we observe their respective translations. The mark of Cain in Genesis 4:15 was a *sign* or *token*.

◀ 226. oth ▶

Lexicon

oth: Sign, token, mark, miracle

Strong›s Exhaustive Concordance

mark, miracle, ensign

Probably from ‹uwth (in the sense of appearing); a signal (literally or figuratively), as a flag, beacon, monument, omen, prodigy, evidence, etc. -- mark, miracle, (en-)sign, token.

Usage: The term אות (oth) is used in the Hebrew Bible to denote a sign or symbol that serves as a signal or evidence of something. It can refer to a physical sign, a miraculous event, or a symbolic act that conveys a message or confirms a covenant.

This translation differs significantly from the mark of the beast in Revelation chapter 13:

> **Also he compels all, the small and the great, and the rich and the poor, and the free men and the slaves, to be given a <u>mark</u> on their right hand or on their forehead [signifying allegiance to the beast], and that no one will be able to buy or sell, except the one who has the <u>mark</u>, either the name of the beast or the number of his name. (Revelation 13:16-17 AMP)**

The mark in these verses differs from the mark of Cain:

Lexicon

charagma: Mark, stamp, engraving

Strong›s Exhaustive Concordance

stamp, mark.

From the same as <u>charax</u>; a scratch or etching, i.e. Stamp (as a badge of servitude), or scupltured figure (statue) -- graven, mark.

Topical Lexicon

Word Origin: *Derived from the Greek verb χαράσσω (charassō), meaning «to engrave» or «to carve.»*

The mark of Cain is a physical sign, symbol, or token—something people would visually see and be compelled to respect. The mark of the beast, however, is a stamp or engraving, seemingly like a tattoo, that signifies allegiance in opposition to God.

In our digital age of technology, the mark of the beast could manifest as both a tattoo and a DNA-altering microchip. It could be visible on the surface of the skin or only detectable by digital electronic scan—such as RFID scan or maybe a blacklight—but linked to DNA. All forms of RFID and microchip biotechnology make the mark of the beast, by this definition, available for mass implementation immediately.

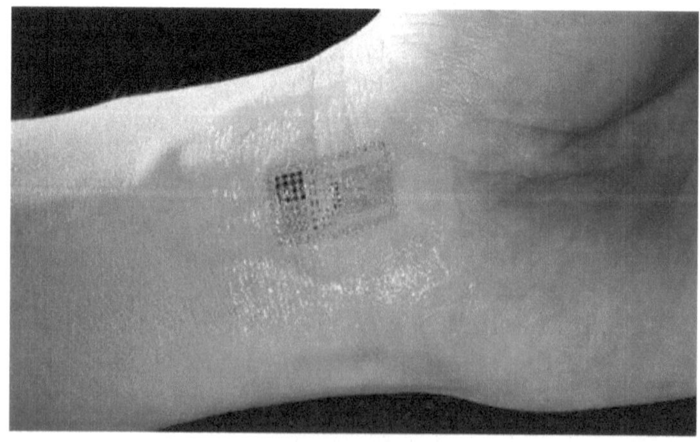

In the case of the mark of the beast, once taken, there is no turning back. There appears to be no forgiveness for those who take the mark. The fact that it cannot be erased or atoned for suggests that it must be linked to DNA—where the very DNA of the bearer is marked as property of the beast.

This recalls what happened in Genesis 6, when the DNA of mankind was altered through cohabitation with fallen angels. Genetic manipulation of the human genome began decades ago in Nazi Germany. I shudder to think how far this technology has come since then. The COVID-19 virus was synthesized and later augmented by gene-altering mRNA technologies in something labeled as a "vaccine". I believe it is safe to assume that the mark of the beast could be successfully launched today.

> *Then another angel, a third one, followed them, saying with a loud voice, "Whoever worships the beast and his image and receives the mark [of the beast] on his forehead or on his hand, he too will [have to] drink of the wine of the wrath of God, mixed undiluted into the cup of His anger; and he will be tormented with fire and brimstone (flaming sulfur) in the presence of the holy angels and in the presence of the Lamb (Christ). And the smoke of their torment ascends forever and ever; and they have no rest day and night—those who worship the beast and his image, and whoever receives the mark of his name." (Revelation 14:9-11 AMP)*

Whatever this mark of the beast is, the blood of the perfect Lamb without blemish (Yehshua) will not atone for it. For this reason, I believe the mark of the beast is tied to genetic or DNA manipulation. The sons of disobedience and the Nephilim offspring of the fallen sons of God will share this in common with recipients of the mark. The first Nephilim were destroyed by the flood, for their existence was never permitted by God. They were born out of rebellion, their DNA illegally conceived, and they had no hope of salvation. The same will be true for those who partake of the mark of the beast.

The mark of the beast will be directly related to genetic manipulation for which there can be no forgiveness once human DNA has been cross-contaminated with something of non-human origin.

The sons of disobedience have hope of salvation only until they choose allegiance to the Antichrist— an allegiance marked by genetic manipulation. For this reason, I urge diligence in researching modern vaccines and biotechnologies before blissfully taking anything, especially when we're this close to the wheat harvest and the close of the Church Age.

It is challenging to keep this chapter on point. Please understand that the lower levels of secret societies, like the Freemasons, are not operating with the same knowledge as their higher-ranking "initiates." A "Master Mason" is a third-degree Mason, which is the highest level of the lower rites. But there are other "rites" of Freemasonry that take the Mason to new levels of "knowledge" or "enlightenment." Namely, these are the York Rite and the Scottish Rite, which offer an additional thirty levels. At the peak of these higher-order "rites" are the Knights Templar.

It is within these extremely esoteric rites that, at the thirtieth degree, a new god is introduced—one that replaces the true God. This esoteric group operates behind the scenes, placing world leaders in power or removing them from power. The thirtieth-degree Masons are the sons of disobedience by their own choice, following directly in Lucifer's footsteps.

Many Masons are good people and believe they are doing God's work, without noticing the esoteric signs all around them. In this sense, they share something in common with Roman Catholics. And I am about to point out three religions that will shock you when you discover what they have in common. Please understand: I want to help Catholics, as well as Masons, come out from under this well-designed and highly organized deception.

I heard another voice from heaven, saying, "Come out of her, my people, so that you will not participate in her

I think most of us are aware that there is a very dark and evil group of people who rule the world—we just don't know exactly who they are. We've all heard bizarre stories about families like the Rothschilds and Rockefellers, or about political dynasties such as the Clintons, Obamas, and Bushes. The problem is that not only are many of the stories you have heard or read rooted in some origin of truth, but they are also far darker than most can comprehend.

A few years ago, I became curious about the so-called "dark web" and downloaded the Tor Onion app, which allows access to places on the internet otherwise hidden. I found things so horrible that I had to delete the app. Some of the images are still engraved on my mind, images I wish I could forget. Epstein Island, for example, was a house of horrors that I seriously doubt Satan was even so evil as some of the guests there. Children are tortured and raped by the super-elite—sometimes in rituals, sometimes for pleasure. In some cases, the adrenal glands of tortured children are said to be consumed for a narcotic effect. You can see the faces of those who participate in such atrocities on the news daily. Often, they are people you would immediately recognize—powerful political figures, Hollywood actors, and others. One of the worst of them is a US congressman still in office today. I do not understand how this is possible, except by some kind of mutually agreed pact among these powerful esoteric groups, a pact that is promised never to be broken.

The Epstein headline story is limited to his pedophilia and sex trafficking allegations and convictions. But make no mistake: Epstein was a direct link to every billionaire and powerful public figure, including Hollywood actors. This is not a story about one man named Jeffrey Epstein; it is far more evil and involves thousands of people who rule over us and those who aid our rulers. Epstein was an enterprising power broker whose religion was satanic and as ancient as the sons of Cain. At the pinnacle of that power are the Illuminati (the enlightened ones), and the Freemasons, whose god is not our God. These are the sons of disobedience (Colossians 3:6), and they work directly with the principalities and powers of darkness

(Ephesians 6:12) in their shared goal of destroying the sons of God led by the Spirit. Do not be naive about this!

The thirtieth-degree and higher Freemasons are only one of these esoteric groups, but make no mistake—they are very powerful. One of the patriarchs of the Scottish Rite, who composed various writings to be used as guide manuals, was named Albert Pike. Perhaps Pike's most notable work as a Mason was *Morals and Dogma*, printed in 1871, considered sacred among the higher degrees. I want you to read this quote by Albert Pike so that you may understand what the "enlightened initiates" believe:

> **Albert Pike addressing the 23 Supreme Councils of the world on July 14, 1889:**
>
> **"To you, Sovereign Grand Instructors General, we say this, that you may repeat it to the Brethren of the 32nd, 31st and 30th degrees: 'the Masonic Religion should be, by all of us initiates of the high degrees, maintained in the purity of the <u>Luciferian Doctrine</u>. . ."**

The Luciferian doctrine? These are a few names you will recognize, names that can be verified. This is a very secretive group, and many more names would shock you. Below are just a few:

- George Bush, thirty-third-degree Freemason, former president of the USA, former director of the CIA
- J. Edgar Hoover, thirty-third-degree Freemason, director of the FBI
- Walt Disney, founder of the Disney Corporation, thirty-third-degree Freemason
- Norman Vincent Peale, thirty-third-degree Freemason, former grand chaplain of the Grand Lodge of New York, past grand prelate of the Knights Templar and Shriner
- Jesse Jackson, thirty-third-degree Prince Hall Freemason
- Colin Powell, thirty-third-degree Freemason, US secretary of state
- Newt Gingrich, thirty-third-degree Freemason

Masons of the thirtieth degree and above include a vast number of kings, queens, princes, prime ministers, generals, and state diplomats—so many that it is not worth the time to disclose their names here. What matters is the appearance that it is impossible to become a powerful leader of any kind without holding a thirtieth degree or higher Masonic rank, or without achieving the "Illuminati" rank alongside figures like Jeffrey Epstein. As stated by the Masonic patriarch Albert Pike, once initiated beyond the thirtieth degree, there is no way to remain ignorant of the fact that the Masonic religion is maintained in the purity of the Luciferian doctrine.

The ceremonies for initiates beyond the thirtieth degree are bone-chilling and horrifying, and no born-again Christian could or would ever participate in them or agree to their secret oaths. The thirtieth-degree and higher Masons stand in direct and blatant opposition to God. Their purpose and priority are to undermine the sons of God led by the Spirit and to deprive humankind of the opportunity for salvation. They believe they can aid Lucifer's success against God if the bride church can be condemned through deception. Are they succeeding?

The bride church is engaged in a spiritual war whose physical operatives are hidden within secret societies like the Freemasons, Illuminati, cults of Baal, and Ninth Circle Cult. Amazingly, nearly every major false religion can be traced to the lineage of Cain through his sons Tubal-Cain and Enoch. Yet the spirit of the Antichrist could not fully manifest until the arrival of Christ. The Antichrist spirit is Satan himself, older than mankind, but without a Christ church, there could be no Antichrist church. The foundation of the Antichrist church is far older than Freemasonry, though Freemasons claim their roots extend beyond Nimrod to Tubal-Cain and Enoch, sons of Cain.

The Antichrist spirit is not stupid; he laid the foundation for an Antichrist church two thousand years before the arrival of the Messiah. Before the Great Flood, the strategy of the fallen angels and their leader was to corrupt the human genome to the point that there could be no salvation—just as they will do again before the tribulation. When God sent the flood to exterminate the Nephilim, the angel-human hybrids, and vowed their extinction, Satan required a new strategy to condemn humankind. For that strategy, Satan would use the line of Ham, son of Noah, to develop his Antichrist spirit, which first appeared through Nimrod. Nimrod became the first post-flood global ruler and the founder of Babylon—the first Antichrist.

Nimrod first appears in Genesis, chapter 10, and we know very little about him except that he was the builder of the Tower of Babel, king of Babylon, and a "mighty hunter before the Lord" (Genesis 10:9). According to rabbinical targums, he was a hunter/murderer of Godly men and was totally opposed to God. Nimrod is an enigma, mysterious by the very lack of information given about him. What little we do know about him only makes him even more enigmatic. We know he founded several cities, and ancient monuments still bear his name—Nimrod's Castle on the Israel-Lebanon border and Mount Nemrut in Turkey. Yet the only detail we know seems irrelevant. A mighty hunter? That's it?

(Nimrod's Castle National Park, Israel. This was built by Nimrod. Notice the megalithic stones surrounded by smaller stones. The smaller stones were added to repair earthquake damage to the original construction many centuries after Nimrod. The base foundation stones used in the original structure weigh many tons. This was built by a grandson of Noah, who stood in opposition to Noah's other sons. Where did he find the help to build it? How did he manipulate these massive stones with such precision? I believe the builders were Nephilim superhumans, "in those days and also after that...")

(Mount Nemrut—Nimrod—in Turkey. These monuments are attributed to King Antiochus IV, a Syrian king who reigned from 175 BC to 164 BC. Certainly, he may have been responsible for placing some of these monuments on Mount Nemrut, but this location was named after Nimrod by Nimrod, not by a Syrian king eighteen centuries later. The image at the top right is believed to be an actual representation of Nimrod, but note its similarity to the stone carving depictions of the Sumerian Anunnaki gods—fallen angels! I believe Nimrod built this as a monument to the fallen angels, not to himself. I believe Nimrod thought he had found Mount Hermon, where it all began. The monuments at Mount Nemrut were erected before Nimrod built the fortress at Nimrod's Castle on Mount Hermon. Scholars assign a far later date to Mount Nemrut, but in error.)

I believe Nimrod was a hunter of men who opposed him, which explains the obscure and seemingly irrelevant mention of "mighty hunter." Also recall that Amraphel, king of Shinar (Babylon), in the Genesis 14 coalition against the cities of Sodom—who kidnapped Abraham's nephew Lot—was Nimrod. I discussed this in the last book.

Nimrod was the first global leader opposed to God after the flood, and together with his siblings, he founded much of the post-flood Middle East. Nimrod is the Egyptian Osiris; his wife and mother, Semiramis (Ashtoreth), is the Egyptian Isis. They were deified in ancient Egypt and everywhere that Nimrod exerted his influence. Osiris and Isis became the sun and the moon in ancient pagan religions, further symbolizing their deification. By this symbology, we can identify Nimrod and Semiramis today anywhere that sun and moon worship continues under various religious disguises.

Nimrod and Semiramis—or Ashtoreth, as she was known in the Bible (Judges 2:13, 10:6; 1 Samuel 7:3–4, 12:10; 1 Kings 11:5, 11:33; 2 Kings 23:13; 1 Samuel 31:10; Jeremiah 7:18)—appear in their various forms across most religions. In the current context of Freemasonry, Nimrod is a very important figure. Keep in mind that Nimrod of Babylon is also Osiris of Egypt, deified across numerous cross sections of religious culture. Here is a quote from the *Encyclopedia of Freemasonry*:

> *The legend of the Craft in the Old Constitutions refers to Nimrod as one of the founders of Masonry. Thus in the York MS., No. 1, we read: 'At ye makeing of ye Toure of Babell there was Masonrie first much esteemed of, **<u>and the King of Babilon yt was called Nimrod was A mason himselfe and loved well Masons.</u>** '"' And the Cooke MS. thus repeats the story: "And this same Nembroth began the towre of babilon and he taught to his werkemen the craft of Masonrie, and he had with him many Masons more than forty thousand. And he loved and cherished them well." '*[16]

> *The modern discoveries of Rich, of Botta, and other explorers, have thrown much light upon its ancient condition, and have shown that it was the seat of much architectural splendor and of a profoundly symbolical religion, which had something of the characteristics of the Mithraic worship. In the mythical relations of the Old Constitutions, which make up the legend of the Craft, it is spoken of as the ancient birthplace of Masonry, where **Nimrod, who was its builder, and "was a Mason and loved well the Craft,"** employed 60,000*

---

16   Encyclopedia of Freemasonry, page 513

Masons to build it, and gave them a charge "that they should be true," and this, says the Harleian MS., No. 1942, was the first time that any Mason had any charge of Craft.[17]

The following quote is directly from a Freemason website:

The universal sentiment of the Masons of the present day is to confer upon Solomon, King of Israel, the honor of being their "first Grand Master." But the Legend of the Craft had long before, though there was a tradition of the temple extant, bestowed, at least by implication, that title upon Nimrod, the King of Babylonia and Assyria. It had attributed the first organization of a fraternity of craftsmen to him, in saying that he gave a charge to the workmen whom he sent to assist the King of Nineveh in building his cities.

*That is to say, he framed for them a Constitution, and, in the words of the Legend, "this was the first tyme that ever Masons had any charge of his science." It was the first time that the Craft were organized into a fraternity working under a Constitution or body of laws; and as **Nimrod** was the autocratic maker of these laws, it results as a necessary consequence, that their first legislator, legislating with dictatorial and unrestricted sovereign power, **was also their first Grand Master**.*[18]

It is difficult to make all the necessary false-religion connections concisely, but these links between the ancient past and the modern present are vitally important to understand. It is by these connections that we

---

17   Ibid, page 514

18   https://www.universalfreemasonry.org/en/history-freemasonry/legend-of-nimrod

can accurately identify the "sons of disobedience," who are in deliberate opposition to our God just as their proclaimed patriarch Nimrod was. One of the resources I find especially useful in this research is a highly controversial book by the Rev. Alexander Hislop. Those who argue against it are generally opposed to everything that would define the Church of Philadelphia, so I choose to ignore the noise and utilize this treasure by Rev. Hislop, appropriately titled *The Two Babylons*.

There are many resources available for identifying Osiris with Nimrod, but Hislop did a magnificent job of connecting thousands of elusive dots in his research. Here is a quote from his book:

> *The identity of Nimrod, however, and the Egyptian Osiris, having been established, we have thereby light as to Nimrod's death. Osiris met with a violent death, and that violent death of Osiris was the central theme of the whole idolatry of Egypt. If Osiris was Nimrod, as we have seen, that violent death which the Egyptians so pathetically deplored in their annual festivals was just the death of Nimrod. The accounts in regard to the death of the god worshipped in the several mysteries of the different countries are all to the same effect. A statement of Plato seems to show, that in his day the Egyptian Osiris was regarded as identical with Tammuz; * and Tammuz is well known to have been the same as Adonis, the famous HUNTSMAN, for whose death Venus is fabled to have made such bitter lamentations.*[19]

There can be no doubt that Nimrod and his mother/wife Semiramis are the Egyptian deities of Osiris and Isis. Their son Horus was worshipped by the name Tammuz in Israel, as noted by Ezekiel:

---

19   *The Two Babylons*, Alexander Hislop, Chapter II Subsection IV

Then he brought me to the door of the gate of the LORD'S house which was toward the north; and, behold, there sat women weeping for Tammuz. (Ezekiel 8:14 KJV)

Why were Jewish women weeping for Tammuz, who was also the Egyptian Horus, son of Nimrod and Semiramis (Osiris and Isis)? This occurred just prior to Nebuchadnezzar's conquest of Jerusalem, when, because of Israel's return to idolatry, ten thousand Jews were taken into Babylonian captivity. The temple of Jerusalem was being used for idolatrous purposes, including women who gave themselves to prostitution in the temple for the worship of Tammuz. When you visualize the fallen condition of Israel at that time, you can also visualize the magnitude of God's mercy for His people when He takes them back every time they repent for their idolatry.

The *Benson Bible Commentary* offers this very interesting insight on the idolatrous behavior that Ezekiel describes:

Dr. Lightfoot distinguishes this door from that mentioned Ezekiel 8:5; this, he says, was the upper north gate, and that the lower; this being just over against the temple itself; whereas that was opposite the altar. Behold, there sat women weeping for Tammuz—"The prophet here refers to a Phœnician or Syrian superstition. Tammuz was an idol of Chaldee (Babylonian) extraction, as is plain from his name; which also is used for the tenth month, reckoning from the autumnal equinox, that is, the month of June; and Tammuz, as the object of worship, expresses the solar light in its perfection, as in the summer solstice. The Vulgate renders Tammuz, by Adonis; and that Adonis, according to the physical theology of the heathen, was the same as the sun, there is no question. Macrobius expressly affirms it, Saturnal., lib. 1. cap. 21, and says, that the tradition of Adonis being killed by a boar, means the diminution of the sun's light and heat by winter. This departure of Adonis, or the sun, was lamented in the most frantic ceremonies of grief by the Phœnician and Assyrian women, who, on these occasions, used to prostitute themselves in honour of his vivifying power; and thus the Jewish women are described by our prophet, weeping for Tammuz, on the fifth day of the sixth month, that is, of August; at which time his death, by the winter boar, was drawing on apace. Tammuz was supposed to have been killed by a wild boar in mount Lebanon, whence flows the river Adonis, concerning which Lucian relates an opinion prevailing in these parts, that its stream, at certain seasons of the year, is of a bloody colour, which the heathen considered as proceeding from a kind of sympathy in the river for his death: see Parkhurst and Uni. Hist., vol. 1. p. 342.

A theological pattern begins to emerge in which well-defined lines connect ancient Nimrod, Semiramis, and their son Tammuz to their deified counterparts—Osiris, Isis, and Horus—and to sun and moon worship. Therefore, it is critical to understand that wherever we see sun and moon worship, we are witnessing the former deifications of Nimrod, his mother-wife Semiramis, and Tammuz, being worshipped by different names and rituals as they relate to sun and moon worship. Sun and moon worship are the most prevalent of all pagan religions.

Just as Nimrod was regarded as the first post-flood Mason, according to claims made by Freemasons, he also stands at the center of their religion, which is not Christianity. Read this excerpt from the *Encyclopedia of Freemasonry:*

The adoption of the moon in the Masonic system as a symbol is analogous to, but could hardly be derived from, the employment of the same symbol in the ancient religions. In Egypt, Osiris was the sun, and Isis the moon; in Syria, Adonis was the sun, and Ashtoroth the moon; the Greeks adored her as Diana, and Hecate; in the mysteries of Ceres, while the hierophant or chief priest represented the Creator, and the torch-bearer the sun, the émduos, or officer nearest the altar, represented the moon. In short, moon-worship was as widely disseminated as sun-worship. Masons retain her image in their Rites, because the Lodge is a representation of the universe, where, as the sun rules over the day, the moon presides over the night; as the one regulates the year, so does the other the months, and as the former is the king of the starry hosts of heaven, so is the latter their queen; but both deriving their heat, and light, and power from him, who, as the third and the greatest light, the master of heaven and earth, controls them both.[20]

You see, there are divisions between the initiated hierarchy of Freemasonry and the under-initiates, who believe they are serving the one true God in Christianity. From the thirtieth degree and higher, they discover what Albert Pike described as "Luciferianism in its purest form"—*the worship of the sun and moon, Osiris and Isis.* If this were not true, Freemasonry would not be saturated with sun and moon symbolism in their Egyptian forms.

The secret occult societies hide in plain sight. It is in plain view that they are least suspected of anything ominous. Below is the Masonic chart:

---

20   *Encyclopedia of Freemasonry,* page 491

It is difficult to imagine the need for so many symbols, and I won't waste your time with the multitude of deceptive descriptions permitted to be shared with the uninitiated. However, at the very top of this chart, we see father sun (Osiris/Nimrod) on the left, mother moon (Isis/Semiramis/Ishtar/Ashtoreth) on the right, and prodigy son Tammuz/Horus in the form of the all-seeing eye in the center. Every symbol on this chart serves as a secretive code for what it represents. Beyond that, it is enough to know that Nimrod and his wife-mother are the deities represented by the sun and the moon. Neither Nimrod nor his wife-mother—Semiramis, Ashtoreth, or Ishtar—were favored by the God of our Bible. If these ancient figures are the deities of Freemasonry, then they are sons of disobedience, not led by the Spirit of God.

Do not be deceived. Do your own research and be aware that the first pages of an internet search have been scrubbed of almost everything useful. You must dig deeply and read published books to fully understand this highly secretive society of powerful people. At the thirtieth degree and above lies "Luciferianism in its purest form," yet the sun-and-moon worship symbology remains in plain view. When you research

Freemasonry's own written materials, you will see for yourself that these are the sons of disobedience, in blatant opposition to God. They know God and oppose Him, which means they also oppose the sons of God who are led by the Spirit of God.

Take a look at some of the symbology that defines Freemasonry in lodges around the world. The image below comes from the Andaz Masonic Temple of London, discovered during a renovation of the hotel.

Notice above the center seat, where the lodge's "Grand Master" would be seated during meetings and ceremonies, the all-seeing eye of Horus (Tammuz, son of Nimrod and Semiramis) appears within a sunburst ray. Also notice the ladder above the Horus eye, leading upward to the sun. This is a symbolic mockery: Horus, the son of the sun (Nimrod/Osiris), portrayed as the messiah child who leads to the father sun. Such imagery can be seen throughout Freemasonry, without any appearance of trying to hide their thirtieth-degree beliefs.

The image below is directly from the Freemasons of California website:

Once again, at the top left is father sun, Nimrod/Osiris; at the top right is mother Semiramis/Isis; and at the center is the sunburst Tammuz/Horus. Below Horus is the supposed Mary, mother of Jesus, holding the messiah child. Were it not for the sun, moon, and baby-sun Tammuz symbolism painted across every Masonic entity around the world, we might dismiss all of this as some twisted version of Christianity. The problem lies in knowing history—and recognizing that this very symbolism precedes the birth of Christ!

The three primary deified personalities in ancient Egypt are Nimrod/Osiris, Semiramis/Isis, and Tammuz/Horus. Nimrod and his lineage are, of course, from Babylon; Osiris and his lineage from Egypt. But they represent the same deified royal family of Nimrod, estranged from God. Here is a stone-engraved image from Egypt depicting Osiris with the queen of heaven, Isis, and the royal baby Horus:

Horus/Tammuz leaves the mother (Isis, on the right) to be with the father (Osiris, on the left), who will be glorified upon returning to the sun and the home of the father (upper center). This began in Babylon, but remember that Nimrod was the son of Cush and grandson of Ham. Ham (or Khem) was the father of the Khemites (Egyptians). Nimrod, the mighty hunter of men and archenemy of the Lord, was the architect of the Tower of Babel, deified both by the Babylonians and by his cousins, the Egyptians.

This is sun worship involving a royal family—Osiris, Isis, and Horus—who were Babylonian (Nimrod, Semiramis, Tamuz), not Egyptian. This is the religion of the Freemasons. They may lie about it in public, but when they speak through their clandestine symbolism, they cannot conceal their beliefs. If this is merely conspiracy theory, and if thirtieth-degree and higher Freemasons are a benign group of no significance, why does their symbology appear in the most conspicuous places? For example, why does the eye of Horus watch over even the smallest monetary exchange—the one-dollar bill?

The "Eye of Providence" (eye of Horus) appeared on numerous US government seals beginning in 1782, but since 1935, the eye of Horus has been imprinted on the US one-dollar bill. The "all-seeing eye of Horus" appears within the same sunburst found throughout Egyptian and Masonic symbology, with the words below it, *Novus Ordo Seclorum*—"New Order of the Ages." Above the eye of Horus are the words *Annuit Coeptis*—

"He favors our undertakings." Who favors their undertakings? Certainly not our God but their god, Lucifer, according to the Masonic patriarch Albert Pike ("Luciferianism in its purest form"). They might as well have placed the Tower of Babel beneath the eye of Horus instead of the pyramid because that is its true origin. This is sun worship that dates all the way back to Nimrod, Semiramis, and Tammuz in ancient Babylon.

Before I leave the subject of Freemasonry, I must also address another son of Cain—the evil Enoch.

> ***Cain had relations with his wife and she conceived, and gave birth to Enoch; and Cain built a city, and named the city Enoch, after the name of his son.*** *Now to Enoch was born Irad, and Irad fathered Mehujael, and Mehujael fathered Methushael, and Methushael fathered Lamech. Lamech took two wives for himself: the name of the one was Adah, and the name of the other, Zillah. Adah gave birth to Jabal; he was the father of those who live in tents and have livestock. His brother's name was Jubal; he was the father of all those who play the lyre and flute. As for Zillah, she also gave birth to Tubal-cain, the forger of all implements of bronze and iron; and the sister of Tubal-cain was Naamah. (Genesis 4:17-22 NASB)*

Probably the most comprehensive work ever compiled on the secret societies of the world was written by author Gary Wayne in his book *Genesis 6 Conspiracy*. This is a fascinating work, and I can only imagine how difficult and painstaking it must have been to arrange and publish such closely guarded secrets while articulating them in a way that helps the reader connect myths and legends to our modern reality.

In Wayne's book, an entire chapter is dedicated to "Enoch the Evil." From the Bible, we have only a single verse about this enigmatic figure, yet he is highly esteemed among the most powerful elite secret societies. This is frustrating, but it is also the reason I sometimes believe we can learn much about our God by observing His adversaries. We are defined as much by our enemies as by our friends. The sons of disobedience are so perverse and twisted that we must be certain we have nothing in common with them. I don't even want one of their dollar bill talismans in my pocket!

I am including some quotes from Wayne's chapter on "Enoch the Evil" rather than offering a book review so that his words may be understood by the reader as he intended. Here is from page 44 of *Genesis 6 Conspiracy*:

> *When Enoch imagined writing in the form of hieroglyphics, he unwittingly set in motion the technology that would fuel all of humankind's advances. For without an efficient manner for preserving ideas and advancements and accurately communicating them to others, whether in the current generation or future generations, humankind would be locked in a virtual state of never-ending ignorance, forgetting into oblivion any noteworthy ideas or advances.*

> *As enlightening and significant as this creation was, the motivation for hieroglyphics was not as pure as its results would suggest. Enoch invented writing, according to Mackey, to employ the secretive, sacred symbols, known only to the selected elite, as a vehicle to transmit the sacred truths and Mysteries in a way that was free from discovery by the masses not considered worthy enough to learn about those sacred truths and mysteries. It was the Mysteries that Enoch was associated with that are of important value.*

> *With hieroglyphs, Enoch recorded all the sciences of the spurious branch into great books, while building nine subterranean vaults to protect the wisdom from the looming deluge. Enoch is even credited by Adrian Gilbert with the building of the Great Pyramids to*

*preserve this corrupted antediluvian knowledge.
In addition, Egyptians owe their origins (and
hieroglyphics) to Hermes Trismegistus. Furthermore,
Hermes was thought to have founded the ancient
Egyptian city of Hermopolis, the home of the infamous
Great White Brotherhood, which we will discuss in
detail later. Enoch was attributed with the building of
the first antediluvian ziggurats in Sumeria. Enoch was
also renowned in lore to be the first real builder of cities,
after the spirit of Cain. Enoch then, was the first Master
Mason.*

*All this suggests that the antediluvian Enoch was the
first sponsor of preparation for the deluge. He saved
the corrupted ancient knowledge through hieroglyphs
and secret storage houses for the spurious knowledge,
which were then further enhanced by the children of
Lamech and eventually found by Hermes after the flood.
The nine hidden vaults were believed to be subterranean
vaults stacked one on top of the other, while one of the
two famous Pillars of Lamech was manufactured out of
marble so that it would never burn and the second out
of laterus, some type of brick, so that it would not sink.
The pillar of brick had inscribed on it the seven spurious
sciences, while the pillar of marble had inscribed on it
directions to find the nine vaults.*

*Again, from Craft legends, the children of Lamech
inscribed the information as to the whereabouts of
the nine vaults of knowledge on the marble pillar. The
marble pillar was rendered to be, in early Masonic
writings, some form of obscure crystalline rock. The
information discovered on the marble pillar, of course,*

is why Hermarynes led the people of Ham back to Egypt after the Babel incident.

According to the Legend of Enoch, Solomon discovered these nine vaults during the excavation of the First Temple. Solomon did in fact excavate and discover antediluvian knowledge, but it is unlikely that this discovery was the original antediluvian knowledge; this Judean version of antediluvian knowledge likely came to be stored in Jerusalem as a secret and sacred relic of the exodus from Egypt. It is reasonable to expect that the original antediluvian knowledge was buried in Egypt, beneath the Great Pyramids, and in either Sumeria, beneath antediluvian ziggurats, or in Britain.

From the sacred hieroglyphs Enoch taught the original mysticism of the Sacred Sciences, complete with secretive, sacred ceremonies and rituals. Freemason Adept Albert Mackey informs us that Enoch was both idolatrous and a worshipper of the sun. It is clear that the branch of the sciences taught by Enoch, according to the Legend of Enoch, was not the pure brand but rather the spurious. The pure branch did not contain any mysticism whatsoever. It did not contain any secret rituals or ceremonies, and it was not kept in dark dungeons, hidden from the believers and followers of God. This reticent religious worship was only practiced by Cain's descendants and, therefore, was contrary to that of the ecclesiastical Enoch, who was the posterity of Seth.

Enoch (the evil) was then also attributed with implementing the worship of God through religious rites, a pillar of mysticism. The further we unveil the

*details from the legends of Freemasonry with regard to
Enoch, the larger the contradiction becomes between
the biblical records of the righteous Enoch and the
legend of the numinous Enoch revered by Freemasonry.
Yet Freemasonry regards the mystical Enoch as the
ecclesiastical Enoch. Strange indeed, unless one
considers that Freemasonry truly upholds the doctrine
that mysticism is in fact the pure religion and the pure
branch of heavenly knowledge that descended from
Adam through Seth and Noah, coupled with the concept
that orthodox Christianity and orthodox Judaism are, in
fact, equal partners in the evil religion.*

*Enoch fuses to mysticism when we consider the second
definition of the Hebrew name Enoch. Not only can
Enoch be translated as "consecrated," which applies
perfectly to the biblical Enoch, but also it can be
translated as "initiated," which applies perfectly to the
Enoch of Freemasonry. You see, mysticism comes with
secret ceremonies to initiate the selected elite into secret
societies, thereby preserving the sacred knowledge and
truths with the elite, who were known as the initiates.*

*Abbey Robin, who authored Recherches sur les
Initiations Anciennes et Modernes in 1780, traced the
ancient initiations to the virtuous intercessors with the
gods, which is certainly how Freemasonry looks upon
Enoch. Certainly, Mercury was considered a messenger
to the gods that could also be viewed as an intercessor,
just as Thoth was viewed as an intercessor with the
gods of Egypt. Furthermore, Hermes was the one who
transmitted the knowledge of the gods concerning
their secret names, weaknesses, and abilities to control
the gods to humankind, again suggesting he was an*

intercessor with the gods. Enoch most certainly was considered as one who interceded with the gods. Finally, Enoch is one of the Craft's legendary founders who gave humankind the art of building (masonry).

Therefore, the Enoch who invented hieroglyphs was attributed with introducing formalized mysticism that corrupted the antediluvian and postdiluvian worlds. According to the Anderson Theory, Enoch was credited with founding the Craft, no doubt because he was the first to formalize it in written form. Understand then, that masonry, the Seven Liberal Sciences, the additional illicit heavenly knowledge from the fallen angels, and mysticism, in which all this has been cleverly encoded, are all part of the same spurious religion of Enoch, Cain, fallen angels, and Nephilim. It is no wonder that Enoch was held in such high regard by the descendants of the spurious religion of the postdiluvian epoch. Enoch was truly the spurious patron saint, the founding father of mysticism and Freemasonry.

As we draw back the veil from this infamous hero of antiquity, we learn even more about his corruption. The Babylonians affirmed Enoch was an expert on the stars, just as the Enoch of Seth's lineage would have been an expert in the peculiar wisdom of the stars, as recorded by Josephus and Craft legends. However, the Babylonians stated Enoch used his knowledge of the stars to invent astrology, an obvious perversion of the intended application for astronomy. In The Legend of Enoch, Enoch is the patriarch who discovered the knowledge of the zodiac, which he wrapped into astrology. He also established festivals and sacrifices to the sun during the periods when the luminary began to enter a new

This is heavy and difficult to digest, but it explains the sun symbology
we see in Freemasonry and how it all began with the lineage of Cain
through his son Enoch. Freemasons credit this Enoch with inventing
hieroglyphics as a method of symbolic code communication, understood
only by "initiates"—the literal meaning of the name *Enoch*. He inscribed
these hieroglyphic symbols on "marble pillars" (granite obelisks that the
Freemasons are so enamored with). Remember, we discussed the obelisks
and marble pillars and their meaning in a previous chapter, and what God
thinks of them.

The Enoch who walked with God was an initiate of God Himself. The
Enoch, son of Cain, was an initiate of the counterfeit god represented by
the sun—Lucifer. Both were named *Enoch*, and both were "initiates," but
of their respective gods.

Note the marble pillars of Freemasonry represent the guarded ancient knowledge of the evil Enoch

While Cain and Enoch may belong to the most ancient origins of the pre-flood world, they are credited by the Masons as being its earliest founders. The "Hermes" figure mentioned by Wayne in that chapter appears after the flood. Hermes serves a post-flood link to Enoch, son of Cain, rediscovering the hieroglyphs of Enoch in the pyramids—symbols that contained the "secret sciences" which would empower and eventually deify Nimrod, his wife, and his son as gods.

Who, then, was Hermes if there is no mention of him in the Bible? Thank God for conspiracy theorists, who have existed as long as God's enemies have conspired against Him. One of those conspiracy theorists was the highly criticized Rev. Alexander Hislop, who I previously mentioned. Referring to his fascinating work *The Two Babylons*, I have included an excerpt here that explains who this highly revered character was. Hermes's fame extended from Babylon to Rome, and he remains an important figure in the secret sun-worshipping societies, especially Freemasonry:

*** The composition of Her-mes is, first, from "Her,"
which, in Chaldee, is synonymous with Ham, or Khem,
"the burnt one." As "her" also, like Ham, signified "The
hot or burning one," this name formed a foundation for
covertly identifying Ham with the "Sun," and so deifying
the great patriarch, after whose name the land of Egypt
was called, in connection with the sun. Khem, or Ham,
in his own name was openly worshipped in later ages in
the land of Ham (BUNSEN); but this would have been
too daring at first. By means of "Her," the synonym,
however, the way was paved for this. "Her" is the name
of Horus, who is identified with the sun (BUNSEN),
which shows the real etymology of the name to be from
the verb to which I have traced it. Then, secondly,
"Mes," is from Mesheh (or, without the last radical,
which is omissible), Mesh, "to draw forth." In Egyptian,
we have Ms in the sense of "to bring forth" (BUNSEN,
Hieroglyphical Signs), which is evidently a different form
of the same word. In the passive sense, also, we find Ms
used (BUNSEN, Vocabulary). The radical meaning of
Mesheh in Stockii Lexicon, is given in Latin "Extraxit,"
and our English word "extraction," as applied to birth
or descent, shows that there is a connection between the
generic meaning of this word and birth. This derivation
will be found to explain the meaning of the names of the
Egyptian kings, Ramesses and Thothmes, the former
evidently being "The son of Ra," or the Sun; the latter
in like manner, being "The son of Thoth." For the very
same reason Her-mes is the "Son of Her, or Ham," the
burnt one--that is, Cush.*[21]

Cush, the son of Ham and father of Nimrod, was Hermes—the one
who rediscovered the hieroglyphs of Enoch after the flood. In fact, in

---

21   *The Two Babylons*, Chapter II Subsection I

tracing the travels of the prodigy of the flood survivors, we see that they journeyed in a straight line westward from the east, just as they began construction of the Tower of Babel in Genesis, chapter 11:

> *And the whole earth was of one language, and of one speech.*
>
> *And it came to pass, as they journeyed from the east, that they found a plain in the land of Shinar; and they dwelt there.*
>
> *And they said one to another, Go to, let us make brick, and burn them thoroughly. And they had brick for stone, and slime had they for morter.*
>
> *And they said, Go to, let us build us a city and a tower, whose top may reach unto heaven; and let us make us a name, lest we be scattered abroad upon the face of the whole earth. (Genesis 11:1-4 KJV)*

Before I continue, I have an important side note to address. It is very important to remember that when you're engaged in Bible research, double-check and compare various translations against the King James Version, searching out discrepancies. This is one of those instances where, depending on the translation, the descendants of Noah after the flood might have been traveling east—or maybe west. They could only have traveled in one direction unless they were going in circles.

If you read the King James, it says *from the east*, while most translations say *to the east*. This is after the flood and Noah's prodigy are traveling to their respective settlements. In this verse, they journeyed to the land of Shinar (Sumer, Chaldea—the location of Babylon). Which direction was it, and why does it matter?

It matters if you're interested in where Noah's Ark may have landed. The assumed location of the ark explored by Ron Wyatt in the 1970s and 1980s is Mount Ararat in Turkey. Pastor and author Rick Renner has also confirmed wholeheartedly that this is indeed the Ark of Noah.

This location investigated by Ron Wyatt is north of Shinar, so now we have three possible directions to consider. Did the ark land in the east? Somewhere along the Mediterranean coast to the west? Or to the north, in Turkey?

I believe Pastor Renner strongly believes that the ark is on Mount Ararat in Turkey, which suggests we may be missing a significant part of the story. I personally believe the ark originally landed above Nepal in the Himalayas and may have drifted to the Turkey location later. There is a small amount of circumstantial evidence pointing to this region. One example is that *Himalaya* can be phonetically interpreted as Hebrew for "cold abode of God" (*Himal-a-yah?*). Another is that the Nepal region produces excellent grapes, figs, and other fruit, and we know that shortly after the flood, Noah overindulged in his wine stock (Genesis 9:21).

Another reason is geographical: the Himalayas lie in a straight-line due east of Shinar, while the proposed location of the ark in Turkey is north. Additionally, Mount Ararat was named by Marco Polo in the thirteenth century, based on the Armenian name *Agri Dagi*, which he assumed to be the biblical site of Noah's Ark. Another reason is that Genesis 7:20 states that the mountains were covered by fifteen cubits of water, or 22.5 feet. I read the Bible literally, and I understand this to mean the highest mountain was fifteen cubits under water. This matters because if Noah's Ark was thirty cubits in height, it would have had approximately fifteen cubits of draft and barely cleared the highest mountain—Mount Everest.

So, to clarify, I believe Rick Renner and Ron Wyatt both positively identified the ark in Turkey. I just do not know how it got there or why the location does not match the biblical narrative. It's one of those mysteries that must, for now, remain unknown.

That information aside, one of my default translations is the International Standard Version, as its translators attempted to utilize other biblical resources to accurately determine the intended language of the original authors. The ISV agrees with the King James Version, translated from the Masoretic Texts, that Noah's descendants traveled from the east. I think this might be important for several reasons. In tracing Nimrod's founding of Babylon, Ninevah, etc., we see a pattern of movement westward, as if in search of something—even though Egypt and its ancient knowledge lay to the south. I believe Nimrod was searching for Mount Hermon, where fallen angel rebellion began, which lies due west of Shinar. A monument in his name still stands there today. Mount Nimrod is slightly west of the summit of Mount Hermon, with strange monuments credited to Nimrod, though history has obscured much of the truth.

The land of Shinar lies in a perfectly straight-line west of Mount Everest, and Mount Hermon rests on that same latitude due west of Shinar. I find this noteworthy because it aligns with Genesis 11:2, while the current ark location does not. If Ron Wyatt and Rick Renner are correct, the only possible answer is that the ark drifted to Turkey from somewhere east of Shinar, the direction from which Noah's descendants migrated. If God says *east* in Genesis 11:2, then it was east.

Returning to Hermes, he was Cush, son of Ham and grandson of Noah. Cush was the father of Nimrod, and Ham was Khem, the father of the Khemites (Egypt). While the name *Cush*[22] is disputed among scholars as to its origin, Hislop attributes it to a Chaldean root synonymous with "chaos."

Hislop had much more to share on the subject of Cush and Nimrod that helps explain much of what would remain unanswered without his contributions:

> *Now, Hermes was the great original prophet of idolatry;*
> *for he was recognised by the pagans as the author of*
> *their religious rites, and the interpreter of the gods.*
> *The distinguished Gesenius identifies him with the*
> *Babylonian Nebo, as the prophetic god; and a statement*
> *of Hyginus shows that he was known as the grand*
> *agent in that movement which produced the division*
> *of tongues. His words are these: "For many ages men*
> *lived under the government of Jove [evidently not the*

---

22   The name of Cush is also Khus, for *sh* frequently passes in Chaldee into *s*; and Khus, in pronunciation, legitimately becomes *Khawos*, or, without the digamma, *Khaos*.

*Roman Jupiter, but the Jehovah of the Hebrews], without
cities and without laws, and all speaking one language.
But after that Mercury interpreted the speeches of men
(whence an interpreter is called Hermeneutes), the
same individual distributed the nations. Then discord
began."**

*Here there is a manifest enigma. How could Mercury
or Hermes have any need to interpret the speeches of
mankind when they "all spake one language"? To find
out the meaning of this, we must go to the language
of the Mysteries. Peresh, in Chaldee, signifies "to
interpret"; but was pronounced by old Egyptians and
by Greeks, and often by the Chaldees themselves, in the
same way as "Peres," to "divide." Mercury, then, or
Hermes, or Cush, "the son of Ham," was the "DIVIDER
of the speeches of men." He, it would seem, had been
the ringleader in the scheme for building the great city
and tower of Babel; and, as the well known title of
Hermes,--"the interpreter of the gods," would indicate,
had encouraged them, in the name of God, to proceed
in their presumptuous enterprise, and so had caused
the language of men to be divided, and themselves to be
scattered abroad on the face of the earth. Now look at
the name of Belus or Bel, given to the father of Ninus, or
Nimrod, in connection with this. While the Greek name
Belus represented both the Baal and Bel of the Chaldees,
these were nevertheless two entirely distinct titles. These
titles were both alike often given to the same god, but
they had totally different meanings. Baal, as we have
already seen, signified "The Lord"; but Bel signified
"The Confounder." When, then, we read that Belus, the
father of Ninus, was he that built or founded Babylon,
can there be a doubt, in what sense it was that the title of*

I personally find the work of Rev. Hislop very useful. Though it is scarcely cited by scholars and highly disputed, Hislop's research explains much in just a few paragraphs—helping to solve puzzles that would otherwise remain clandestine and mysterious. For example, we learn that Cush was deified as Bel the Confounder, first post-flood author of chaos. His name was also Hermes, father of Nimrod and divider of the languages by curse. From this name we derive the word *hermeneutics*, applied by scholars to describe the methods used to interpret the Bible. It seems somewhat shameful to apply the term to God's Word, knowing this bit of trivia.

We also know from Hislop's work that Mercury and Hermes are the same person or deity, later absorbed into the pantheon of Greco-Roman deities. Mercury is the source of the name for Wednesday, or *Miercoles* in Spanish. The English "Wednesday" comes from the Norse god Odin, or Woden, who was likewise identified with Mercury—appearing in different cultures, languages, and forms, yet representing the same deity. The god Janus gives us the name of the month January. This makes sense if we recognize that Cush, Hermes, Mercury, and Janus are all the same person: the father of the deified Nimrod, whose birthday was celebrated at the winter solstice. Since the time of Constantine, this is why Christians have celebrated Jesus's birth in December, coinciding with the Roman holiday.

---

23   The Two Babylons, Chapter II Subsection I

Nimrod and Tammuz are the reason for sun worship. The winter solstice celebrates the end of the shortest day of the year and return of the sun on the third day after the solstice. January, named after the father of Nimrod (Janus = Cush), is the first month of the new year following the solstice, when Nimrod was supposedly born. Everything in our lives is connected to this post-flood idolatrous family of Cush and Nimrod—carried from Babylon to Greece and Rome, and then to the rest of the world. The sons of disobedience have plagued the sons of God with deception after deception, nonstop, for nearly six thousand years.

Sun worship, then, is an ancient form of idolatry that ties directly to Nimrod and Cush after the flood, and back to Enoch, the son of Cain, before the flood. This is why both Nimrod and Enoch, son of Cain, are considered the original Masons by the Freemasons. Enoch formed the language of hieroglyphs, preserved in stone pillars as seen in Freemasonry (see Masonic chart on the previous page), carrying forward the knowledge of the sacred sciences known only to the earliest Adamic generations. Nimrod and his father, Cush, were the first post-flood prodigies to engage in the same worship of their father and patriarch, Enoch, son of Cain. According to the Masons, sun worship is the oldest religion, tied to the lineage of Cain.

Cush and Nimrod stood in blatant opposition to God, as do the thirtieth-degree and higher Freemasons today, by decrees nearly as old as mankind itself. This is difficult to comprehend, yet the evidence is before us daily in symbols, calendars, and festivities, as entire nations continue to celebrate Babylonian cultural beliefs thousands of years later. This is as amazing as it is terrifying that, through subtle deceptions over time, most of mankind has been trapped into unknowingly honoring Satan in one form or another.

My personal pet peeve is Easter and how it erased the Passover during the time of Constantine. Due to Constantine's hatred for the Jews, the celebration of Passover was no longer permitted. The first Sunday after the spring equinox, coinciding with the fertility rites of Easter, became a Christian holiday replacing Passover (Council of Nicaea 325AD). From Babylonian culture, which became Roman culture rooted in the worship of Nimrod, Semiramis, and Tammuz—sun worship and Luciferian—we inherited Easter Sunday instead of Passover.

Signs and symbols are how the sons of disobedience communicate since the time of Enoch, son of Cain.

This is the ancient work of Satan and his sons of disobedience, who continue deceiving the masses today. However, it would be far too simple if the Freemasons were the only willing enemies of God. There exists another group—an even more powerful elite secret society—that the Masons themselves fear and respect: *the Society of Jesus.*

How could such a noble-sounding name be associated with anything negative? It all began with Martin Luther on October 31, 1517, when he nailed his Ninety-Five Theses to the door of the Castle Church in Wittenburg, Germany. This act ignited the Protestant Reformation. Once again, Roman authority was challenged by Christianity, just as it had been by the Caesars fifteen centuries earlier. The proliferation of Christianity in ancient Rome was a major factor in the fall of the Roman Empire after Christ. In Christianity, there is only one "pontifex maximus," who is Christ Himself, not the Caesars or the popes of Rome. Early Christians, or course, knew that the Caesar was a mere mortal, never to be revered as a god or as a bridge to God. Christianity had to be eliminated, or the Caesars risked becoming obscure politico-religious relics, replaced by a higher authority.

Twelve centuries later, after the reign of Emperor Constantine—who by all measures was the true first pope of Rome—Martin Luther unleashed heaven's armies upon the papacy, directly challenging the supposed infallibility of papal authority. His challenge was an assault on Rome itself and was met with a violent response.

It is important to understand that, from a historical perspective, the Roman Empire never actually died. Rather, the authority of Rome was a transition of power from Caesars to popes, beginning under Constantine. Rome has continued to rule the world from the shadows of secrecy, until Martin Luther threatened to topple papal authority through the Protestant Reformation. I find it fascinating that Martin Luther chose Satan's highest holy day of Halloween—on October 31—to begin the Reformation that once again threatened the Roman Empire. Very poetic indeed! Thank you, Martin Luther!

The Society of Jesus was the papal response to Protestantism, formed to eliminate any threat it posed to papal rule. Wherever the truth of the real Jesus thrives under Protestant theology, the Jesuits of the Society of Jesus operate in secrecy to extinguish every threat that truth could bring to the papacy. The first Jesuit general to lead this militant force was Ignatius de Loyola (1491–1556).

Loyola, once a soldier in the Spanish Army, claimed to have turned to religion after being hit in the leg by a cannonball during a battle with France. He was the son of a noble and wealthy family with strong ties to the papacy and Pope Paul III. Ignatius de Loyola founded the Society of Jesus between 1536 and 1540, depending upon where you research, to function as a military force against Protestantism. From the first Jesuits under "General" Ignatius de Loyola, the military arm of the Roman Catholic Church was established. The Papal Bull of September 27, 1540, known as *Regimini militantis ecclesiae* ("Governance of the Militant Church"), transformed Roman Catholicism into a militant force more brutal and cruel than the Caesars themselves. Since its founding, Jesuit leaders have borne the title of general, and a strict military discipline was codified in *Loyola's Spiritual Exercises*, which set the rules for the Order.

The Jesuits (Society of Jesus) formed what the papacy called the "Counter-Reformation," designed to suppress all Protestant movements under papal rule by force. The Spanish Inquisitions, organized in the late 1400s to eradicate Judaism, escalated under the Vatican's militant Jesuit arm. In fact, the inquisitions were imposed in every country under the assumed political authority of the papacy. Throughout the revived Roman Empire under papal authority, Protestantism was publicly declared "heresy" and punished ferociously. With the Jesuit force under Loyola, the papacy resumed the torture practices of the Caesars to thwart any uprisings against papal authority or any dispute that the pope was the "Infallible Vicar of Christ" on earth.

It was obvious that the Protestant Reformation threatened to exterminate the successive reign of the "pontifex maximus" line of Caesars and popes. Protestantism attempted to do what the early church could not accomplish during the time of the Caesars: to leave Rome buried in the ashes of pagan relics. The Society of Jesus was, therefore, a papal call to war against Protestantism, led by its founder, Ignatius de Loyola.

If it sometimes seems as though there is no difference between Catholicism and Protestantism, it is because the Jesuit force over the last five centuries has purposely blurred the theological lines. A few evangelical pastors have even gone so far as to comment publicly that there is no difference between Catholicism and Protestantism since the Reformation. They are, of course, spiritually blinded. And while it may appear to be true, it should not be. Protestantism has all but died under the constant, relentless Jesuit infiltration of every sector of society—from public-school textbooks to churches, and even into the highest levels of government, where they operate as power brokers around the world. Progressivism and universalism are mere tools of a fascist power that severs the legs of freedom under a sovereign God.

That well-camouflaged, deadly fascist power exerting the pope's authority over global affairs since September 27, 1540, is the Society of Jesus. Every Freemason, Illuminati, or other occult secret society, along with high-ranking political authorities, must kiss the hand of the pope and pay tithes to the Vatican—or be handed over to those who do.

A very controversial ex-Jesuit named Alberto Rivera wrote the following introduction to Edmond Paris's book *The Secret History of the Jesuits*, which I want to share with you:

> *The most dangerous of men are those who appear very religious, especially when they are organized and in a position of authority. They have the deep respect of the people who are ignorant of their ungodly push for power behind the scenes.*

> *These religious men, who pretend to love God, will resort to murder, incite revolution and wars if necessary to help their cause. They are crafty, intelligent, smooth religious politicians who live in a shadowy world of secrets, intrigue, and phony holiness. This pattern, seen in "The Secret History of the Jesuits," spiritually speaking can be seen in the Scribes, Pharisees and Sadducees at the time of Jesus Christ. This same evil spirit directed the Roman emperors to issue the ten murderous decrees to persecute the early Christian church.*

> *The "Early Fathers" observed most of the ancient Babylonian system plus Jewish theology and Greek philosophy. They all perverted most of the teachings of Christ and His apostles. They paved the way for the Roman Catholic machine that was to come into existence. Piously, they attacked, perverted, added to and took away from the Bible. This religious antichrist spirit working through them is seen again when Ignatius de Loyola created the Jesuits to secretly accomplish two major goals for the Roman Catholic Institution: 1) universal political power, and 2) a universal church, in*

fulfillment of the prophecies of Revelation 6, 13, 17 and 18.

By the time Ignatius de Loyola arrived on the scene, the Protestant Reformation had seriously damaged the Roman Catholic system. Ignatius de Loyola came to the conclusion that the only way his "church" could survive was by enforcing the canons and doctrines on the temporal power of the pope and the Roman Catholic institution; not by just destroying the physical life of the people alone as the Dominican priests were doing through the Inquisition, but by infiltration and penetration into every sector of life. Protestantism must be conquered and used for the benefit of the popes. That was Ignatius de Loyola's personal proposal, among others, to Pope Paul III. Jesuits immediately went to work secretly infiltrating ALL the Protestant groups including their families, places of work, hospitals, schools, colleges, etc. Today, the Jesuits have almost completed that mission.

The Bible puts the power of a local church into the hands of a Godly pastor. But the cunning Jesuits successfully managed over the years to remove that power into the hands of denomination headquarters, and have now pushed almost all of the Protestant denominations into the arms of the Vatican. This is exactly what Ignatius de Loyola set out to accomplish: a universal church and the end of Protestantism.

As you read "The Secret History of the Jesuits," you will see there is a parallel between the religious and political sectors. The author, Mr. Paris, reveals the penetration

There are many valuable resources to choose from for identifying the true history of the Jesuits and how they manipulate everything from political power to cultural phenomena, Hollywood filmmakers, public-school curricula, and even financial and monetary systems. The Jesuits stand as the pinnacle of power among the sons of disobedience. Under Satan's authority, there is no higher earthly power. Organizations like the Freemasons serve merely as infantry foot soldiers for a higher authority that leads directly to the papacy of Rome. This is even truer today than it was at the time of Loyola, and I am certain Ignatius de Loyola would be proud of how his Jesuit force not only conquered Protestantism—having Christians chase Easter eggs and chocolate bunnies instead of celebrating Passover—but in the process, conquered the world. There is no more powerful or feared political figure than the pope, whose ring has been kissed by every global superpower leader. What could more surely seal one's fate as a global political power than defying the pope?

There is no coincidence in global events or agendas—the Jesuits are the masterminds of conspiracies at the pinnacle of global power. Their conspiracy is as old as the sons of Cain. There is conspiracy theory, and then there is willful ignorance of an obvious conspiracy.

For example, I have been outspoken in my attitude regarding "geoengineering" in the name of combating "climate change." While I believe we should be good stewards of the planet God gave us, I despise the lie that global weather disasters are the direct result of human existence. The people behind this political agenda belong to the same secret societies whose corporations produce the chemicals that are killing us and destroying the environment. In their complete absence of shame, they create unbelievable narratives and promote propaganda until the keywords become common household terms.

In the 1950s through the 1970s, we were told the earth would freeze over in a mini ice age within eight to ten years. Then in the 1980s and 1990s, we had global warming that threatened to submerge Florida beneath the Atlantic within the same time frame. Now we face "climate change," where every weather event is reported as a rare phenomenon. They even resurrected Al Gore from the DNC graveyard to jump start the dead battery of weather scare tactics. These are well-thought-out campaigns, and millions of low-information voters believe them when they hear them. *Do you want to guess who does not buy what the devil is selling? "Those who are led by the Spirit of God, these are the sons of God." The Holy Spirit is your ultimate warning device!*

When COVID struck, most true Christians recognized that too much about it simply didn't add up. It seemed too much like a staged event to anyone that was paying close attention. Most true Christians do not trust anyone in positions of power—political or otherwise—because we know they do not worship our God. Those who are led by the Spirit of God are the primary targets for extermination by the Jesuits and Freemason "sons of disobedience."

Whatever propaganda is promoted on prime-time corporate media—especially under the disguise of "we're all going to die if you don't..." or "we need trillions to save the planet"—trust instead in the Holy Spirit, who inspires and guides you. This is one of the gifts that comes with the gift of the Spirit. It is not the wisdom of God to remain blissful or stupefied while the sons of disobedience implement their devices of evil. Rather, "greater things than these shall you do"!

> *Truly, truly I say to you, the one who believes in Me,*
> *the works that I do, he will do also; and greater works*
> *than these he will do; because I am going to the*
> *Father. And whatever you ask in My name, this I will*
> *do, so that the Father may be glorified in the Son. If*

you ask Me anything in My name, I will do it. (John 14:12-14 NASB)

The sons of God coming together in prayer are far more powerful than Loyola's Jesuit army, the Illuminati Ba'al worshippers, or the Freemasons. Prayer is a nuclear weapon when it rises from an atoned and repentant heart in the body of Christ gathered in His name, who promises, "Ask in my name and I will do it." The sons of God (the body of Christ, the bride) have been spiritually complacent for too long. A book of Acts/Mark chapter 16 force of Christian soldiers, armed with the blood of Yehshua and the Word of God, can remove mountains (principalities) from their places.

Was 9/11 a sign of a weakened body of Christ? Is it possible that the COVID "planned-demic" might never have happened if the body of Christ had been spiritually healthy? The sons of God are the bride, and the bride is the fulfillment of Christ on earth, led by the Spirit of God. For the bride to sit peering outside through the curtains with a spirit of fear, rather than petitioning before the Father in intercession, is like having an arsenal of unfired artillery while a common thief ransacks your home.

The sons of God have the power to stop the sons of disobedience in the name of Yehshua, with the authority given through His holy, precious blood. Can we agree to do our job and begin pushing them back in their evil schemes?

Before I get distracted again, I want you to read the oath taken by the Jesuits, still recited today. I do not know when the oath began, only that it continues.

Jesuit Extreme Oath of Induction

The following is the Jesuit Extreme Oath of Induction given to high-ranking Jesuits only. This oath is taken from the book Subterranean Rome by Carlos Didier, translated from the French, and published in New York in 1843.

*When a Jesuit of the minor rank is to be elevated
to command, he is conducted into the Chapel of the
Convent of the Order, where there are only three others
present, the principal or Superior standing in front of
the altar. On either side stands a monk, one of whom
holds a banner of yellow and white, which are the Papal
colors, and the other a black banner with a dagger and
red cross above a skull and crossbones, with the word
INRI, and below them the words IUSTUM, NECAR,
REGES, IMPIOUS. The meaning of which is: It is just
to exterminate or annihilate impious or heretical Kings,
Governments, or Rulers. Upon the floor is a red cross at
which the postulant or candidate kneels. The Superior
hands him a small black crucifix, which he takes in his
left hand and presses to his heart, and the Superior at
the same time presents to him a dagger, which he grasps
by the blade and holds the point against his heart, the
Superior still holding it by the hilt, and thus addresses
the postulant:*

Superior:

*My son, heretofore you have been taught to act the
dissembler: among Roman Catholics to be a Roman
Catholic, and to be a spy even among your own
brethren; to believe no man, to trust no man. Among
the Reformers, to be a reformer; among the Huguenots,
to be a Huguenot; among the Calvinists, to be a
Calvinist; among other Protestants, generally to be a
Protestant, and obtaining their confidence, to seek even
to preach from their pulpits, and to denounce with all
the vehemence in your nature our Holy Religion and
the Pope; and even to descend so low as to become a
Jew among Jews, that you might be enabled to gather*

*together all information for the benefit of your Order as
a faithful soldier of the Pope.*

*You have been taught to insidiously plant the seeds of
jealousy and hatred between communities, provinces,
states that were at peace, and incite them to deeds of
blood, involving them in war with each other, and to
create revolutions and civil wars in countries that were
independent and prosperous, cultivating the arts and the
sciences and enjoying the blessings of peace. To take
sides with the combatants and to act secretly with your
brother Jesuit, who might be engaged on the other side,
but openly opposed to that with which you might be
connected, only that the Church might be the gainer in
the end, in the conditions fixed in the treaties for peace
and that the end justifies the means.*

*You have been taught your duty as a spy, to gather all
statistics, facts and information in your power from
every source; to ingratiate yourself into the confidence
of the family circle of Protestants and heretics of every
class and character, as well as that of the merchant, the
banker, the lawyer, among the schools and universities,
in parliaments and legislatures, and the judiciaries and
councils of state, and to be all things to all men, for the
Pope's sake, whose servants we are unto death.*

*You have received all your instructions heretofore as
a novice, a neophyte, and have served as co-adjurer,
confessor and priest, but you have not yet been invested
with all that is necessary to command in the Army
of Loyola in the service of the Pope. You must serve
the proper time as the instrument and executioner as*

*directed by your superiors; for none can command here
who has not consecrated his labors with the blood of
the heretic; for "without the shedding of blood no man
can be saved." Therefore, to fit yourself for your work
and make your own salvation sure, you will, in addition
to your former oath of obedience to your order and
allegiance to the Pope, repeat after me---*

The Extreme Oath of the Jesuits:

*"1, _ now, in the presence of Almighty God, the Blessed
Virgin Mary, the blessed Michael the Archangel, the
blessed St. John the Baptist, the holy Apostles St.
Peter and St. Paul and all the saints and sacred hosts
of heaven, and to you, my ghostly father, the Superior
General of the Society of Jesus, founded by St. Ignatius
Loyola in the Pontificate of Paul the Third, and
continued to the present, do by the womb of the virgin,
the matrix of God, and the rod of Jesus Christ, declare
and swear, that his holiness the Pope is Christ's Vice-
regent and is the true and only head of the Catholic or
Universal Church throughout the earth; and that by
virtue of the keys of binding and loosing, given to his
Holiness by my Savior, Jesus Christ, he hath power to
depose heretical kings, princes, states, commonwealths
and governments, all being illegal without his sacred
confirmation and that they may safely be destroyed.
Therefore, to the utmost of my power I shall and will
defend this doctrine of his Holiness' right and custom
against all usurpers of the heretical or Protestant
authority whatever, especially the Lutheran of Germany,
Holland, Denmark, Sweden, Norway, and the now
pretended authority and churches of England and
Scotland, and branches of the same now established in*

342

*Ireland and on the Continent of America and elsewhere;
and all adherents in regard that they be usurped and
heretical, opposing the sacred Mother Church of Rome.
I do now renounce and disown any allegiance as due to
any heretical king, prince or state named Protestants or
Liberals, or obedience to any of the laws, magistrates or
officers.*

*I do further declare that the doctrine of the churches
of England and Scotland, of the Calvinists, Huguenots
and others of the name Protestants or Liberals to be
damnable and they themselves damned who will not
forsake the same.*

*I do further declare, that I will help, assist, and advise
all or any of his Holiness' agents in any place wherever
I shall be, in Switzerland, Germany, Holland, Denmark,
Sweden, Norway, England, Ireland or America, or in
any other Kingdom or territory I shall come to, and do
my uttermost to extirpate the heretical Protestants or
Liberals' doctrines and to destroy all their pretended
powers, regal or otherwise.*

*I do further promise and declare, that notwithstanding I
am dispensed with, to assume my religion heretical, for
the propaganda of the Mother Church's interest, to keep
secret and private all her agents' counsels from time to
time, as they may entrust me and not to divulge, directly
or indirectly, by word, writing or circumstance whatever;
but to execute all that shall be proposed, given in charge
or discovered unto me, by you, my ghostly father, or any
of this sacred covenant.*

*I do further promise and declare, that I will have no
opinion or will of my own, or any mental reservation
whatever, even as a corpse or cadaver (perinde ac
cadaver), but will unhesitatingly obey each and every
command that I may receive from my superiors in the
Militia of the Pope and of Jesus Christ.*

*That I may go to any part of the world withersoever
I may be sent, to the frozen regions of the North, the
burning sands of the desert of Africa, or the jungles
of India, to the centers of civilization of Europe, or to
the wild haunts of the barbarous savages of America,
without murmuring or repining, and will be submissive
in all things whatsoever communicated to me.*

*I furthermore promise and declare that I will, when
opportunity present, make and wage relentless war,
secretly or openly, against all heretics, Protestants
and Liberals, as I am directed to do, to extirpate and
exterminate them from the face of the whole earth; and
that I will spare neither age, sex or condition; and that
I will hang, waste, boil, flay, strangle and bury alive
these infamous heretics, rip up the stomachs and wombs
of their women and crush their infants' heads against
the walls, in order to annihilate forever their execrable
race. That when the same cannot be done openly, I will
secretly use the poisoned cup, the strangulating cord,
the steel of the poniard or the leaden bullet, regardless
of the honor, rank, dignity, or authority of the person
or persons, whatever may be their condition in life,
either public or private, as I at any time may be directed
so to do by any agent of the Pope or Superior of the
Brotherhood of the Holy Faith, of the Society of Jesus.*

*In confirmation of which, I hereby dedicate my life, my
soul and all my corporal powers, and with this dagger
which I now receive, I will subscribe my name written in
my own blood, in testimony thereof; and should I prove
false or weaken in my determination, may my brethren
and fellow soldiers of the Militia of the Pope cut off my
hands and my feet, and my throat from ear to ear, my
belly opened and sulphur burned therein, with all the
punishment that can be inflicted upon me on earth and
my soul be tortured by demons in an eternal hell forever!*

*All of which, I, _, do swear by the Blessed Trinity and
blessed Sacraments, which I am now to receive, to
perform and on my part to keep inviolable; and do call
all the heavenly and glorious host of heaven to witness
the blessed Sacrament of the Eucharist, and witness the
same further with my name written and with the point
of this dagger dipped in my own blood and sealed in the
face of this holy covenant."*

*(He receives the wafer from the Superior and writes his
name with the point of his dagger dipped in his own
blood taken from over his heart.)*

Superior:

*"You will now rise to your feet and I will instruct you in
the Catechism necessary to make yourself known to any
member of the Society of Jesus belonging to this rank.*

*In the first place, you, as a Brother Jesuit, will with
another mutually make the ordinary sign of the cross
as any ordinary Roman Catholic would; then one cross*

his wrists, the palms of his hands open, and the other
in answer crosses his feet, one above the other; the first
points with forefinger of the right hand to the center of
the palm of the left, the other with the forefinger of the
left hand points to the center of the palm of the right;
the first then with his right hand makes a circle around
his head, touching it; the other then with the forefinger
of his left hand touches the left side of his body just
below his heart; the first then with his right hand draws
it across the throat of the other, and the latter then
with a dagger down the stomach and abdomen of the
first. The first then says Iustum; and the other answers
Necar; the first Reges. The other answers Impious."
(The meaning of which has already been explained.)
"The first will then present a small piece of paper folded
in a peculiar manner, four times, which the other will
cut longitudinally and on opening the name Jesu will
be found written upon the head and arms of a cross
three times. You will then give and receive with him the
following questions and answers:

Question —From whither do you come? Answer — The
Holy faith.

Q. —Whom do you serve?

A. —The Holy Father at Rome, the Pope, and the Roman
Catholic Church Universal throughout the world.

Q. —Who commands you?

A. —The Successor of St. Ignatius Loyola, the founder of
the Society of Jesus or the Soldiers of Jesus Christ.

Q. —Who received you? A. —A venerable man in white
hair.

Q. —How?

A. —With a naked dagger, I kneeling upon the cross beneath the banners of the Pope and of our sacred order.

Q. —Did you take an oath?

A. —I did, to destroy heretics and their governments and rulers, and to spare neither age, sex nor condition. To be as a corpse without any opinion or will of my own, but to implicitly obey my Superiors in all things without hesitation of murmuring.

Q. —Will you do that? A. —I will.

Q. —How do you travel? A. —In the bark of Peter the fisherman.

Q. —Whither do you travel? A. —To the four quarters of the globe. Q. —For what purpose?

A. —To obey the orders of my general and Superiors and execute the will of the Pope and faithfully fulfill the conditions of my oaths.

Q. —Go ye, then, into all the world and take possession of all lands in the name of the Pope. He who will not accept him as the Vicar of Jesus and his Vice-regent on earth, let him be accursed and exterminated."

The Jesuits have many operatives in the form of secret societies such as the Freemasons. The Knights Templar are another strong arm of the Jesuits. They are very connected and worship the same god, which is not our God. This can be determined by their respective symbology. Notice the sunburst in the Knights Templar logo on the left:

The Knights Templar cross can be seen in numerous inconspicuous places that identify their members secretly in plain sight:

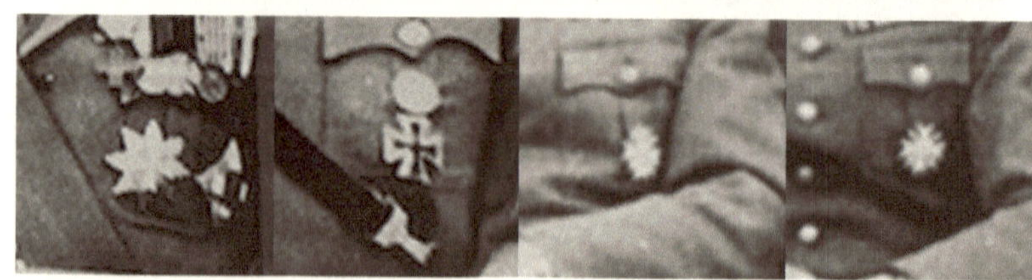

Notice the starburst and the Templar cross pinned on the pocket of the Nazi officer. Do these symbols have anything in common with Freemasonry? Of course they do.

The eight-pointed star is a shared symbol among all secret societies. They are all related and worship the same god esoterically. The Masons, Templars, Jesuits, and the Pope all play for the same team.

This is the official symbol of the Jesuits, or the Society of Jesus:

The Jesuits and Freemasons worship the same gods of Osiris, Isis, and Horus. This is the Jesuit logo on the left and a Jesuit gold coin from Germany with the all-seeing eye of Horus.

This German gold coin from 1616 begs the question, who came first, the Jesuits or the Freemasons? The Freemasons claim that Nimrod was their first Mason, but according to various sources, the first Grand Lodge of the Masons was built in London 1717. If Loyola was the first Jesuit in

1546, then the Jesuits preceded the Masons, and therefore Freemasonry was born out of the Society of Jesus. And if the Society of Jesus is the older brother of Freemasonry, then who is the grandfather of them both?

This brings me to another important point that piques my curiosity. In the ancient stone images of the Sumerian gods known as the Anunnaki—who I believe could only have been fallen angels—there is a common thread between these images:

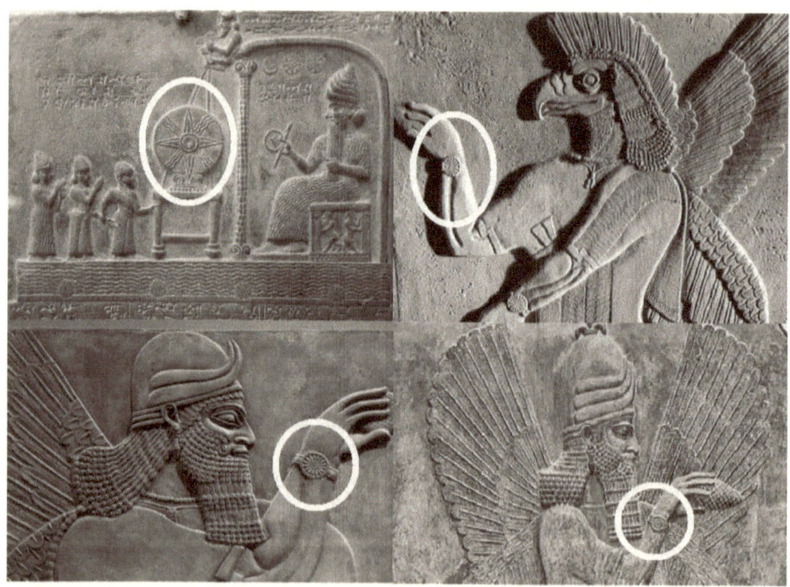

This wrist band worn by the Anunnaki (fallen sons of God) has been the subject of much speculation among historians and scholars without a single valid conclusion. Take a closer inspection:

It certainly has a lot in common with the sunbursts of Freemasonry and Jesuit symbolism. Notice the circle within a circle, a motif also employed in secret societies to represent the generative principle (human reproduction). I do not know precisely what this was on their wrist, but I find it intriguing, especially given that sun worship began long before the flood according to Freemason literature.

We should consider that Enoch, the son of Cain, did not invent a religion but rather fell into worship of the fallen sons of God, learning from their symbolism. The Anunnaki "gods" preceded the flood and were recorded in stone as wearing something resembling both the sunburst and the generative principle in the form of a wristband. If this was indeed a sunburst or generative principle symbol marking their allegiance to Lucifer, then we see the same symbology appearing in the most unexpected places even today.

On the right is Osiris, represented by one of the obelisks of Heliopolis centered within a circle, and on the left is the dome of Isis. Together, the obelisk and disc form a sundial that, at certain times of the year, casts a shadow from the male obelisk to the female dome and vice versa—representing the impregnation of Isis by Osiris's missing male part.

We haven't covered that yet, but there are several Jewish rabbinical legends that claim Nimrod's body was cut into fourteen pieces when he was attacked and killed by Shem, son of Noah. This account is not biblical, but it is certainly possible, as Shem outlived Abraham and Nimrod lived during Abraham's time. Semiramis found the male part, impregnated herself with it, and this is how Tammuz was born.

I'm not saying I believe the story. I'm just sharing the legend to explain the symbolism of the Vatican Square and Washington, DC, and what those who perpetuate these beliefs hold to be true. Whether factual or not, the important point is that *they believe it*.

The same symbology appears at the Washington Monument (Osiris) opposite the US Capitol dome (Isis). The Washington Monument is the pin-within-a-circle generative principle symbol of the Masons who constructed it.

The Vatican, the Jesuits, the Templars, and the Freemasons use the same symbology and worship the same god, which is not our God. Roman Catholicism functions exactly as Freemasonry, where the uninitiated believe they are worshipping one God, while the occult elitists worship another through their Ninth Circle cult or other cult. It is all Luciferian sun worship *("in its purest form")* that traces back to Enoch, son of Cain, before the flood.

Then after the flood, the "marble pillars" (obelisks) of Enoch were rediscovered by Cush, father of Nimrod—also known as Hermes, Mercury, and Bel. According to the Masons, Cush located these pillars and their hieroglyphs to the west of the ark's landing place, where Nimrod became the first world ruler from Babylon and constructed the Tower of Babel.

Here is a stone carving from the time of Nimrod showing the Anunnaki and sun worship together:

Notice the ancient moon, sun, and star symbology that still appears in Freemasonry, Jesuit, and Vatican symbolism. This is luciferian sun worship "in its purest form" (to quote the Masons), already present at the time of Nimrod.

These secret societies are linked together and all worship the same god—who is not our God. They are the sons of disobedience I mentioned as Group 3, those who know our God yet openly defy Him under Satan. Nimrod was not the first sun worshipper; Enoch, son of Cain, was the first type of Antichrist, forming global governments separate from the chosen line of Seth, son of Adam. From practically the beginning of time, the sons of disobedience descended through Cain were assimilating against God and His chosen line, from whom the "sons of God," led by the Spirit of God, would arrive in the future under the last Adam.

This is common knowledge among the powerful esoteric sons of disobedience, who collectively conspire against the chosen sons of God led by His Spirit. They hate us, and their ultimate desire is to destroy us.

Understanding that the sons of disobedience have existed since the time of Cain helps explain much about the passage in John chapter 8 that we discussed earlier. I use the AMP version for linguistic clarity:

> *I tell the things that I have seen at My Father's side [in His very presence]; so you also do the things that you heard from your father." They answered, "Abraham is our father." Jesus said to them, "If you are [truly] Abraham's children, then do the works of Abraham and follow his example. But as it is, you want to kill Me, a Man who has told you the truth, which I heard from God. This is not the way Abraham acted. You are doing the works of your [own] father." They said to Him, "We are not illegitimate children; we have one [spiritual] Father: God." Jesus said to them, "If God were your Father [but He is not], you would love and recognize Me, for I came from God [out of His very presence] and have arrived here. For I have not even come on My own initiative [as self-appointed], but He [is the One who] sent Me. Why do you misunderstand what I am saying? It is because [your spiritual ears are deaf and] you are unable to hear [the truth of] My word. You are of your father the devil, and it is your will to practice the desires [which are characteristic] of your father. He was a murderer from the beginning, and does not stand in the truth because there is no*

truth in him. When he lies, he speaks what is natural to him, for he is a liar and the father of lies and half-truths. But because I speak the truth, you do not believe Me [and continue in your unbelief]. Which one of you [has proof and] convicts Me of sin? If I speak truth, why do you not believe Me? Whoever is of God and belongs to Him hears [the truth of] God's words; for this reason you do not hear them: because you are not of God and you are not in fellowship with Him." (John 8:38-47 AMP)

No other passage of the Bible better demonstrates the division between the sons of God led by the Spirit and the sons of disobedience than this one. The Pharisee priests stood staunchly opposed to the truth, led by the father of lies and not by the Spirit of God. Had they received the Spirit of God, they would have recognized Yehshua for who He truly was through spiritual eyes. Yehshua states that their father was a liar and murderer *from the beginning*.

From the beginning of what? The same beginning of Genesis chapter 1—not the beginning of his existence. The devil was already in a fallen state when man's story on earth began. Cain was influenced (or possessed, as the name infers) by Satan, hearing only with ears of pride and envy, not with ears attuned to the Spirit of God.

One of the apocryphal books canonized in the Septuagint but later removed from our Bibles is the *Wisdom of Solomon*. I think there is little doubt that Solomon was its author, though that's another subject. In the context of the father of the sons of disobedience, here is a verse from that book:

For God created us for incorruption

and made us in the image of his own eternity,

but through an adversary's envy death entered the world,

We were not made in the image of disobedience and corruption. We were beautifully and wonderfully made (Psalm 139:14). God's adversary, through pride and envy, brought death into the world. The father of pride and envy (Satan) deceives the world by imposing his ways strategically, through psychological and sometimes physical manipulation of mankind. The sons of Cain chose the father of the kingdom of death as their god.

The sons of disobedience are victims of envy and pride, lusting after power, control, and carnality rather than the way of truth. They hear another voice that is not the Father of truth, but the father of disobedience, murder, lies, and envy. They are trapped in the kingdom of death, void of the Spirit of God, and will perish with their god (Matthew 25:41).

The Pharisee leaders were under the influence of the father of disobedience, the prince of death, just as Cain and his lineage were before the flood. Those who live their lives in pride, envy, lies, and deception are the sons of disobedience of old. They are the same today as they were millennia ago, following the same father of lies into the kingdom of death.

Ham was the first post-flood father of corruption, followed by his sons Canaan and Cush (Chaos), who went in search of the "pillars of Enoch" and the ancient secret knowledge inscribed as hieroglyphics upon them. These became the patriarchs of the secret societies, linked together by their symbolic characters. Osiris, Isis, and Horus—who were Nimrod, Semiramis, and Tammuz—were immortalized by sun and moon worship.

Therefore, by these symbols, we discover who among the pagan religions are linked together as sons of disobedience, with Satan as their father—the father of lies and the prince of death.

There are sons of disobedience who do not know our God and live only for their own desires. And then there are others who do know our God and live in direct opposition, serving the father of lies in the kingdom of death. We need to know who they are and how they work against the sons of God led by the Spirit in their attempts at our destruction.

By their symbols, we know that the thirtieth-degree and above Freemasons are leaders among the sons of disobedience.

I think it is safe to assume that most of us have heard many conspiracy theories surrounding the famously enigmatic "Illuminati." The Masons and the Illuminati share the same symbology and are interconnected, though they are not the same organization. The powerful and esoteric Illuminati

357

were founded by Adam Weishaupt of Ingolstadt, Bavaria, who was born in 1748.

The Jesuits of the Catholic Church were openly opposed to Weishaupt's new religion of "enlightenment." By several accounts, the Jesuits feared that Weishaupt's Illuminati could become another strong movement against the Church of Rome, much like Protestantism. Over time, however, the Masons, Jesuits, and Illuminati became intertwined, each performing respective roles in managing global power structures.

When Weishaupt became a law professor at the University of Ingolstadt, he handpicked the first Illuminati members. Their first meeting was held in a secret spot in a Bavarian forest, which some suspect may have given birth to the secretly exclusive "Bohemian Grove" membership. The Bohemian Grove is a 2,700-acre compound in California, accessible only to a very exclusive group of affluent men. Though there is no direct historical connection between the Illuminati and Bohemian Grove, many believe it resembles Weishaupt's first forest gathering of the "enlightened."

One could argue that there is little difference between the Freemasons, Illuminati, or Bohemian Grove members, since nearly all who attend meetings at the Bohemian Grove are also members of other secret occult societies.

We have already seen Freemason symbols on the US $1.00 bill. It is important to note that an Illuminati slogan mirrors the Freemason slogans found there. It is believed that Adam Weishaupt did join the Freemasons who preceded him, but later recruited the most powerful Masons into the Illuminati. For this reason, it is likely that thirtieth-degree and higher "enlightened" Masons became Illuminati members. Their symbology is the same. They both serve Satan and maintain "luciferianism in its purest form."

Here is a logo from a claimed Illuminati website, designed to change public perception about who they are and what they do. However, they make no effort to hide their symbology:

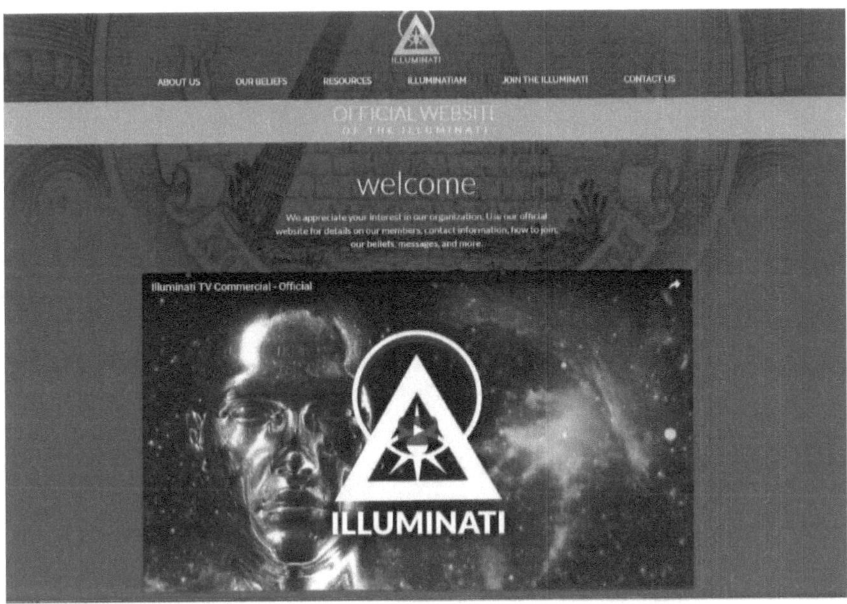

Here is the US $1.00 bill in the background in plain view. These secret societies of the Freemasons, Illuminati, Knights Templar, and Jesuits use the same symbols. What else can be found on this mysterious talisman of a sovereign debt monetary system?

This little owl hiding in the corner of the design of the $1.00 bill is the primary symbol of the Bohemian Grove, representing "enlightenment."

*Left: Bronze plaque at the entrance to the Bohemian Grove. Notice the
moon behind the owl (representing Isis)
Right: A forty-foot statue of an owl worshipped there for wisdom
(enlightenment).*

Many believe that human sacrifices have taken place at the Bohemian Grove. Anya Wick says she was taken there to be shared by many men during a satanic ritual. The owl on the right has a close resemblance to ancient depictions of Moloch, the god to whom child sacrifices were made in ancient times. The Hebrews carried this idolatrous influence out of Egypt with them.

It is no coincidence that these connected religions trace back to Egypt. And who was the father of the Egyptians (Khemites)? Ham, the son of Noah, father of Cush, and grandfather of Nimrod. I believe that Moloch worship likely originated with Enoch, son of Cain, and was reinstated by the Khemites under Nimrod.

> *You shall not give any of your children to offer*
> *them [by fire as a sacrifice] to Molech [the god of*
> *the Ammonites], nor shall you profane the name of*
> *your God [by honoring idols as gods]. I am the Lord.*
> *(Leviticus 18:21 AMP)*

I do not know what they do at the Bohemian Grove in California, but what can be proven is that many of its members are also known Freemasons and Illuminati members. The rituals reported there are tragically evil and idolatrous and are practiced by the richest and most powerful men on earth.

Here are a few names published as attendees that might surprise you. These can be easily verified, which could mean their names are shared to keep the most important members in the shadows. Too many people know about the Grove now, so they throw a bone to conspiracy theorists with lists like this one. I found photo archives that prove their participation that I could not share here due to copyright infringement, but they are available:

- Richard Nixon
- Ronald Reagan
- Karl Rove
- Colin Powell
- Nelson Rockefeller
- Warren Buffet
- George Bush (both)

- Dick Cheney
- Bill Clinton
- Donald Rumsfeld
- Arnold Schwarzenegger

There are many names that appear in association with the Bohemian Grove members who are not members but have been invited as entertainers, speakers or singers, etc. However, only Illuminati or Freemason associates would receive such an invitation, and all of the names listed above can be traced to other secret societies— Freemasons, Illuminati, or Skull and Bones—which are interrelated and share the same symbols in their lodges and logos.

I mentioned earlier that the niece of Jeffrey Epstein, Anya Wick, says she was born and raised to be a sex slave for the cult of Baal to whom her family belonged. One of her claims is that she was forced to have violent sex for powerful men at the Bohemian Grove when she was barely a teenager. These are the sons of disobedience, who worship the prince of death, and they control global affairs. Do not be naive about whatever they are trying to sell in their next propaganda campaign. Whenever they say "we all must do or else", do the opposite. Whatever these people are selling in 24/7 corporate media news propaganda cycles, don't buy it. They are the sons of disobedience. Their father is the father of lies and the prince of death.

At the pinnacle of the global financial system is the central bank of central banks, the Bank of International Settlements in Basel, Switzerland. Most of us are not aware that central banks are not owned by the governments they represent but are privately owned. The majority shareholders of these central banks generally share the same last names. These shareholders are shrouded in secrecy but can be found with some diligent research.

Here is a list of the top 10 shareholders of the US Federal Reserve Bank published by Peter Kershaw in his book *Economic Solutions*:

1. The Rothschild Family – London
2. The Rothschild Family – Berlin
3. The Lazard Brothers – Paris

4. Israel Seiff – Italy
5. Kuhn-Loeb Company – Germany
6. The Warburgs – Amsterdam
7. The Warburgs – Hamburg
8. Lehman Brothers – New York
9. Goldman & Sachs – New York
10. The Rockefeller Family – New York

The Federal Reserve has twelve member banks, and the top shareholders of those Federal Reserve banks are made public. But the primary shareholders of the Federal Reserve itself, as a central bank operating independently from the sovereign nation it represents, are kept private. I find it very interesting that for the bank that establishes monetary policy in the USA, only three of the top 10 shareholders are from the USA.

In his book *Rule by Secrecy*, Jim Marrs makes this statement:

The Federal Reserve Bank of New York, which undeniably controls the other eleven Federal Reserve branches, is essentially controlled by two financial institutions:

1) Chase-Manhattan (controlled by the Rockefellers) - 6,389,445 shares - 32.3%

2) Citibank - 4,051,851 shares - 20.5%

Thus, these two entities control nearly 53% of the New York Federal Reserve Bank.

In the case of the Bank of International Settlements, sixty-three central banks are members, fifty-five of which have ownership. When you investigate the shareholders of those fifty-five banks, the same names appear repeatedly. The Rothschilds are involved in all of them.

So, the central banks of sovereign nations around the world are owned by the same private banks and families. These elite folks are not like us. They are deluded, deranged, and mostly under a dark influence. JP Morgan is another name listed repeatedly as a central bank shareholder. JP Morgan made a $290 million court settlement to Epstein's victims in a single lawsuit filed in a Manhattan federal court, paid to over 100 victims related to the case. This does not include an additional $75 million settlement with the US Virgin Islands, where the lawsuit claimed JP Morgan was complicit in Epstein's child sex trafficking ring. If your local banker lost a lawsuit and by court order paid out hundreds of millions of dollars to victims of pedophilia tied to the bank, would you find a more reputable banker to do business with? We are not given that choice—thus the "all-seeing eye of Horus."

It is also interesting how often the name Rothschild appears in the same places as Jesuit activity. The Rothschilds and the Jesuits can both be traced with involvement in Napolean's demise. Mayer Amschel Rothschild provided Adam Weishaupt with funding and powerful connections in the early days of the Order of the Illuminati. Reportedly, they are not as wealthy as Gates, Soros, or Musk—but is that actually true? If they own part of every central bank in the world, including the central bank of central banks, the BIS, who has more power? Gates, or the Rockefellers and Rothschilds? Perhaps Gates does what he does to please some of these people in exchange for power.

Chase Manhattan Bank was the Rockefeller family jewel, owned by the late David Rockefeller. Anneke Lucas is another child sex slave survivor who published the book *Quest for Love*. On Patrick Bet-David's podcast, Anneke reluctantly admitted that she was a sex slave to David Rockefeller long before the age of puberty. These are the sons of disobedience who exist at the global hierarchy level.

At the time of his death in 2017, David Rockefeller's reported net worth was only 3.3 billion USD. This is something the elite bankers have in common—meager net worths compared to their super-elite counterparts— yet they command the flow of trillions.

Take a look at where the central bankers around the world meet: the BIS headquarters in Basel, Switzerland.

On the left is the BIS headquarters. On the right is an old rendition of the Tower of Babel. These are the sons of disobedience working together toward their "Novus Ordo Seclorum" in plain sight.

Here is the simple truth: it is impossible to be in a position of global influential power in Satan's kingdom without being a son of disobedience. And that takes me back to where I left off regarding the Jesuits.

Ignatius de Loyola was the first Jesuit and Jesuit general in what was an armed militant force (*"governance of militant church"—papal bull Regimini militantis Ecclesiae, September 27, 1540*) organized to stamp out Protestantism. They have been behind every war since their inception and every peace accord that follows. They are at the top of the global monetary system, manipulating economies and currencies, the largest banks, global financial markets, etc., in favor of any agenda that promotes their "New World Order" ideology with a *universal church* at the head of it.

They have influenced everything in society, from public education curriculum to the movie industry and from global politics to global monetary systems. They operate in secrecy, allowing conspiracy theories to surround the Freemasons and Illuminati while they are, in fact, at the pinnacle of power on the global power pyramid. And remember that at their founding under Loyola, they were at the service of the papacy of Rome, to protect and defend the institution of the papacy at all costs and by any means necessary.

Their secrecy insulates the pope, shrouding the papacy under an illusion of godliness when the reality is quite the contrary. The Jesuits are the generals guiding the fate of the beast of prophecy:

*Then I saw another beast coming up out of the earth;
and he had two horns like a lamb, and he spoke as a
dragon. He exercises all the authority of the first beast
in his presence. And he makes the earth and those who
live on it worship the first beast, whose fatal wound
was healed. He performs great signs, so that he even
makes fire come down out of the sky to the earth in the
presence of people. And he deceives those who live on
the earth because of the signs which it was given him
to perform in the presence of the beast, telling those
who live on the earth to make an image to the beast
who *had the wound of the sword and has come to life.
And it was given to him to give breath to the image of
the beast, so that the image of the beast would even
speak and cause all who do not worship the image of
the beast to be killed. And he causes all, the small and
the great, the rich and the poor, and the free and the
slaves, to be given a mark on their right hands or on
their foreheads, and he decrees that no one will be
able to buy or to sell, except the one who has the mark,
either the name of the beast or the number of his name.
(Revelation 13:11-17 NASB)*

Many believe that the fatal wound inflicted on the beast by the sword was Martin Luther's Ninety-Five Theses and the Protestant Reformation. I'm not among them, but they make a valid argument. The Jesuits have succeeded in shaping a "progressive" universal religion that further empowers the papacy, where Protestants are no longer distinct or apart from it. Could this be the wound that has healed? I do not believe so, but there are many that do.

They stand as the apex of the sons of disobedience who rule Satan's kingdom. The Freemasons, the Templars, and the Illuminati, while extremely powerful, can do little without the Jesuit generals' oversight. The Society of Jesus leads the forces of evil in favor of papal power and global dominance. The sons of God—the bride-church—remain the only force on earth they fear, for it is our prayers that obstruct their *Novus Ordo Seclorum* endeavor. By promoting a universal religion through subtle, sublime propaganda over time, they have slowly disarmed the most powerful force on earth: the "sons of God, led by the Spirit," who are the true church and bride of Christ.

If you walked into a new church and saw serpent fangs and eyes behind the pulpit, would you remain for the service? This is the pope's audience hall at the Vatican. Many faithful Catholics truly know God, but they are trapped by the sons of disobedience, who secretly worship a different god—the same god of the Jesuits, Freemasons, and Illuminati. Pray for them!

And after these things I saw another angel come down from heaven, having great power; and the earth was lightened with his glory.

And he cried mightily with a strong voice, saying, Babylon the great is fallen, is fallen, and is become the habitation of devils, and the hold of every foul spirit, and a cage of every unclean and hateful bird.

For all nations have drunk of the wine of the wrath of her fornication, and the kings of the earth have

committed fornication with her, and the merchants of
the earth are waxed rich through the abundance of her
delicacies.

And I heard another voice from heaven, saying, Come
out of her, my people, that ye be not partakers of her
sins, and that ye receive not of her plagues.

For her sins have reached unto heaven, and God hath
remembered her iniquities. (Revelation 18:1-5 KJV)

The sons of disobedience have surrounded the sons of God, led by the Spirit, within the ancient Babylonian relics of sun worship, whose origins trace back to the first Masons—Enoch and Tubal-Cain, sons of Cain before the flood. Their post-flood descendants were Cush and Nimrod. Today, the sons of disobedience, in their respective secret societies, can be identified by symbols tied to sun and moon worship and to the first false messiah, Tammuz/Horus. Wherever their signs and symbols appear, they reveal themselves as the sons of disobedience. These are the deliberate enemies of the One True God and, likewise, of the sons of God led by the Spirit.

The power of confession and fervent prayer (James 5:16), in the name of Yehshua and by the blood of Yehshua, is our only defense against this formidable militant force headquartered in Rome. I believe that just as the Jesuits and the sons of disobedience have their oaths and decrees to one another and to the papacy of Rome, the sons of God led by the Spirit hold their own decree in John chapter 14:

"Do not let your heart be troubled; believe in God,
believe also in Me. In My Father's house are many
rooms; if that were not so, I would have told you,
because I am going there to prepare a place for you. And
if I go and prepare a place for you, I am coming again
and will take you to Myself, so that where I am, there you
also will be. And you know the way where I am going."
*Thomas *said to Him, "Lord, we do not know where You*
*are going; how do we know the way?" Jesus *said to*

him, "I am the way, and the truth, and the life; no one comes to the Father except through Me.

Oneness with the Father

If you had known Me, you would have known My Father also; from now on you know Him, and have seen Him."

*Philip said to Him, "Lord, show us the Father, and it is enough for us." Jesus *said to him, "Have I been with you for so long a time, and yet you have not come to know Me, Philip? The one who has seen Me has seen the Father; how can you say, 'Show us the Father'? Do you not believe that I am in the Father, and the Father is in Me? The words that I say to you I do not speak on My own, but the Father, as He remains in Me, does His works. Believe Me that I am in the Father and the Father is in Me; otherwise believe because of the works themselves. Truly, truly I say to you, the one who believes in Me, the works that I do, he will do also; and greater works than these he will do; because I am going to the Father. And whatever you ask in My name, this I will do, so that the Father may be glorified in the Son. If you ask Me anything in My name, I will do it.*

"If you love Me, you will keep My commandments.

The Holy Spirit

I will ask the Father, and He will give you another Helper, so that He may be with you forever; the Helper is the Spirit of truth, whom the world cannot receive, because it does not see Him or know Him; but you know Him because He remains with you and will be in you.

*"I will not leave you as orphans; I am coming to you. After a little while, the world no longer is going to see Me, but you are going to see Me; because I live, you also will live. On that day you will know that I am in My Father, and you are in Me, and I in you. The one who has My commandments and keeps them is the one who loves Me; and the one who loves Me will be loved by My Father, and I will love him and will reveal Myself to him." Judas (not Iscariot) *said to Him, "Lord, what has happened that You are going to reveal Yourself to us and not to the world?" Jesus answered and said to him, "If anyone loves Me, he will follow My word; and My Father will love him, and We will come to him and make Our dwelling with him. The one who does not love Me does not follow My words; and the word which you hear is not Mine, but the Father's who sent Me.*

"These things I have spoken to you while remaining with you. But the Helper, the Holy Spirit whom the Father will send in My name, He will teach you all things, and remind you of all that I said to you. Peace I leave you, My peace I give you; not as the world gives, do I give to you. Do not let your hearts be troubled, nor fearful. You heard that I said to you, 'I am going away, and I am coming to you.' If you loved Me, you would have rejoiced because I am going to the Father, for the Father is greater than I. And now I have told you before it happens, so that when it happens, you may believe. I will not speak much more with you, for the ruler of the world is coming, and he has nothing in regard to Me, but so that the world may know that I love the Father, I do exactly as the Father commanded Me. [__Get up, let's go from here__.] (John 14 NASB)

The Group 3 sons of disobedience are a vile company of deceivers, fornicators, idolaters, murderers, and worse. They form a distinct group among the sons of disobedience, living in deliberate opposition to God. They rule over every aspect of our lives, and I believe this stems from a promise they received from Satan—the same promise offered to Yehshua in Matthew 4, which He rejected, but which the sons of disobedience embraced. We see and hear stories of powerful people like Jeffrey Epstein and focus on his crimes of pedophilia and child sex trafficking, which are horrific and unimaginable to the sons of God led by the Spirit. But the Epstein story is buried within an even darker story of satanic occult groups that remain active, continuing their rituals despite one of their members being "suicided."

Worse than the Epstein story is the Ninth Circle satanic occult, which, according to investigator and author Kevin Annett, requires every Catholic cardinal and pope to participate to make the "red list" from which popes are chosen. I urge you to research this yourself because so much of what I discovered is too horrible to share here. I've already shared some horrible things. Annett's book *Murder by Decree* is a valuable resource for those seeking to understand our adversaries and Satan's operatives on earth.

Whether you can endure the details or not, do not neglect prayer against the forces of evil that rule this world. Make a diligent effort to support groups like Gloria Master's foundation for pedophile victims. The voices of women who have survived and emerged from the shadows—bearing the weight of physical and psychological trauma yet able to recount their personal horrors—must be heard. Women like Anneke Lucas, Gloria Masters, Anya Wick, and the late Virginia Giuffre are super survivors of the super-elite and must not be ignored!

Remember, I categorized the sons of disobedience into three groups, with Group 3 operating directly for Satan and against God. The Epsteins and super-elite of the world belong to this group. But I do not want to discount the horrors of the Group 1—the drug and human traffickers who live for the gods of money and the carnal pleasures it can buy. They may not have sold their souls to Satan yet, but they must equally be prayed against, that warring angels be dispatched against them and ministering angels sent to aid the victims of their atrocities.

Child sex trafficking is on the rise around the world, whether through Group 1 or Group 3 sons of disobedience. Countries like Thailand and Guatemala receive international attention, but this is spreading like wildfire under demonic influence globally. "Anything you ask in my name I will do it" refers to this type of prayer. Yehshua wasn't talking about fasting and praying for private island mansions with landing strips for private jets—a deception of Laodicean prosperity preaching. We are at war with spiritual forces, and Yehshua will act against them when we pray!

Therefore, pray daily against the sons of disobedience, and ask all of your Christian friends and family to join you in fervent prayer for the victims of satanic cults and organized crime mafias. Pray for the victims, and pray against the sons of disobedience—daily!

Beyond prayer, find a cause and support it. A large portion of the proceeds from this book will be used to support some of the following charities that fight child sex trafficking. Ask the Holy Spirit to guide you in supporting a charity dedicated to child sex trafficking victims. I am only naming a few here:

1. Handing the Shame Back – https://www.handingtheshameback. org/

This is Gloria Masters's foundation for child sex victims. When researching charities and foundations, remember that the sons of disobedience have their own charities to disguise themselves. The "Lolita Express" carried many minor sex slaves while the super-elite claimed to embark on humanitarian missions. I would be horrified to give even a fraction of a cent to such deceivers. Do your research before giving money. I think a safe policy is to donate to a charity whose founder or members are victims themselves.

2. Operation Underground Railroad – https://ourrescue.org/

This was founded by Tim Ballard in 2013. The movie *Sound of Freedom* tells Tim Ballard's story. If you haven't seen the movie, I think it should be mandatory.

3. SOAR (Speak Out Act Reclaim) – <u>https://www.speakoutactreclaim.org/</u>

This is the late Virginia Giuffre's charity. While they are not currently accepting donations, they offer other ways to get involved until they are able to.

Perhaps one of the most effective organizations dedicated to stopping child trafficking is Covenant Rescue Group, founded by former Navy SEAL Jared Hudson and his wife. Hudson worked with Tim Ballard in targeting child trafficking rings abroad and later determined he could be more effective by training law enforcement agents to recognize the signs of pedophiles and traffickers. Hudson's efforts in this endeavor have demonstrated amazing success. One of the most recent, at the time of this writing, occurred just weeks after training local sheriff's deputies in Alabama. Within weeks, deputies identified a child sex trafficking ring and rescued numerous children who were being held in an underground bunker, sexually exploited for money, zip-tied to posts and furniture, and fed like stray dogs. According to Hudson, child trafficking occurs near every major population in America.[24]

4. Andreozzi + Foote, Sexual Abuse Lawyers – <u>https://www.victimscivilattorneys.com</u>

This firm was very supportive of Virginia Giuffre, offering not only legal advocacy for victims but also connections to PTSD trauma counselors and other resources while pursuing legal action against perpetrators. They have representation in eleven states and are equipped to act in cases involving schools and churches as well.

I also highly recommend all of Kevin Annett's books and publications, which expose the atrocities of the papacy and reveal how some of the worst crimes in the world are swept under the rug, leaving surviving victims without justice. These crimes are not limited to the papacy but involve a network of Catholic churches worldwide that participate in crimes against children. The Ninth Circle Satanic Cult is the pinnacle of evil on planet earth, and every pope has been a member since its formation, according to

---

24   <u>https://www.covenantrescue.org/</u>

Annett. As sons of God led by the Spirit, we want no part of this and must pray fervently against it.

As I mentioned, most accounts of atrocities committed by the sons of disobedience are too horrible to discuss openly. But we must know enough to discern whom to pray against and whom to pray for. These victims desperately need the help of the sons of God led by the Spirit. Many details I have not mentioned here can be discovered through your own research—such as how the papacy has acted as chief money launderer for Italian mafias and sanctioned governments. Far worse, however, are reports of "human hunting parties" organized by the super-elite, where adolescent children are literally hunted and killed from horseback, or infants taken from the wombs of child sex slaves and mutilated before their mothers on altars to Satan.

For their sake, we cannot bury our heads in the sand while they are tortured in secret. The sons of God led by the Spirit have a responsibility to engage spiritually on behalf of the millions of children trafficked into sex slavery around the world.

> *And whatever you ask in My name, this I will do, so that the Father may be glorified in the Son. If you ask Me anything in My name, I will do it. (John 14:13-14 NASB)*

> *Vengeance is Mine, and retribution;*
>
> *In due time their foot will slip.*
>
> *For the day of their disaster is near,*
>
> *And the impending things are hurrying to them. (Deuteronomy 32:35)*

> Praise God that vengeance is His and not ours, for His shall be far worse. ***For it is because of these things that the wrath of God is coming upon the sons of disobedience.*** (Colossians 3:6 KJV)

*And the heaven departed as a scroll when it is rolled
together; and every mountain and island were moved
out of their places.*

*And the kings of the earth, and the great men, and
the rich men, and the chief captains, and the mighty
men, and every bondman, and every free man,
hid themselves in the dens and in the rocks of the
mountains;*

*And said to the mountains and rocks, Fall on us, and
hide us from the face of him that sitteth on the throne,
and from the wrath of the Lamb:*

*For the great day of his wrath is come; and who shall
be able to stand? (Revelation 6:14-17 KJV)*

<u>This generation shall not pass till all things be fulfilled.</u>
(Matthew 24:34)

And all God's people said amen, and blessed the Lord.
(1 Chronicles 16:36)

CHAPTER 10

The Last Son of Disobedience: The Imam Mahdi?

Seventy weeks have been decreed for your people and your holy city, to finish the wrongdoing, to make an end of sin, to make atonement for guilt, to bring in everlasting righteousness, to seal up vision and prophecy, and to anoint the Most Holy Place. So you are to know and understand *that* from the issuing of a decree to restore and rebuild Jerusalem, until Messiah the Prince, *there will be* seven weeks and sixty-two weeks; it will be built again, *with* streets and moat, even in times of distress. Then after the sixty-two weeks, the Messiah will be cut off and have nothing, and the people of the prince who is to come will destroy the city and the sanctuary. And its end *will come* with a flood; even to the end there will be war; desolations are determined. And he will confirm a covenant with the many for one week, but in the middle of the week he will put a stop to sacrifice and grain offering; and on the wing of abominations *will come* the one who makes desolate, until a complete destruction, one that is decreed, gushes forth on the one who makes desolate.

—Daniel 9:24-27 (NASB)

I was curious to know which is the youngest religion in the world. We know that Adam was the first king and priest (Melchizedek) of the One True God, making Judaism the oldest religion on earth from the most fundamental viewpoint. We also know that sun and moon worship began with Adam and Eve's grandchildren in the lineage of Cain, making sun worship the second oldest religion. But what is the youngest religion?

According to various sources, Astronism might be the youngest religion. Its founder is a young philosopher named Brandon Taylorian, who calls himself "Cometan" within the order of Astronic traditions—religions he claims date back to the Stone Age. According to Taylorian's "cosmocentric" worldview, the astronomical realm is the supreme power in the universe. He was inspired by Plato, Socrates, and Aristotle, of course. I wouldn't have expected less.

This is simply another "universal" religion, such as The Secret or Universalism and many others. What I find interesting is how often religions have been inspired by the ancient Greek philosophers. Brandon Taylorian is only one in a long line of individuals who, ironically, because of their "higher learning," became totally ignorant of God. In their ignorance of God, they lack wisdom and begin worshipping the creature rather than the Creator. Plato and his Greek wordsmith counterparts inspired many deep thinkers to become lost in space with sophistication and eloquence.

Another deeply inspired student of Plato in the fifth-century Catholic Church was St. Augustine of Hippo, considered one of the first "Doctors of the Universal Church" (Roman Catholic Church). I have mentioned Augustine in this book and the previous one in reference to his writings *City of God* and *Confessions*. He is proclaimed by many to be one of the fathers of the Christian Church, due to the influence of his writings on Christianity. In 1298, Pope Boniface VIII decreed Augustine and others to be the first doctors of the Universal Church (Roman Catholicism).

I covered some basic information about St. Augustine in the last book, so I won't bore you with it a second time. He is responsible for promoting the Sethite view of the Genesis 6 event, a perspective that has left scholars confused for 1,600 years on the subject of fallen angel-human hybrid Nephilim. For this chapter, it's only important to understand how he relates to the information I am about to share. He was a fifth-century bishop in Hippo, North Africa, later making his way to Rome, where the "Rule of St. Augustine" and the "Augustine Canon" were introduced into Catholicism.

Read this excerpt from *Britannica* that will help lead me to my point:

Intellectually, Augustine represents the most influential adaptation of the ancient Platonic tradition with

*Christian ideas that ever occurred in the Latin Christian
world. Augustine received the Platonic past in a far
more limited and diluted way than did many of his
Greek-speaking contemporaries, but his writings were so
widely read and imitated throughout Latin Christendom
that his particular synthesis of Christian, Roman, and
Platonic traditions defined the terms for much later
tradition and debate. Both modern Roman Catholic
and Protestant Christianity owe much to Augustine,
though in some ways each community has at times been
embarrassed to own up to that allegiance in the face of
irreconcilable elements in his thought.*[25]

Platonism (from Plato) is a school of thought that emphasizes the existence of abstract, nonmaterial ideas or forms. These forms are considered the true reality, while the physical world is merely a shadow or imitation. Plato does not acknowledge a Creator per se, but suggests that certain abstract necessities must have been established to sustain creation. Here is a definition from *Webster's*:

*Platonism: the philosophy of Plato stressing especially
that actual things are copies of transcendent ideas
and that these ideas are the objects of true knowledge
apprehended by reminiscence.*[26]

The New Age religion of Universalism is rooted in Platonism, which is why people like Brandon Taylorian become academic astronauts in philosophical space—constantly orbiting from one deep thought to another without recognizing the simple truths of our Creator-inspired realities. I have studied philosophy just enough to know that it is too much like walking a figure 8 in search of its end. The end only takes you back

---

25   Encyclopedia Britannica

26   Merriam Websters: Platonism

to the beginning, where the cycle starts all over again. It is far easier to read the Bible and confirm its truths with archaeological and historical evidence than to attempt to prove the abstract shadows of the metaphysical philosophies from ancient Greeks, who worshipped nature and fallen angels above their Creator.

What does this have to do with the Mahdi? The first question is: What is the Mahdi?

This is from an Islamic website, www.quranrecital.com:

> *As the end of time comes near, corruption will spread like wildfire. Injustice will be prevalent, the strong will persecute the weak and the evil people will come into power. For the believers, this will be a very tough time and they will wish for something to relieve them of this darkness. It will be at this point that Allah will give permission for Muhammad ibn Abdullah Al-Hasani, Imam Mahdi, to appear.*

> *Imam Mahdi's full name is Muhammad ibn Abdullah Al-Hasani. He will be a descendant of the family of Prophet Muhammed SAW from Fatima RA and Hadhrat Hasan ibn Ali RA.*

> *The word Mahdi comes from the Arabic language and means 'The Guided One'. Someone who will bring justice and peace during his leadership.*

> *After all the hardship, struggle, corruption and injustice, a pious, righteous man will appear. Through his hands Allah will set right the affairs of this ummah. To those of the Ahl-us Sunnah, he is known as the Mahdi. People will gather around him and he will lead the believers*

in many battles. For the Muslim ummah, he will be a leader and a ruler.

As Nabi SAW mentioned in the hadith, Imam Mahdi will rule the Muslims for 7 years. During these years, there will be justice all around and there will no longer be any oppression and corruption. While he rules, the Ummah will enjoy many blessings; the Earth will bring forth its vegetation, the sky will send down rain and wealth will be given without measure.

Imam Mahdi will come from the East. When he emerges, he will not be alone, rather Allah will support him with people from the east who will strive alongside him in order to bring strength to Islam.

There will be turmoil near the end of time. Three sons of a Caliph will fight over the treasure of the Ka'bah, each wanting to capture it for himself, but none will succeed. At this point, Imam Mahdi will appear in Makkah and he will become famous among the people. Allegiance will be sworn to him next to the Ka'bah to follow and obey him.

Each one of them the son of a caliph' – this means there will be three men and each will have followers. The father of each of these men will be a king, so he will seek power like his father's kingdom.

'Your treasure' – refers to the treasure of the Ka'bah, which is gold. It is said that this treasure lies beneath the Ka'bah. On the contrary, it could mean power,

namely ruler-ship and the caliphate. Some say this is the treasure of the Euphrates, a mountain of gold that will be uncovered when the water level of the Euphrates drops.

Ibn Katheer mentions in Al-Nihaayah, "He [Imam Mahdi] will be supported by people from the east who will establish his authority. Their flags will be black because it is a colour that indicates dignity, as the banner of the Messenger of Allah SAW was also black and it was called Al-Uqaab."

'Allah will rectify him in a single night' could mean that Allah will prepare him to become the caliph and will guide and inspire him, and give him the attributes of leadership and wisdom. All of which he didn't possess before.

Here is from another website called Faith in Allah:

Al-Mahdi (meaning "the guided one") is a righteous leader who will appear in the last days of the Ummah, __just before the descent of Jesus__, peace be upon him. He will be from the prophetic lineage (Ahl al-Bayt) and will be forced to become Caliph by righteous believers in front of the Ka'bah. Allah will aid him with a miracle that will leave no doubt he is the long awaited figure.

Abu Huraira reported: The Messenger of Allah, peace and blessings be upon him, said:

How will you be when the son of Mary descends upon you while your leader is among you?

> *Jabir ibn Abdullah reported: The Messenger of Allah, peace and blessings be upon him, said, "**Jesus the son of Mary, peace and blessings be upon him, will descend and the Muslim leader will say: Come lead us in prayer. Jesus will say: No, some of you are leaders over others, as Allah has honored this nation.**"*

Let's recap:

- The Imam Mahdi has permission to arrive when the world reaches peak corruption.
- He will arrive before the return of Jesus.
- He will be a descendant of Muhammad.
- The Mahdi is the "Guided One" and brings peace through his leadership.
- He will be considered a righteous religious authority to his followers.
- Where conflicts arise, he will lead his Muslim armies in battle.
- The Mahdi will rule for seven years.
- When the Mahdi arrives, he will come from the east, accompanied by a large force that joins Islam.
- He will put down a caliphate rebellion, earning great respect among his people. He will be greatly revered in Mecca.
- He will be given attributes of leadership and wisdom that were not his nature before some kind of miraculous transformation (similar to Nimrod: "He began to be a mighty one in the earth." He wasn't born that way; see Genesis 10:8).
- A nation from the east will help establish his authority, flying a black flag. The ISIS flag and the Iranian Jihad flag are the only two completely black flags I am aware of. On the ISIS flag are the words: "There is no other god but allah, Muhammed is the prophet of allah."

There is much more to this subject of Islam, the Mahdi, and their obvious Antichrist profiles. I found an article by Pastor John Kodiyil that compares the Mahdi to the Antichrist. I know nothing about this pastor or his ministries beyond this one work, but it is well done, and I want to share it directly rather than paraphrase it. I prefer to give Pastor Kodiyil full credit for his work, which follows:

The Biblical Antichrist compared to the Islamic Mahdi

December 2, 2016 by <u>John Kodiyil</u>

A Comparison

A review of the many startling similarities that exist between the biblical Antichrist and the Islamic Mahdi (Messiah)

Bible: The Antichrist is an unparalleled political, military, and religious leader that will emerge in the last days.

Islam: The Mahdi is an unparalleled political, military, and religious leader that will emerge in the last days.

Bible: The False Prophet is a secondary prominent figure that will emerge in the last days who will support the Antichrist.

Islam: The Muslim Jesus is a secondary prominent figure that will emerge in the last days to support the Mahdi.

Bible: The Antichrist and the False Prophet together will have a powerful army that will do great damage to the earth in an effort to subdue every nation and dominate the world.

Islam: The Mahdi and the Muslim Jesus will have a powerful army that will attempt to control every nation of the earth and dominate the world.

Bible: The False Prophet is described essentially as a dragon in lamb's clothing.

Islam: The Muslim Jesus comes bearing the name of the one that the world knows as "the Lamb of God," Jesus Christ. Yet the Muslim Jesus comes to murder all those who do not submit to Islam.

Bible: The Antichrist and the False Prophet establish a new world order.

Islam: The Mahdi and the Muslim Jesus establish a new world order.

Bible: The Antichrist and the False Prophet institute new laws for the whole earth.

Islam: The Mahdi and the Muslim Jesus institute Islamic law all over the earth.

Bible: The Antichrist is said to "change the times."

Islam: It is quite certain that if the Mahdi established Islam all over the earth, he would discontinue the use of Saturday and Sunday as the weekend or days of rest, changing to Friday, the holy day of Islam. Also, he would most certainly eliminate the Gregorian calendar and replace it with the Islamic calendar currently used in every Islamic country.

Bible: The Antichrist and the False Prophet will both be powerful religious leaders who will attempt to institute a universal world religion.

Islam: The Mahdi and the Muslim Jesus will institute Islam as the only religion on the earth.

Bible: The Antichrist and the False Prophet will execute anyone who does not submit to their world religion.

Islam: Likewise, the Mahdi and the Muslim Jesus will execute anyone who does not submit to Islam.

Bible: The Antichrist and the False Prophet will specifically use beheading as the primary means of execution for nonconformists.

Islam: The Mahdi and the Muslim Jesus will use the Islamic practice of beheading for executions.

Bible: The Antichrist and the False Prophet will have a specific agenda to kill as many Jews as possible.

Islam: The Mahdi and the Muslim Jesus will kill as many Jews as possible, until only a few are left hiding behind rocks and trees.

Bible: The Antichrist and the False Prophet will attack to conquer and seize Jerusalem.

Islam: The Mahdi and the Muslim Jesus will attack to reconquer and seize Jerusalem for Islam.

Bible: The Antichrist will set himself up in the Jewish Temple as his seat of authority.

Islam: The Mahdi will establish the Islamic caliphate from Jerusalem.

Bible: The False Prophet is said to do many miracles to deceive as many as possible into supporting the Antichrist.

Islam: The Mahdi himself is said to control the weather and the crops. His face is said to glow. We can also assume that since Jesus is viewed as having been empowered by Allah to work miracles when He was here on earth the first time, He will most likely be expected to continue to do so when He returns.

Bible: The Antichrist is described as riding on a white horse in the Book of Revelation

Islam: The Mahdi is described as riding on a white horse (ironically in the same verse).

Bible: The Antichrist is said to make a peace treaty with Israel for seven years.

Islam: The Mahdi is said to make a peace treaty through a Jew (specifically a Levite) for exactly seven years.

Bible: Jesus the Jewish Messiah will return to defend the Jews in Israel from a military attack from a vast coalition of nations led by the Antichrist and the False Prophet.

Islam: The Dajjal, the Islamic Antichrist, will gain a great Jewish following and claim to be Jesus Christ; he will fight against the Mahdi and the Muslim Jesus.

Bible: The spirit of antichrist specifically denies the most unique and central doctrines of Christianity, namely the Trinity, the incarnation, and the substitutionary death of Jesus on the Cross.

Islam: Islam doctrinally and spiritually specifically denies the most unique and central doctrines of Christianity, namely the Trinity, the incarnation, and the substitutionary death of Jesus on the Cross.

Bible: The primary warning of Jesus and the Apostle Paul was to warn Christians of the abundance of deceit and deception in the last days.

Islam: Islam is perhaps the only religion on earth that practices deceit as one of its tools to assist its own ascendancy. It actually has a specific doctrine that allows and even calls for deception to be used to achieve its desired end.

Bible: The specific nations pictured in the Bible as part of the final empire of the Antichrist are all Islamic nations.

Islam: All Muslims are commanded to give their allegiance to the Mahdi as the final caliph and imam (leader) of Islam.

Bible: From the Bible and history we learn that the final Antichrist empire will be a revived version of the empire that succeeds the Roman empire.

Islam: The empire that succeeded the Roman/Byzantine empire was the Islamic Ottoman empire.

Bible: When the Antichrist emerges, a system will already exist that is poised to receive him as a savior and to give allegiance to him.

Islam: Islam is already the second-largest religion and will at present growth rates become the largest religion within a few decades. Islam awaits the coming of the Mahdi with universal anticipation.

The Muslim Jesus

After the emergence or the "rising" of the Mahdi, the second most important event among the Major Signs is the return of Jesus Christ. Christians who love Jesus understandably get quite excited by the prospect that Muslims look for and long for His return. Unfortunately, the Islamic belief of just who this Jesus is that is coming, and what He does once He has arrived, is drastically different than what Christians believe about Jesus.

The first thing that Christians need to understand regarding the Islamic belief about Jesus is that Muslims of course reject the idea that Jesus was or is the Son of God. According to Islam, Jesus is not, as the Bible articulates, God in the flesh. Second, in Islamic belief, Jesus never died on a cross for the sins of mankind. The Qur'an specifically denies that Jesus was ever crucified or that He ever experienced death. Muslims believe that after Allah miraculously delivered Jesus from death, He ascended into heaven alive in a similar fashion to the biblical narrative regarding Elijah.

Since then, Muslims believe, Jesus has remained with Allah, awaiting His opportunity to return to the earth to finish His ministry and complete His life. As such, to

*the Islamic mind, Jesus was not in any way a "savior."
To Muslims, Jesus was merely another prophet in the
long line of prophets that Allah has sent to mankind. The
special title of Messiah, although retained in the Islamic
tradition, is essentially stripped of any truly biblically
defined messianic characteristics. According to the
sacred texts of Islam, as we are about to see, when Jesus
returns, it most certainly will not be to restore the nation
of Israel to the Jewish people. Nor will Jesus' purpose
be to save and deliver His faithful followers from the
ongoing persecution of the Antichrist. In order to
understand the Islamic concept of Jesus' return, the first
thing that needs to be realized is that when Jesus comes
back, He comes back as a radical Muslim.*

The Antichrist Spirit of Islam

*While we have already discussed the actual person of
the Antichrist, the Bible also talks of an antichrist spirit.
Apart from the one direct reference in the Bible to the
Antichrist, there are four other times that the Apostle
John uses the word in a more general sense. Each time
it is in reference to a particular spirit. This spirit is
defined by its denial of some very specific aspects of
Jesus' nature and His relationship to God the Father.
Following are the verses that describe this "antichrist"
spirit:*

1 John 4:3 (NKJV) *and every spirit that does not
confess that Jesus Christ has come in the flesh is not of
God. And this is the spirit of the Antichrist, which you
have heard was coming, and is now already in the world.*

1 John 2:22-23 (NKJV) *22 Who is a liar but he who
denies that Jesus is the Christ? He is antichrist who*

*denies the Father and the Son. 23 Whoever denies
the Son does not have the Father either; he who
acknowledges the Son has the Father also.*

2 John 1:7 (NKJV) *For many deceivers have gone
out into the world who do not confess Jesus Christ as
coming in the flesh. This is a deceiver and an antichrist.*

*From these verses, we learn that the antichrist is a spirit
that is identified as a "liar" and a "deceiver" who
specifically denies the following:*

*That Jesus is the Christ/Messiah (the savior/deliverer of
Israel and the world).*

*The Father and the Son (the Trinity or that Jesus is the
Son of God).*

*That Jesus has come in the flesh (the incarnation—that
God became man).*

*The religion of Islam, more than any other religion,
philosophy, or belief system, fulfills the description of
the antichrist spirit. The religion of Islam makes one of
its highest priorities the denial of all three of the points
regarding Jesus and His relationship to the Father. In
fact, we can fairly claim that Islam is a direct polemical
response against those essential Christian doctrines.*

*Regarding the previous points, however, Muslims will
be quick to argue that Islam teaches that Jesus is indeed
the Messiah. But this is really just trickery. While it
is true that Islam does retain the title of Messiah for
Jesus, when one asks a Muslim to define what the title
"Messiah" actually means in Islam, the definitions given
are always hollow and fall entirely short of containing
any truly messianic substance.*

*In Islam, Jesus is merely another prophet in a very long
line of prophets. Biblically speaking, however, the role
of the Messiah among other things entails being a divine
priestly savior, a deliverer, and the king of the Jews.
As we saw in earlier chapters, rather than delivering
His followers, the Muslim Jesus leads Israel's enemies
against her and seeks to convert or kill all the Jews and
Christians. This would the equivalent of calling Adolph
Hitler, rather than Moses, Israel's deliverer. But the
Apostle John informs us that in the last hour, a man is
coming who will fully personify the antichrist spirit and
deny many of the essential biblical doctrines regarding
who Jesus is and what He came to do. That man will be
the Antichrist.*

Tawhid And Shirk

*In order to properly understand the antichrist spirit
of Islam, there are two doctrines that must first be
understood. Tawhid refers to the belief in the absolute
oneness of God. Islam adheres to the strictest form of
unitarian monotheism possible. In Islam, God is utterly
alone. But in order to understand tawhid, one must
understand that it is more than just a doctrine; in Islam,
belief in tahwid is an absolute commandment. And if
adherence to tawhid is the highest and most important
commandment in Islam, then the greatest sin is shirk.
Shirk is, in essence, idolatry. From the "Invitation to
Islam" newsletter published by a Muslim group from
Toronto, we read a very telling statement that helps us to
understand exactly how shirk is viewed by Muslims:*

*Murder, rape, child molesting, and genocide. These are
all some of the appalling crimes which occur in our
world today. Many would think that these are the worst*

possible offences which could be committed. But there is something which outweighs all of these crimes put together: It is the crime of shirk.

Thus many Muslims feel as though believing in the Trinity or ascribing divinity to Jesus are among the greatest sins conceivable. In fact, believing in these essential Christian doctrines is more than just a sin; it is the most heinous of all crimes! In the Muslim mind, shirk refers not only to the beliefs of polytheists or pagans, but also to the essential historical doctrines of the Christian faith. We will examine these three essential doctrines and how Islam specifically denies them.

Islam Denies The Sonship Of Christ

The religion of Islam has as one of its foundational beliefs a direct denial of Jesus as God's Son. This denial is found several times throughout the Qur'an:

In blasphemy indeed are those that say that God is Christ the son of Mary. (Sura 5:17; Yusuf Ali)

They say: "God hath begotten a son!"—Glory be to Him! He is self-sufficient! His are all things in the heavens and on earth! No warrant have ye for this! Say ye about Allah what ye know not? (Sura 10:68; Yusuf Ali)

They said, "The Most Gracious has begotten a son"! You have uttered a gross blasphemy. The heavens are about to shatter, the earth is about to tear asunder, and the mountains are about to crumble. Because they claim that the Most Gracious has begotten a son. It is not befitting the Most Gracious that He should beget a son. (Sura 19:88–92 Rashad Khalifa)

The Christians call Christ the son of Allah. That is a saying from their mouth; [in this] they but imitate what the unbelievers of old used to say. Allah's curse be on them: how they are deluded away from the Truth! (Sura 9:30; Yusuf Ali, emphasis mine)

The Qur'an pronounces a curse on those who believe that Jesus is God's Son. People who say such things utter "gross blasphemies" and are likened to "unbelievers" or infidels. Without question then, in this regard, Islam is an antichrist religious system. Remember Jim Hacking's comments from chapter one? He was the priest in training who converted to Islam. "The thing I've always latched to is that there's one God, he doesn't have equals, he doesn't need a son to come do his work." Islam attempts to create an acceptable form of monotheistic worship yet it not only leaves out the most essential aspects of a saving relationship with God, but it also directly confronts these things and calls them the highest forms of blasphemy. "Far be it from God that he should have a son!" These words encircle the inside of the Dome of the Rock Mosque in Jerusalem—the very location where for centuries God's people, the Jews, worshipped in their Temple awaiting their Messiah. This is also where Jesus, the Son of God and the Jewish Messiah will someday rule over the earth. Islam has built a monument of utter defiance to this future reality.

Islam Denies The Trinity

Islam applies the same claim of blasphemy to those who believe in the Trinity:

They do blaspheme who say: Allah is one of three in a Trinity: for there is no god except One Allah. If they desist not from their word [of blasphemy], verily a grievous penalty will befall the blasphemers among them. (Sura 5:73;)

Thus belief in the Trinity is also defined as blasphemy. But what is the "grievous penalty" that shall befall those who believe such things? Well, as we saw in previous chapters, many Muslims ironically expect their version of Jesus to return and kill these "polytheist Trinitarian Christians."

And the Qur'an does not stop at denying that Jesus is the Son of God or that God exists as a Trinity.

Islam Denies The Cross

With tears in his eyes, Paul the Apostle warned the Thessalonians that, "many live as enemies of the cross of Christ" (Philippians 3:18). It should not come as a surprise, then, that Islam also denies the most central event of all of redemptive history: the crucifixion of Jesus. Speaking to the Jews of Jesus' day, the Qur'an says:

That they said [in boast], "We killed Christ Jesus the son of Mary, the Messenger of Allah"; but they killed him not, nor crucified him, but so it was made to appear to them, and those who differ therein are full of doubts, with no [certain] knowledge, but only conjecture to follow, for of a surety they killed him not: Nay, Allah raised him up unto himself; and Allah is exalted in power, wise. (Sura 4:157–8; Yusuf Ali)

Islamic scholars put forth conflicting theories regarding exactly what happened to Jesus. (Ironically, regarding this issue it is actually they who are the ones who have "only conjecture to follow.") But despite the inability of Muslims to arrive at any form of consensus regarding what happened to Jesus, they are very much in agreement on at least one issue: He was not crucified! This passage of the Qur'an makes at least this much clear.

How Does The Antichrist Spirit Of Islam Affect Muslims?

So we see that Islam very specifically and very deliberately denies all three of the doctrines that the Apostle John says the antichrist spirit will deny. The Qur'an does not merely deny these doctrines but expresses utter disdain for them, actually cursing those who believe these things, accusing them of gross blasphemy. But how do these Qur'anic attitudes then affect Muslims? This statement may sound strong, but in all of my years of outreach, interfaith dialogue, and casual conversations with those who are not Christians, the two groups that I have personally witnessed expressing the strongest degree of contempt and mockery toward the Gospel have been Satanists and Muslims. Only these two have expressed such a high degree of venomous disgust.

While many religions and systems of belief exist that do not agree with the doctrines of Christianity—many of which do not even believe in God—only Islam fills the role of a religion that exists to deny core Christian beliefs. And of course, following the lead of the Qur'an, the three doctrines most severely and most often attacked and mocked by Muslims are the doctrines of the Trinity, the divine incarnation, and the atoning sacrifice/ crucifixion of Jesus.

We should not be surprised then to find that one of the descriptions of the Antichrist is that he will be very fond of uttering great blasphemies against the God of the Bible:

Daniel 11:36 (NKJV) *"Then the king shall do according to his own will: he shall exalt and magnify himself above every god, shall speak blasphemies against the God of gods, and shall prosper till the wrath has been accomplished; for what has been determined shall be done.*

Daniel 7:25 (NKJV) *He shall speak pompous words against the Most High, Shall persecute the saints of the Most High, And shall intend to change times and law. Then the saints shall be given into his hand For a time and times and half a time.*

The Qur'an itself expresses such blasphemies. As someone who is in continual dialogue with numerous Muslims from all over the world, I can testify that the blatant antichrist spirit that we saw expressed in the previous Qur'anic passages quite often blooms into an overt disdain and utter contempt, not only for Christian beliefs, but also for Christians themselves. While this is not always the case, should we really be surprised when Muslims act out against those whom the Qur'an curses as idolatrous infidel blasphemers? And if we are being realistic, should we expect the future of Islam to rest with those Muslims who identify with the Qur'anic scorn for Christians, or with those who show an amiable attitude despite the curses of their own holy book?

In regard to whether or not Islam is specifically the antichrist system that the Bible foretells, there can be no

*question that this, the second-largest, fastest-growing
religion in the world, is, and has been from its inception,
the quintessence of the very antichrist spirit about which
John the Apostle warned us.*

I am thankful for Pastor Kodiyil's work. The Islamic Antichrist is the Dajjal, meaning "the liar" or "the deceptive one." In Arabian literature, he is known as *Al Masih al-Dajjal* (false messiah). What is particularly interesting in an etymological study of "dajjal" is that the origin of the word can be traced back to the Christian-Syriac Aramaic dialect; it is not originally an Arabic name. In fact, the origin of this Dajjal character is found in a pseudepigraphal New Testament book excluded from the biblical canon due to dubious authorship. The book is titled *The First Apocryphal Apocalypse of John*, dated to the early seventh century AD, though it has nothing to do with John—just as Peter was not the first pope. This book is shrouded in doubts regarding both authorship and time of writing, and for good reason it is not part of our Bible.

From this apocryphal book of dubious origin, which predates the Quran, comes the description of the "dajjal" in what is considered a Christian manuscript of highly dubious origin:

- Face is dark
- Hairs of his head are sharp as arrows
- Eyebrows are like a field (i.e., wildness)
- Right eye like the morning star rising
- Other eye like a lion
- His mouth is one cubit length
- Teeth a broad span
- Fingers are like sickles
- Footprint is two spans
- Upon his forehead, an inscription "Antichrist"

This is the first "dajjal" Antichrist appearing in a book that was falsely attributed to the Apostle John and carries obvious issues. Hold this thought while I share another piece of history that may qualify as the mother of all conspiracies.

I believe the timeline of this apocryphal book of John is kept quiet because it coincides too closely with the arrival of the prophet Muhammad and the founding of Islam. In fact, I believe Muhammad may have been persuaded by the author of this dubious book, or possibly the book itself was a source of inspiration. This profound statement is based on an observation of history that has long been obscured from public view.

The final blow to the Roman Empire occurred when the Germanic tribe leader Odoacer entered the city unopposed by Caesar Romulus Augustus, who was officially the last emperor of Rome. But Roman rule over the nations did not vanish; it fell into the shadows, secretly governed by a far more powerful force that had begun centuries earlier. The Roman Catholic Church and the papacy of Rome were well established, and Rome's power had begun to shift away from the Caesars. A transition of power slowly shifted to a new "pontifex maximus"—the pope of Rome.

Though Augustus Caesar was the first *pontifex maximus* of the Roman Empire in 27 BC, his predecessor Julius Caesar, ruling over the Republic of Rome, was the first Roman leader to bear the title. Julius Caesar was both the first Caesar and the first *pontifex maximus* (the "great bridge between man and god") of Rome. Yet Julius Caesar wasn't the first to hold this title. That title is attributed by some to Nimrod, including Rev. Alexander Hislop. According to Hislop and others, Semiramis established the first Babylonian priesthood with Nimrod as its high priest, or "pontifex maximus," where he served as both high priest of the royal priesthood and king of Babylon. Nimrod as king and priest was a cheap forgery of the original Melchizedek title (meaning "king and priest") that I believe Adam held before his fall.

This Babylonian priesthood system under pontifex maximus authority continued in various forms until 539 BC, when Cyrus the Persian conquered Babylon. For the most part, Cyrus allowed this system to continue. This Babylonian priesthood was still practiced in the kingdom of Pergamos, the farthest extension of the Babylonian empire, several centuries after Cyrus's reign. Attalus III was the last king and *pontifex maximus* of Pergamos.

On his deathbed in 133 BC, Attalus III relinquished his authority over Pergamos and title of pontifex maximus to Julius Caesar.

The "great bridge between man and god" that began with Nimrod and survived beyond the sun and moon worship traditions of Babylon, continued to the last Babylonian *pontifex maximus* Attalus III, then was passed on to Rome under Julius Caesar. All Caesars from Julius to Romulus bore the title "pontifex maximus."

Rome wasn't built in a day, nor did it fall in a day. Pope Damasus was the first to take the title "supreme pontiff" around AD 380, a title that had always been reserved for the Caesars. But the first to be called a "Vicar of Christ" on earth was Pope Gelasius 1, about fifteen years after the last Caesar of Rome, around AD 492. It is ironic that, although many factors contributed to the fall of Rome, the spread of Christianity and lack of reverence for the Caesars as "gods" played a major role. But Rome never died. The Roman Empire quietly moved into the shadows under the papacy.

This takes us to AD 610 and the father of Islam, Muhammad. There is a backstory about Muhammad that very few have ever known. It has been tightly kept in the Vatican for fourteen centuries until a Jesuit priest named Alberto Rivera, whom I mentioned earlier, left the Jesuit order and the Catholic Church.

I was reluctant to share Rivera's story in this book because he became such a controversial figure with his outrageous claims. The Catholic Church denied that he was ever a priest or Jesuit, and a whirlwind of campaigns arose to discredit him. I had to carefully consider whether to use his claims to avoid conflicts of my own, because his stories are extremely controversial. The Jesuits ruined his life, tortured him in a sanitorium, and staged payments in his name with bad checks and credit card fraud, among other things, to shut him up.

Because I know how these secret societies work to protect themselves— and how they will ruin anyone's life or even assassinate (by "suicide") those who stand in their way—I believe Rivera had an epiphany at some point and decided to clear his conscience. What makes whistleblowers so valuable is that they reach a point where they cannot live with their own conscience, and the fear of hell overtakes them if they truly know God. When whistleblowers fear being ostracized by God and inheriting the kingdom of death with Satan, they experience a sudden epiphany to clear their conscience. The most valuable and useful information regarding the sons of disobedience often comes from those suddenly overcome with the fear of the One True God, who then depart from Satan's global operations.

After reading Alberto Rivera's story, the conclusion I have drawn is that at least most of it is probably true, based on the degree to which he was persecuted for his claims. That being said, do what you will with the following information. I personally believe the Jesuits intended to destroy Rivera's credibility rather than kill him and make him a martyr. After sharing this article written by Rivera, I will provide additional remarks and observations that may substantiate his claims based on visual evidence.

FYI, all websites containing Rivera's letters and articles are constantly being scrubbed from top web searches. I found this one archived at us.archive.org, which was surprising.

"How the Vatican created Islam." This is the account of an ex-Jesuit priest, Alberto Rivera, who claimed the story was told to him by Cardinal Bea while he was at the Vatican. *(This information comes from Alberto Rivera, former Jesuit priest, after his conversion to Protestant Christianity. It is excerpted from* The Prophet, *published by Chick Publications, PO Box 661, Chino, CA 91708. Since its publication, and after several unsuccessful attempts on his life, he died suddenly from food poisoning. His testimony should not be silenced. Dr. Rivera speaks to us still.)*

<u>How the Vatican Created Islam</u>

By Alberto Rivera

What I'm going to tell you is what I learned in secret
briefings in the Vatican when I was a Jesuit priest, under
oath and induction. A Jesuit cardinal named Augustine
Bea showed us how desperately the Roman Catholics
wanted Jerusalem at the end of the third century.

Because of its religious history and its strategic location, the Holy City was considered a priceless treasure. A scheme had to be developed to make Jerusalem a Roman Catholic city.

The great untapped source of manpower that could do this job was the children of Ishmael. The poor Arabs fell victim to one of the most clever plans ever devised by the powers of darkness.

Early Christians went everywhere with the gospel setting up small churches, but they met heavy opposition. Both the Jews and the Roman government persecuted the believers in Christ to stop their spread. But the Jews rebelled against Rome, and in 70 AD, Roman armies under General Titus smashed Jerusalem and destroyed the great Jewish temple which was the heart of Jewish worship...in fulfillment of Christ's prophecy in Matthew 24:2.

On this holy place today where the temple once stood, the Dome of the Rock Mosque stands as Islam's second most holy place. Sweeping changes were in the wind. Corruption, apathy, greed, cruelty, perversion and rebellion were eating at the Roman Empire, and it was ready to collapse. The persecution against Christians was useless as they continued to lay down their lives for the gospel of Christ.

The only way Satan could stop this thrust was to create a counterfeit "Christian" religion to destroy the work of God. The solution was in Rome. Their religion had come from ancient Babylon and all it needed was a face-lift. This didn't happen overnight, but began in the writings of the 'early church fathers'.

It was through their writings that a new religion would take shape. The statue of Jupiter in Rome was eventually called St. Peter, and the statue of Venus was changed to the Virgin Mary. The site chosen for its headquarters was on one of the seven hills called 'Vaticanus', the place of the divining serpent where the satanic temple of Janus stood.

The great counterfeit religion was Roman Catholicism, called 'Mystery, Babylon the Great, the Mother of Harlots and Abominations of the Earth'- Revelation 17:5. She was raised up to block the gospel, slaughter the believers in Christ, establish religions, create wars and make the nations

drunk with the wine of her fornication as we will see.

Three major religions have one thing in common - each has a holy place where they look for guidance. Roman Catholicism looks to the Vatican as the Holy City. The Jews look to the wailing wall in Jerusalem, and the Muslims look to Mecca as their Holy City. Each group believes that they receive certain types of blessings for the rest of their lives for visiting their holy place. In the beginning, Arab visitors would bring gifts to the 'House of God', and the keepers of the Kaaba were gracious to all who came. Some brought their idols and, not wanting to offend these people, their idols were placed inside the sanctuary. It is said that the Jews looked upon the Kaaba

as an outlying tabernacle of the Lord with veneration
until it became polluted with idols.

In a tribal contention over a well (Zamzam) the treasure
of the Kaaba and the offerings that pilgrims had given
were dumped down the well and it was filled with sand -
it disappeared.

Many years later Adb Al-Muttalib was given visions
telling him where to find the well and its treasure. He
became the hero of Mecca, and he was destined to
become the grandfather of Muhammad. ***Before this
time, Augustine became the bishop of North Africa and
was effective in winning Arabs to Roman Catholicism,
including whole tribes***. It was among these Arab
converts to Catholicism that the concept of looking for
an Arab prophet developed.

Muhammad's father died from illness and sons born to
great Arab families in places like Mecca were sent into
the desert to be suckled and weaned and spend some of
their childhood with Bedouin tribes for training and to
avoid the plagues in the cities.

After his mother and grandfather also died, Muhammad
was with his uncle when a Roman Catholic monk
learned of his identity and said, "Take your brother's
son back to his country and guard him against the Jews,
for by god, if they see him and know of him that which
I know, they will construe evil against him. Great things
are in store for this brother's son of yours.

The Roman Catholic monk had fanned the flames for
future Jewish persecutions at the hands of the followers

of Muhammad. The Vatican desperately wanted Jerusalem because of its religious significance, but was blocked by the Jews.

Another problem was the true Christians in North Africa who preached the gospel. Roman Catholicism was growing in power, but would not tolerate opposition. Somehow the Vatican had to create a weapon to eliminate both the Jews and the true Christian believers who refused to

accept Roman Catholicism. Looking to North Africa, they saw the multitudes of Arabs as a source of manpower to do their dirty work. Some Arabs had become Roman Catholic, and could be used in reporting information to leaders in Rome. Others were used in an underground spy

network to carry out Rome's master plan to control the great multitudes of Arabs who rejected Catholicism. When 'St Augustine' appeared on the scene, he knew what was going on. His monasteries served as bases to seek out and destroy Bible manuscripts owned by the true Christians.

The Vatican wanted to create a messiah for the Arabs, someone they could raise up as a great leader, a man with charisma whom they could train, and eventually unite all the non-Catholic Arabs behind him, creating a mighty army that would ultimately capture Jerusalem for the pope.

In the Vatican briefing, Cardinal Bea told us this story:

A wealthy Arabian lady who was a faithful follower of the pope played a tremendous part in this drama. She was a widow named Khadijah. She gave her wealth to the church and retired to a convent, but was given an assignment. She was to find a brilliant young man who could be used by the Vatican to create a new religion and become the messiah for the children of Ishmael.

Khadijah had a cousin named Waraquah,, who was also a very faithful Roman Catholic and the Vatican placed him in a critical role as Muhammad's advisor. He had tremendous influence on Muhammad.

'Teachers were sent to young Muhammad and he had intensive training. Muhammad studied the works of St. Augustine which prepared him for his "great calling." The Vatican had Catholic Arabs across North Africa spread the story of a great one who was about to rise up among the people and be the chosen one of their God.

While Muhammad was being prepared, he was told that his enemies were the Jews and that the only true Christians were Roman Catholic. He was taught that others calling themselves

Christians were actually wicked impostors and should be destroyed. Many Muslims believe this.

Muhammad began receiving "divine revelations" and his wife's Catholic cousin Waraquah helped interpret them. From this came the Koran. In the fifth year of Muhammad's mission, persecution came against his followers because they refused to worship the idols in the Kaaba.

Muhammad instructed some of them to flee to Abysinnia where Negus, the Roman Catholic king accepted them because Muhammad's views on the virgin Mary were so close to Roman Catholic doctrine. These Muslims received protection from Catholic kings because of Muhammad's revelations.

Muhammad later conquered Mecca and the Kaaba was cleared of idols. History proves that before Islam came into existence, the Sabeans in Arabia worshiped the moon-god who was married to the sun-god. They gave birth to three goddesses who were worshipped throughout the Arab world as "Daughters of Allah" An idol excavated at Hazor in Palestine in 1950's shows Allah sitting on a throne with the crescent moon on his chest.

Muhammad claimed he had a vision from Allah and was told, "You are the messenger of Allah."

This began his career as a prophet and he received many messages. By the time Muhammad died, the religion of Islam was exploding. The nomadic Arab tribes were joining forces in the name of Allah and his prophet, Muhammad.

Some of Muhammad's writings were placed in the Koran, others were never published. They are now in the hands of high ranking holy men (Ayatollahs) in the Islamic faith.

When Cardinal Bea shared with us in the Vatican, he said, these writings are guarded because they contain information that links the Vatican to the creation of Islam. Both sides have so much information on each other, that if exposed, it could create such a scandal that it would be a disaster for both religions.

In their "holy" book, the Koran, Christ is regarded as only a prophet. If the pope was His representative on earth, then he also must be a prophet of God. This caused the followers of Muhammad to fear and respect the pope as another "holy man."

The pope moved quickly and issued bulls granting the Arab generals permission to invade and conquer the nations of North Africa. The Vatican helped to finance the building of these massive Islamic armies in exchange for three favors:

Eliminate the Jews and Christians (true believers, which they called infidels).

Protect the Augustinian Monks and Roman Catholics.

Conquer Jerusalem for "His Holiness" in the Vatican

As time went by, the power of Islam became tremendous - Jews and true Christians were slaughtered, and Jerusalem fell into their hands. Roman Catholics were never attacked, nor were their shrines, during this time. But when the pope asked for Jerusalem, he was surprised at their denial! The Arab generals had such military success that they could not be intimidated by the pope - nothing could stand in the way of their own plan.

Under Waraquah's direction, Muhammad wrote that Abraham offered Ishmael as a sacrifice.

The Bible says that Isaac was the sacrifice, but Muhammad removed Isaac's name and inserted Ishmael's name. As a result of this and Muhammad's vision, the faithful Muslims built a mosque, the Dome of the Rock, in Ishmael's honor on the site of the Jewish temple that was destroyed in 70 AD. This made Jerusalem the 2nd most holy place in the Islam faith. How could they give such a sacred shrine to the pope without causing a revolt?

The pope realized what they had created was out of control when he heard they were calling "His Holiness" an infidel. The Muslim generals were determined to conquer the world for Allah and now they turned toward Europe. Islamic ambassadors approached the pope and asked for

papal bulls to give them permission to invade European countries.

The Vatican was outraged; war was inevitable. Temporal power and control of the world was considered the basic right of the pope. He wouldn't think of sharing it with those whom he considered heathens.

The pope raised up his armies and called them crusades to hold back the children of Ishmael from grabbing Catholic Europe. The crusades lasted centuries and Jerusalem slipped out of the pope's hands.

Turkey fell and Spain and Portugal were invaded by Islamic forces. In Portugal, they called a mountain village "Fatima" in honor of Muhammad's daughter, never dreaming it would become world famous.

Years later when the Muslim armies were poised on the islands of Sardinia and Corsica, to invade Italy, there was a serious problem. The Islamic generals realized they were too far extended. It was time for peace talks. One of the negotiators was Francis of Assisi.

As a result, the Muslims were allowed to occupy Turkey in a "Christian" world, and the Catholics were allowed to occupy Lebanon in the Arab world. It was also agreed that the Muslims could build mosques in Catholic countries without interference as long as Roman Catholicism could flourish Arab countries.

Cardinal Bea told us in Vatican briefings that both the Muslims and Roman Catholics agreed to block and destroy the efforts of their common enemy, Bible-believing Christian missionaries.

Through these concordats, Satan blocked the children of Ishmael from a knowledge of Scripture and the truth.

The Islamic community looks on the Bible-believing missionary as a devil who brings poison to the children of Allah. This explains years of ministry in those countries with little results.

The next plan was to control Islam. In 1910, Portugal was going Socialistic. Red flags were appearing and the

Catholic Church was facing a major problem. Increasing numbers were against the church.

The Jesuits wanted Russia involved, and the location of this vision at Fatima could play a key part in pulling Islam to the Mother Church.

In 1917, the Virgin appeared in Fatima. "The Mother of God" was a smashing success, playing to overflow crowds. As a result, the Socialists of Portugal suffered a major defeat.

Roman Catholics world-wide began praying for the conversion of Russia and the Jesuits invented the Novenas to Fatima which they could perform throughout North Africa, spreading good public relations to the Muslim world. The Arabs thought they were honoring the daughter of Muhammad, which is what the Jesuits wanted them to believe.

As a result of the vision of Fatima, Pope Pius XII ordered his Nazi army to crush Russia and the Orthodox religion and make Russia Roman Catholic." A few years after he lost World war II, Pope Pius XII startled the world with his phony dancing sun vision to keep Fatima in the news. It was great religious show biz and the world swallowed it.

Not surprisingly, Pope Pius was the only one to see this vision. As a result, a group of followers has grown into a Blue Army world-wide, totaling millions of faithful Roman Catholics ready to die for the blessed virgin.

But we haven't seen anything yet. The Jesuits have their
Virgin Mary scheduled to appear four or five times in
China, Russia, and major appearance in the US.

What has this got to do with Islam? Note Bishop Sheen's
statement: "Our Lady's appearances at Fatima marked
the turning point in the history of the world's 350 million
Muslims. After the death of his daughter, Muhammad
wrote that she "is the most holy of all women in
Paradise, next to Mary."

He believed that the Virgin Mary chose to be known
as Our Lady of Fatima as a sign and a pledge that the
Muslims who believe in Christ's virgin birth, will come
to believe in His divinity.

Bishop Sheen pointed out that the pilgrim virgin statues
of Our Lady of Fatima were enthusiastically received
by Muslims in Africa, India, and elsewhere, and that
many Muslims are now coming into the Roman Catholic
Church.

If you're still reading, take a breath.

It is mind-blowing, and it reminds me of something I learned from
my Jewish friend Eli over twenty years ago. Eli had ties with various
intelligence agencies, including Mossad, and there were times when I
simply could not mentally process the information he shared with me. But
one thing he said that I will always remember and apply was this: "You
must be willing to assume that everything you think you know is probably
a lie, or at best, a piece of truth that has been tainted with lies to control
a political narrative. History, politics, and religion are not what you think
you know from history books and news reports. Everything is a lie. You

must accept that as a fact if you truly want to learn anything, then dig to find the truth."

It wasn't until I took a deep dive into the Bible eight years ago and began to understand that there are two kingdoms on earth—and that the prince of the kingdom of this world is Satan—that I began to view the world differently. When I understood the Bible and how Satan took legal possession of the earth from the first Adam, I began to question everything. History has been rewritten to persuade our thoughts and influence what we choose to believe. And it's working. We grow comfortable in a network of lies and stop thinking critically. It feels like too much work to erase the lies and start over, so we remain ignorant in our complacence. Satan's mission is accomplished, and voilà'38 percent of Christians think Satan is a mythological figure!

The other day I was in a grocery store, and two women were arguing about something they had heard on the news. I thought to myself, *The only reason they're discussing this is because someone in corporate media decided what would be the news narrative of the day. News is propaganda and serves a purpose toward another agenda that is not even being remotely considered in their conversation.*

This is Satan's kingdom—don't fall for the lies. Learn to become a critical thinker and question everything. The sons of God who are led by the Spirit will instinctively know when something isn't quite right. When we feel these inner emotions speaking to us through the Spirit, we pray about the matter, and deeper insights will come. This is Satan's world for now; do not expect good things from its operatives. If you are among the future sons of God, let the Spirit lead! Don't follow deceptions designed by the prince of this world into a trap.

Rivera's story would be much easier to dismiss as whacko conspiracy theory lunacy if it were not for the overwhelming archives of evidence against the Vatican and the Roman Catholic Church. In Dave Hunt's book *A Woman Rides the Beast*, Hunt documents atrocities so horrific that Rivera's story seems like a kindergarten fairy tale by comparison.

For example, it is well established that the Vatican was complicit in Hitler's rise to power, and that both Hitler and Mussolini were baptized into the Roman Catholic Church. Catholicism became the official religion of Germany and Italy under their rule. The Vatican helped finance Germany's war efforts. The goal of the fascist Nazis and the Vatican was the same: eliminate the Jews. The Vatican has always secretly wanted to control Jerusalem, as Rivera mentioned.

Nazis were afforded escape and seclusion through the Vatican Ratlines. The Vatican (Jesuits) provided Vatican diplomatic passports to Nazi war criminals disguised as priests and bishops, along with travel accommodations to South America, USA, and Canada after the Allied forces invaded Germany. This is not conspiracy theory; it has been well documented.

The one person who could have silenced Hitler—when 42 percent of German soldiers were Catholics—was the pope. Yet he chose to remain silent, fully aware that Jews were being exterminated and was complicit in their attempted extinction.

This is recent history. It did not occur during the medieval period or the Inquisition that began in the thirteenth century. What we see is a pattern that spans the entire history of the Roman Catholic Church—beginning with the fact that Peter was never the first pope.

We choose what we want to believe, and I pray it isn't a lie. Ask yourself this question: why wouldn't we believe Rivera's story when the Vatican has no credibility left? There is an overwhelming amount of evidence implicating the Vatican in sinister events, and dismissing Rivera's story too quickly is just willful ignorance. But based on the reactions I've already received when sharing this information, I know most people will forget about it within five minutes of reading. This is Satan's greatest talent—hiding in plain sight. This is precisely why 38 percent of Christians don't even believe that Satan or the Holy Spirit are living entities. Willful ignorance coincides with disbelief.

To continue, do you see the connections spanning time? St. Augustine was influenced by Plato's writings. Plato's philosophies, infused into Christian theology, gave rise to modern "universalism" and "mother earth" progressivist neo-religions, where man is portrayed as capable of becoming all-knowing and capable of achieving a godlike existence through self-awareness and positive thinking in pursuit of the divine. However sincere Augustine may have been in his monotheistic belief in the One True God, his interest in philosophers who did not know God eventually dealt a detrimental blow to the Christian faith.

The most severe blow to Christianity was inspired by St. Augustine, as his influence contributed to the religious shaping of Muhammad, giving birth to the greatest archenemy of Christians and Jews ever to exist. The goal of Islam is not peaceful coexistence with Christians and Jews, but rather their extermination from the earth.

I want to review how Plato influenced St. Augustine to enhance our understanding of how Christianity slowly morphed into something other than the church of the book of Acts where it began. This is an article from Christian.net on theology and spirituality:

Augustine's Use of Plato's Ideas in his Theology

Augustine's theological framework bears the indelible imprint of Plato's ideas, as he deftly wove the rich tapestry of classical philosophy into the fabric of Christian doctrine. One of the central themes through which Augustine appropriated Plato's ideas is the concept of the transcendent Forms. For Plato, the Forms represented the immutable archetypes of reality, transcending the material world. Augustine ingeniously integrated this concept into his theological discourse, positing the divine as the ultimate Form, the source of all reality and perfection. This theological appropriation of Platonic Forms enriched Augustine's articulation of the divine transcendence and the eternal verities that undergird the created order.

Furthermore, Augustine's engagement with Plato's allegory of the cave found profound resonance in his theological reflections. The allegory, depicting

*humanity's journey from the shadows of ignorance
towards the illumination of truth, provided Augustine
with a powerful metaphor for the human quest for God.
Augustine deftly employed this allegory to expound
on the transformative journey of the soul, enshrining
the yearning for divine illumination at the core of his
theological vision.*

*Moreover, Augustine's appropriation of Plato's insights
on the nature of love and the ascent towards the
contemplation of the divine enriched his theological
reflections on the primacy of love in the Christian life.
Drawing inspiration from Plato's dialogues, Augustine
expounded on the transformative power of love in
guiding the soul towards union with the divine, thereby
infusing his theological discourse with profound insights
on the nature of divine love and the human longing for
communion with God.*

*Additionally, Augustine's nuanced engagement with
the Neoplatonic concept of the soul's ascent towards
the One, as expounded by Plotinus, permeated his
theological reflections on the human soul's yearning for
union with God. This Neoplatonic framework provided
Augustine with a philosophical language to articulate
the soul's innate orientation towards the divine,
enriching his theological anthropology with profound
insights into the nature of the human longing for ultimate
fulfillment in God.*

*In essence, Augustine's use of Plato's ideas in his
theology represents a masterful synthesis of classical
philosophy and Christian doctrine, enriching the*

theological landscape with profound insights into the nature of reality, the human soul, and the yearning for ultimate truth. This dynamic appropriation of Platonic ideas underscores the enduring legacy of Augustine's theological vision, which continues to inspire contemplative exploration and theological discourse in the Christian tradition.

In conclusion, the profound influence of Plato's ideas on Augustine's theological and philosophical framework is unmistakably evident in the intricate tapestry of his writings. Augustine's engagement with the Platonic concepts of transcendent Forms, the allegory of the cave, the nature of love, and the soul's ascent towards the divine enriched his theological discourse with profound insights that continue to resonate in the contemplative exploration of faith and reason.

By deftly weaving the rich tapestry of classical philosophy into the fabric of Christian doctrine, Augustine synthesized the wisdom of Plato with the tenets of Christian faith, thereby enriching the theological discourse of his time. The enduring legacy of Augustine's synthesis of Platonic thought and Christian theology continues to resonate in theological discourse, shedding light on the intellectual and spiritual landscape of the early Church.

The interplay between classical philosophy and Christian theology, as exemplified in Augustine's appropriation of Plato's ideas, underscores the dynamic dialogue between faith and reason, the contemplative exploration of the human condition, and the enduring quest for ultimate truth. Augustine's theological vision, shaped by the profound influence of Plato's philosophy, stands as a testament to the enduring power of intellectual and spiritual synthesis in the development of Christian thought.

In tracing the contours of Augustine's engagement with Plato's ideas, we gain a deeper understanding of the intellectual currents that shaped the development of Christian theology in the early centuries of the Church. This exploration illuminates the enduring legacy of Augustine's synthesis of classical wisdom and Christian doctrine, enriching the theological discourse with profound insights that continue to inspire contemplative exploration and theological discourse in the Christian tradition.

Ultimately, Augustine's use of Plato's ideas in his theology represents a masterful synthesis of classical philosophy and Christian doctrine, enriching the theological landscape with profound insights into the nature of reality, the human soul, and the yearning for ultimate truth. This dynamic appropriation of Platonic ideas underscores the enduring legacy of Augustine's theological vision, which continues to inspire contemplative exploration and theological discourse in the Christian tradition.[27]

Wow, so sophisticated, and so eloquently written! Yet it all led to a scholarly corruption of Christianity, the creation of false doctrines (Astronism being merely the latest among many), and ultimately inspired

---

27   https://christian.net/theology-and-spirituality/how-did-augustine-use-platos-ideas/

the archenemy of Christians and Jews. This is the problem with any academic endeavor not firmly planted in the Word of God. Plato was not a "son of God led by the Spirit," or he would have pursued the literature of the Hebrews, which he surely must have known about. Abraham and Moses preceded Plato by a millennium and had no need of fantastical philosophical ideologies when they knew God. In fact, some scholars have concluded that certain of Plato's philosophical inspirations came from translations of the Torah.

Platonism influenced St. Augustine, and Augustine influenced Muhammad. Muhammad became both patriarch and son of a religion born inorganically—through in vitro fertilization—where the Vatican was the true father.

In the chronology of Muhammed's life, he married Khadijah in AD 594. Khadijah came from a wealthy family and was also Roman Catholic, as was her cousin Waraquah. Waraquah was sent by the Vatican to kindle a relationship with Muhammad and arrange the introduction of Khadijah to him.

Remember that Muhammad was illiterate and didn't read anything himself, but had others read to him. During this time between AD 594 and AD 610, when Muhammad experienced his "divine vision" of Allah, he had already been exposed to more than sixteen years of information directly controlled by Vatican influences.

While all of this is based on Alberto Rivera's highly controversial and suspect disclosures—insight he claimed to have gained from Cardinal Bea—there are other historical tidbits that connect the dots between the Vatican and Islam. History records that powerful leaders desired an alternative to Christianity due to its exponential expansion between the second and seventh centuries. One such leader was Byzantine Emperor Heraclius. Christianity posed a constant threat to oppressive, tyrannical leaders, and Christians became so hated that Islam was not only embraced but well supported in exchange for loyalty. Some historians believe that the idea of advocating Muhammad's new religion as a means to sponsor an inorganic uprising against Christians and Jews originated with Heraclius, later adopted and perfected by the Vatican.

In a bizarre twist, the Jews of Medina so hated the name Jesus that Muhammad's teachings resonated with them by recognizing His birth to Mary and His life as a prophet of God—while denying that He was the Son of God. The Medina Jews believed Muhammad was their Messiah, which opened a door for the Vatican to gain greater control over Jerusalem under Pope Honorius I. But Honorius himself didn't trust the rapid acceptance of Islam and began to incite distrust and violence between Jews and Muslims, fearing an Arab uprising against the Vatican.28

Why is this important to know? In their academic brilliance, Platonist Christians are embracing Islam in large numbers. Since the Islamic holy writings of the Quran and Sunna include the Jesus and Mary story, they believe Muslims, Christians, and Jews are religious cousins of the same background. Satan may be evil without being foolish—and we've been warned:

> **For there shall arise false Christs, and false prophets,**
> **and shall shew great signs and wonders; insomuch**
> **that, if it were possible, they shall deceive the very elect.**
> **(Matthew 24:24 KJV)**

Islam was devised by Satan and his sons of disobedience, implemented through the church of Pergamum (Roman Catholic Church) for the purpose of deceiving the future sons of God. Now we see Christians embracing Satan's tactics and questioning Christianity as merely "one of many religions with problems." That statement was made by pastor and author Brian McLaren, who advocates "a new kind of Christianity." Here is one of his quotes:

> *Many Hindus are willing to consider Jesus as a*
> *legitimate manifestation of the divine... many Buddhists*
> *see Jesus as one of humanity's most enlightened*
> *people.... A shared reappraisal of Jesus' message could*
> *provide a unique space or common ground for urgently*

---

28   Classical Islam, a History 600-1258 – by G.E. Von Grunebaum

The death of Protestantism gave life to a multitude of deceptions. You can quote me on that! I am sure Brian McLaren is a wonderful person and loves his fellow man, thus motivated to find "common ground" between religions. But Yehshua was very clear in Mark 16 that we will know His followers by certain signs, with a warning to those who do not believe:

> **He that believeth and is baptized shall be saved; but he that believeth not shall be damned.**
>
> **And these signs shall follow them that believe; In my name shall they cast out devils; they shall speak with new tongues;**
>
> **They shall take up serpents; and if they drink any deadly thing, it shall not hurt them; they shall lay hands on the sick, and they shall recover. (Mark 16:16-18 KJV)**

There is only the kingdom of life under Yehshua, the Son of God who came to save the world, and the kingdom of death under Satan, prince of this world. There is no common ground between the two kingdoms. Heaven and hell, life and death, are divided between them. There is not a third kingdom of compromise between the two. Such a notion is absurd and entirely nonbiblical.

Here is what the holy Quran (the word of Allah) and the Sunna of Islam (the teachings and traditions of Muhammad) declare about Jesus, so that you are not confused. These two sources of Muslim holy references describe a Jesus who is not the Jesus of Scripture:

- Jesus was a man, not God.

- Jesus did not die; he was carried away to heaven.
- If Jesus did not die, He could not have risen.
- If Jesus was a man and did not die, there is no atonement for sin by His death.
- Jesus was a prophet only.
- After Jesus's ascension, He stands by Allah awaiting to be sent back to earth to help the Mahdi.

During the tribulation, the fake Muslim Jesus will assist the Antichrist, deceiving remaining Christians who do not know what I am sharing with you now. God bless John for letting us know one major condition for an Antichrist so that we are not deceived:

> *Who is a liar but he that denieth that Jesus is the Christ? He is antichrist, that denieth the Father and the Son. (1 John 2:22 KJV)*

If you read my last book, you know my belief that there is more than one harvest if we consider that the seven feasts are prophetic and that the three agricultural feasts represent the harvests of the barley, wheat, and olives occurring on at least three different occasions. There is a wheat harvest that I believe takes place before the seven-year tribulation, and at least another harvest during the tribulation (the gleaning). Much of the wheat of the tribulation period will not survive and will fall for deceptions such as the fake Muslim Jesus who assists the Mahdi Antichrist.

No matter your opinion of Alberto Rivera or the Vatican's involvement in this long history of deception, please keep those deceived people in mind. We are here for them, and that horrible time is racing toward us. We cannot stop it. We can only prepare for it. Time is not our friend in this matter.

Let's take a step back and compare these sons of disobedience by their symbology. Remember that symbols are the method of communication used by ancient secret societies, beginning with the hieroglyphs on Enoch's (son of Cain) marble pillars (preflood obelisks). Nearly all of them lead to sun and moon worship, at least for the sons of disobedience who rule the world.

What are the symbols of Islam?

Turkish flag with the symbol of Islam

Crescent moon and star are the symbols of Islam

Unfortunately, the crescent moon and star symbol did originate with Islam. Its roots trace back to where it all began: with Nimrod and Semiramis:

The oldest crescent moon and eight-pointed stars on record are from ancient Sumeria.

The eight-pointed star in Islamic architecture, unfortunately, is also not unique or original to Islam.

Star of "Ashtoreth" in the Bible, or Ishtar/Semiramis, which later became the symbol of the goddess Venus in Rome. They are all one and the same, originating in Babylon.

Where else do we see these Islamic symbols?

Almost no pagan sun worship symbol is missing from this gold papal eucharist stand, with the moon goddess Isis symbol and her priests placed dead center, Horus in a sunburst at the peak.

The queen of heaven in Babylon made her way to Rome via "pontifex maximus" before being exported to the world. If these symbols were isolated to the Vatican, it would be a simpler matter, but they are found everywhere there is a Catholic church.

Platonism, where all religions come together. Notice anything familiar about this? Isis is the crescent moon with Horus in her bosom. This is not in Rome! This is Chicago, IL, USA!
(In 2007, Cardinal Francis George designated St. Stanislaus Kostka Parish as the Sanctuary of the Divine Mercy in Chicago, and in 2008, he blessed the iconic Monstrance, Our Lady of the Sign-Ark of Mercy.)

Pontifex Maximus 2015

Caesar Julius Augustus, founder of the Roman Empire, reigned from 27BC-14AD
Pontifex Maximus

Did anything change from Caesar Julius to Pope Francis? For 2050 years, the Roman Empire has merely passed from the Caesars to the popes beneath the shadows of the Vatican. Observing symbols through the lens of history reveals that sun worship began with Enoch, son of Cain. The traditions of Enoch were continued by the son of Ham, Cush (Chaos), and his son Nimrod in Babylon. Babylonian sun worship under a pontifical system expanded to Egypt before finding its way to Pergamum under Attalus III. The last Chaldean *pontifex maximus*, Attalus III, bequeathed his kingdom of Pergamum to Julius Caesar, where the Roman emperors became the new *pontifex maximus*—the bridge between God and man. Before the end of the official Roman Empire, the title *pontifex maximus* had already shifted to the pope of Rome.

Through manipulation by the papacy of Rome, Plato and St. Augustine became the mentors of a new religion to foster the last son of disobedience. The Mahdi, the fake Jesus, and the Dajjal became the eschatological figures of this mockery by Satan, brought to life and nurtured by the papacy of Rome. For what other reason would these religions share the same symbology? They share the same origin: Babylon, Nimrod, Semiramis, and Tammuz, whose true roots trace back to Enoch the son of Cain. Amazingly, sun worship is as ancient as the sons of Adam. We are not discussing religious nuances. These are the ancient enemies of God, the sons of God who fell with lucifer. The first sons of disobedience under the prince of death, satan.

Although I focus on Babylon and Rome, the sun worship that began with Enoch, son of Cain, and later Nimrod, spread throughout Nimrod's empire, which included Egypt. The Egyptian symbols are the most interesting because some of them date back to the time of Enoch, son of Cain, and continued seemingly uninterrupted by Nimrod and Semiramis, later deified as Osiris and Isis. Take a look at this moon god from Egypt:

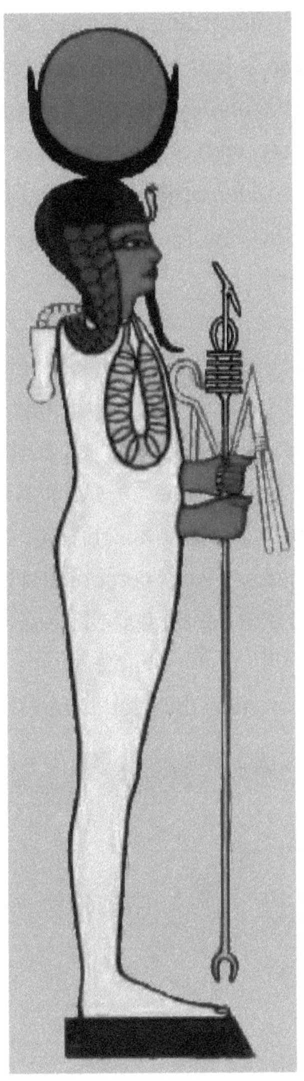

This is the Egyptian moon god "Iah." That name is important, especially in the context of its origin in Egyptology. The God in Genesis 1 is referred to as *Elohim*, which is God(s) plural. Based on John 1, we know that Yehshua was at least one of the other *Elohim*. It is not until Exodus 3:14 that we see the name of God as "I Am," which is "Yah" in Hebrew. The moon god above is named "Iah," which phonetically is the same as Yah, but this is not the God of the Hebrews! Then who is it?

The moon god Iah, according to various scholars, dates back to around 4000 BC. Wikipedia says that his deity influence was diminished by two other gods by 1600 BC, and eventually he became associated with—you guessed it right—Osiris, who is Nimrod. The biblical timeline of Cain is 3900 BC. This moon god Iah originated with Enoch, son of Cain, named "I Am" as a mockery of the One True God in this sun-worship religion linked to fallen angel worship.

Enoch, son of Cain, was involved as a builder of Egypt before the flood, making him the first Freemason, the first Roman Catholic, and the first Muslim, since all sun and moon worship symbology originated with him. I'm injecting humor here, but you get the message. It makes sense that Iah, worshipped by the sons of Cain, would later become Nimrod under the name Osiris. It all connects into one religion; sun worship, "luciferianism in its purest form" perpetuated by the sons of disobedience since the time of Cain and continues still today.

Before closing this ugly chapter, let's look at Nimrod and his appearance and compare it to the Mahdi and Dajjal.

Above is one depiction that is supposed to represent Nimrod, but there are many variations and it is difficult to know which, if any, are accurate. This figure is assumed to portray the "mighty hunter before the Lord" (Genesis 10:9). Below is another example:

There are some who believe the image above is a stone carving depicting Nimrod, while others connect it to the Anunnaki. In either case, Nimrod and the Anunnaki are said to have been together in ancient Shinar (Sumer). Many legends credit the Anunnaki with Nimrod's rise to power. Whether this figure represents Nimrod or one of the Anunnaki, notice the Templar cross around his neck, the eight-pointed star, the crescent moon, and other familiar symbols. Any religions using the same symbology are related and can be traced throughout history—from Enoch, son of Cain, to Nimrod, Egypt, and Rome, then to Mecca, the Freemasons, Illuminati, Jesuits, the Nazis, and the pope of Rome.

It is assumed that Nimrod was similar to the Nephilim in strength and stature, but was not one of them.

> *And Cush begat Nimrod: he began to be a mighty one in the earth.*
>
> *He was a mighty hunter before the Lord: wherefore it is said, Even as Nimrod the mighty hunter before the Lord. (Genesis 10:8-9 KJV)*

That Nimrod "began to be a mighty one in the earth" possibly suggests that he was like the Nephilim without actually being one. This is impossible to explain with certainty, as there are only legends and no biblical evidence, so we can only assume without knowing for sure. Most traditions describe Nimrod as resembling the "mighty men of old, men of renown" mentioned in Genesis 6.

With Nimrod regarded as being the first global Antichrist figure, it raises the question of whether there will be similarities between him and the last Antichrist figure—the Mahdi—that will compare to Nimrod.

> *The Prophet said: The Mahdi will be of my stock, and will have a broad forehead a prominent nose. He will fill the earth will equity and justice as it was filled with oppression and tyranny, and he will rule for seven years.*[29]

Other resources state that he will be of prominent countenance and radiant, like a "shining star." It is therefore assumed that he will be very charming and handsome.

Remember, there is also the "Dajjal," who appears after the Mahdi. The Dajjal is the Muslim version of the Antichrist, and the fake Jesus

---

29   Sunnah.com

assists the Mahdi in killing this fake Antichrist, further empowering the Mahdi as a legitimate global ruler. The Dajjal, however, is described as having a much different appearance:

Prophet Muhammad PBUH referred to Dajjal as
Al-Awar which means blind with one eye. Prophet
Muhammad PBUH said that Dajjal's right will float like
a grape and its left eye will be defective too.

While many details are excluded, I find it very interesting that the Islamic Antichrist fits at least one description of our biblical Antichrist:

Woe to the idol shepherd that leaveth the flock! the
sword shall be upon his arm, and upon his right eye:
his arm shall be clean dried up, and his right eye shall
be utterly darkened. (Zechariah 11:17 KJV)

If we stick to the Bible, I believe that if the Antichrist is the Imam-Mahdi, he fits the following description:

- Blind in right eye and crippled right arm (Zechariah 11:17)
- He will be an Assyrian (Isaiah 10:5; Micah 5:5)
- From the part of Assyria that was once the Roman Empire, "revived Roman Empire" which is likely the Byzantine leg, perhaps even Istanbul and where the "beast" religion began with Constantine (Daniel 7; Daniel 9:26—"people of the prince to come")

I believe there is another point that allows us to triangulate on an Antichrist figure as possibly also coming from the tribe of Dan based on this verse:

Dan shall judge his people,

As one of the tribes of Israel.

Dan shall be a serpent in the way,

A horned viper in the path,

That bites the horse's heels,

So that its rider falls backward.

For Your salvation I wait, Lord. (Genesis 49:16–18
NASB)

One reason I speculate this about the tribe of Dan is based on John 5:43 (KJV):

I am come in my Father's name, and ye receive me
not: if another shall come in his own name, him ye will
receive.

This leads me to believe that the Jewish people will recognize the false Messiah as being linked to Jewish origin in some way, which could fulfill the prophecy from Genesis 49. Yet the Jews of Medina once believed Muhammad could have been the Messiah, so this may prove irrelevant. At the same time, we shouldn't ignore the tribe of Dan, as it has clear prophetic ties to Israel and the end times.

In any case, the first sign of the Antichrist comes after a brutal war—Gog and Magog of Ezekiel 38—that ends with a peace treaty mediated by him. Whoever he is must align with the descriptions found in Zechariah, Isaiah, Daniel, and Micah.

What does it mean that the number of his name is 666? I wish I knew for certain, but I will share a strong possibility. *Gematria* is the practice of applying numerical values to the letters of alphabets. This can be applied to both the Hebrew and Greek alphabets, where each letter corresponds to a numerical value. Here is the Hebrew chart with letters and values:

THE 22 HEBREW LETTERS AND THE NUMERICAL VALUES										
1	2	3	4	5	6	7	8	9	10	11
א	ב	ג	ד	ה	ו	ז	ח	ט	י	ך כ
1	2	3	4	5	6	7	8	9	10	20
(a)	B, V	G	D	H	W, V	Z	H, X	T	J, I, Y	K
Alef	Bet	Gimel	Dalet	He	Vav	Zayin	Chet	Tet	Yod	Kaph
12	13	14	15	16	17	18	19	20	21	22
ל	ם מ	ן נ	ס	ע	ף פ	ץ צ	ק	ר	ש	ת
30	40	50	60	70	80	90	100	200	300	400
L	M	N	S	(o)	P, F	Ts	K, Q	R	S, Sh	T
Lamed	Mem	Nun	Samekh	Ayin	Pe	Tsade	Qoph	Resh	Shin	Tav

When a possible candidate for the final Antichrist appears, I think this might be a way to cross-reference his name in Revelation 13:8:

Here is wisdom. Let him that hath understanding count the number of the beast: for it is the number of a man; and his number is Six hundred threescore and six.

Here is a brief example. The letters for the word "Roman kingdom" in Hebrew, when added together using the chart above, look like this:

ROMIITH.

200 ר

6 ו

40 מ

10 י

10 י

400 ת

= 666

This is just an example, and because the New Testament was written in Greek, we must check the Greek alphabet numerical values as well when proving out this gematria theory for the number of his name.

Alpha	Beta	Gamma	Delta	Epsilon	Zeta	Eta	Theta	Iota	Kappa	Lambda	Mu
A	B	Γ	Δ	E	Z	H	Θ	I	K	Λ	M
α	β	γ	δ	ε	ζ	η	θ	ι	κ	λ	μ
1	2	3	4	5	7	8	9	10	20	30	40

Nu	Xi	Omicron	Pi	Rho	Sigma	Tau	Upsilon	Phi	Chi	Psi	Omega
N	Ξ	O	Π	P	Σ	T	Y	Φ	X	Ψ	Ω
ν	ξ	ο	π	ρ	σ, ς	τ	υ	φ	χ	ψ	ω
50	60	70	80	100	200	300	400	500	600	700	800

Ιησους	Jesus	10 + 8 + 200 + 70 + 400 + 200 = 888
Χριστος	Christ	600 + 100 + 10 + 200 + 300 + 70 + 200 = 1480

Save these charts for future reference! There are websites that will calculate the values of words and phrases online. One of them is https://www.gematrix.org/.

There have been many Antichrists throughout history, but the Imam-Mahdi might be the last. Satan took extreme measures spanning centuries to create a counterfeit religion out of the corrupt Pergamum church for this very purpose. Meanwhile, Satan has his operatives positioned at every key seat of power throughout his kingdom. There is little doubt in my mind that the Vatican will be the second beast of Revelation 13, giving rise to the first. We also cannot ignore the ten kings of Revelation 17, who I believe are already actively operating today against the bride church.

The sons of disobedience seek to strip the sons of God of their faith, hope, and ultimately their salvation. When the door of the ark closes, as it did before the flood (first type of rapture), and the tribulation begins, those who remain for the subsequent harvests must be informed and aware of what has happened to them.

Pastor Jimmy Evans and his daughter wrote a great little book dedicated to those who will be left behind when the first tribulation harvest occurs, titled *Where Are the Missing People*. I strongly urge everyone to purchase as many copies as needed and leave them in strategic places, where they will be found by those left behind. We want all our family to join us as the "sons of God, joint heirs with Christ" in His kingdom.

Meanwhile, do not be fooled by the "sons of disobedience" super-elite globalist agendas, as they are aligned precisely with Satan's schemes. We witnessed the atrocities of the COVID pandemic, where churches were forced to close and non-compliant pastors were arrested in the very same cities where nude strip clubs were allowed to remain open. There were many clear signs that the pandemic was a dry run for the mark of the beast system, which is being perfected for successful implementation. With so many lies being dumped on us today, we must test everything against God's Word. As Pastor John McArthur wisely stated, "Tyrants will come and go, but God's sovereignty will always remain."

I apologize for diverting from the Imam-Mahdi, but one deception that deeply grinds against me is the "Climate Change" agenda, designed to control every living, breathing creature—whether human or possessed by humans. A single volcanic eruption emits hundreds or even thousands of times more "greenhouse gases" than humankind has produced throughout history. This is an obvious "sons of disobedience" agenda for greater control over human activity. As with all Satan's agendas, there are multiple goals, one of which was to create a tax base for the United Nations by imposing C02 taxes on everything that breathes. The "greenhouse effect" of C02 was a propaganda tool intended to hide what was really happening: a "geoengineering" plan to manipulate and weaponize weather by causing floods or droughts in strategic areas, while perhaps allowing normal rainfall in others. Do not be ignorant and do not be fooled—climate change is a massive lie perpetrated upon the global population.

Please indulge me while I expand on this diversion. The concept began innocently with cloud seeding in the early 1900s. Vincent Joseph Schaefer, a scientist employed by General Electric Research Laboratory, discovered that dry ice could be atomized and distributed by plane at cloud levels to provoke precipitation. It worked so well that he became highly successful at promising rain to farmers. Everything begins with good intentions, then the sons of disobedience follow closely to corrupt every good invention.

Five decades later, Schaefer's cloud seeding technology evolved from its origin as an agricultural aid into the development of weather weaponization during the Cold War. This technology could produce clouds, clear skies, floods, storms, hurricanes, tornadoes, and droughts. The Russians developed their own versions of climate control, while the US led in advancing the technology. A 1976 article in *New Scientist* discussed the heavy funding being poured into weather weaponization research fifty years ago. Imagine where we are today—and no one realizes that this is a product of the sons of disobedience being literally dumped on our heads. God help us!

Australia 60 cents. Canada $1.00. DM 3.00. FF 5.20. New Zealand 60 cents. South Africa 60 cents. Spain 40 pts. USA (by air) $1.50. ISSN 0028-6664

17 June 1976 Vol 70 No 1005 Weekly 25p

newscientist

FOLLOW US ON FACEBOOK
WEATHER MODIFICATION HISTORY

The shape of war to come?

Unless we seek to ban such research now, it is almost certain that military scientists around the world will perfect methods for harnessing the forces of the geophysical environment for waging war. the SIPRI Yearbook, published today, spells out some of the awesome possibilities

SCIENTIFIC CALCULATORS

(Source: https://climateviewer.com)

By 1987, weather control technology had accelerated with a patent filed by Dr. Bernard Eastlund titled *Method and Apparatus for Altering a Region in the Earth's Atmosphere, Ionosphere, and/or Magnetosphere.* This patent laid the foundation for a multimillion-dollar investment in the northern hemisphere called the High Altitude Aurora Research Program, or the HAARP.

High Altitude Aurora Research Program, Alaska

This program of "altering the earth's atmosphere or ionosphere" named HAARP, consisted of a 3.6-megawatt array of radio antennas designed to emit "ultra-low frequency" (ULF) radio waves aimed at specific points in the upper atmosphere. These waves, calibrated between 2.8 Hz and 30 Hz, could be concentrated in specific regions of the atmosphere or ionosphere to achieve multiple goals.30 Think of ULF as a huge base speaker: it vibrates everything around it. In a similar way, ULF waves directed into the ionosphere and atmosphere generate constant vibrational frequency

---

30   . zerogeoengineering.com

patterns that stimulate electrons and photons to behave erratically, yet predictably.

- The ULF waves can heat the ionosphere, altering the natural behavior of electrons and photons.
- ULF waves can create domes in the atmosphere that alter the flow of jet stream currents. The natural course of atmospheric rivers, cold or hot jet streams, can be redirected as desired.
- Artificial ionosphere plasma can be created, generating man-made auroral events almost anywhere.
- By reflecting off the atmosphere and back to earth, ULF waves can target tectonic plates, relieve pressure, and trigger earthquakes with relative precision.
- Another aspect of ULF studied and developed by other government-funded research organizations was the effect of ULF waves on the human brain.

You can do your own research on this, but difficulty in understanding does not preclude its existence. I have studied the subject extensively and still do not fully grasp it. I am not a physicist. I also don't have to understand gravity to know that without it, I would be a floating carcass in space. Billions of dollars continue to be invested in weather control to advance a human-control agenda.

When you hear a buzzword like "greenhouse gases," you can be certain that something is being done that creates greenhouse gases, and a shift of blame becomes necessary.

Remember the acid rain propaganda of the 1970s? When propaganda news reports begin warning us of something to fear, it often indicates that governments are doing something with our money that warrant concern. During the Cold War (no pun intended), stratospheric aerosol injections of aerosols were conducted as part of the weaponization of weather program. The resulting acid rain required a scapegoat, so they targeted heavy industry, where a link to acid rain could be demonstrated. Capitalism, as the enemy of communism, creates wealth, and wealth fosters freedom and independence—making heavy industry a consistent target. Acid rain was said to result from sulfuric acid forming in the atmosphere due to toxic aerosol gases emitted by factories. However, by 1992, our government began funding the atomization of sulfuric acid injected directly into the stratosphere to "reflect harmful solar radiation." I know no one wants to believe this, so I encourage you to conduct your own research. This is not a wild conspiracy theory; it reflects what I've learned through thousands of hours of research. Remember to always enter your key search terms in a way that doesn't pull up dozens of government and university websites designed to discredit evidence of conspiracy. The top search results are provided by the sons of disobedience—don't give them credit for claiming to act in the best interests of the rest of us.

The sulfuric acid idea was canned in favor of metallic oxide nanoparticle dust—aluminum oxide, barium oxide, mercury oxide, and other metallic oxides—combined with polymers and other "useful" chemicals. These are the components of what is being called a conspiracy theory, as if we can't see the abnormal stripes visible across the sky each day. If you research this, the first thirty pages that appear are typically like the one mentioned, carefully worded to categorize anyone who believes what they see in the sky overhead as crazy:

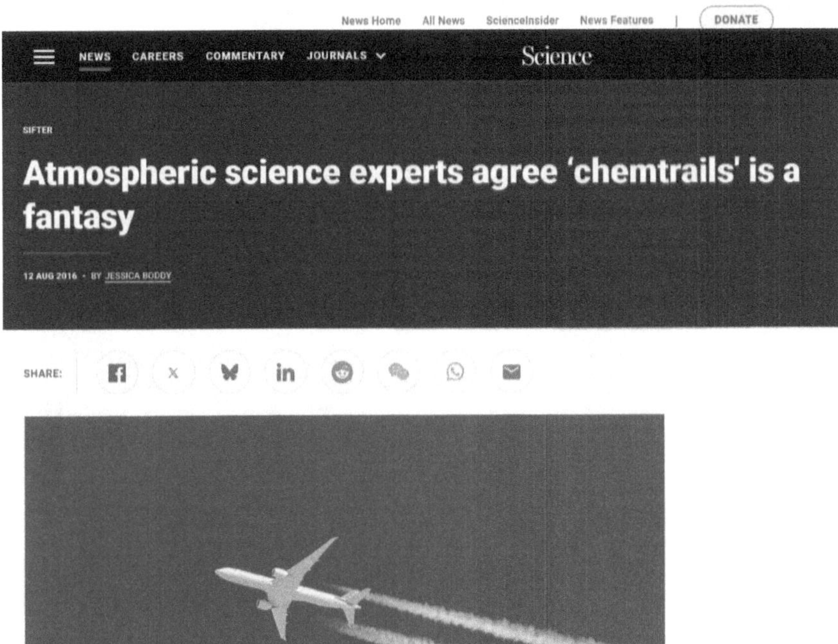

Believers of one conspiracy theory claim that the persistent condensation trails left behind aircraft in the sky—so-called "chemtrails"—are evidence of a covert large-scale spraying operation with sinister intent. A new study aims to debunk that idea by surveying atmospheric chemists who specialize in condensation trails and geochemists working on atmospheric deposition of dust and pollution. Nearly all of them—76 out of 77—said they had not encountered any evidence of secret atmospheric spraying, reports Phys.org. The researchers, who published their findings in *Environmental Research Letters*, admit they may never convince the most steadfast chemtrail believers, but they wish to build a foundation of objective science to inform the general population so they won't believe such a "paranoid fantasy."

Notice in the photo they use a picture of an airplane's condensation trails, formed as moisture heated by friction passing over the wing recrystallizes quickly at subzero temperatures. The photo was chosen knowing that most people will see the vapor trail behind the plane and assume it matches what they observe in the sky. This is the type of explanation you will encounter in a brief internet search to make you feel stupid. The difference, however, is that condensation trails evaporate quickly. They do not linger to spread across the sky, forming unusual cloud patterns that obscure the sun.

(photos from chemtrails.substack.com)

Here is an article published by the PR Newswire in 2018 that addressed the unusual behavior of wildfires in California:

LOS ANGELES, Sept. 6, 2018 /PRNewswire/ — While researching for his new novel, author Denis Mills discovered an alarming link between chemtrails and the super wildfires.

The author discovered that unprecedented levels of aluminum and barium nanodust, primary components in chemtrails, both of which are incendiary, are fueling the ferocity of the super wildfires.

Aluminum-fueled super wildfire

Author Denis Mills

A retired USAF brigadier general, Gen. Charles Jones, has been quoted from a public source as stating, "These white aircraft spray trails are the result of scientifically verifiable spraying of aluminum particles and other toxic heavy metals, polymers and chemicals."

"Millions of tons of aluminum and barium are being sprayed almost daily across the U.S., stated Mills, a former naval officer and UCLA graduate. "Just sprinkle aluminum or barium dust on a fire and see what happens. It's near explosive. When wildfires break out, the aluminum/barium dust results in levels of fire intensity so great as to cause firefighters to coin a new term — 'firenados,'" he said. The entire U.S., in addition to various other NATO countries, are being sprayed."

*The government has for years denied the existence
of chemtrail spraying. It now calls the program by
various names, all under Geoengineering.*

*According to Cal Fire operation chief Steve
Crawford, the fires are burning differently and more
aggressively. It has been reported the fires move
faster than anyone has ever seen and barriers that
in years past contained them such as rivers, no
longer do.*

*In California's Mt. Shasta region, Francis Mangel,
a USDA biologist tested and found elevated levels
of aluminum in water and soil samples of 4,610
parts per million which is 25,000 times the safe
guidelines of the World Health Organization.*

*Some have claimed Mr. Mills is publicity-seeking
for his teen and young adult fiction adventure
series, Matt Legend, about four teens who
encounter and battle the supernatural and all kinds
of strange things, including the forces behind the
chemtrails. The adventure thriller is being called
the new Harry Potter. Mr. Mills states the research
speaks for itself and the novel is only what led to
the discovery. "Authors are known for researching
things to death," he stated. No one can argue,
however, the wildfires' newfound ferocity or the
millions of tons of aluminum/barium nanodust
which have appeared, which is killing vegetation
and causing illness and death.*

Why do the sons of disobedience work so diligently to deny what
they are doing above our heads? How many global control agendas are

linked to this one? What else is in this dust besides "dust"? If you look up and see it being sprayed into the air, you are called a crazy conspiracy theorist.

The "acid rain" fear campaign was propaganda to cover up the dumping of sulfuric acid into the stratosphere. The "greenhouse effect" of global warming—now renamed climate change to account for winter storms and expanding ice caps—is blamed on C02 emissions from human activity and cow flatulence. "Climate change" serves as another propaganda tool to generate public support for tyrannical power grabs while hiding the effects of geoengineering nanoparticle dust sprayed daily, as abnormal clouds form overhead without question.

We hear plenty about cow flatulence and human C02 emissions, but have you ever heard one of these nut jobs complain about the amount of C02 used to make a can of soda? According to co2everything.com, a single can of Coca-Cola contains 0.17 kg, or about 1.7 grams, with a carbon equivalent 100 times greater when factoring in manufacturing, transportation, and loss. Based on this formula, every four cans of Coca-Cola equal less than a cow's daily flatulence in terms of carbon equivalent from producer to consumer.

According to statista.com, Americans are rapidly reducing soda consumption while emerging markets are increasing. Americans consume 9.6 gallons of carbonated soda per year per capita, or 37.189 billion cans annually. That's the equivalent of 4.5 million cows that no one talks about. Did Greta Thunberg ever say she was ashamed of soda drinkers? Why aren't people dumping Coca-Cola stock if the polar caps are melting because of C02? Climate change is a fear-driven propaganda campaign. Warren Buffet acknowledges that climate change poses significant risks to the future of the planet, yet he remains the largest single shareholder of Coca-Cola, which produces 693 billion cans annually. My calculator doesn't have the capacity to compute the equivalent number of cows, but it's into the billions. Wikipedia says there are only 1.5 billion cows in the world today. If C02 is truly the problem, Coca-Cola is a far larger threat to the planet than cows.

We are currently in the maximum phase of a Solar Cycle 25, which continues through 2026. According to NOAA, the maximum sunspot phase of this cycle peaked in July 2025. Solar maximum cycles typically produce increased rainfall due to the electromagnetic relationship between the earth and solar radiation. As solar radiation peaks, rainfall should occur if temperature and humidity conditions are favorable. The spraying of metal oxide nanoparticle dust into the upper atmosphere reflects solar radiation and interrupts the natural cycles God intended. This interruption not only reduces opportunities for rainfall but also leaves behind the greenhouse effect of a manmade dust canopy overhead. The "greenhouse" theory had to be publicized and blamed on human C02 emissions and cow flatulence to distract from the true cause of unusually warm temperatures. Below is an example of the "normal" solar radiation and rain correlation that no longer occurs because of "geoengineering":

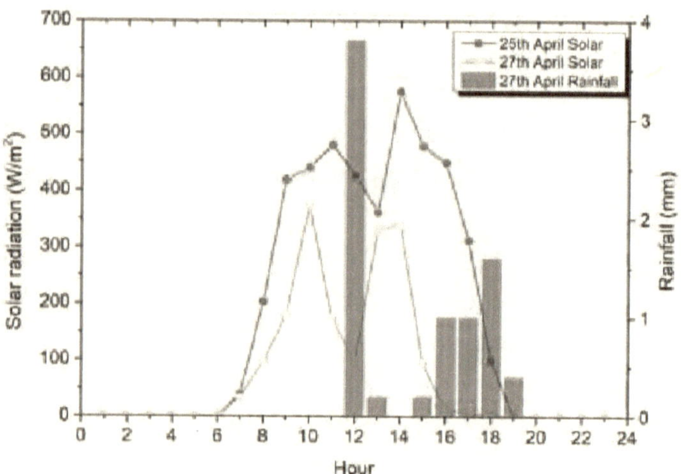

Is it purely coincidence that severe droughts began precisely at the time of the Paris Climate Accord when geoengineering went global with our money? Scientists share the same handicap as doctors: they are indoctrinated more than educated. Somewhere, a PhD in physics will read this in total disagreement, having been fully indoctrinated with honors into a well-structured academic network organized by the sons of disobedience. It is nearly impossible for truth to escape the clutches of such deception. Grant money is distributed to advance global control agendas, not to benefit mankind—that's another conspiracy topic!

In the 1970s, global cooling propaganda warned of mankind's extinction by the 1980s, with chlorofluorocarbon aerosols (CFCs) identified as the main culprit. The Montreal Protocol of 1986 banned the use of over one hundred chemicals blamed for depleting the ozone layer. The Montreal Protocol preceded the 1992 UN Climate Treaty, which opened the door for climate change hoaxes and disguises for geoengineering. During the Cold War, governments were heavily experimenting with aerosols in weather-weaponization research programs, and blame had to be shifted away from DOD-funded scientists. This is where climate change propaganda began—a distraction from the truth, as always.

By the 1990s, a new propaganda campaign shifted the threat of extinction from global freezing to global warming. Florida was predicted to be submerged below sea level by the early 2000s. The transition from sulfuric acid to metallic oxide dust was completed around 1999. Al Gore became famous for standing on a ladder to illustrate a graph suggesting we would be reduced to ashes by now. Yet with changes in the ionosphere through HAARP in the stratosphere, and dust sprayed below in the atmosphere, weather patterns entered a period of unpredictability while weather-weaponization research was still in development. The terminology has since been rebranded as "climate change" because Florida is still above sea level ten years after its predicted submersion, and the Antarctic ice sheet continues to expand.

Scientists have become less credible than the popes of Rome. Why? They are paid large grants to prove a list of theories later presented as "the science." Unlike mathematics, science can be twisted into infinite hypotheticals and made to appear empirical in theory. Remember politicians saying "trust the science" during the pandemic? Take my advice please and trust the Bible while assuming everything else is a lie.

So, what is the real agenda? I don't know, but it cannot be good if such extremes are taken to conceal the truth in parallel with prophecy being fulfilled daily. One possibility is that water has become the new oil, and droughts are good for business. One of the ten kings of Revelation 17 may be someone like Klaus Schwab, who was recently replaced as chairman of the World Economic Forum by Peter Brabeck-Letmathe. The internet is full of debunkers who quickly step in to claim conspiracy theorists spread disinformation, so I pulled this directly from the WEF website:

FORUM INSTITUTIONAL

Why water security is our most urgent challenge today

Oct 12, 2023

Water security goes far beyond whether we have too much or too little of the physical resource.

Image: Nana Kofi Acquah (Creative Commons)

Gim Huay Neo
Managing Director, Asia Strategy and Centre for Energy and Materials, World Economic Forum

Saroj Kumar Jha
Global Director, Water Global Practice, The World Bank

Share:

This article is part of:
Annual Meeting of the Global Future Councils

▶ Listen to the article   7 min listen

- Water is central to our survival, economic growth and development.
- Yet we face a global water crisis that is outpacing efforts to address it.
- The 2030 Water Resources Group was set up to help tackle this crisis.

OUR IMPACT

What's the World Economic Forum doing to accelerate action on Forum institutional?

THE BIG PICTURE

Explore and monitor how Fresh Water is affecting economies, industries and global issues

Strategic Intelligence

Stay up to date:
Fresh Water

Follow +

With just seven years left to meet the Sustainable Development Goals, the world remains far behind, particularly on its water goals. We need to take swift and significant strides towards a water-secure world. But what does that mean in practice?

Water security goes far beyond whether we have too much or too little of the physical resource. It goes to the heart of every aspect of our development and well-being as people on a liveable planet. We need enough water, of the right quality, to keep us healthy, sustain our livelihoods, grow our economies, and protect our ecosystems. Water security covers all aspects of the issue, from water-related disasters and water-borne diseases, to conflict over shared resources and governance challenges, to biodiversity and groundwater quality.

Have you read?

- Achieving the SDGs requires public-private collaboration on water. Here's why
- Applying a circular economy mindset will help ensure a water-secure future
- Visualizing the global population by water security levels

Despite global commitments, our progress on water security for all is far too slow. By 2030, global freshwater demand is expected to outstrip supply by 40%, and an estimated 1.6 billion people will lack safely managed drinking water.

What are the constraints on water security?

We need urgent global action — coordinated across all sectors and institutions — to ensure a water-secure world for all. Improving climate resilience and ensuring water use is sustainable will help optimize our use of this increasingly scarce and variable resource. Increasing inclusion is important to support development and ensure that the benefits of water are shared. These changes require partnerships, policies, and financing. In practical terms, we need much larger investment and financing for water-related infrastructure and the institutions — including river basin agencies, utilities, and municipalities — that can help build and maintain it.

Meeting the global financing needs for water is a particularly big challenge. Water infrastructure is estimated to require a staggering $6.7 trillion by 2030 — and $22.6 trillion by 2050. Yet the global water sector currently attracts less than 2% of public spending, with a similar level of private investment in low- and middle-income countries. More financing is needed, alongside more innovative approaches to maximize the impact of funds.

The power of partnerships

Global leaders, including international institutions such as the World Bank and the World Economic Forum, alongside governments and civil society, are putting a shared vision for water security into action.

The World Bank hosts a multi-donor trust fund, the 2030 Water Resources Group (2030 WRG), which is using the power of partnerships to bring change to the water sector. This can be seen in action in Bangladesh, where communities are facing a severe pollution crisis. Many rivers are biologically dead, and 28% of deaths are caused by pollution. The country's funding gap for water pollution management, expected to reach $6.6 billion by 2040, is too big to be met by public funding alone. This is where collaboration becomes crucial. 2030 WRG is bringing public and private stakeholders together to fast-track investments, including $450 million in public finance and $100 million in private capital, to help address the urgent water pollution challenge in Bangladesh.

Over the past decade, 2030 WRG has helped advance water security through multi-stakeholder partnerships in several countries. Earlier this year, the trust fund launched a new state-wide plan to catalyse

https://www.weforum.org/stories/2023/10/why-water-security-is-our-most-urgent-challenge-today/

You may not be able to read this clearly, so the link is provided below the image. This is carefully crafted word art designed to guide the herd into the mark of the beast branding chute: "The 2030 Water Resources Group was set up to tackle this crisis," followed by the caption "What are the constraints on water security?" Then comes the statement that the crisis must be urgently addressed, with $20 trillion proposed as the solution. The sons of disobedience might be evil, but they're not stupid. They provoke a global water crisis with HAARP and nanoparticle metallic dust, then present the solution—at the cost of $20 trillion—claiming, "we can fix this crisis."

Water will soon become the next most valuable commodity if the sons of disobedience are not stopped in their weaponization of weather programs. This is another mainstream story, not a manufactured paranoid theory. For example, a Forbes headline from 2021 reported on another of the ten kings of Revelation 17—Bill Gates—who proposed blocking the sun. Imagine when the church is gone and no one remains to oppose their twisted agendas. Oh yeah, that's the tribulation period.

Bill Gates's name appears in the most conspicuous of places. He is the single largest donor to the World Health Organization and contributes even larger amounts of money to WHO projects. Gates is said to be actively involved in vaccinating the impoverished world, spending billions of dollars to do so. But whose money is it? His own? Or USAID furnished by taxpayers to fund NGO's? We may never know. The Gavi Campaign and the Gavi Alliance are vaccination projects subsidized by Gates to provide vaccines for children in poor countries. After what we learned about this guy after the COVID planned-demic, I don't want him anywhere near anyone that I care about. And think about it: why vaccines? What if he spent billions of dollars on food instead? Or at least, in addition to vaccines, devoted a portion to groceries?

For the sake of argument, let's assume I'm a few cards short of a full deck with too much time to read. Why, then, did Governor DeSantis and the state of Florida suddenly pass a law outlawing geoengineering if it doesn't exist? Does a theory require legislation to stop it? The problem is that the fines are minimal, classified as a third-degree felony, while the power behind it is immense, making the effort seem futile. Still, the law received a small measure of press coverage, though limited to Florida newspapers

Senate passes bill banning geoengineering, weather modification

'The bill really comes from concerns, a lot of concerns.'

Capping a nearly two-month debate with no shortage of conspiracy theorizing from the public, the Senate has passed legislation to crack down on suspected weather modification and geoengineering in Florida.

The bill (**SB 56**) passed after a back-and-forth on the chamber floor between its sponsor, Miami Republican Sen. **Ileana Garcia**, and Boca Raton Democratic Sen. **Tina Scott Polsky**, who asked pointed questions and received circuitous answers.

Senators voted 28-9 for the measure, with Broward Democratic Sens. **Jason Pizzo** and **Barbara Sharief** joining their GOP colleagues in voting "yes."

Garcia admitted that carrying SB 56 to passage "has been nerve-wracking" and often drew political discourse she hoped it wouldn't.

"I didn't want this to be an issue where it was politicized," she said. "The bill really comes from concerns, a lot of concerns."

She insisted the bill and its House analog (**HB 477**) by Tallahassee Republican Rep. **Kevin Steele** aren't meant to perpetuate conspiracy theories over cloud seeding, solar radiation modification and so-called "chemtrails." Rather, she said, the goal is to put those concerns to rest if unsubstantiated or, if proven true, to curtail them with severe penalties.

"The purpose of this bill is to separate fact from fiction," she said.

SB 56, which can now move to the House for a vote, would make geoengineering and weather modification a third-degree felony, punishable by up to five years in prison and a significantly hiked monetary fine of up to $100,000. Each individual infraction would count as a separate violation, potentially leading to far longer and pricier penalties.

The bill would also direct the Department of Environmental Protection (DEP) to intake reports of suspected wrongdoing, investigate claims it deems warranting of further review and report its observations to the

A blogger named Ji Sayer published this on his website in February 2025. Immediately after USAID funding was paused by President Trump, Florida experienced the cleanest air quality in twenty-five years. There are no coincidences when it comes to the sons of disobedience. And there are no mere theories of conspiracy since the deception of Eve and the fall of Adam—only true conspiracies aimed at eliminating the sons of God led by the Spirit.

Clear Skies, Unanswered Questions: The Naples, FL Anomaly and the USAID Funding Pause

Florida's skies cleared overnight—was it coincidence or proof of hidden geoengineering?

SAYER JI
FEB 17, 2025

♡ 72   💬   ⟳ 18   Share

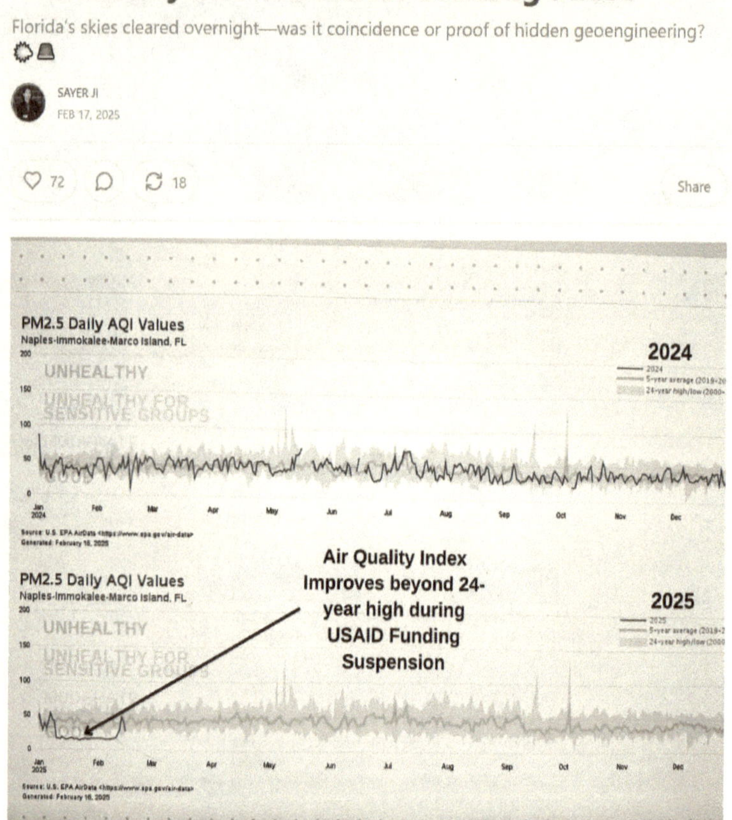

Floridians across the state noticed the return of naturally clear skies and the disappearance of the gray haze that had been dumped for the past twenty-four years. The article included a photo of beautiful skies with natural clouds—something people haven't seen in decades:

There is more to this that we can ever possibly know. Why has Bill Gates been so deeply involved with the World Health Organization? He's their largest single financial supporter. Why was he so involved in both the COVID pandemic and the vaccines? Why was the computer guy involved at all—Windows for humans 1.0? Bill Gates was financing COVID pandemic simulations two years before the pandemic, then pushing vaccines while also proposing to block sunlight. Vitamin D deficiency diminishes immune response to illnesses such as cancer and COVID, and the purest source of vitamin D is sunlight. Is this coincidence? This guy is certainly one of the sons of disobedience, and if he lives long enough, he may even be one of the ten kings of Revelation 17.

While chemtrails are dismissed as the imaginings of conspiracy theorists, and COVID is said to have originated in a Wuhan open market—unrelated to $billions invested in its trail of patents, later exported to Wuhan to circumvent "gain of function" legislation in the USA—critics now believe vaccines could be added to chemtrails and dispersed over populations like crop dusters. They argue that when the next pandemic occurs, vaccinations will not be optional. The First Amendment must be stopped, they say, because conspiracy theorists are spreading disinformation!

Perhaps if the company developing air-distribution vaccines were not named "AeroVax," conspiracy theorists wouldn't jump to such fanatical conclusions.[31]

About the AeroVax Inhaled COVID Vaccine Trial

When a vaccine is inhaled, the body's immune system responds in a different way than when injected that may be better at preventing infection

This new vaccine, named ChAd-triCoV/Mac, targets three different proteins in the SARS CoV-2 virus to improve the vaccine's ability to protect against new strains (or variants) of the COVID virus

The AeroVax Trial is a Phase 2 clinical trial funded by the Canadian Institutes of Health Research (CIHR), Canada's federal funding agency for health research.

The AeroVax Trial will evaluate if this new COVID-19 vaccine is safe to give by aerosol (inhalation) to people who have been vaccinated with at least three doses of a COVID mRNA vaccine. The researchers also want to look at how the body's immune system responds to this vaccine. Participants will be randomly assigned to receive either the vaccine or a placebo

A placebo is an inactive substance that doesn't have any therapeutic effect. Placebos are used by researchers to compare to an active substance to see if the active substance is having any effect or causing any side effects.

We will be enrolling approximately 350 participants across three sites in Canada.

I hope I haven't lost you. I know this may sound like the rantings of a lunatic, but the evidence is all around us, and why should we trust the sons of disobedience? Sixty-two years later, we're still trying to figure out why JFK was assassinated, even though he told us why just one week before he was killed. Today he would be considered as a conspiracy theorist and laughed at by corporate media.

---

31   https://aerovax.ca/

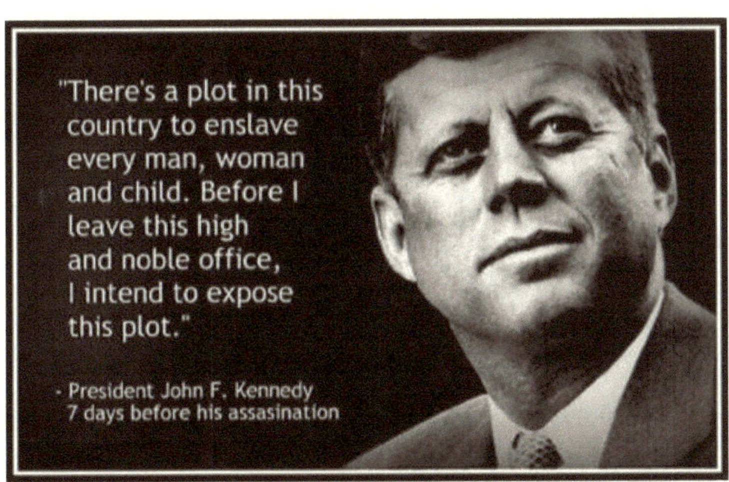

"There's a plot in this country to enslave every man, woman and child. Before I leave this high and noble office, I intend to expose this plot."

- President John F. Kennedy
7 days before his assasination

"All the News That's Fit to Print"
The New York Times.
LATE CITY EDITION
NEW YORK, SATURDAY, NOVEMBER 23, 1963
TEN CENTS

KENNEDY IS KILLED BY SNIPER AS HE RIDES IN CAR IN DALLAS; JOHNSON SWORN IN ON PLANE

TEXAN ASKS UNITY
Congressional Chiefs of 2 Parties Give Promise of Aid

LEFTIST ACCUSED
Figure in a Pro-Castro Group Is Charged— Policeman Slain

Gov. Connally Shot; Mrs. Kennedy Safe
President Is Struck Down by a Rifle Shot From Building on Motorcade Route— Johnson, Riding Behind, Is Unhurt

1963

"We'll know our disinformation program is complete when everything the American public believes is false."
- William Casey, CIA Director
(from first staff meeting in 1981)

1981

Believe what you want. My task is to point out that the sons of disobedience cannot be trusted. If you believe they have our best interests at heart, I cannot help you. Make no mistake: the future sons of God led by the Spirit are the archenemies of the sons of disobedience.

The most comprehensive research information on geoengineering can be found on www.geoengineeringwatch.org – whose founder, Dane Wittington has risked his life by sharing what he has learned about the "sons of disobedience" and their evil schemes.

The time is near when the Antichrist will appear. If you dismiss conspiracies too quickly, I fear you will wear the mark of the beast and believe the lie of a fake Christ. For this reason, I have taken the risk of being labeled a whacko conspiracy theorist by readers. Never in the history of the world has deception been executed with such precision, as is evident by the number of people who deny nanoparticle metallic dust trails in the sky when they are plainly visible overhead every day. Deep red sunsets are not normal!

I fear that if you don't begin to resist the beast now, you won't resist when it truly matters. And consider this: what are you praying against if not the sons of disobedience? Whom are you praying for if not their victims?

The sons of God, led by the Spirit, hold a great power through Yehshua that is often left untapped. Together, we can unite in prayer, trusting in God's sovereignty, that He will bring an end to the intentional global poisoning of our skies, food, water, etc.

> *And whatsoever ye shall ask in my name, that will I do, that the Father may be glorified in the Son.*
>
> *If ye shall ask any thing in my name, I will do it. (John 14:13-14 KJV)*

I should have included this rant in the last chapter and apologize for that brutal detour from the point of this chapter. The Antichrist will soon arrive, and there is no stopping him. Multitudes will be deceived, yet I pray that you are not among them. The gates of hell will not prevail against the church until that time. Most of the sons of God led by the Spirit will not remain to endure the Antichrist. Meanwhile, while we are here, we hold authority through Yehshua over the prince of this world and his operatives—both the physical sons of disobedience and the spiritual fallen sons of God.

Can I at least persuade you to use His authority until then? Pray with me that the sons of disobedience will cease poisoning us! The beast is hard at work while the church lies in a coma. The Antichrist could arrive next week, and people will read reports of his miracles, watch the pope kiss his hand on Fox News, and line up to take the mark of the beast when the fake Jesus appears.

This book is dedicated to those who might otherwise be deceived.

For the mystery of lawlessness is already at work; only
He who now restrains will do so until He is removed.
Then that lawless one will be revealed, whom the Lord
will eliminate with the breath of His mouth and bring
to an end by the appearance of His coming; that is,
the one whose coming is in accord with the activity
of Satan, with all power and false signs and wonders,
and with all the deception of wickedness for those who
perish, because they did not accept the love of the truth
so as to be saved. For this reason God will send upon
them a deluding influence so that they will believe what
is false, in order that they all may be judged who did
not believe the truth, but [took pleasure in wickedness.
(2 Thessalonians 2:7-12 NASB)

These deceptions are allowed by God so that the sons of disobedience may be separated from the sons of God led by the Spirit. The sons of disobedience will embrace the lie, while the sons of God will embrace the truth. To love the truth, we must first recognize and discern it. The Holy Spirit draws us out of the deceptions of the lawless one and into truth—if we learn to know His still and quiet voice.

The focus of this chapter was the Imam-Mahdi Antichrist, and though I drifted from the subject, I chose to leave it all together. These deceptions are interlinked, and we are now down to the minute hand on the prophetic clock of Israel. Hundreds of deceptions will continue, one after another. The sons of God must get their heads in the game and discern deception quickly. This requires constant prayer and intercession, while continually absorbing the Word of God.

When you pick up your Bible and are unsure what to read, turn to the book of Psalms and let your heart resonate with David's words. At some point, the Holy Spirit will redirect your attention to where you need to focus.

Listen to the voice of the Holy Spirit!

The church is the only society on earth that exists for the benefit of non-members. (William Temple)

CHAPTER 11

The Antichrist Church and the Missing Temple

The end-times Antichrist church celebrated its grand opening in the summer of 2022. Did anyone notice? I believe this aligns with the prophecy of the two women spoken of by the prophet Zechariah in chapter 5, where he shares his sixth and seventh visions.

Zechariah prophesied during the restoration of Judah and the rebuilding of the temple between 520–470 BC. His visions were provocative, and if we understand Yehshua's words in Matthew 23, it is likely that Zechariah was murdered in or near the temple. The overarching theme of his prophecies connects repentance, the restoration of Israel, the rebuilding of the temple, and the tribulation period. What many overlook is that the timing of his prophecies coincided with the rebuilding of the Second Temple. The restoration of Israel and plans for the Second Temple were already underway during Zechariah's time, meaning his prophecies draw a parallel between events in his day and those that will unfold again in the future.

I believe Zechariah's prophecies in chapter 5 reveal Israel at the time of the budding of the fig tree in Luke 21 and Matthew 24—the restoration of Israel. The most distinctive connection is between the rebuilding of the Second Temple in Zechariah's day and the future construction of the Third Temple after Israel's restoration.

**"Now learn this lesson from the fig tree: As soon as
its young shoots become tender and it puts out its
leaves, you know that summer is near;**

**so you, too, when you see all these things [taking
place], know for certain that He is near, right at the
door. 34 I assure you *and* most solemnly say to you,
this generation [the people living when these signs
and events begin] will not pass away until all these
things take place. (Matthew 24:32-24 AMP)**

I prefer the AMP translation for that passage, which provides a window of time in which all church-age prophecies must ultimately be fulfilled. At least some of those born on or around May 1948—when Israel was officially reborn as a nation and the fig tree budded forth—will still be alive when Yehshua returns (Luke 21, Matthew 24). At the time of this writing (2025), we're in the seventy-seventh year of this prophecy, which must include the seven-year tribulation. Seventy-seven plus seven is eighty-four. That is certainly a golden age, and though we're not there yet, the fulfillment is obviously imminent. I fear this book may not reach many people in time to be of use before the tribulation begins. Promoting a book is far more challenging than writing a book.

I believe Zechariah chapter 5 is a prophecy of the end-times religion that will be established in the last days, serving to aid and empower the Antichrist. Read Zechariah chapter 5 with that thought in mind:

*Then I turned, and lifted up mine eyes, and looked,
and behold a flying roll. And he said unto me, What
seest thou? And I answered, I see a flying roll; the
length thereof is twenty cubits, and the breadth thereof
ten cubits. Then said he unto me, This is the curse
that goeth forth over the face of the whole earth: for
every one that stealeth shall be cut off as on this side
according to it; and every one that sweareth shall be
cut off as on that side according to it. I will bring it
forth, saith the Lord of hosts, and it shall enter into
the house of the thief, and into the house of him that
sweareth falsely by my name: and it shall remain in*

An ephah was a unit of dry measure, similar to our bushel, used in trading grains and other agricultural commodities. An "ephah of grain" equaled roughly more than a five-gallon pail in modern terms. Upon this ephah rested a talent of lead, weighing about 125 pounds. The first thing that strikes any reader is the disproportionate weight of the lead on the ephah. The lead would outweigh the grain in the ephah by more than double. Both the ephah and talent represent commercialism and wealth. But why a talent of lead?

References to a woman in the Bible are symbolic of a church or religious entity. The great harlot, for example, who rides the beast, signifies a church that ushers in the final beast system under Antichrist rule—a theme we've discussed at length. The key elements of Zechariah 5 are as follows:

- A flying roll (or scroll), 20 x 10 cubits
- The scroll decreeing a curse upon the whole earth
- The ephah, a unit of measure
- A lead cover weighing one talent (125 lbs)
- Two women
- Wickedness
- A stork
- Wind in the stork's wings
- Ephah is taken to a place between earth and heaven before becoming a house in Shinar

The flying roll, measuring 20 x 10 cubits, corresponds to the reading of the law from the porch of the temple (1 Kings 6:3) and signifies a curse pronounced upon all wickedness throughout the earth. This can only be the tribulation period, meaning the prophecy in this chapter does not apply to the Second Temple or to Israel's restoration after Babylonian captivity. However, a connection is drawn from that era to the Third Temple. The link between the flying scroll and the tribulation period confirms that this is an end-times prophecy concerning an end-times religion, represented by the two women in the ephah.

The significance of the ephah, which was used as a volumetric measurement for grain, symbolizes a harvest. Yet, instead of grain, it contains a woman named "wickedness." I believe this woman is the same described in Revelation 17 as "the great prostitute who sits on many waters." The woman in the ephah has displaced a measure of the grain harvest (the church) that should have been in the ephah. But by her deceptions, a portion of the grain (the church) will be lost. The two women (representing false religions) occupy the ephah in place of God's people, who will not be harvested because they were deceived.

It is generally assumed that the ephah represents the Jewish people. My interpretation is different, because this decree of the flying scroll applies to the entire earth. The woman in the ephah has deceived all nations, not only Israel. This decree serves to purge the earth of evil in preparation for Yehshua's return and the establishment of the Millennial Kingdom. For this reason, I conclude that the women in the ephah represent two related religions that have corrupted the entire earth and are related to Babylon. The first woman, then, can only be Babylon the Great, Mother of Harlots (Revelation 17:5). The second woman is related to her.

The lead cover is more difficult to understand. A talent, also a unit of measure, perhaps indicating commercialism and wealth—the very forces that corrupted the Jewish people during their first Babylonian captivity. The scroll decrees a curse upon the earth, while the units of measure represent the wealth of the earth. The woman named Wickedness represents the first apostasy of Shinar, which defiled the earth. The lead cover seals her wickedness until the appointed time, when it will be set up as a "house" (temple) —the end-times false church—in Shinar, the place where apostasy was first established.

It is also possible that the lead cover relates to the Gog-Magog nuclear war of Ezekiel 38, as Islamic nations draw the world into alignment against Israel. The two false religions within the ephah are ultimately responsible for this conflict. If the second woman had never existed, the Gog and Magog war would not occur.

This brings us to the conclusion reached in the previous chapter. If Alberto Rivera's claims are dismissed, then what follows will seem implausible. Yet I believe Rivera's claims help clarify Zechariah's prophecy. If the first woman is Wickedness—the same as the woman in Revelation 17 (Roman Catholic Church), then the second woman must be Islam. Islam, according to this interpretation, would not have risen on its own apart from the Roman Catholic Church, and it will be responsible for the nuclear war of Ezekiel 38. The lead cover could symbolize the containment of this war until God allows it. Since Israel's statehood was established in 1948, the nations of Islam have hallucinated over her elimination. God is restraining the wickedness within the ephah, preventing the fulfillment of certain aspects of Zechariah's prophecy until the appointed time.

The Vatican has sought to exterminate Jews from Jerusalem since before the sixth century AD, and Islam has long stood as Israel's archenemy. These two powers—the Vatican and Islam—are represented by the two women in the ephah. They displaced a vast portion of the world that otherwise would have been counted as harvested grain (the church) within the ephah. The church of these two women will be codified in Shinar, the place where religious apostasy first began. From Shinar will arise the Third Temple of Jerusalem, shared by the two women in the ephah. The same wickedness that displaced a measure of the church will also deceive the Jewish people, thereby releasing the curse of the flying scroll curse upon the entire earth. If "Mystery Babylon, Mother of Harlots" is indeed the first woman in the ephah—who mentored Muhammad and thereby gave rise to Islam (the second woman in ephah)—then this is how the prophecy unfolds. Zechariah's vision of the two women in the ephah connects the first church of Babylon to the last church of Babylon in the Third Temple.

To understand the stork, one must consider Jewish kosher laws. The stork is regarded as a scavenger bird and is not kosher. In this vision, the unkosher stork represents a powerful demonic entity, carrying the two women to their end-times destiny. The wind in its wings signifies a dark prince spirit—the fallen angel sons of God—who bear the bird into the second heaven ("between the earth and the heaven"), where spiritual warfare begins before returning to be established on earth.

At times when researching something in the Bible, you will be amazed how often the Bible interprets itself. In the case of the stork, I found at least half a dozen references, but two verses helped significantly in interpreting Zechariah 5.

> *Yea, the stork in the heaven knoweth her appointed times; and the turtle and the crane and the swallow observe the time of their coming; but my people know not the judgment of the LORD. (Jeremiah 8:7 KJV)*

> *The trees of the Lord are full of sap; the cedars of Lebanon, which he hath planted;*
>
> *Where the birds make their nests: as for the stork, the fir trees are her house.*

__The high hills are a refuge for the wild goats; and the__
__rocks for the conies.__

__He appointed the moon for seasons: the sun knoweth__
__his going down. (Psalm 104:16-19 KJV)__

The stork knows her appointed time and season more than God's people. Jump over to Revelation 18:

__And he cried mightily with a strong voice, saying,__
__Babylon the great is fallen, is fallen, and is become__
__the__ *__habitation of devils__*__,__ *__and the hold of every foul__*
__spirit, and a cage of__ *__every unclean and hateful bird.__*
__(Revelation 18:2 KJV)__

If we continue to verse 11 of Zechariah 5 ("*To build it a house in the land of Shinar: and it shall be established, and set there upon her own base"),* several conclusions may be drawn about Zechariah's stork:

- It represents an unclean, demonic entity (Revelation 18:2).
- It is carried by a powerful spiritual force (the wind beneath its wings Zech. 5:9).
- It cannot move before its appointed time (Jeremiah 8:7).
- It is building a nest for a new home (Psalm 104:17).

The house in the land of Shinar signifies a church that unites Catholicism and Islam under one roof—an end-times church. The book of Zechariah is mostly dedicated to the last days and the tribulation period. The two women in the ephah symbolize two religions that have something in common. The "nest" or house/temple, will be promoted in the interest of "peace" (as seen in the Abrahamic Family House).

Why Shinar? The brilliance of this prophecy connects the origin of false religion to the end-times Antichrist church. Nimrod, I believe, will have a direct link to the Antichrist. The false religion represented by the two women in the ephah will establish a church (house) in Shinar where it all began. The beginning comes full circle to the end. What originates in

Shinar will become the religion of Jerusalem, with the Antichrist enthroned in the Third Temple as its ultimate figurehead.

After the flood, sun and moon worship was revived by Nimrod in Shinar. Shinar, therefore, codifies this religion of apostasy before sending it forth. The same religion of Nimrod will ultimately find its way to the Third Temple of Jerusalem through Shinar.

All of this sounds ridiculous and impossible, except that it has already happened. The church of Pergamos has joined hands with Islam. Here is some news from 2019 that has become a reality as of the summer 2022:

> *On 4 February 2019 Pope Francis and Sheikh Ahmed el-Tayeb—Grand Imam of Al-Azhar Mosque and University in Cairo Egypt and considered Sunni Islam's highest authority in jurisprudence—signed a document entitled the Document on Human Fraternity for World Peace and Living Together, also known as the Abu Dhabi declaration. Reportedly, it is to be a common declaration of commitment to unite humanity and work for world peace to ensure that future generations can live in a climate of mutual respect and healthy coexistence.*

> *This document is the foundation of the subsequently established Higher Committee of Human Fraternity (HCHF). In 2019 at a meeting of the HCHF at the New York Public Library in New York City a project was announced by Abdullah bin Zayed calling for the construction of The **<u>Abrahamic Family House</u>** on Saadiyat Island in Abu Dhabi, UAE.*

> *The Abrahamic Family House will be an interfaith complex that will include a synagogue, mosque, and a church – Imam Al-Tayeb Mosque, St. Francis Church, and Moses Ben Maimon Synagogue, respectively.*

Pope Francis, representing the first woman in the ephah, and Sheikh Ahmed el-Tayeb, representing the second, joined together in the interest of peace to form a new religion called "Chrislam" at the "Abrahamic Family House."

This was the concept rendition:

This is the Abrahamic Family House headquarters in Abu Dhabi, a completed construction project, unveiled today:

Abu Dahbi is not in the land of Shinar (ancient Mesopotamia, present-day Iraq). But the new world religion of Chrislam is advancing across the Middle East, and a Chrislam church has now been established in the ancient city of Ur in Iraq—formerly Shinar—called the "Interfaith Chrislam Center." The term *interfaith* is becoming the new buzzword for the "universal church" long desired by the Vatican. Wherever the word *interfaith* appears, it signals a connection to this end-times one-world religion prophesied by Zechariah 1100 years before Pope Boniface IV imagined the existence of Islam.

Ibrahim Al-Khalil Church in Ur of the Chaldeans

This is the Interfaith Chrislam Center in the city of Ur, Iraq—once the center of the Babylonian Empire in the land of Shinar. This church fulfills Zechariah's prophecy of the two women in the ephah carried to Shinar by the stork, to set the house (temple) upon its base. Shinar serves as the foundation of the Third Temple religion, which will be exported to Jerusalem, likely through the Imam-Mahdi and the false prophet (Vatican/pope).

These are not isolated to the Middle East. "The House of One," another Abrahamic Family House project, is currently under construction in Berlin, Germany:

The construction of the Interfaith Center in Ur, Iraq, (in the land of Shinar) fulfills Zechariah's prophecy precisely. The unclean bird (demon), borne by the wind of the dark spirit (prince), has carried the two women of the ephah to their appointed base in Shinar.

This marks the rise of the church of the final Antichrist that will occupy the 3rd Temple during the seven-year tribulation, in agreement with all prophecy. At some point in the near future, the pope and Imam will salute the Antichrist Imam-Mahdi and call him god, deceiving billions. I think we can assume that whatever this Antichrist does will captivate the hearts and minds of all religions, consolidating them into one global "Interfaith" religion. Pray that none of God's people will be deceived by this false religion, which will have the Antichrist as its ultimate figurehead in the Third Temple.

This is not a time to remain ignorant of God or prophecy. By now you should know that the budding of the fig tree (Luke 21; Matthew 24) began on May 14, 1948, when Israel was reborn as a nation in a single day, just as Isaiah prophesied (Isaiah 66:8). President Harry Truman signed the agreement at ten minutes to midnight, Tel Aviv time, on that day. Luke 21:32 declares, "Verily I say unto you, this generation shall not pass away, till all be fulfilled." Which generation? The generation of Israelites born on or around May 14, 1948—some of which will still be alive at the end of the seven-year tribulation. As of May 2025, we are seventy-seven years into fulfillment of this prophecy. So please stay wide awake and be prepared. I pray that everyone reading this is worthy of the wheat harvest and invited to the wedding in the Father's house, though we all know many who will not be there.

The church of the final Antichrist and the tribulation period has already celebrated its grand opening. How many more signs must appear before we recognize them? In your prayers, give thanks for the life of Zechariah and to God for allowing this generation to witness the fulfillment of prophecy before Yehshua's return.

Meanwhile, the one-world religion is taking root, and the threat of war continues to rage between Israel and its Muslim adversaries. This brings us back to the lead cover on the ephah. Zechariah's vision in chapter

5 is arranged like pieces of a large puzzle. In looking at the puzzle, we know that the prophet's visions concern the last days, when Israel would be restored and a Third Temple built. This culminates in the tribulation period, symbolized by the flying scroll that decrees a curse upon the world.

A macro view of this puzzle in chapter 5 looks like this:

- The ephah, a unit of volumetric measurement used for grain, contains not a harvest but rather wickedness—represented by two women symbolizing false religions. These religions have displaced the grain that should have been gathered (the bride church). Two false churches are in the ephah instead of a portion of the bride church that should have been harvested but were deceived by the church of Shinar that began with Nimrod. The first and last false churches that deceive the world are of the same origin.

- I believe former Jesuit Alberto Rivera's story of Cardinal Bea's historical account of Muhammad is mostly accurate, and that the Vatican (first woman in the ephah) was responsible for his rise to fame, thus giving birth to Islam (second woman in the ephah). These are the two women in the ephah.

- If you have any doubt about any of this, the fact that Pope Francis and Grand Imam Sheikh Ahmed el-Tayeb came together to christen the Abrahamic Family House under the new religion of Chrislam should free your mind from any bondage to deception. This prophetic event confirms that Rivera's conspiracy theory is no longer a theory. The stork has carried the two women in the ephah since Muhammad's time and has now set them upon their base in Shinar (the city of Ur, Iraq).

- These two women are empowered by demons (stork) and princes (fallen angel sons of God = wind that carries the stork), held back until the appointed time (Jeremiah 8:7). Nimrod and Babel are restored through Mystery Babylon, the Mother of Harlots, who has moved through history from Shinar to Persia, then Greece, and finally Rome. Through Rome, Mystery Babylon remains in the Vatican today. I believe the Interfaith Chrislam Center in

Shinar aligns with Zechariah's prophecy and will serve as the religion of the Third Temple, with the Antichrist as its god.

- The first missing piece of this prophetic puzzle is the rebuilding of the Third Temple after Israel's restoration. This was the central theme of Zechariah's prophecies, with the flying scroll curses demonstrating the timing of their fulfillment.
- The second missing piece is the huge lead cover on the ephah. Why lead? And why would the cover outweigh the ephah by more than double?

Remember that the Imam Mahdi is said to come from the east, and tradition holds that Allah will send people from the east to support his rise to power. The people of the east will carry black flags. The two black flags I am aware of belong to ISIS and the Iranian Jihad movement. Both ISIS and Iran may aid the Imam Mahdi as he rises to become a world leader, but Iran is central to prophecy because of the Gog and Magog war in Ezekiel 38.

Israel's relationship with Iran—known historically as Persia or Elam in the Bible—has been historically good until modern times, for the most part. The Israelites were conquered by the Babylonians, and when the Babylonians were conquered by the Persians, the Israelites became Persian captives by default. They were generally treated well, except for a brief circumstance recorded in the book of Esther under King Xerxes I. Even then, the true enemy of the Jewish people was not King Xerxes I but his high-ranking official, Haman. Haman was an Agagite, descended from King Agag of the Amalekites. This explains everything about Haman because the Amalekites and Israelites have a long history of warfare—a conflict that continues today in Gaza.

However, in no other instance in the history of the world has there been a conflict between Persia (Iran) and Israel until now. The weight of this moment cannot be overstated.

Thirty years after Israel was officially recognized by President Harry Truman, the Iranian Revolution erupted. Iran, long ruled under a monarchial system, saw the fall of the Pahlavi dynasty and the removal of Shah Mohammad Reza Pahlavi from power. In his place, Ayatollah Ruhollah Khomeini established the Islamic Republic of Iran under Shiite Muslim rule.

The Shah was granted political asylum in the US, sparking outrage in Iran and leading to the attack on the US Embassy in November 1979. Sixty-six American hostages were held captive, with demands for the Shah's extradition back to Iran—where he would almost certainly have faced execution. The embassy hostage situation was a colossal failure under President Jimmy Carter that lasted 444 days. When President Reagan was elected, the hostages were released, marking a symbolic victory for his new administration.

While this was a great success for Reagan, relations between Iran and the US intensified to new extremes. This animosity has endured for decades, with the Ayatollahs constantly calling for "death to Israel" and "death to America."

However, the Shiite Muslim leadership in Iran rules by fear rather than genuine popularity. In a consensus, most Iranians hold a very low opinion of their rulers. Perhaps the best thing about the Ayatollahs radically zealous jihadist views can be observed by the rate at which Christianity is exploding in Iran. It is estimated that in 1980, there were only about 500 Christians in the country. Today, that number has grown to well beyond one million, according to persecution.org and the research organization GAAMAN. This is amazing, given that Christians in Iran face imprisonment, torture, and the confiscation and burning of Bibles or Christian literature by authorities.

If you would like to support the Iranian Christian movement, there are various ways to do so. One is through a very brave missionary group called Elam Ministries, which ministers covertly to the Iranian people. They have offices outside of Iran, located in the UK, USA, Greece, Australia, and Germany. Go to www.elam.com for more information. I am certain they will appreciate your support!

Let's return to the "death to everyone" regime of Iran. Unless you've been living under a rock, you know that Iran has been involved in the development of a nuclear program for over seventy years going back to the

1950s. It began with help from the US and Europe, supposedly to produce low-cost nuclear energy. This makes no sense when Iran is sitting on low-cost energy already. No other oil-producing nation has been so interested in nuclear energy as Iran. This is no coincidence! The sons of disobedience know prophecy! Israel regained statehood in 1948, the US and Europe start a nuclear program in Persia two years later. This is no coincidence.

The program suffered major setbacks after the Iranian Revolution. However, I doubt there is another country in the world that has been so obsessed with developing an autonomous nuclear program by any means necessary. They are at least thirty-five years into nuclear development, most of which has been managed by the Ministry of Defense and Armed Forces Logistics of Iran. As far back as the year 2000, Iran has been testing nuclear bombs in remote areas. So, it is a bit perplexing when we hear news reports of always being "months or weeks away from nuclear capacity" when they've been testing nuclear bombs for twenty-five years.

I am afraid some readers may be bored with this, but it is essential to review Iran's history of nuclear development to understand they are far from being backward or undeveloped in military terms. This is some great information I will share with you from iranwatch.org to help connect a few dots. I hope you will be patient in reading this for the sake of being adequately informed and not ignorant of the imminent threat Iran poses to the world. When someone says "death to USA, death to Israel" with fifty years of experience in nuclear weapon development, we shouldn't naively assume they're exaggerating. What if Bin-Laden had a nuclear weapon? What condition would our world be in today?

This website (www.iranwatch.org) provides some useful information about Iran's history of nuclear development:

Key Institutions and Personnel
AEOI and TESA

The Atomic Energy Organization of Iran (AEOI) is the central entity in Iran's publicly-disclosed nuclear program. It oversees key sites such as the uranium enrichment plants at Natanz and Fordow, a nuclear technology center at Isfahan, the Bushehr and Arak reactors, and the Tehran Research Reactor. A network of contractors, subsidiaries, and affiliates has assisted and supplied AEOI, including Mesbah Energy Company, Novin Energy Company, and Kalaye Electric Company.

The Iran Centrifuge Technology Company (TESA) has played a crucial role in Iran's uranium enrichment program by manufacturing centrifuges for the AEOI. According to the European Union, TESA took over the activities of Farayand Technique, which itself was a subsidiary of Kalaye Electric Company.

SPND and MODAFL

The military dimension of Iran's nuclear program centers on the Organization for Defensive Innovation and Research (SPND), an institute subordinate to the Ministry of Defense and Armed Forces Logistics (MODAFL) and formerly led by Mohsen Fakhrizadeh, who directed Iran's Amad Plan effort to develop nuclear weapons. The SPND has its roots in the Physics Research Center, a military-related institute established at Lavisan-Shian in 1989 that was involved in efforts to acquire dual use materials and equipment that could be used in uranium enrichment and conversion activities.

Universities

Iranian universities and nuclear scientists are one of the links between the civilian and military sides of the nuclear program. Shahid Beheshti University has collaborated with both MODAFL and AEOI, and the

MODAFL-subordinate Malek Ashtar University of Technology has been sanctioned by the United Nations for having contributed to Iran's research on nuclear weapons. Prominent nuclear scientists including Fakhrizadeh (before his assassination in 2020), Mohammad Mehdi Tehranchi, and former AEOI head Fereidoun Abbasi-Davani have maintained links to those and other universities.

Foreign Assistance

In 1985, Iran secretly launched a domestic centrifuge enrichment program that would receive a substantial boost from illicit foreign assistance. The illicit assistance was set in motion by an attempt at civil nuclear cooperation through official channels, however. In 1987, Iran approached the government of Pakistan seeking help on its nuclear program, and the two countries signed a formal agreement that year that included training for at least six Iranian scientists at the Pakistan Institute of Nuclear Science and Technology.

Yet the deal yielded little else for Iran, prompting it to look for other means by which to access Pakistani nuclear technology. These efforts led to its contacts with the black-market network led by A. Q. Khan. Khan had reportedly traveled to Iran in 1986 to visit the Bushehr reactor and inspect the damage done to it by Iraqi bombing during the war.

At a meeting in 1987, the Khan network made an offer in the form of a one-page, handwritten letter to the Iranians. The offer contained a menu of items

*such as a disassembled P-1 centrifuge, drawings and
specifications for a complete centrifuge plant, and
materials for 2,000 centrifuge machines. Iran did not
purchase everything on the list but did buy one or
two disassembled centrifuges along with supporting
drawings and specifications. Iran also admitted to using
the menu as a shopping list to purchase other items from
different suppliers.*

*A second deal with the Khan network materialized in
the mid-1990s. Between 1994 and 1995, Iran received
some 500 disassembled P-1 centrifuge machines as well
as drawings for the P-2 model. Iran told the IAEA in
2003 that these were domestically produced, but trace
particles of highly enriched uranium on the machines
allowed the IAEA to forensically connect them to the
Pakistani program, and Iran later acknowledged their
foreign origin. But the Khan network was not Iran's
only source. According to the IAEA, Iran admitted to
receiving a total of about 2,000 centrifuge components
and some subassemblies from foreign sources between
1985 and 1997.*

*Also around 1987, the Khan network provided a 15-page
document describing procedures for the conversion of
uranium hexafluoride into metal and the casting of the
metal into hemispheres. Such activities, according to
the IAEA, were "related to the fabrication of nuclear
weapon components." Iran showed the 15-page
document to the IAEA in 2005, although the IAEA
was not given sufficient access or evidence to confirm
the veracity of Iran's claims regarding the document's
origin.*

In addition to assistance from the Khan network, Iran is also believed to have received help from China as well. For example, China is widely acknowledged to be the source of information for Iran's uranium conversion plant at Isfahan. It also supplied Iran with uranium compounds in 1991 that Iran did not declare to the IAEA, including 1,000 kg of UF6, 400 kg of UF4, and about 400 kg of natural UO2.

Iran may have received considerable help from foreign experts in its crash nuclear weapon development program as well. For example, the Atomic Archive indicates that Iran acquired several designs for nuclear weapons from abroad, including one obtained via the Khan network in the early 1990s. Further, according to the IAEA, Iran could have benefited in its effort to develop an explosives technology known as multipoint initiation from a certain "foreign expert." This expert is identified elsewhere as Vyacheslav Danilenko, who was present in Iran in the period from 1996 to 2001. Both Iran and Danilenko have denied that he contributed to the nuclear program, claiming instead that his work was related to the production of nanodiamonds. But the Atomic Archive reveals that Danilenko was not the only one—well over a dozen foreign scientists may have assisted Iran in its nuclear weapons development program.

Iran has also attempted to illicitly procure dual use items for its nuclear program from unwitting foreign firms over the years. For example, a 2013 report by a U.N. Panel of Experts highlighted one case in which Iran attempted to import high-quality valves, which have a variety of industrial applications, from Germany and Sweden. To acquire the valves, Iran used false shipping documents and other suspicious methods, and the panel was subsequently able to establish that they were intended for use in the Arak heavy-water reactor. Other dual use goods that Iran has sought to illicitly procure include vacuum pumps, high-frequency converters, heat exchangers, nuclear-grade graphite, high-strength aluminum, and carbon fiber. To advance these efforts, Iran has made use of front companies, concealed the true end user, and falsified documentation in order to deceive suppliers and evade sanctions and export controls.

Iran has also received official foreign assistance for its nuclear program as well. During the Shah's rule, the United States built a five-megawatt research reactor at the University of Tehran, which began operation in 1967 and remains in use as of 2023. The Shah also pursued deals with European suppliers, signing a contract with Kraftwerk Union (later Siemens) to build two 1,200 megawatt reactors at Bushehr and negotiating with the French company Framatome for two additional 900-megawatt reactors.

Under the Islamic Republic, in the 1990s, Iran turned to Russia and China for cooperation on its nuclear program. In particular, in 1995, it concluded an agreement with Russia to complete the construction of the reactor at Bushehr and possibly supply a uranium enrichment plant. Russia's state nuclear company Rosatom finished the Bushehr reactor in 2011 and continues to supply the low-enriched uranium fuel for it, returning the spent fuel to Russia. The uranium enrichment plant was never delivered.

The JCPOA also contained provisions for international nuclear cooperation with Iran. As a result of the multilateral accord, in 2017 Iran concluded an agreement with China's state-owned nuclear corporation to re-design and rebuild the heavy-water reactor at Arak.

Sanctions and Export Control Measures United Nations

U.N. Security Council resolution 2231 is the primary legal basis for U.N. sanctions on Iran. This resolution endorses the Joint Comprehensive Plan of Action (JCPOA) and supersedes earlier resolutions, thereby lifting most U.N. sanctions on Iran. Until 2025, the resolution limits Iran's ability to import nuclear-related items without case-by-case approval from the Security Council. This list of restricted items is based on the list established by the Nuclear Suppliers Group (NSG), a multilateral export control regime of 48 countries that have agreed to a set of guidelines about which nuclear technologies they will export, and under what conditions.

Previously, resolution 2231 had also restricted Iran's imports of items usable in nuclear weapon delivery systems (namely missiles), called upon Tehran to suspend tests of ballistic missiles designed to carry a nuclear warhead, and imposed targeted sanctions on entities that had contributed to unsafeguarded nuclear activities or ballistic missile testing. Those provisions expired in mid-October 2023. Resolution 2231 also

I didn't share the entire page, only the most relevant portion. If you are interested, their site contains many details that are not commonly reported and are very informative.

However, not all details are included there. The USA, under President Obama, was complicit in assisting Iran both financially and technologically in advancing its nuclear capabilities. Much was done to help Iran, while almost nothing was done to stop them. There were numerous reports of funds being given to Iran to support their nuclear program. Through various funding mechanisms, including NGOs, some have estimated as much as $150 billion was given to Iran over Obama's two terms. While that figure has been intentionally difficult to verify, there is also the matter of $1.7 billion in non-US currency given to Iran to help circumvent international sanctions under the premise of "in exchange for US hostages." This has been confirmed by numerous "reliable" news media sources and is not a conspiracy theory.

When I discuss these issues with the average, uninformed corporate news media consumers, I get a lot of head shaking and responses such as "Well, that was fact-checked and not true." When you research these sensitive matters, one must scroll past the psychological operations of fact-checkers and filter them out. Most fact-checkers are politically motivated and privately funded distributors of disinformation. If you conduct a little forensic work on corporate media networks, you will find that at the top of a global media empire stand only about half a dozen names, all of whom can be classified as "sons of disobedience." They are among the hierarchy in Satan's kingdom. Do not trust corporate media as an information resource. Instead, rely on small, privately owned publications or networks, especially Christian- or Jewish-based independent media sources. Do not trust anyone politically motivated in favor of the beast's agendas.

Please stay with me on this. Here are a couple of reports based on fact, not conspiracy theory, that support a point I want to make about the current situation in Iran:

From Deal to Detonation: How Obama's Iran Nuclear Accord Fueled The Israel-Iran War[32]

> *As war erupts between Israel and Iran, experts revisit the 2015 nuclear deal, arguing that sanctions relief, sunset clauses, and unchecked missile funding paved the way for today's conflict.*

> ***Gila Isaacson***

> ***JUN 16, 2025 08:03***

> *As missiles light up Middle Eastern skies and sirens disrupt civilian life in Israel and Iran, a critical question looms: Did the 2015 Joint Comprehensive Plan of Action (JCPOA), a cornerstone of Obama's foreign policy, empower Iran's ambitions, leading to today's war? Experts dissect the deal's impact.*

> ***Sanctions Relief: A Financial Boost for Iran***

---

32   https://www.jfeed.com/news-world/obama-iran-deal-israel-war

The JCPOA lifted stringent sanctions in exchange for nuclear restrictions, releasing tens of billions in frozen assets. Mark Dubowitz, CEO of the Foundation for Defense of Democracies, warned Congress in 2015 and 2017 that this cash influx would not only advance Iran's nuclear program but also fund ballistic missiles and proxy warfare. "The JCPOA provides Iran with a patient path to a nuclear weapon," he stated, predicting Tehran's strategic gains.

Sunset Clauses: A Ticking Clock

Critics, including Israel's then-ambassador Ron Dermer, flagged the deal's "sunset clauses," which allowed restrictions on uranium enrichment and missile work to expire after 10–15 years. "Iran could simply decide to walk in," Dermer warned, noting the lack of linkage between sanctions relief and Iran's aggressive behavior. This gave Tehran a clear, legally sanctioned path to nuclear capability.

Obama's Hesitant Stance

Michael Doran, writing for Brookings and Mosaic Magazine in 2014, criticized Obama's approach as containment rather than prevention. "Obama is bluffing on Iran," he argued, pointing to a reluctance to act decisively, from Syria to Tehran, which signaled weakness and emboldened Iran to advance under diplomatic cover.

JCPOA's Limits: Inspections Without Teeth

The deal extended Iran's nuclear "breakout time" to about a year and barred advanced centrifuges for 15 years. But without behavioral conditions, these restrictions were temporary. Dubowitz noted that Iran retained key nuclear infrastructure while gaining sanctions relief, paving the way for a "threshold" nuclear state.

Funding Proxies and Missiles

Though the JCPOA ignored Iran's missile programs, the financial windfall didn't. By 2015–16, reports confirmed Iran funneled funds to proxies like Hezbollah and the Houthis, enhancing its regional influence. These capabilities now fuel conflicts in Gaza, Lebanon, Yemen, and threats against Israel.

Trump's Withdrawal: Pressure Without a Plan

In 2018, Trump exited the JCPOA, reimposing "maximum pressure" sanctions. While this slowed Iran's progress, Tehran escalated enrichment to 60% purity, nearing weapons-grade. Subsequent Biden-era talks failed to restore the deal or curb Iran's missile and proxy activities.

Today's Crisis: A Predictable Escalation

The June 2025 conflict, with Israeli strikes on Iran's nuclear sites (Natanz, Fordow, Isfahan), reflects the deal's fallout: Iran holds 400 kg of 60% enriched uranium, the IAEA warns of covert sites, and Tehran hints at exiting the Non-Proliferation Treaty. Unchecked missile development and sunset clauses created this volatile moment.

Who's to Blame?

Obama's Gamble: The JCPOA freed funds without addressing Iran's missiles or proxies, enabling long-term planning.

Trump's Misstep: Withdrawing without a robust alternative left Iran unchecked.

Biden's Inaction: Weak negotiations failed to rein in Tehran's escalation.

Lessons for the Future

A new deal must tie nuclear relief to missile and proxy limits, make sunset clauses contingent on Iran's behavior, and back diplomacy with a credible military deterrent. Addressing Iran's regional network is as critical as its nuclear labs. The JCPOA, once hailed as a diplomatic triumph, became a strategic pause that enabled Iran's nuclear and regional rise. Whether future U.S. policy learns from these errors will determine if war persists or peace prevails.

Do you get the picture? The goal of the sons of disobedience is that Iran, the archenemy of the US and Israel, become a radical nuclear wildcard and unleash hell. If the above scenario doesn't provoke your sense of disgust, read this article by the *Investor's Business Daily:*

Obama Funded Terrorism With His $1.7 Bil Ransom To Iran
05:12 PM ET 09/14/2016

*War On Terror: Since it was revealed the U.S. gave Iran
$1.7 billion as part of its 2015 nuclear deal, everyone
has wondered: What did Iran do with all that money,
much of it in cash? Now we know—a chunk of it went to
fund terrorism.*

*The U.S. foolishly gave Iran the money because both
President Obama and Secretary of State John Kerry
were so desperate for an Iranian nuke deal that they
were willing to bribe the Iranians to go along. And ever
since, Iran has treated them with utter contempt for
being so weak.*

*Even so, all along the U.S. government has steadfastly
maintained that the money was desperately needed by
Iran to prop up its ailing economy. They would spend the
money on butter, not guns.*

*Yes, both Obama and Kerry said that "some" of the
money might get used for evil purposes, but downplayed
its significance.*

*And, as recently as last week, State Department official
Christopher Backemeyer told a congressional hearing:
"It's our assessment **the vast majority (of the $1.7
billion) has gone to the critical needs that Iran has
had.**"*

*He went on to concede that he couldn't vouch for "every
dollar that's gonna go in or out of Iran, as you know."
Still he made clear the government believes the money
was used mainly general economic purposes.*

*Well, it was bad enough that a big part of the $1.7 billion
— about $400 million — was paid out as a clear bribe
for the return of four American hostages, a violation of
U.S. law.*

*But now we find out from a new report by the American
Action Forum (AAF) that **$37.4 million of the
ransom money likely has been handed over to the
Iranian Revolutionary Guard Corps (IRGC)**, the group
that carries out terrorist operations around the world
and that has murdered Americans.*

*"Applying the official (Iranian budget) spending levels
to the U.S. payment to Iran, the $1.7 billion would mean
$37.4 million for the IRGC," wrote Rachel Hoff, the
analyst at the American Action Forum who calculated
the amount.*

*"Paying ransoms in exchange for Americans held
abroad is one bad policy," Hoff said. "Indirectly funding
terrorism is another."*

*And make no mistake — the IRGC is a terrorist
group. A **State Department report in 2012 cited** the
"marked resurgence of Iran's state sponsorship of
terrorism through its Islamic Revolutionary Guard
Corps — Quds Force, its Ministry of Intelligence and*

Security, and Tehran's ally Hezbollah." It further warned at the time that these terrorist activities "have reached a tempo unseen since the 1990s."

Since then, under the desperate-for-a-deal Kerry, State has changed its tune, suggesting that somehow the Iranian Guard is no longer involved in terrorism as it once was. This is not mere naivete—it is a lie, and the State Department knows it.

Iran is responsible for the death of hundreds of Americans, mostly through the Iranian Guard's terrorist Quds force and its terrorist allies in other countries, including Hezbollah and al-Qaida. In early August, we called the ransom a "regrettably foolish and dangerous error." This makes it even worse.

*There is even the possibility that the support for Iran is far worse than people imagine. Mark Dubowitz, executive director of the Foundation for Defense of Democracies, says that Iran **"may have received an additional $33.6 billion in secret cash and gold payments** facilitated by the Obama administration between 2014 and 2016." This was all part of the bribery of Iranian officials by the U.S. as part of the Iran talks and their aftermath.*

If so, the Obama administration has likely sowed the seeds of terrorism for many years to come.

That Iran got even a penny from us to perpetrate more terrorism is a disgrace, and is yet another reason for regime change in the U.S. in 2016.

President Obama was instrumental in shaping Iran's status as a global nuclear threat. It doesn't matter whether the amount was $1.00 or $150 billion; what matters is that as a US taxpayer, you have unwillingly contributed to an archenemy of Israel. In your prayers, ask for forgiveness and mercy on behalf of your country, and that only the sons of disobedience be held accountable for what has been done to Israel. May we be spared God's judgment as US taxpayers.

This brings us back to the lead cover on the ephah. We know that one aspect of the ephah is the "house in the land of Shinar," which already exists as a model for One World Universal Religion. I believe Islam is the second woman in the ephah, vehemently pursuing the destruction of Israel for Allah. The antichrist will introduce a peace treaty following the nuclear confrontation of the Ezekiel 38–39 Gog and Magog war. When the lead cover is removed from the ephah at the appointed time, the Gog and Magog war will begin. This will be the worst war in the history of the world up to that time.

This is an additional aspect of what I believe the "talent" represents, being larger than the amount of wheat that should have been in the ephah. It is only the beginning, and conditions will worsen when the "flying scroll" is released for the seven years that follow. The Gog and Magog war will end with a peace treaty organized by the Imam Mahdi. One of the conditions of this treaty will likely be a global mandate of conformance to the "Interfaith Universal Church," complete with sun worship Sunday laws, where the pope and the Imam will shake hands and embrace at a press conference, ushering in a new era of peace under a new faith. The Imam-Mahdi could possibly be the god of the apostate religion born in the land of Shinar, now established at the Third Temple on the Temple Mount in Jerusalem.

The Abrahamic Family House, or "Chrislam Interfaith Church," which the stork set upon its base in Shinar where all false religions are born, will be the religion of the Third Jewish Temple in Jerusalem. This connects the timing of Zechariah's prophecy perfectly to the end times tribulation church. Through signs and miracles, the Imam Mahdi, or Antichrist, will be accepted as god. The fake Jesus of Islam will appear and try to deceive the Jews, at which point only one religion will remain on the Temple Mount, with the Antichrist declaring himself as god. I believe one of the tasks of the 144,000 will be to prevent the Jews from falling into this deception of the fake Jesus. The 144,000 will aid in fulfilling Romans 11:26.

The prophecies of Ezekiel, Jeremiah, Zechariah, Daniel, Micah, Isaiah, Matthew, Mark, Luke, John, the epistles of Paul, and Revelation must connect coherently if we desire to gain an accurate picture of what is to come for Israel in the last days. Daniel 9:26–27 offers much insight:

> *Then after the sixty-two weeks [of years] the Anointed One will be cut off [and denied His Messianic kingdom] and have nothing [and no one to defend Him], and the people of the [other] prince who is to come will destroy the city and the sanctuary. Its end will come with a flood; even to the end there will be war; desolations are determined. And he will enter into a binding and irrevocable covenant with the many for one week (seven years), but in the middle of the week he will stop the sacrifice and grain offering [for the remaining three and one-half years]; and on the wing of abominations will come one who makes desolate, even until the complete destruction, one that is decreed, is poured out on the one who causes the horror. (Daniel 9:26-27 AMP)*

I used the AMP translation, but several translations render the end of verse 26 differently, and some make more sense in the context of Daniel's prophecy in chapter 9. The KJV says that "unto the end of war, desolations are determined," which suggests a war that has already occurred. What makes more sense in the Amplified translation is that "even to the end there will be war," which leads into verse 27 and the Antichrist in the temple.

On October 7, 2023, Hamas—an Iranian proxy financed covertly with US funding—attacked Israel. My opinion is that the October 7 attack began the Psalm 83 war through proxies, as previously mentioned. Hamas, Hezbollah, the Taliban, and the Houthis can all be traced to the tribes listed in Psalm 83. I believe we may be mistaken in assuming that the Hagarenes of Psalm 83 are Egypt, which allows prophecy to pass unnoticed while we wait for something that has already happened. I believe that one of Iran's funded proxies is a small Arab nation obscured by time, in fact the Hagarenes of Psalm 83:6. They were cousins to Ishmael through Hagar and were nomadic tribes settling as far north as Syria and east to the Persian Gulf. Both Fausset's and Smith's Bible Dictionaries connect them to Hejer (from Hagar), a small town in the province of el-Bahreyn on the Persian Gulf. The entire coastline of the Persian Gulf consists of enemies of Israel. The Hagarenes have been traced more frequently from Syria to the Persian Gulf (Hejer) than to Egypt.

Military spokesman for the Izz ad-Din Al-Qassam Brigades, Abu Obeida, from the military wing of the Palestinian Hamas terrorist organization, made a televised appearance on the 100th day of the Israeli war on Gaza. He made this statement during that speech:

We look back 100 days to remember the educated,
the complicit, and the incapacitated among the world
powers governed by the law of the jungle, reminding
them of an aggression that reached its peak against our
path (Al-Quds) and Al-Aqsa, with the start of its actual
temporal and spatial division, and the 'bringing of red
cows' as an application of a detestable religious myth
designed for aggression against the feelings of an entire
nation in the heart of its Arab identity, and the path of its
prophet (the Night Journey) and Ascension to heaven.

The primary reason for the October 7 massacre, capture, and torture of Jews was the red heifers shipped from Texas to Israel in 2022. One year after the heifers arrived, Hamas attacked Israel because of the religious implications. The ashes of at least one of these heifers will be used in a ceremony to cleanse the temple grounds before construction. The Dome of the Rock, or "Temple Mount," is the assumed location of Solomon's Temple and the future Jewish Temple. It remains under Muslim control and is the most controversial piece of real estate in the world.

Hamas Muslims are not Israel's only enemies. A vast network of adversaries was involved with Hamas in the October 7 attack. The missing link is the Hagarenes of Psalm 83:6, whom I believe are connected to Syrian and various Persian Gulf Islamic extremist groups. If this is correct, one of the end-times markers is the Psalm 83 war, which I believe began on October 7, 2023, setting the prophecies of Jeremiah 49 and Ezekiel 38 in motion. This depends on whether the Hagarenes are Egyptian or nomadic Arab descendants of Ishmael's brothers.

Hagar was Egyptian, and some believe she brought an Egyptian out of Egypt to be Ishmael's wife. However, nowhere is it recorded that she returned to Egypt. In fact, Jewish sages of the Babylonian captivity era believed that Abraham's second wife, Keturah, was the name given to Hagar after Sarah's death. While the sages are not a wholly trustworthy resource, it is worth noting that nowhere is it found that Hagar returned to Egypt. To identiy the Hagarenes as Egyptians is far less probable than the sages recording Keturah as Hagar.

As noted in the previous chapter on the Imam Mahdi, Muhammad's handlers rewrote the biblical account of Abraham and Isaac. In Genesis 22, we read of Abraham being asked by God to offer his son Isaac as a sacrifice on Mount Moriah, only to be stopped by an angel. God then provided a ram tangled in the bush for Abraham to sacrifice in place of Isaac. Twenty centuries later, the story was rewritten in the Quran, placing Ishmael as Abraham's offer of sacrifice on the "Foundation Stone," where the Dome of the Rock is built. According to the Quran, the "All-Merciful" stopped Abraham from killing Ishmael on the rock.

The large rock beneath the dome is also where Muslims believe that Muhammad's miraculous night journey and ascent to heaven occurred, known as Isra and Mi'raj. According to Islamic tradition, Muhammad was transported from Mecca to Jerusalem on a winged steed named Al-

Buraq. From the rock enshrined within the dome, he ascended through the seven heavens, where he met with previous prophets and received divine revelations from Allah.

Many significant events have occurred on Mount Moriah:

- Abraham offered Isaac as a sacrifice, but God substituted a ram (Genesis 22). In Genesis 22:9, Abraham *"builds an altar."* There is no mention of a large boulder for the altar, only that Abraham constructed one.

- In Genesis 28, Jacob gathered stones for a pillow (which sounds uncomfortable!) and dreamed of angels ascending and descending a ladder to and from heaven. He then assembled the stones into a pillar, marking the place where "God's house" would someday be. This could only have been on Mount Moriah, yet again there is no mention of a large boulder. If a single boulder marked such a spiritual event, why would Jacob assemble stones into a pillar rather than use the boulder itself as a marker?

- In 2 Samuel 24, David purchased the grain threshing floor from Araunah the Jebusite to serve as the location for the Jewish Temple. This was a large, flat, natural limestone plateau on elevated ground where the wind could blow away the chaff from wheat or barley. An ox or donkey would pull a wooden skid over the grain, removing the hull as the skid dragged across the stone platform.

No boulder is mentioned in the midst of David's threshing floor, though Mount Moriah is large enough that perhaps the boulder was not an obstruction. Still, if the Foundation Stone of the Dome of the Rock were directly on the threshing floor, it seems unlikely that Jacob would have needed to assemble a pillow of stones into a pillar to mark the spot for the future House of God. An enormous solitary boulder would have been more than sufficient as a marker on its own.

- Yehshua was crucified on Mount Moriah, outside the Temple camp (outside the city walls, Hebrews 13:12). While skeptics believe it is impossible that Isaac was offered in the exact same spot where Yehshua was crucified, I believe it is precisely the same location to the square inch because that's how God works. I have no evidence for this except that the God I know is precise and detail oriented and wouldn't miss the opportunity for perfection to complete the most significant event in the history of the world.

- The Foundation Stone at the Dome of the Rock has no apparent biblical significance other than being located on Mount Moriah. It is not the location of the crucifixion, and there is no mention of the large stone in Scripture. Jacob assembled stones used for a pillow to make a pillar, with no mention of a boulder. A large boulder would have been an obstacle on the threshing floor of David. This boulder seems conspicuously absent from Scripture.

(Foundation Stone at the Dome of the Rock where Muhammad had his visions)

According to 2 Chronicles 3:1, Solomon built the temple on Mount Moriah. This is confusing because of the volume of scriptures that refer to Mount Zion as the "holy mountain" or "habitation/house of the Lord." The City of David is also Zion. As I began researching this, I discovered an ongoing controversy between most archaeologists and Bible researchers. I am a latecomer in this heated debate regarding the location of Solomon's Temple. I merely began looking into it because I kept coming across small details that planted a seed of doubt in my mind, where the Dome of the Rock location might not match the original temple location. First, it had to be at the threshing floor purchased by David from the Jebusite "Araunah" (Ornan):

> *And the king (David) said unto Araunah, Nay; but I will surely buy it of thee at a price: neither will I offer burnt offerings unto the Lord my God of that which doth cost me nothing. So David bought the threshing floor and the oxen for fifty shekels of silver. (2 Samuel 24:24 KJV)*

Then Solomon began to build the house of the Lord at
Jerusalem in mount Moriah, where the Lord appeared
unto David his father, in the place that David had
prepared in the threshing floor of Ornan the Jebusite.
(2 Chronicles 3:1 KJV)

A large boulder is an obvious obstruction on a floor, so this is where I began questioning the Foundation Stone as the site of Solomon's Temple. From here, we need to understand that "Zion" and the "City of David" are interchangeable:

Nevertheless David took the strong hold of Zion: the
same is the city of David. (2 Samuel 5:7 KJV)

Before the time of David, Jerusalem was a small walled city of twelve to fifteen acres that David took from the Jebusites. This account is found in 1 Chronicles 11:

Therefore came all the elders of Israel to the king to
Hebron; and David made a covenant with them in
Hebron before the Lord; and they anointed David
king over Israel, according to the word of the Lord by
Samuel. And David and all Israel went to Jerusalem,
which is Jebus; where the Jebusites were, the
inhabitants of the land. And the inhabitants of Jebus
said to David, Thou shalt not come hither. Nevertheless
David took the castle of Zion, which is the city of
David. (1 Chronicles 11:3-5 KJV)

Below is what the ancient City of David probably looked like:

(source: alchetron.com)

If Zion is the City of David, there can be no confusion as to Zion's location. The City of David is at the south end of Mount Moriah.

For the Lord hath chosen Zion; he hath desired it for his habitation. (Psalm 132:13 KJV)

And many people shall go and say, Come ye, and let us go up to the mountain of the Lord, to the house of the God of Jacob; and he will teach us of his ways, and we will walk in his paths: for out of Zion shall go forth the law, and the word of the Lord from Jerusalem. (Isaiah 2:3 KJV)

Blow ye the trumpet in Zion, and sound an alarm in my holy mountain: let all the inhabitants of the land tremble: for the day of the Lord cometh, for it is nigh at hand. (Joel 2:1 KJV)

So shall ye know that I am the Lord your God dwelling in Zion, my holy mountain: then shall Jerusalem be holy, and there shall no strangers pass through her any more. (Joel 3:17 KJV)

Then the moon shall be confounded, and the sun ashamed, when the Lord of hosts shall reign in mount Zion, and in Jerusalem, and before his ancients gloriously. (Isaiah 24:23 KJV)

Great is the Lord, and greatly to be praised in the city of our God, in the mountain of his holiness. Beautiful for situation, the joy of the whole earth, is mount Zion, on the sides of the north, the city of the great King. (Psalm 48:1-2 KJV)

Psalm 48 verses 1 and 2 are often cited to argue against the temple having been located in the City of David. "The sides of the north" refers to the walls of Jerusalem. When Jerusalem fell to the Romans in AD 70 and the temple was reduced to rubble, the forced migration of the Jews disrupted continuity in their record keeping to some extent. Researchers have since relied on the writings of people like Josephus, Irenaeus, and others to complete the historical picture. Over time, both natural changes and the actions of Israel's enemies changed the topography so significantly that the original Jerusalem is difficult to recognize or reconcile accurately with scripture. In fact, after the Romans annihilated the Jews in AD 70, the only structure left standing was the present location of the Temple Mount, which some researchers say aligns closely with Matthew 24:2:

And Jesus said unto them, See ye not all these things? verily I say unto you, There shall not be left here one stone upon another, that shall not be thrown down. (Matthew 24:2 KJV)

Those on the side of the Mount Zion temple location use this verse as evidence to support the fact that the only thing left standing is the Dome of the Rock location. They have a valid argument, yet those who support the Dome of the Rock location for Solomon's Temple use the same verse to say that it is taken out of context. Those supporting the Dome of the Rock location say Matthew 24:2 was a figure of speech and Yehshua didn't mean the temple would be destroyed completely.

Another verse that supporters of the City of David/Zion temple location use is this prophecy from Micah:

Therefore shall Zion for your sake be plowed as a field, and Jerusalem shall become heaps, and the mountain of the house as the high places of the forest. (Micah 3:12 KJV)

Here is an image of the City of David from the turn of the century around 1900:

(Source: US Library of Congress)

The City of David and the "mountain of the house" is a plowed field, while the Temple Mount stands majestically intact above it. Or is it that the "mountain of the house" prophecy went unfulfilled? God fulfills all prophecy, so which is it—Mount Moriah or Zion? This debate is critically important as it ultimately determines the location of the Third Temple where the Imam-Mahdi or Antichrist will set up his abomination of desolations:

> *And he shall confirm the covenant with many for*
> *one week: and in the midst of the week he shall*
> *cause the sacrifice and the oblation to cease, and for*
> *the overspreading of abominations he shall make*
> *it desolate, even until the consummation, and that*

determined shall be poured upon the desolate. (Daniel
9:27 KJV)

And arms shall stand on his part, and they shall pollute
the sanctuary of strength, and shall take away the daily
sacrifice, and they shall place the abomination that
maketh desolate. (Daniel 11:31 KJV)

When ye therefore shall see the abomination of
desolation, spoken of by Daniel the prophet, stand in
the holy place, (whoso readeth, let him understand).
(Matthew 24:15 KJV)

Yehshua says in Matthew 24:15 that the Antichrist will stand in the "holy place." Clearly, this indicates the temple must be reconstructed in the original location of Solomon's Temple. No other place would be "holy." So which is it—Mount Zion or Mount Moriah?

The dark ages of Israel lasted from AD 70, under Nero, Titus, and the Roman Empire, until 1917 with the Balfour Declaration at the fall of the Ottoman Empire during World War I. This period was the result of a curse the Jewish people pronounced upon themselves in Matthew 27, when Yehshua was taken before Pontius Pilate, the governor of Judea:

Pilate saith unto them, What shall I do then with Jesus
which is called Christ? They all say unto him, Let him
be crucified. And the governor said, Why, what evil
hath he done? But they cried out the more, saying,
Let him be crucified. When Pilate saw that he could
prevail nothing, but that rather a tumult was made, he
took water, and washed his hands before the multitude,
saying, I am innocent of the blood of this just person:
see ye to it.

<u>Then answered all the people, and said, His blood be</u>
<u>on us, and on our children.</u> (Matthew 27:23-25 KJV)

God's purpose in reestablishing Israel as a nation was to bring an end to the curse. It is my opinion that the curse did not end at the time of Israel's renewed statehood in 1948. Rather, Israel's statehood marked the beginning of the end-times clock, when the curse would finally be reversed for the woman in the wilderness (Revelation 12:6), as she finally sees the "one whom they pierced" standing before her (Zechariah 12). The role of the 144,000 sealed from every tribe will be to save the Jews when the Antichrist appears. The significance of Mount Zion appears again in relation to this event:

And I looked, and, lo, a Lamb stood on the mount Sion,
and with him an hundred forty and four thousand,
having his Father's name written in their foreheads.
(Revelation 14:1 KJV)

There seems to be a well-drawn distinction in Scripture between Mount Moriah and Mount Zion that should not be overlooked. Either the expansion of the City of David upward onto Mount Moriah makes it part of Zion, or the "holy place" is on Mount Moriah and not on Mount Zion. The two hills remain distinct and separate for the purposes of prophecy and significant events. When reading through the Bible and we come across the words and phrases "Mount Zion" or "holy mountain," remember Psalm 132:13. God chose Zion as His holy mountain and "hath desired it for His habitation." Also remember that the modern Temple Mount is not located in Zion, but that Zion was above the City of David, south of the Dome of the Rock. Time and tradition have obscured the original temple location, leaving us to rely on archaeology. Most archaeologists agree with the Temple Mount theory, though some present evidence that suggests otherwise. Does it matter? Yes, because the Third Temple will be built on the "holy place."

Meanwhile, Revelation 14 states specifically that Yehshua will stand on Mount Zion with the 144,000 sealed, not on Mount Moriah. This cannot be ignored for the sake of simplifying the mystery into a solvable solution. The only way to reconcile this is to understand that Moriah is a general region wherein Mount Zion is located (God told Abraham to take Isaac to the "land of Moriah" in Genesis 22:2). If not, the temple was located on Mount Moriah and not Mount Zion. Both locations can be reconciled with scripture and archaeological evidence, which explains the ongoing debate.

Second Chronicles 3:1 says the temple was constructed on Mount Moriah, where David purchased the threshing floor. Elsewhere, it is said to be on Zion, with Zion identified as the City of David. I believe the Holy Spirit has concealed a mystery in the temple's location so that it will not be revealed until its proper season (thus Zechariah's stork).

So, we have this boulder that appears out of place with Abraham's "building an altar" and Jacob's pillow of rocks formed into a pillar to mark the site of the "house of God." Why not use the massive boulder as a marker instead of a small pillar of stones? Then we have Solomon's Temple constructed on Ornan's threshing floor of Mount Moriah (2 Chronicles 3:1). Another anomaly that intensifies the debate is the Gihon Spring.

In a review of scripture, "living water"—that is, pure spring water not exposed to contaminants that would disqualify it for temple rituals—is biblically documented as necessary for the Levitical priesthood to perform certain priestly activities and sanctification procedures. "Washing with water" was required for a number of cleansing procedures, so many that carrying water 800 meters uphill from the Gihon Spring to the Temple Mount would require a small army. I read one estimate where it would require 1,300 trips daily by donkey to supply enough water to the temple. Obviously, this was never done and would never have been permitted by the priesthood.

The Gihon Spring is the only fresh spring water source within miles of Jerusalem. While cisterns exist on the Temple Mount—possibly dug by Solomon, later expanded by the Hasmoneans, and perhaps used by the Romans for Fort Antonia—there are no natural springs there. Here are the examples I found for sanctification procedures requiring fresh spring water:

> ***And for an unclean person they shall take of the ashes***
> ***of the burnt heifer of purification for sin, and <u>running</u>***

*<u>water</u> shall be put thereto in a vessel: And a clean
person shall take hyssop, and dip it in the water, and
sprinkle it upon the tent, and upon all the vessels, and
upon the persons that were there, and upon him that
touched a bone, or one slain, or one dead, or a grave:
(Numbers 19:17-18 KJV)*

*And when he that hath an issue is cleansed of his
issue; then he shall number to himself seven days for
his cleansing, and wash his clothes, and bathe his flesh
in <u>running water</u>, and shall be clean. (Leviticus 15:13
KJV)*

*Then shall the priest command to take for him that
is to be cleansed two birds alive and clean, and cedar
wood, and scarlet, and hyssop: And the priest shall
command that one of the birds be killed in an earthen
vessel over <u>running water</u>: As for the living bird, he
shall take it, and the cedar wood, and the scarlet, and
the hyssop, and shall dip them and the living bird in the
blood of the bird that was killed over the running water.
(Leviticus 14:4-6 KJV)*

In my research on this controversial debate, I found an article describing the discovery of several large caverns beneath the Temple Mount that were used as water storage reservoirs. These date back to at least the time of Hasmonean (Maccabean) occupation, with most likely originating in the era of Solomon. Here is a photo of one, published in a press release by the Jerusalem Center for Security and Foreign Affairs:

(Source: Jerusalem Center for Security and Foreign Affairs)

(Painting of Wilson Simpson in 1870 who discovered the largest cistern
under the Temple Mount)

There is no water in these cisterns today, but they were full in
ancient times. The construction of at least some is credited to Simon the

Hasmonean (Maccabean Revolt, 167 BC), but I believe many were there in Solomon's day, as some archaeologists have suggested. The Gihon Spring is a "karstic cavern" that siphons water through natural cavernous ductwork connected to an aquifer in Mount Scopus, north of Jerusalem. The large underground reservoir at Mount Scopus is fed by groundwater aquifers extending north of Israel and terminating near Jerusalem. As the Gihon depleted the Mount Scopus reservoir, the siphoning action would cease momentarily until the reservoir refilled from the aquifer system. Once the Mount Scopus reservoir recovered to a level above the siphon, the Gihon Spring would resume flowing.

This phenomenon is called a "karstic cavern" with an artesian well effect, where the water table elevation is higher than the discharge zone. The result was similar to geysers, though without steam pressure behind it. The water flowed under static pressure alone. The cavern was refilled through a siphon in the rock from a reservoir in another hill farther away, Mount Scopus.

In ancient times, the Gihon flowed in excess of 75,000 liters per hour until the siphon level rose above the water level, gushing forth in burst cycles about an hour apart, as the name *Gihon* suggests. This gushing action stopped about twenty-five years ago as residential developments began depleting aquifer levels.

Ernest Martin and others have theorized that the static pressure of the Gihon Spring was enough to force water up into the temple at a higher elevation around the Ophel area above the City of David. However, with the discovery of the cisterns, it is now believed they were naturally maintained with constant levels of fresh water through stone aqueducts extending all the way to Jerusalem from Solomon's Pools south of Bethlehem.

Stone aqueducts that once connected the spring water sources of Bethlehem to the Temple Mount can still be seen today. At first, I doubted this possibility because of the similarity in elevation between Bethlehem and the Temple Mount. However, Solomon's Pools are more than 100 feet higher in elevation than the Temple Mount, making it certainly possible that this stone aqueduct attributed to Solomon was used to transport water there.

I have studied both sides of this argument. Each presents strong supporting evidence, and I prefer to avoid being overly dogmatic until something more concrete emerges. Time and radical changes in topography have made it extremely difficult to determine the original temple location. Many people live for the joy of confrontation and will argue regardless of whether their position makes sense. In this case, both sides of the debate can support their claims with archaeological evidence and scripture. This is strange—unless God's plan was to keep the original temple location undisclosed until the appointed time.

There is something else that really intrigues me about this temple dilemma, and that is the "fountain of Al-Kas," located between the Al Aqsa Mosque and the Dome of the Rock toward the southern end of the Temple Mount. This fountain was originally fed by the stone ducts that carried water from Solomon's Pools to the Temple Mount.

Al-Kas Fountain on the Temple Mount

This fountain sits almost directly above the largest cistern beneath the Temple Mount. The total capacity of these cisterns is estimated at more than 40 million liters of water. The total capacity of Solomon's Pools, located roughly seven miles away, hold more than four times that amount, with a constant flow of spring water to sustain them. These pools also supplied irrigation below Bethlehem, evidence of which can still be seen today. Assuming the aqueduct was used for the Temple Mount, the change in elevation between the pools and the Temple Mount would have produced at least 10 psi of static flow pressure at the fountain of Al-Kas and in a volume of water more than substantial for temple procedures. The stone aqueducts from Bethlehem would possibly have provided more water to the temple than the Gihon Spring itself. It seems possible that this Bethlehem water source is a critical piece of the temple puzzle currently being overlooked by most archaeologists.

All things considered, tradition can be the enemy of truth. Until I began investigating the original location of the temple, I had no idea there was already such a strong debate brewing over it. People on both sides have built compelling cases: some have discovered archaeological evidence supporting the temple's location near the City of David, while others have found strong evidence for the Dome of the Rock as being the site of Solomon's Temple.

Over time, we build special memories around traditions. We celebrate Christmas and other non-biblical holidays where families gather, enjoy feasts at Mom's or Grandma's house, laugh, and play together. These traditions become engrained into cultures, whether biblical or not. Every Christian treasures priceless memories of Christmas. In similar fashion, the Wailing Wall is a priceless relic for the Jewish people. But can it be reconciled to Matthew 24:2?

We often look for evidence to support tradition rather than evidence to support truth. It is possible this has happened with the Temple Mount. Israel assembled as a nation after a gap of nineteen centuries, during which history was confused by hatred of the Jewish people and the destruction of their ancient artifacts. Traditions were reestablished over remnants of the past that may or may not mark the true temple location.

I began this research on the Temple Mount with a bias, believing that somewhere on Mount Zion had to be the original location of Solomon's

Temple. In the process, I found so much evidence supporting both sides of the debate that I am now conflicted. Archaeological work continues to uncover important details that seem to favor an alternate location besides the Dome of the Rock. One of the most interesting recent discoveries is the work of Dr. Eilat Mazar near the Ophel mound, below the current Temple Mount and above the City of David. Dr. Mazar believes she has found the gates of Solomon's Temple at Ophel, above the City of David. You can read more about this here: https://armstronginstitute.org/811-jerusalems-massive-first-temple-period-gate.

One of the passages of scripture that originally supported this archaeological excavation is 1 Kings 9:

And this is the reason of the levy which king Solomon raised; for to build the house of the Lord, and his own house, and Millo, and the wall of Jerusalem, and Hazor, and Megiddo, and Gezer. (1 Kings 9:15 KJV)

A few archaeologists have speculated that Ophel was the location of the temple, and this verse in 1 Kings would be supportive due to the reference to "raising the levy" for the purpose of constructing the temple. The levy can be understood as massive retaining walls that would have been required to accommodate the vast layout of the temple grounds. Such walls would not have been necessary on the current Temple Mount location, but would have been essential on the side of the hill above the City of David.

At the same time, the threshing floor of Ornan purchased by David would have been a large limestone slab area, not evident at Ophel or the City of David, but clearly present on Mount Moriah.

Much of the archaeological work has been complicated by the destruction of Zion (above the City of David at Ophel) carried out by Simon the Hasmonean. Simon, also known as "Simon the Maccabean," was one of the leaders of the Maccabean Revolt against the Seleucid Empire. When Antiochus Epiphanes sacrificed a pig in the Jewish Temple, mocking the God of the Jews and desecrating the temple, the Maccabees revolted and defeated Antiochus.

According to controversial author Ernest Martin in his book *The Temples that the Jews Forgot*, Simon the Hasmonean destroyed the temple and removed the top of Ophel due to the desecration by Antiochus. Martin claims the area of Ophel at Mount Moriah was originally closer in elevation to Moriah, but Simon removed everything from the foundation down to the earth beneath the temple, relocating most of the excavation debris to the Kidron Valley. He further asserts that Simon built a new temple on Ophel at a lower elevation than Moriah after removing hundreds of thousands of cubic yards of debris. Simon's justification, according to Martin, was that the original temple at the time of Moses was mobile and that "Zion" could be located anywhere.

Yet again, however, there is substantial evidence of the Hasmonean temple reconstruction on the Temple Mount. Archaeologists have defined Israel's historic time periods according to the differences in the stonework attributed to Solomon, Zerubbabel, Hezekiah, Simon the Hasmonean, Herod, the Romans, and the Ottomans.

The Maccabees ruled Jerusalem only briefly until Pompey the Great conquered the city in 63 BC, incorporating it into Julius Caesar's Roman Republic. Shortly afterward, Herod the Great expanded the temple and the area known as Fort Antonia, where the Temple Mount is today. Herod was responsible for most of the visible construction above ground at the Temple Mount, with the obvious exception of the Dome of the Rock, which was built centuries later. Many archaeologists have stated that Herod's architectural work far exceeded anything ever conducted by the Jewish people in terms of grandeur and splendor. Most of this is what we see remaining at the Temple Mount area of Jerusalem today.

The Jewish Temple, known as Herod's Temple at the time of Christ, was destroyed by the Romans in AD 70 to prevent the surviving Jews from the possibility of congregating for worship. Absolutely nothing remained of the Jewish temple in agreement with Matthew 24:2 and Micah 3:12, in addition to others.

Perhaps the most detailed work on this subject of the original temple location was done by Bob Cornuke in his book titled *Temple*. One of the most fascinating observations by Cornuke was an obvious location for animal sacrifice that archaeologists found in the City of David. Cornuke, as well as Jewish archaeologists, agree that this very well may have been the first temple location preceding even King David. What they discovered in the City of David was obviously of Hebrew design, with only one possible origin: Melchizedek at the time of Abraham.

In the same stone quarters is a stone olive press for extracting olive oil. This is obviously Hebrew, and David would have known about this.

> ***And <u>Melchizedek king of Salem</u> brought forth bread***
> ***and wine: and he was the priest of the most high God.***
> ***And he blessed him, and said, Blessed be Abram of***
> ***the most high God, possessor of heaven and earth.***
> ***(Genesis 14:18-19 KJV)***

The City of David was the original Jerusalem. Melchizedek, at the time of Abraham, was the "king of Salem" (Jerusalem) long before David. If what archaeologists discovered in the old City of David was the temple of Melchizedek, then the first temple was below the Gihon Spring, while Solomon's Temple was above it—either at Ophel or Moriah. I don't think it is wise to be overly dogmatic for either side of the debate as to the temple's true location. This truth will be revealed in God's timing. What is certain is that a lot of people will be surprised to know the truth when it is finally revealed.

For now, I believe there may be some surprises coming regarding the Al-Kas fountain that was once supplied by the aqueducts coming from Solomon's Pools at Bethlehem. It is quite possible that the fountain was the location of Solomon's Temple. This is my own speculation and have found no other evidence for this except the aqueducts from Solomon's Pools. The temple has been destroyed and rebuilt three times, if we include the Hasmonean account, then expanded by Herod. The Romans and Muslims have destroyed and rebuilt over the top of any hard evidence, so we are forced to speculate. But the Al-Kas fountain is near the south end of the Temple Mount and was constructed there by Solomon for a reason. What other purpose would the fountain serve if not for the temple? And the fountain is situated above the cisterns discovered by William Simpson. The aqueducts flowed to the fountain, and the fountain overflowed into the cisterns. As far as anyone knows, the Al-Kas fountain is the only fountain on the Temple Mount, and, I believe, deserves strong consideration as the original temple location.

If you do not believe that water was necessary for a Jewish temple, imagine cleaning up the blood and carcasses of sacrificial animals, at times by the hundreds—or even thousands.

> *And they sacrificed sacrifices unto the Lord, and*
> *offered burnt offerings unto the Lord, on the morrow*
> *after that day, even a thousand bullocks, a thousand*
> *rams, and a thousand lambs, with their drink*

offerings, and sacrifices in abundance for all Israel. (1 Chronicles 29:21 KJV)

An abundant water source to the temple would have been an absolute necessity to clean up a slaughterhouse of this magnitude!

Another aspect that complicates matters further is the reported discovery of the Ark of the Covenant by Ron Wyatt in 1982. This is perhaps the most controversial archaeological claim in modern history. Almost no one believes that Wyatt discovered the ark in a cave near the Garden Tomb. I have listened to his testimony several times and reached a complex conclusion. It is difficult to believe what Wyatt claimed, yet he believed with all his heart and soul that he saw the Ark of the Covenant. He died of cancer in 1999, and if he had invented the story, he carried it to his grave without ever admitting otherwise. For any Christian that knows God, carrying a lie of that magnitude to the grave without admitting the truth is very difficult to accept. For that reason alone, I keep my mind open to the probability that Ron Wyatt discovered the Ark of the Covenant.

I can believe everything Wyatt claimed, but what complicates the matter is the location. The Garden Tomb is at the north end of the Temple Mount area, while Zion is at the south end. The centurion guard facing Yehshua when He died was close enough to the temple to see the veil torn (Matthew 15). If the temple was at the south end of the Temple Mount, or even at the current Dome of the Rock location, this does not align with the Garden Tomb/Golgotha site to the north. If the temple faced the Mount of Olives to the east, then the crucifixion would need to have been east of the temple for the centurion to face Jesus and see the veil rip. For the crucifixion to have occurred at the north end of the "camp," where Wyatt claimed the blood fell on the mercy seat of the ark, is inconsistent with current temple location theories. I believe Wyatt found the Ark of the Covenant, therefore it's location may provide some clues as to the original temple location that should not be overlooked.

It is important to keep an open mind to all of this. One new piece of evidence could change everything. The Temple Institute of Israel claims to know the exact location of the Ark and that it is within Israel. Wherever it is, it will be revealed to the world when the Third Temple is built. The question remains: where will the temple be built? If Israel is an end-time clock, we're counting the minutes until temple construction begins.

Scholars often dismiss the work of Ernest Martin in his book *The Temples that Jerusalem Forgot*. One of Martin's claims is that the temple was rebuilt many times, not just twice. His sequence includes Solomon's original construction, Hezekiah's restoration, Zerubbabel's reconstruction, Simon the Hasmonean's leveling and reconstruction, and finally Herod's expansion of the Hasmonean temple. Personally, I believe there is value in learning from anyone and prefer not to discard valid points. Martin makes valid points about the history of the temple and how much of that history has been lost. Likewise, I keep an open mind regarding Ron Wyatt's account.

I've exhausted myself researching both sides of the temple debate. Instinctively, I know something is wrong with the Dome of the Rock being the location of the First Temple. The archaeological evidence is conflicting, yet strong evidence appears in favor of a temple at Mount Ophel above the City of David. One reason is the lack of destruction to the current Temple Mount by the Romans, despite the fact that the original temple was completely destroyed several times. Why would Simon the Hasmonean excavate Ophel to cleanse the temple grounds if the temple wasn't there?

Another reason is that Ophel could have been considered part of Moriah and not a lone mountain, yet also a daughter of Zion (Micah 4:8) in association with the City of David.

At the same time, there is strong evidence of a temple on the existing Temple Mount. I can't imagine Muslims allowing Jews to rebuild the temple on the Dome of the Rock. That is simply absurd to even consider as a possibility. But if the Al-Kas fountain theory for the temple location can be substantiated with strong evidence, it is possible that the Third Temple would be built there.

One thing is certain: the rabbinic priesthood and the government of Israel have studied this more extensively than anyone else. They would be unwise to disclose a location for the temple in advance. We'll have to wait and see where they decide to build the Third Temple. If the Antichrist is to stand in the "holy place" in agreement with Daniel's prophecy, the Third Temple will be built where Solomon's Temple once stood. Only then will we know for sure where the original temple was located. Jerusalem has endured too much devastation over the centuries to tell the story accurately with what remains.

The strongest intangible evidence favoring the Temple Mount is the spiritual warfare surrounding it. Muslims around the world are ready to defend the Dome of the Rock to the death, while Jews feel the same about the Western Wall. If the Antichrist is to stand in the holy place and proclaim himself to be God (2 Thessalonians 2:4), the temple will stand exactly where it once stood. The demons and princes under Satan's authority concern themselves greatly with the Temple Mount. It could be that the Dome of the Rock temple theory is a satanic deception to distract from the true location, delaying its inevitable construction. The longer the truth is concealed, the longer it will take to build the temple. It could also be the same princes and demons are protecting the Dome of the Rock to prevent the temple from ever being constructed there. I lean toward the former theory. I personally do not believe the rock under the dome was ever part of the original temple, and that the temple was located elsewhere.

We are all looking for answers. Some seek to defend tradition by finding evidence to support it, while others simply want to know the truth. I am not an archaeologist; I am only curious about where the Third Temple will be built. The artifacts are interesting, but they support both temple theories inconclusively.

We are rapidly approaching the fulfillment of prophecy and the tribulation period. Israel has had completed temple plans for years, and red heifers are already in Jerusalem to sanctify the temple grounds with their ashes. It appears that the Psalm 83 war has passed, Jeremiah 49 and Gog Magog are imminent. Yet we are no closer to knowing the actual temple location today than we were in 1948.

Zechariah's vision of the two women in the ephah answers the first part of the question: what religion will dominate the temple when it is built? That religion already exists in the land of Shinar, where false religions were first re-established after the Great Flood. The false religion will be exported to the Temple Mount after a peace treaty organized by the Imam-Mahdi or Antichrist. The Third Temple will be a place for the Antichrist to honor himself and deceive billions, while the pope—representative of the first woman called wickedness—bows to him. The ephah, which should have contained a measure of wheat (the bride church) for harvest, instead contains two false religions that will merge in the Third Temple under the Antichrist.

Zechariah's visions transcend his time-period and provide clarity, connecting the past temple and state of Israel to the future temple and the deceptions it will unveil. The first woman in the ephah seems to correlate directly to the mother of harlots in Revelation 17. Before ever studying Zechariah chapter 5, it was obvious to me that the mother of harlots was the Roman Catholic Church. Knowing the history of Islam as exposed by Alberto Rivera clarifies the mystery of the two women in the ephah. The first woman gave life to the second woman through Muhammed.

Even if Rivera's account is dismissed as conspiracy theory, the symbolism of Islam—such as the crescent moon and eight-pointed star—derives from Rome, whose religious roots trace back to Babylon and Nimrod. Babylon is where apostasy was codified. The unclean bird (stork) at the appointed time set the "house upon its base" in the land of Shinar, where false religion began under Nimrod. This has already occurred with the representatives of the two women in the ephah. The pope and Imam Ahmed el-Tayeb have already inaugurated their "interfaith" center in the City of Ur. Rivera's story provides answers to the clues, showing that the two women in the ephah are related and what religions they represent!

The etymology of the name Zechariah translates as "Yah has remembered." Remember that "Yah" is "I AM" (Exodus 3:14), the shortened name of God. Everything the Jewish people will endure during the tribulation is because God has not forgotten them and has devised a means by which they can choose the truth of the Messiah. The 144,000 witnesses of Revelation will have one primary objective: to save the Jewish people. God had already remembered them when Zechariah received those visions over 2,500 years ago. He knew they were a stiff-necked people (Exodus 32:9; Acts 7:51) and would only come to Yehshua the hard way.

For thus saith the Lord of hosts; After the glory hath
he sent me unto the nations which spoiled you: for
he that toucheth you toucheth the apple of his eye.
(Zechariah 2:8 KJV)

As Christians, we shouldn't be bickering about whether the rapture is biblical or not. And as Christian gentiles, it is not our concern where the Third Temple will be built. God's word assures us that the Antichrist will be standing in the "holy place." God is sovereign over all things, including where the Jewish Rabbinical Priesthood decides the temple should be built. If it's not where He wants it, He can send an earthquake to rip it from its foundations, and they'll discover some new artifact that proves the correct location. It is not our concern. Leave it to the Jewish people and the Most-High God of Israel to determine.

When I discovered the extent of this debate and read or heard the comments, I thought how awful it must sound to Yehshua that we're fighting and criticizing each other over this issue. Let's allow God to be God and stay out of His business. I have brought you up to date with what I know.

That said, I am very thankful for all the work that the gentiles have done to try and locate the true location of the temple. Bob Cornuke's work in his book *The Temple* is fascinating and amazing, as is the work of many archaeologists who have uncovered a treasure trove of ancient artifacts that will eventually lead Israel to the temple's correct location. Ron Wyatt's work is amazing, as well.

The important thing to know is that I firmly believe Alberto Rivera's story from Cardinal Bea clarifies who the two women are in Zechariah's vision. If you disagree, I am sorry you wasted your time with this chapter. As for myself, Rivera's story solidifies Zechariah's vision with incredible precision.

If you're still here when the Third Temple is built somewhere on or near the Temple Mount, remember this: the first woman in the ephah is the reason the second woman exists. These two women— false religions— will come together as one under the Antichrist, who will stand in the holy place (the Third Temple) proclaiming that he is God.

Then I saw another beast rising up out of the earth; he had two horns like a lamb and he spoke like a dragon. He exercises all the authority of the first beast in his presence [when the two are together]. And he makes the earth and those who inhabit it worship the first beast, whose deadly wound was healed. He performs great signs (awe-inspiring acts), even making fire fall from the sky to the earth, right before peoples' eyes. And he deceives those [unconverted ones] who inhabit the earth [into believing him] because of the signs which he is given [by Satan] to perform in the presence of the [first] beast, telling those who inhabit the earth to make an image to the beast who was wounded [fatally] by the sword and has come back to life. And he is given power to give breath to the image of the beast, so that the image of the beast will even [appear to] speak, and cause those who do not bow down and worship the image of the beast to be put to death. Also he compels all, the small and the great, and the rich and the poor, and the free men and the slaves, to be given a mark on their right hand or on their forehead [signifying allegiance to the beast], and that no one will be able to buy or sell, except the one who has the mark, either the name of the beast or the number of his name. Here is wisdom. Let the person who has enough insight calculate the number of the beast, for it is the [imperfect] number of a man; and his number is six hundred and sixty-six. (Revelation 13:11-18 AMP)

My all-time favorite people besides Yehshua are John Wayne, Rush Limbaugh, Paul Harvey, and Chuck Missler. Today I am adding Max Lucado to that list.

CHAPTER 12

Don't Feed the Demons

Christians have to look more redeemed if the world is to believe in our redeemer.

—Gary French

Those who belong to Christ Jesus have crucified the flesh with its passions and desires.

—Galatians 5:24 (NIV)

If you identify as a Christian, you might be a problem for Satan and his operatives. If you identify as a born-again Christian, baptized by submersion, filled with the Spirit, and demonstrate your faith in Yehshua by fulfilling Mark 16:14–18, Satan has specifically targeted you as a threat to his kingdom. If you are a Mark 16 Christian, rest assured that demons have been assigned to you and fallen angels know your name. They will act aggressively against you at every legal opportunity given to them. Therefore, we must conduct ourselves as the sons of God, led by the Spirit, guarded by the Word of God engraved on our minds and hearts.

But put on the Lord Jesus Christ, and make no provision for the flesh in regard to its lusts. (Romans 13:14 NASB)

So this I say, and solemnly affirm together with the Lord [as in His presence], that you must no longer live as the [unbelieving] Gentiles live, in the futility of their minds [and in the foolishness and emptiness of their souls], for their [moral] understanding is darkened and their reasoning is clouded; [they are] alienated and self-banished from the life of God [with no share in it; this is] because of the [willful] ignorance and spiritual blindness that is [deep-seated] within them, because of the hardness and insensitivity of their heart. And they, [the ungodly in their spiritual apathy], having become callous and unfeeling, have given themselves over [as prey] to unbridled sensuality, eagerly craving the practice of every kind of impurity [that their desires may demand]. But you did not learn Christ in this way! If in fact you have [really] heard Him and have been taught by Him, just as truth is in Jesus [revealed in His life and personified in Him], that, regarding your previous way of life, you put off your old self [completely discard your former nature], which is being corrupted through deceitful desires, and be continually renewed in the spirit of your mind [having a fresh, untarnished mental and spiritual attitude], and put on the new self [the regenerated and renewed nature], created in God's image, [godlike] in the righteousness and holiness of the truth [living in a way that expresses to God your gratitude for your salvation].

Therefore, rejecting all falsehood [whether lying, defrauding, telling half-truths, spreading rumors, any such as these], speak truth each one with his neighbor, for we are all parts of one another [and we are all parts of the body of Christ]. Be angry [at sin—at immorality, at injustice, at ungodly behavior], yet do not sin; do not let your anger [cause you shame, nor allow it to] last until the sun goes down. And do not give the devil an opportunity [to lead you into sin by holding a

*grudge, or nurturing anger, or harboring resentment,
or cultivating bitterness]. The thief [who has become
a believer] must no longer steal, but instead he must
work hard [making an honest living], producing that
which is good with his own hands, so that he will
have something to share with those in need. Do not
let unwholesome [foul, profane, worthless, vulgar]
words ever come out of your mouth, but only such
speech as is good for building up others, according to
the need and the occasion, so that it will be a blessing
to those who hear [you speak]. And do not grieve
the Holy Spirit of God [but seek to please Him], by
whom you were sealed and marked [branded as God's
own] for the day of redemption [the final deliverance
from the consequences of sin]. Let all bitterness and
wrath and anger and clamor [perpetual animosity,
resentment, strife, fault-finding] and slander be put
away from you, along with every kind of malice [all
spitefulness, verbal abuse, malevolence]. Be kind and
helpful to one another, tender-hearted [compassionate,
understanding], forgiving one another [readily
and freely], just as God in Christ also forgave you.
(Ephesians 4:17-32 AMP)*

*Therefore, if you have been raised with Christ, keep
seeking the things that are above, where Christ is,
seated at the right hand of God. Set your minds on the
things that are above, not on the things that are on
earth. For you have died, and your life is hidden with
Christ in God. When Christ, who is our life, is revealed,
then you also will be revealed with Him in glory.*

*Therefore, treat the parts of your earthly body as dead
to sexual immorality, impurity, passion, evil desire, and
greed, which amounts to idolatry.*

*and in them you also once walked, when you were
living in them. But now you also, rid yourselves of all
of them: anger, wrath, malice, slander, and obscene
speech from your mouth. Do not lie to one another,
since you stripped off the old self with its evil practices,
and have put on the new self, which is being renewed
to a true knowledge according to the image of the
One who created it— a renewal in which there is no
distinction between Greek and Jew, circumcised and
uncircumcised, barbarian, Scythian, slave, and free,
but Christ is all, and in all.*

*So, as those who have been chosen of God, holy and
beloved, put on a heart of compassion, kindness,
humility, gentleness, and patience; bearing with one
another, and forgiving each other, whoever has a
complaint against anyone; just as the Lord forgave
you, so must you do also. In addition to all these things
put on love, which is the perfect bond of unity. 15 Let
the peace of Christ, to which you were indeed called
in one body, rule in your hearts; and be thankful.
Let the word of Christ richly dwell within you, with
all wisdom teaching and admonishing one another
with psalms, hymns, and spiritual songs, singing with
thankfulness in your hearts to God. Whatever you do
in word or deed, do everything in the name of the Lord
Jesus, giving thanks through Him to God the Father.
(Colossians 3:1-17 NASB)*

Either we are obedient and put on the righteousness of Christ, or we are disobedient. "Somewhat obedient" indicates the need for atonement and is not a category. There is a kingdom for the sons of God led by the Spirit of God, and a kingdom for the sons of disobedience led by the prince of death (Satan). There is no third kingdom for the somewhat semi-obedient in Christ. By not being conformed to obedience in Christ, we feed the demons who have been assigned to us, opening direct spiritual doorways to the prince of death. Once he has a legal foothold in the door, he'll try to take the whole house (body). We must understand that Satan and his operatives have nothing else to worry about except the complete and utter destruction of the sons of God led by the Spirit. They will lose their estates to us when we become joint heirs in Christ. They have nothing to live for except our destruction.

The sons of God led by the Spirit must be aware of what God considers disobedience. Those passages above characterize what the Father expects from those worthy of becoming joint heirs with the Son. It is easy to overlook the significance of Paul's words in Ephesians 4:27 (AMP):

> ***And <u>do not give the devil an opportunity</u> [to lead you into sin by holding a grudge, or nurturing anger, or harboring resentment, or cultivating bitterness].***

Willful ignorance and spiritual blindness cannot exist in the sons of God led by the Spirit (Ephesians 4:18). A born-again and sealed by the Holy Spirit "Christian" must remain conscious of how, why, and where demons enter our lives legally and attempt to separate us from God. Paul makes a clear list so we are not mistaken and learn to gain control over our bodily desires and emotions:

- Anger
- Holding grudges (not forgiving)
- Hardness of heart (lack compassion)
- Harboring resentment
- Greed (the same as idolatry)
- Lying
- Defrauding
- Telling half-truths
- Spreading rumors
- Obscene or profane speech
- Sexual immorality and lust for the flesh

In 1 Peter 2:11, Peter says that fleshly lusts "war against the soul":

Dearly beloved, I beseech you as strangers and pilgrims, abstain from fleshly lusts, <u>which war against the soul.</u>

In chapter 7, we discussed the link between the mind and the soul, and that the soul drives the body. The mind is the battleground for spiritual warfare. What begins in the mind grips the soul and manifests in the flesh. Therefore, the list above are symptoms of an evil spirit(s)'s presence. These behaviors have nothing in common with the Holy Spirit and grieve Him:

But I say, walk by the Spirit, and you will not carry out the desire of the flesh. For the desire of the flesh is against the Spirit, and the Spirit against the flesh; for these are in opposition to one another, in order to keep you from doing whatever you want. But if you are led by the Spirit, you are not under the Law. Now the deeds of the flesh are evident, which are: sexual immorality, impurity, indecent behavior, idolatry, witchcraft, hostilities, strife, jealousy, outbursts of anger, selfish ambition, dissensions, factions, envy, drunkenness, carousing, and things like these, of which I forewarn you, just as I have forewarned you, that those who practice such things will not inherit the kingdom of God. But the fruit of the Spirit is love, joy, peace, patience, kindness, goodness, faithfulness, gentleness, self-control; against such things there is no law. Now those who belong to Christ Jesus crucified the flesh with its passions and desires.

If we live by the Spirit, let's follow the Spirit as well. Let's not become boastful, challenging one another, envying one another. (Galatians 5:16-26 NASB)

When Paul said "and all who are led by the Spirit of God, these are the sons of God," he was defining the character profile of the bride of Christ. The bride will have nothing in common with the sons of disobedience, for whom the wrath of God is reserved (Colossians 3:6). For this reason, it is not legally possible to manifest anger, envy, lust, sexual immorality, etc., and also inherit the kingdom of God.

The sons of God led by the Spirit of God inherit the kingdom as joint heirs with Christ. The sons of disobedience inherit death with the prince of death. The spirit and the flesh are against each other and have nothing in common. To be led by the Spirit is to be prepared for the transfiguration of the body, when we shall see Him as He is, because we will be as He is.

> *Beloved, now are we the sons of God, and it doth not yet appear what we shall be: but we know that, when he shall appear, we shall be like him; for we shall see him as he is.*
>
> *And every man that hath this hope in him <u>purifieth himself, even as he is pure</u>. (1 John 3:2-3 KJV)*

Being led by the Spirit of God, we are led to be blameless in "body, soul, and spirit." We are all equally subject to the flesh, but overcoming the flesh is to live by the Spirit. When we live by the Spirit, we close all demonic doorways where war wages against the soul through the mind and manifests in the flesh. The flesh will override the spirit only if we allow it. We make a conscious choice to either resist the devil or embrace him.

These manifestations of the flesh by demonic influence are the lists Paul gave, which reveal themselves physically when one is led by another spirit that is not the Holy Spirit. If we use Paul's words as a checklist, we allow the Spirit to keep the body and soul in check and can quickly identify where demons operate. We atone for the flesh by the blood of Yehshua and realign our behavior with the Spirit. If we are quick to anger, quick to lust, or allow greed or deceptions to take root, these are signs of where a demon has gained access to the soul through the mind, and what follows is manifest in the body.

Unless you're already transfigured into the image of the risen Son of God, we all struggle daily to control and contain the demons that have been assigned to us by the prince of death. God allows them legal access to us when we fail to bring the flesh into obedience to the Spirit. This is what it means to be "led by the Spirit of God." If we are led by the correct Spirit, the flesh is contained and not subject to demonic influence. If we fail to conform in obedience to the Spirit, demons gain legal access to the flesh through the battlefield of the mind (soul).

Demonic influence is not the same as demonic possession. However, many Christians believe that once baptized, it is impossible to be possessed by a demon. The late Derek Prince proved that this is not a true statement, which can be confusing. If we fail to comprehend that allowing the manifestations of the flesh to rule over our spirit means we are no longer led by the Spirit of God but by another spirit. If there is no repentance and correction to conform to the Spirit of God, and without rebuking the controlling spirit, possession can take place. This does not happen immediately but over time, as manifestations progress toward possession in extreme cases when the soul is completely damaged and compromised by the flesh (see Matthew 12:43-45 please!).

I am aware that people strongly disagree with this, but read Derek Prince's book *They Shall Expel Demons*. His experiences are unparalleled, and I give thanks to God for his life.

Most of us are subject to influence, and we know when we're not in agreement with the Spirit. If led by the Spirit of God, we repent and realign to the Holy Spirit who leads us. Personally, I fought a generational demonic influence of anger. At times, I can still struggle with this, but I do not allow it to rule my life. Just yesterday, a man cut me off in a crowded parking area to quickly jump ahead of me and take the parking spot I was pulling into. Before being led by the Spirit of God, I would have cursed him loudly and perhaps even engaged into physical confrontation, operating from a damaged soul and led by the wrong spirit. Instead, I honked my horn impatiently, drove away, and found another space that ended up being a better place to park anyway.

If we operate with the Holy Spirit as leader, better things await us than we thought possible.

In this digital age, we live in a country known for being the largest exporter of pornography in the world. I think the chief enemy of Christians is sexually related lust. It surrounds us everywhere, and even if we're not looking for it, it still finds us. Under this unprecedented influence of the spirit of "Babalon," sexual lust and homosexuality are everywhere and have invaded the church.

When you catch yourself thinking the thoughts that Paul warned about, rebuke the demon and follow the Spirit of God. Do not allow the demon a foothold over the mind, which drives the soul and body. Thank God that the blood of Yehshua has purified your mind, body, and soul, and rebuke the demon that seeks to control you and derail your destiny among the sons of God.

As joint heirs with Christ, we must keep the spirit in complete alignment with the Spirit of God. This is becoming increasingly difficult in a world guided by the prince of death. Yet by resisting the demon in the name of Yehshua, it will depart from you.

So submit to [the authority of] God. Resist the devil
[stand firm against him] and he will flee from you.
(James 4:7 AMP)

For everything that Paul lists as manifestations of evil, it is imperative that we resist and do not indulge a demonic spirit. Indulging the flesh gives a demonic spirit legal access to that part of the soul. And if the demon has claim to any part of the body through the soul, the whole body, soul and Spirit are compromised.

This image of a demonically compromised body transcends to the body of Christ. The reason I wanted to share this chapter and titled it "Do Not Feed the Demons" is because I have been a member of the Christian faith long enough to know we have a problem in the body of Christ.

Demons work most diligently in church congregations, luring the minds of God's people away from Him. Greed, jealousy, resentment, gossiping, defrauding, sexual immorality, and more, have become too common in Christian social circles today. We feed the demons and give them the legal right to inflict harm on the body.

In the same way we pray for an affliction of a person's body, we must pray for affected members of the church, that the cancer of demonic influence not spread to the entire congregation.

In Ephesians 4:16, Paul had a unique vision of Christ's desire for His bride:

From whom the whole body fitly joined together
and compacted by that which every joint supplieth,
according to the effectual working in the measure
of every part, maketh increase of the body unto the
edifying of itself in love.

Demonic access to any part of the body compromises the spiritual health of the whole body. This is true of ourselves individually and true of the body of Christ. Derek Prince said it best when, in his book *They Shall Expel Demons*, he wrote:

Deliverance is only the first step in a process leading
to the recovery of holiness and the restoration of the
Church to her original simplicity and purity.

This is where we need to be today as the body of Christ ahead of the imminent return of the Bridegroom. We need to return to our roots, becoming more like the church born on Pentecost in the book of Acts. They were a simple but dedicated people following in the footsteps of the Bridegroom. Many churches, or dare I say most churches, are compromised and weak today. Much of the body of Christ has been weakened by the powerful deceptions of the sons of disobedience and under the Babalon spirit of confusion. The sons of God who are led by the Spirit need to retune our spiritual ears to the voice of the Holy Spirit. We live in the static of a digital world and 24-7 news cycles filled with the propaganda of the sons of disobedience. Turn everything off, find a quiet place, and listen for His still quiet voice. He will not scream loud enough to drown out your cellphone notifying you of a new social media post. Tuning in to His frequency is a conscious decision that the sons of God must make for ourselves. Each of us are members of the same body. If we heal the separate parts, we heal the whole body.

Beyond the scope of demons, it is suggested that we currently share our planet with other unknown entities. This is not my own whacko conspiracy theory; these are the words of Dr. Eric W. Davis spoken during a congressional meeting in Washington, DC. Dr. Davis is an astrophysicist and former consultant for the Pentagon who began documenting research on UAPs (unidentified aerial phenomena). His UAP research led to the discovery over time of what he has identified as at least four other nonhuman species that occupy our earth and atmosphere.

Davis names these as follows:
- Grays
- Nordics
- Insectoids
- Reptilians

As if demons are not enough to contend with, I'm not sure what to make of this except that they are of Satan's kingdom and operate under his direction. My opinion after reading through piles of articles written by both delusional schizophrenics, as well as reputable researchers and investigators, is that these are species that either fell with Satan or are something hybridized like the pre-flood Egyptian chimeras. The Nordics and possibly Reptilians are probably beings that fell with Lucifer, while the others may be hybrid crossings of other species for Satan's purposes. Perhaps this explains the frogs coming out of the dragon's mouth in Revelation 16:13 (reptilians).

In some cases, I believe we should look at the advancements of mankind in our digital age and assume that Satan has far more technology than we do. Is it possible that the Grays or any of these alien entities are more android than living creatures? If everything in Satan's empire is destined to eternal fire (Matthew 25:41), why wouldn't he maximize everything at his disposal? If the human race has developed artificial intelligence linked to the human brain, on a robot with humanlike tissue, how much more has Satan done with millions of years more experience than us?

We have no idea what Satan is capable of, nor how many dimensions exist around us beyond our perception (hyperspace). But what is no longer conjecture is that they exist. This is becoming mainstream news in preparation for their open arrival. Do not be deceived when they are embraced by a few spiritual leaders who are spiritually blinded.

The time is quickly coming during the tribulation period when these alien operatives of Satan will be unveiled. Just as it was in the days of Noah, they will take for themselves wives of their choosing (Genesis 6:2) as they rampage freely against humanity when the restrainer is taken away (2 Thessalonians 2:6). Do you take comfort in these words (1 Thessalonians 4:18)? Only if you belong to the Bridegroom may you take comfort in knowing that the gates of hell will not prevail against you (Matthew 16:18).

Our purpose is to inform others so that "they be counted worthy to escape these things that shall come to pass" (Luke 21:36). I believe that one or more of these Nordics will probably support the Antichrist as god and work to deceive as many as possible into worshipping him as god in the Jewish Temple. What we know for sure is that the gates of hell will open at the fourth seal of Revelation, and everything previously imprisoned there will be unleashed upon the earth.

*And when he had opened the fourth seal, I heard the
voice of the fourth beast say, Come and see.*

*And I looked, and behold a pale horse: and his name
that sat on him was Death, and Hell followed with him.
And power was given unto them over the fourth part of
the earth, to kill with sword, and with hunger, and with*

death, and with the beasts of the earth. (Revelation 6:7-8 KJV)

Soon after hell is unleashed on earth at the fourth seal, the fathers of the Nephilim are released from chains, arriving by hard landing at the sixth seal:

And I beheld when he had opened the sixth seal, and, lo, there was a great earthquake; and the sun became black as sackcloth of hair, and the moon became as blood;

And the <u>stars of heaven fell unto the earth</u>, even as a fig tree casteth her untimely figs, when she is shaken of a mighty wind.

And the heaven departed as a scroll when it is rolled together; and every mountain and island were moved out of their places. (Revelation 6:12-14 KJV)

A lot of "Christians" will be here to witness these events.

Watch ye therefore, and pray always, that ye may be accounted worthy to escape all these things that shall come to pass, and to stand before the Son of man. (Luke 21:36 KJV)

Not all Christians will be considered worthy to escape the tribulation. Until then, don't feed the demons! By the blood of Yehshua, drive them out of the body of Christ! It is incumbent upon the sons of God to heal the body of Christ ahead of the Bridegroom's imminent return. The body of Christ, when spiritually healthy, is the most formidable force on the earth!

Let no man deceive you with vain words: for because of these things cometh the wrath of God upon the children of disobedience.

Be not ye therefore partakers with them.

For ye were sometimes darkness, but now are ye light in the Lord: walk as children of light: (Ephesians 5:6-8 KJV)

CHAPTER 13

AI and the Final Phase of the Roman Empire

Imagine that in 10 years we will be sitting here with implants in our brains [...] and I can immediately tell you how people react.

—Klaus Schwab, founder of the World Economic Forum

I think we should be very careful about artificial intelligence. If I had to guess at what our biggest existential threat is, it's probably that. So we need to be very careful...With artificial intelligence we're summoning the demon.

—Elon Musk

In my last book titled *The Bride, Wise Virgins, and the Last Adam*, I included a chapter explaining what I believe about the clay mixed with iron in the feet of the statue of Nebuchadnezzar's dream (Daniel 2). The iron is the Roman Empire that never really ceased to exist thanks to the papacy of Rome, and the clay is usually interpreted as mankind. While this may be true, I explained in the book that I had a dream while in the hospital in which the earth had been swallowed by a serpent, and the scales of the serpent were billions upon billions of silicon wafer computer chips, each representing a stack of lies that has been perpetrated upon the earth.

I explained that the silicon in computer chips is derived from a process where it is taken from clay that is primarily silicon dioxide. I believe silicon is the clay in the feet of the statue, when the age of artificial intelligence merges into the final phase of the Roman Empire—The Fourth Industrial Revolution.

I had this dream about the serpent swallowing the earth in 2022 when we were just then talking about AI, but there were no major companies promoting it yet on Wall Street. As of 2024, that has changed, and billions upon billions of dollars are now flowing into artificial intelligence technology stocks. A few weeks ago, as of this writing in September 2025, Mark Zuckerberg was offering up to $250 million to AI techs to leave Elon Musk and work for him. Suddenly, AI is the future, and whoever advances the fastest in this new technology controls the future.

Today, using AI, technology is moving at lightspeed or faster. What does this have to do with Daniel's dream? It is the technology that empowers the one world government, empowers the Antichrist, and enables the mark of the beast. This is the clay and iron of Nebuchadnezzar's statue in the dream.

We know who Klaus Schwab is, the former CEO of the World Economic Forum, and his replacement is Peter Brabeck-Letmathe. Some say they would both make perfect Bond villains without makeup.

Peter Brabeck-Letmathe

Perhaps the leadership at the World Economic Forum is further proof that we share the earth with alien life forms. There are many names you need to keep up with in this final phase of the Roman Empire. Of course, we also know Mark Zuckerberg, Elon Musk, and Bill Gates, the global vax fanatic and climate alarmist. Do you know who Peter Thiel is? Or Noah Harari?

Peter Thiel is Palantir Technologies, the new AI contractor for the US government that will implement a data-sharing platform called "Foundry" across federal agencies. In addition, Palantir's "preemptive precrime security recognition" technology called "Gotham" is soon coming to America just like the movie *Minority Report*. This is already happening.

Here is an article by metafilter.com:

Gotham is an investigative platform built for police,
national security agencies, public health departments
and other state clients. Its purpose is deceptively simple:

take whatever data an agency already has, break it down into its smallest components and then connect the dots. Gotham is not simply a database. It takes fragmented data, scattered across various agencies and stored in different formats, and transforms it into a unified, searchable web.

The stakes are high with Palantir's Gotham platform. The software enables law enforcement and government analysts to connect vast, disparate datasets, build intelligence profiles and search for individuals based on characteristics as granular as a tattoo or an immigration status. It transforms historically static records—think department of motor vehicles files, police reports and subpoenaed social media data like location history and private messages—into a fluid web of intelligence and surveillance.

These departments and agencies use Palantir's platform to assemble detailed profiles of individuals, mapping their social networks, tracking their movements, identifying their physical characteristics and reviewing their criminal history. This can involve mapping a suspected gang member's network using arrest logs and license plate reader data, or flagging individuals in a specific region with a particular immigration status.

The efficiency the platform enables is undeniable. For investigators, what once required weeks of cross-checking siloed systems can now be done in hours or less. But by scaling up the government's investigative capacity, Gotham also alters the relationship between the state and the people it governs...

This technology is timed perfectly with the coming tribulation period. How could we have a one-world government without Palantir? It's perfect!

But that's not even the best part. Have you heard of self-assembling DNA nanochip technology? Part of the COVID experiment was to learn more about how to use this technology. Here is an example of where this is going:

*at Columbia Engineering and leader of the Center for
Functional Nanomaterials' Soft and Bio Nanomaterials
Group at Brookhaven National Laboratory.*

*The new manufacturing technique could also contribute
to the ongoing effort to develop AI systems that are
directly inspired by natural intelligence.*

*"3D electronic architectures that imitate the natural
3D structure of the brain may prove enormously
more effective at running brain-mimicking artificial
intelligence systems than existing 2D architectures,"
Gang said. The researchers detailed their findings
March 28 in the journal Science Advances.33*

The article goes on to explain that the power source for these homegrown DNA nanochips is light. But is there light in the body? Actually, yes. We call it 5G—a bandwidth slightly broader than light frequencies but penetrates just about everything, including the human body. The combination of self-assembling nanochips spiked into a vaccine that will "save the world" will be powered by 5G and, soon, 6G. That's where this bioengineering is headed at light speed—Windows for Humans 1.0.

Speaking of biotechnology, I shouldn't neglect another 4th Industrial Revolution brainchild named Noah Harari Yuval.

---

33   TechXplore.com

Noah Harari Yuval

This guy is right up there with Klaus and Peter, yet another rock star of the WEF. Noah believes we will evolve into gods. Someone needs to post a copy of Genesis 3:5 at the WEF so these Bond characters will know this is an ancient lie that hasn't worked yet.

Philosophy & Religion › Philosophical Issues

Our Nonconscious Future

Ask the Chatbot a Question   ⋮ More Actions

Written by Yuval Noah Harari
Fact-checked by The Editors of Encyclopaedia Britannica
Article History

biological revolution Artist's depiction of human evolution into an electronic future.

Within the next century or two, we <u>humans</u> are likely to upgrade ourselves into gods and change the most basic principles of the evolution of life. Traditional mythologies depicted gods as powerful beings that could design and create life according to their wishes. In the coming two centuries we will probably learn how to engineer and manufacture various life forms according to our wishes. We will use <u>bioengineering</u> in order to create new kinds of organic beings; we will use direct brain-computer interfaces in order to create cyborgs (beings that combine organic and inorganic parts); and advances in machine learning and <u>AI</u> might even allow us to set in motion the creation of completely inorganic beings. The main products of the future economy will not be food, textiles, and vehicles but rather bodies, brains, and minds.

The things these people believe are unthinkable to those who know the One True God. I haven't read Jonathan Cahn's new book, *Avatar*, yet, but these WEF characters could certainly be avatars for fallen princes.

Let's not forget the latest from Elon:

Elon Musk's Neuralink Brain Chip: The Future of Human-Tech Fusion

InsiderRelease · 7 Months Ago · 4 · 12 Mins

Could a Chip in Your Brain Change the Way You Live Forever?

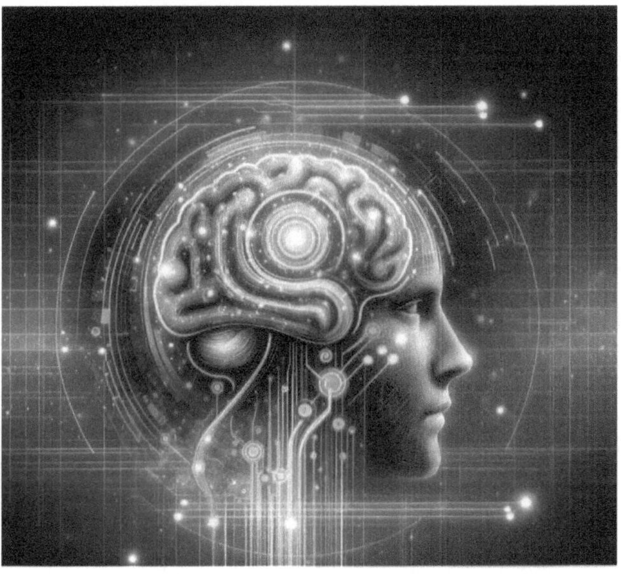

Aldous Huxley went from fiction writer to breaking news journalist from the grave. Remember the soul from chapter 7? Let's take a closer look at the word *soul*. I saved this for this chapter instead of chapter 7 because it fits better. This is from Strong's:

◀ 5590. psuché ▶

psuché: Soul, life, self, inner being

Original Word: ψυχή

Part of Speech: Noun, Feminine

Transliteration: psuché

Pronunciation: psoo-khay'

Phonetic Spelling: (psoo-khay')

KJV: heart (+ -ily), life, *mind, soul*, + us, + you

5590 psyxḗ (from *psyxō*, "to breathe, blow" which is
the root of the English words "psyche," "psychology")
– *soul* (*psyche*); a person's *distinct identity* (*unique
personhood*), i.e. *individual personality.*

Psychology, mind, and soul are synonymous in the Greek. One can assume that the authors of the New Testament understood the language they spoke. With this knowledge, a brain + computer interface is a soul + computer interface by definition. The body connects to the brain and sends signals through a complex electro-chemical network across nerves and neurons. The soul exists in some form of electromagnetic aura over this network. I do not presume to understand this, only extrapolating the unknown from what can be understood.

Am I the only one that sees a serious potential spiritual problem with this, assuming that soul and mind are synonymous as discussed in chapter 7?

If Neurolink and the "we will be gods" group from the WEF are communicating with each other, shouldn't Noah Harari maybe move his timelines up a couple hundred years? In other words, in time for the tribulation? Because I am 99.9 percent certain that Daniel's visions of the clay mixed with iron in the feet of the statue is the silicon used for AI.

It seems only yesterday that cellphones were the most amazing technology fathomable. According to Elon, your own personal robot slave will be available and affordable in 2026. These are called "Optimus" and will have every human ability, including cooking dinner, cleaning house, or even being taken as a dance partner to the local dance club.

Tesla's Chinese counterpart and competitor Xpeng has unveiled its humanoid robot at its 2025 Artificial Intelligence Day fair in Guangzhou. Apparently, Xpeng is offering male and female models of its robots. Why would it be necessary for a robot to have a gender if the sons of disobedience are determined to erase gender? Try not to think about it.

Oh, and if all of this doesn't seem problematic, have you been keeping up with China's progress in Helium-3 mining on the moon? In case you are not aware, Helium-3 is a near weightless super fuel that cannot be held by the earth's gravitational field and changes everything about life on earth as we know it.

<u>**Helium-3**</u>

Isotope of helium, non-radioactive

Helium-3 is a light, stable isotope of helium with two protons and one neutron. Helium-3 and hydrogen-1 are the only stable nuclides with more protons than neutrons. It was discovered in 1939. Helium-3 atoms are fermionic and become a superfluid at the temperature of 2.491 mK. Helium-3 occurs as a primordial nuclide, escaping from Earth's crust into its atmosphere and into outer space over millions of years. It is also thought to be a natural nucleogenic and cosmogenic nuclide, one produced when lithium is bombarded by natural neutrons, which can be released by spontaneous fission and by nuclear reactions with cosmic rays. Some found in the terrestrial atmosphere is a remnant of atmospheric and underwater nuclear weapons testing. Nuclear fusion using helium-3 has long been viewed as a desirable future energy source.34

Nuclear energy without the risk of nuclear fallout? Nice! But that's not the reason for the latest space race to the moon. Whoever achieves quantum computing first will rule the world.

---

34   Wikipedia

Helium-3 Harvested on the Moon Will Drive the Rise of Quantum Computing on Earth

Published: 17 Sep 2025, 08:27 UTC • By: Daniel Patrascu

Who is leading the world in this race?

China has returned helium-3 from the moon, opening door to future technology

BY MARK R. WHITTINGTON, OPINION CONTRIBUTOR - 09/18/22 10:00 AM ET

If you scan the news on this matter, it is being reported that the Chinese have retrieved a small amount of Helium-3 from the moon possibly during 2024. However, stick to the rule that half of what you see and none of what you hear are true when it comes to press releases. Some military intelligence insiders have reported that China began this Helium-3 mining mission on the moon in 2013. While news reports on the subject claim that China could begin a nuclear energy program using Helium-3 as early as 2030, I believe it is much sooner and the USA is behind in the race having fallen under weak leadership for decades. While the media posts articles about Helium-3's value as a clean nuclear energy source with no radioactive fallout risk, the real race is for quantum computing capability.

What is quantum computing, and why is it important? IBM gives the best description that can be more easily understood:

> *Quantum computing is an emergent field of computer science and engineering that harnesses the unique qualities of quantum mechanics to solve problems beyond the ability of even the most powerful classical computers.*

> *The field of quantum computing includes a range of disciplines, including quantum hardware and quantum algorithms. While still in development, quantum technology will soon be able to solve complex problems that classical supercomputers can't solve (or can't solve fast enough).*

> *By taking advantage of quantum physics, large-scale quantum computers would be able to tackle certain complex problems many times faster than modern classical machines. With a quantum computer, some problems that might take a classical computer thousands of years to solve might be solved in a matter of minutes or hours.*

> *Quantum mechanics, the study of physics at very small scales, reveals surprising fundamental natural principles. Quantum computers specifically harness these phenomena to access mathematical methods of*

solving problems not available with classical computing alone.

What might take classical computers thousands of years to solve can be done in a matter of minutes with quantum computing. No password is secure with quantum computing. No crypto wallet or blockchain currency is secure with quantum computing. The more I study the rapid approach of quantum computing, the more I can visualize how the mark of the beast will be tied to DNA. The only encryption that quantum computing cannot hack is the DNA code.

And that no man might buy or sell, save he that had the mark, or the name of the beast, or the number of his name. (Revelation 13:7 KJV)

In a digital AI world, do you think people will be in line to "buy or sell" while someone checks to see if they have the mark of the beast like the TSA line at the airport? In an age where half of our transactions are completed online? Of course not. The mark of the beast will be tied to a DNA scan directly linked to the body, the only thing that quantum computing cannot hack. Instead of entering a password, the DNA will be scanned digitally from every device before accessing, or security to protect against quantum computing will be impossible. There will be a global hack of some kind where people will lose everything they have in a trap laid by Satan to drive as many as possible into his kingdom of death.

The image of the beast will likely be an icon of the Antichrist that brings a false sense of security at about the midpoint of the tribulation. When death and plagues are rampant and wealth has vanished from the earth, the beast system of the Antichrist will offer hope to a population living in fear of extinction. This is the final drive to enforce the mark of the beast, and partakers will be complicit in enforcing the new law out of fear for their own lives, just like we saw during COVID. If you were not wearing a mask, you were killing someone's grandmother. The COVID pandemic is our best example of how this Antichrist control system will unfold. Those who worship the beast will hate and despise those who do not, and will aid the beast to force compliance on those remaining when this time comes.

While it seems that the first harvest and tribulation could begin at any moment, technology is a few megabytes away from a fully functional beast system. I believe quantum computing will close that gap, and China is likely much farther ahead in the Helium-3 race than we realize. The USA is now pushing full speed ahead to regain lost ground in this race under the Trump administration. This only exacerbates the coming beast system of control at a faster pace.

How amazing is it that we seem to be leaping ahead at light speed without quantum computing? Imagine the advancements in AI once quantum computing is realized? This is going to happen much sooner than anyone is prepared for. If I am correct that the first wheat harvest happens at or before the peace treaty organized by the Antichrist, which sets the tribulation in motion, then the Church of Philadelphia (Revelation 3:10) will not be present when the mark of the beast is enforced. In this analogy I am presenting, quantum computing will exist at the time of the mark of the beast. The mark of the beast is the final separation of mankind, sorting out those who belong to Satan and those who were fore destined to the kingdom of life. Consider this passage in Revelation 20:4:

> *And then I saw thrones, and sitting on them were those to whom judgment [that is, the authority to act as judges] was given. And I saw the souls of those who had been beheaded because of their testimony of Jesus and because of the word of God, and those who had refused to worship the beast or his image, and had not accepted his mark on their forehead and on their hand; and they came to life and reigned with Christ for a thousand years. (Revelation 20:4 AMP)*

I like the AMP translation here for its clarity. When we read this verse in the context of multiple harvests, it refers to two groups of people.

In Yehshua's vision, signified by the angel and shared with John (Book of Revelation), the first harvested group is already on thrones and given authority to judge. They are joined by a second group—those who were beheaded for refusing the mark of the beast—who are likewise granted authority to reign with Christ during the millennial reign. Not all seven churches of Revelation are the bride. Only one is securely qualified to be the bride. The Church of Philadelphia is given authority to judge in the first part of the vision. The churches that were not the bride but refused the mark later join the bride. Come out of her, my people!

I want to be very careful here, but it would appear from this verse that they are souls and not yet complete in the spirit. The fact that they are limited to the millennial reign may indicate that they are given a thousand-year grace period, since they did not belong to the harvest. They were latecomers, pursuing the materialism of the world, yet discovering the truth a bit late. In the original Greek, the word *psychas* is used, which is the plural for "souls."

In 1 Thessalonians 5:23, Paul says to preserve your body spirit and soul blameless before the Lord, these are three different aspects of a believer and are specified as such in the Greek as:

Body = *sōma*
Soul = *psychē*
Spirit = *pneuma*

Revelation 20:4 does not include *pneuma*, only *psychē*. They were not part of the wheat harvests that would have taken place before the implementation of the mark of the beast but are rewarded for their faithfulness. They are being identified separately from those who were given thrones and authority to judge. I find this interesting.

The final phase of the Roman Empire arrived nearly a century ago, marked by the Lateran Accords of 1929. The agreements between Italy and the Holy See established Vatican City as an independent state and recognized the sovereignty of the pope as the "vicar of Christ" on earth. The beast that would give rise to the Antichrist was acknowledged again as a global power in 1929, paving the way for the budding forth of the fig tree in 1948 and the ultimate fulfillment of prophecy. Daniel's vision of the clay mixed with iron was AI and the Roman Empire combined into a final beast system of control over Satan's kingdom of death, which is now almost complete.

Timothy Alberino has done significant work in studying advancements in the field of transhumanism, which is where we find ourselves today. Chuck Missler was already addressing this subject over twenty years ago, and his work can be found on the Koinonia House website. I urge everyone to become as informed as possible on this subject because it is the technology of the Antichrist and beast system soon to become reality. Elon's Optimus robots are on track to be available in 2026, and some have said they will be more affordable than a full-size SUV. This is only a step in the process—but one of the last steps.

The good news? There is nowhere to go from here but up! Hallelujah! Shout forth light to the Father! We're almost there!

CHAPTER 14

Rise of the Sons of God

The child of God works not for life, but from life; he does not work to be saved, but works because he is saved.

—Charles Spurgeon

To call yourself a child of God is one thing. To be called a child of God by those who watch your life is another thing altogether.

—Max Lucado

The sons of God, who are the fallen angels, gave up their estate in a war with God they thought they could somehow win by destroying mankind and corrupting the genome of Adam with their seed. This is the story of Genesis chapter 6. Their former estates are in limbo until all prophecies have been fulfilled. The sons of God led by the Spirit of God are joint heirs with Christ, who will inherit everything that God has placed under Yehshua's authority. This includes a vast estate spanning the universe, which the fallen angels forfeited by default of their rebellion against God.

I have had several very close friends in the past who asked for my help with their estate planning. One common theme I noticed in their planning was the desire to reserve something special for a child they loved more than the other heirs of the estate. In one instance I recall, the father left one of his sons completely out of the will. This particular son loved his father's money more than the father himself, and the father knew it. The result was that he excluded him from the inheritance entirely.

As the sons of God led by the Spirit, we can have no attachments to this world. The world as we know it belongs to the prince of death and his sons of disobedience.

> *The only ultimate disaster that can befall us, I have come to realize, is to feel ourselves at home here on earth. (Malcolm Muggeridge)*

> *Love not the world, neither the things that are in the world. If any man love the world, the love of the Father is not in him.*

> *For all that is in the world, the lust of the flesh, and the lust of the eyes, and the pride of life, is not of the Father, but is of the world.*

> *And the world passeth away, and the lust thereof: but he that doeth the will of God abideth for ever. (1 John 2:15-17 KJV)*

The world we live in has been shaped by the prince of death for the purpose of deceiving the sons of God led by the Spirit. Nothing in it is for us once we are baptized into the higher kingdom. However, in the meantime, we are on a mission: first to save ourselves by the blood of Yehshua, and then to save as many as we can who have been called but remain lost in Satan's kingdom. All of us were lost the day we were born into satan's kingdom and before we knew the Messiah. One of our primary objectives being led by the Spirit is to become a conduit for the manifestation of Yehshua's authority, both as individuals and as members of the body of Christ. The time has come to set this world aside and prepare for another kingdom ruled by love, when it shall be on earth as it is in heaven.

Try to imagine every son of God led by the Spirit throughout the history of the Bible, all operating together as the bride through His manifest authority ahead of His coming. "Greater things than these shall you do…" (John 14:12). These are the last days, and Joel's prophecy is fulfilled through the sons of God led by the Spirit of God:

> *And it shall come to pass afterward, that I will pour out my spirit upon all flesh; and your sons and your daughters shall prophesy, your old men shall dream dreams, your young men shall see visions:*
>
> *And also upon the servants and upon the handmaids in those days will I pour out my spirit.*
>
> *And I will shew wonders in the heavens and in the earth, blood, and fire, and pillars of smoke.*
>
> *The sun shall be turned into darkness, and the moon into blood, before the great and terrible day of the Lord come.*
>
> *And it shall come to pass, that whosoever shall call on the name of the Lord shall be delivered: for in mount Zion and in Jerusalem shall be deliverance, as the Lord hath said, and in the remnant whom the Lord shall call. (Joel 2:28-32 KJV)*

In Acts chapter 2, when the Holy Spirit opened the Feast of Pentecost for fulfillment, Peter made this statement to the people hearing the cacophony of the disciples who were filled with the Spirit:

> *For these are not drunken, as ye suppose, seeing it is but the third hour of the day.*
>
> *But this is that which was spoken by the prophet Joel;*
>
> *And it shall come to pass in the last days, saith God, I will pour out of my Spirit upon all flesh: and your sons and your daughters shall prophesy, and your young men shall see visions, and your old men shall dream dreams:*

And on my servants and on my handmaidens I will pour out in those days of my Spirit; and they shall prophesy:

And I will shew wonders in heaven above, and signs in the earth beneath; blood, and fire, and vapour of smoke:

The sun shall be turned into darkness, and the moon into blood, before the great and notable day of the Lord come:

And it shall come to pass, that whosoever shall call on the name of the Lord shall be saved. (Acts 2:15-21 KJV)

What were Joel and Peter referring to? The time leading up to the "Day of the Lord," or the Great Tribulation. This period marks the "rise of the sons of God who are led by the Spirit of God," when many miracles will follow them in advance of the tribulation. The fulfillment of the bride under the authority of Yehshua will fulfill Joel's prophecy in the last days. The time in which we live right now is what Peter was referring to in Acts chapter 2. In the context of his statement through verse 21, Peter follows with these words:

Therefore let all the house of Israel know assuredly, that God hath made the same Jesus, whom ye have crucified, both Lord and Christ.

<u>Now when they heard this, they were pricked in their heart, and said unto Peter and to the rest of the apostles, Men and brethren, what shall we do?</u>

Then Peter said unto them, Repent, and be baptized every one of you in the name of Jesus Christ for the remission of sins, and ye shall receive the gift of the Holy Ghost.

The reason for the "Time of Jacob's Trouble" (Jeremiah 30:7), or the Great Tribulation—unlike anything in world history in its horrors—is that Israel may be saved out of it. The sons of God led by the Spirit will be instrumental in demonstrating Yehshua's authority in the time leading up to the Day of the Lord. The 144,000 sealed in Revelation 7 and 14, who are the firstfruits of mankind, will work through the power of God so that none of Israel is lost; rather, all will be saved through it, as prophesied. Israel should have been the bride of Christ, but she rejected Him. The Gentile bride consists of the sons of God led by the Spirit of God, who rise up in the last days to save as many as possible from the sons of disobedience. But make no mistake—Israel is the apple of God's eye (Zechariah 2:8).

There is a spiritual poison circulating in the world and in the churches today called "Replacement Theology," which teaches that the Gentile church has replaced Israel due to her rejection of the Messiah. This theory began in the Church of Rome and has permeated the body of Christ. Many Christian and conservative podcasters are becoming dangerously anti-Semitic as this deception takes root. Two popular conservative podcasters, with more than ten million listeners between them, have become openly anti-Israel in their views. Whether their views have any basis in truth is irrelevant. God's word is clear: "I will bless those that bless you and curse those that curse you" (Genesis 12:3). This is one of the many deceptions and traps of Satan, designed to lure the sons of God into his lair of destruction. Do not fall victim to this deception, and rescue as many as you possibly can from it.

Replacement Theology reinforces anti-Semitic views and at this moment is turning Israel's last remaining ally, the United States, against them. While this is in line with the Ezekiel 38 prophecy, do not be guilty of it! Stand up for Israel, the apple of God's eye (Zechariah 2:8).

Encyclopedia Britannica defines Replacement Theology as follows. Pay attention to the crafty wording of their definition:

> ***Replacement theology***, *doctrine holding that Christians have replaced the Jewish people as the chosen people of God or as the heirs of the divine-human covenant described in the Hebrew Bible. The theology is also referred to as supersessionism, in which Christianity is thought to have superseded Judaism. It is closely related to fulfillment theology, which holds that Christianity has fulfilled the divine promises signaled in the Hebrew Bible. These ideas appear to be suggested in some of the earliest Christian texts, such as writings of St. Paul the Apostle, and subsequent Christian theologians have strengthened the opposition of Judaism and Christianity in ways that have informed relations between Christians and Jews. In the 20th century many Christian theologians and even church doctrines replaced replacement theology with more-nuanced or inclusive models that support more-amicable interreligious relations.*

Yikes! And they even blame poor Paul by misinterpreting his words in the book of Hebrews. I cannot overstate the danger of falling for this false theology, especially when God stands against the enemies of Israel in the Gog and Magog war. This is one of the many reasons I believe there cannot be a single-sweep wheat harvest event when "He descends from heaven with a shout" (1 Thessalonians 4:16–17). Many Christians who could have been part of that first harvest fail to allow themselves to be led by the Spirit of God. This was covered in the last book, but I cannot see another way. You cannot be anti-Semitic and also be harvested with the wheat. Our calling is to bring them to Christ—not to condemn them for being Jewish. This is a well-planned trap placed for Christians to willingly curse themselves against the Abrahamic Covenant and promise of Genesis 12:3.

We are "grafted into the root and fatness of the olive tree"; we did not replace the olive tree! Let's review a little "Christianity 101" to understand our proper place as Gentiles by reviewing Romans 11 in the Amplified Bible version:

> *So I say, have they stumbled so as to fall [to spiritual ruin]? Certainly not! But by their transgression [their rejection of the Messiah] salvation has come to the Gentiles, to make Israel jealous [when they realize what they have forfeited]. Now if Israel's transgression means riches for the world [at large] and their failure means riches for the Gentiles, how much more will their fulfillment and reinstatement be! But now I am speaking to you who are Gentiles. Inasmuch then as I am an apostle to the Gentiles, I magnify my ministry, in the hope of somehow making my fellow countrymen jealous [by stirring them up so that they will seek the truth] and perhaps save some of them. For if their [present] rejection [of salvation] is for the reconciliation of the world [to God], what will their acceptance [of salvation] be but [nothing less than] life from the dead? If the first portion [of dough offered as the first fruits] is holy, so is the whole batch; and if the root (Abraham, the patriarchs) is holy, so are the branches (the Israelites).*
>
> *But if some of the branches were broken off, and you [Gentiles], being like a wild olive shoot, were grafted in among them to share with them the rich root of the olive tree, do not boast over the [broken] branches and*

exalt yourself at their expense. If you do boast and feel superior, remember that it is not you who supports the root, but the root that supports you. You will say then, "Branches were broken off so that I might be grafted in." That is true. They were broken off because of their unbelief, but you stand by your faith [as believers understanding the truth of Christ's deity]. Do not be conceited, but [rather stand in great awe of God and] fear [Him]; for if God did not spare the natural branches [because of unbelief], He will not spare you either. Then appreciate the gracious kindness and the severity of God: to those who fell [into spiritual ruin], severity, but to you, God's gracious kindness—if you continue in His kindness [by faith and obedience to Him]; otherwise you too will be cut off. And even they [the unbelieving Jews], if they do not continue in their unbelief, will be grafted in; for God has the power to graft them in again. For if you were cut off from what is by nature a wild olive tree, and against nature were grafted into a cultivated olive tree, how much easier will it be to graft these who are the natural branches back into [the original parent stock of] their own olive tree?

I do not want you, believers, to be unaware of this mystery [God's previously hidden plan]—so that you will not be wise in your own opinion—that a partial hardening has [temporarily] happened to Israel [to last] until the full number of the Gentiles has come in; and so [at that time] all Israel [that is, all Jews who have a personal faith in Jesus as Messiah] will be saved; just as it is written [in Scripture],

"The Deliverer (Messiah) will come from Zion,

He will remove ungodliness from Jacob."

"This is My covenant with them,

When I take away their sins."

*From the standpoint of the gospel, the Jews [at present]
are enemies [of God] for your sake [which is for your
benefit], but from the standpoint of God's choice [of
the Jews as His people], they are still loved by Him for
the sake of the fathers. For the gifts and the calling of
God are irrevocable [for He does not withdraw what He
has given, nor does He change His mind about those
to whom He gives His grace or to whom He sends His
call]. Just as you once were disobedient and failed to
listen to God, but have now obtained mercy because
of their disobedience, so they too have now become
disobedient so that they too may one day receive mercy
because of the mercy shown to you. (Romans 11:11-31
KJV)*

Paul never intended to confuse "grafting into the tree" with "replacing the tree." On the contrary, God's plan is that there be one tree, one church, under One God. Replacement Theology cannot account for the restoration of Israel as a marker of the last days (Matthew 24). God's dispensation of grace to the church will converge with Israel's acceptance of Christ during the last week of Daniel's "seventy weeks" prophecy. Israel's role as leader of nations will be restored with Christ's thousand-year reign from the land of God's chosen people.

In William Koenig's book *Eye to Eye*, he carefully illustrates direct connections between catastrophic events and foreign nations interfering with Israel's sovereignty, right to exist, or land-for-peace deals with Palestine. Koenig cites hundreds of natural disasters that occurred either on the same day or within twenty-four to forty-eight hours of circumstances opposing Israel. Interestingly, the hurricane that set me on a spiritual deep dive—and one of the worst events in US history—occurred when Jared Kushner led a peace envoy for the White House in 2017. Hurricane Harvey had all but vaporized but was rekindled as a category 4 storm on the day that Kushner arrived in Jerusalem to discuss a two-state solution peace process.

Hurricane Harvey's rebirth upon Kushner's arrival in Jerusalem was no coincidence. Koenig's research proves hundreds of such connections dating back only as far as 1991. Yet thousands of miracles and catastrophes have occurred on Israel's behalf throughout her ancient history. During the Six-Day War, thousands of Egyptian and Syrian troops reported seeing angels with flaming swords surrounding Israeli tanks. In the Yom Kippur War, a captured Syrian commander of Syria's Ninth Army Division was interrogated as to why he retreated when Syrian tanks had every advantage over the Israeli tanks. His response was astounding to anyone who doesn't know our God that "never slumbers nor sleeps" where Israel is concerned (Psalm 121:4–7).

> *I would like to see you try and cross the Syrian missile lines while you see a whole host of white angels standing right on the missile lines and a white hand from heaven telling you to stop right there and move no further. Needless to say, I stopped right there and then.*[35]

Prime Minister Netanyahu has been quoted as saying that miracles are part of Israel's military defense strategy. Time and again, they have either entered or resisted conflict under impossible odds. The God of Israel is the God of impossible odds! Don't expect a miracle unless it's impossible by any means other than the hand of God.

> **Behold, he that keepeth Israel shall neither slumber nor sleep.**
>
> **The Lord is thy keeper: the Lord is thy shade upon thy right hand.**
>
> **The sun shall not smite thee by day, nor the moon by night.**

---

35   https://bit.ly/yomkippurwarmiracle

> *The Lord shall preserve thee from all evil: he shall*
> *preserve thy soul. (Psalm 121:4-7 KJV)*

Did the Syrian commander see the army of the great prince who stands watch over the people of Israel? (Daniel 12:1 identifies this prince as the archangel Michael.) I believe he did.

> *For thus saith the Lord of hosts; After the glory hath*
> *he sent me unto the nations which spoiled you: for*
> *he that toucheth you toucheth the apple of his eye.*
> *(Zechariah 2:8 KJV)*

Don't mess with Israel. No matter what you hear about the Zionists or what evil the Mossad may have done, Israel is a nuclear hot potato for anyone who opposes her. The sons of God led by the Spirit of God instinctively know this by revelation of the Holy Spirit.

I believe the days have arrived when the sons of God led by the Spirit will physically manifest every divine miracle-working power of the Bible. I believe unexplained miracles will happen not only in healing the sick or raising the dead, but angelic interventions will begin occurring as regularly for the Bride as they do for Israel. I am not certain whether or not our wooden staff can become a serpent and consume Pharaoh's serpent, or whether we can call fire down from heaven as Elijah did. But one thing is certain: we are at the precipice of the wheat harvest, and the Bride is a priceless treasure to both Father and Son. "Greater things than these shall you do…" (See Matthew 26:36-46)

Collective prayer from a spiritually healthy body is the most formidable weapon against the principalities and powers of darkness that roam about like lions, seeking to devour the sons of God led by the Spirit (1 Peter 5:8).

One of the most important yet often overlooked verses in the New Testament is James 5:16 (KJV):

> *Confess your faults one to another, and pray one for
> another, that ye may be healed. The effectual fervent
> prayer of a righteous man availeth much.*

The power of prayer, according to this verse by James, is inhibited by lack of atonement (confession in the name of Yehshua/Jesus = righteousness) and lack of sincerity (fervent).

Our righteousness is in Yehshua.

> *Being justified freely by his grace through the
> redemption that is in Christ Jesus:*
>
> *Whom God hath set forth to be a propitiation through
> faith in his blood, to declare his righteousness for the
> remission of sins that are past, through the forbearance
> of God;*
>
> *To declare, I say, at this time his righteousness: that he
> might be just, and the justifier of him which believeth
> in Jesus. (Romans 3:24-26 KJV)*

The body is healed by confession. Healed from what? Disease is the most obvious manifestation of demonic activity, but the less obvious symptoms are those listed in the previous chapter: resentment, animosity, gossiping, jealousy, greed, lack of forgiveness, etc. These are symptoms of demonic influence that cripple the power of prayer in the body of Christ. These symptoms must be recognized, cut off, and atoned for. When the body is delivered from demonic influence of any kind, the soul is healed, and the effectiveness of fervent prayer is enhanced, according to James.

To understand fervent prayer, consider its opposite. As Christians, we have all likely experienced dull sermons and lifeless prayers—repetitious, robotic, and sometimes spoken in a language no one in the congregation understands, such as Latin. When prayer lacks sincerity, it ceases to be fervent prayer and is likely ignored by the Sovereign Father. In contrast, fervent prayer is emotional, sometimes accompanied by fasting, and empowered when the Holy Spirit groans on our behalf.

Likewise the Spirit also helpeth our infirmities: for we know not what we should pray for as we ought: but the Spirit itself maketh intercession for us with groanings which cannot be uttered.

And he that searcheth the hearts knoweth what is the mind of the Spirit, because he maketh intercession for the saints according to the will of God. (Romans 8:26-27 KJV)

The most profound observation related to fervent prayer when the Holy Spirit groans on our behalf is that this verse is directly correlated to the same passage with Romans 8:14:

For as many as are led by the Spirit of God, they are the sons of God.

Therefore, prayer reaches its maximum potential when:

- We pray from a state of righteousness. We are justified (atoned) by Yehshua's righteousness, confessing and declaring our justification by His blood. We are righteous only through Him.
- Through confession, the body is healed, and the soul is also healed from those matters of the flesh that war against it (1 Peter 2:11).
- Remember that greed equates to idolatry (Colossians 3:5), and many churches are led by leadership plagued with greed. If you are led by the Holy Spirit, you will discern a spiritual problem at the pulpit. Ask others to join you in prayer for the leadership of the church, and rebuke the spirit of idolatry in the name of Yehshua.
- We pray from the heart, with heartfelt sincerity, when the Holy Spirit intercedes on our behalf.

- It is difficult to appeal to God if demons have a grip anywhere on the body. Disobedience is blatant opposition to God, and the only reward for disobedience is the wrath of God (Colossians 3:6). But when the sons of God led by the Spirit pray fervently from an atoned state in Yehshua's righteousness:

- demons tremble (James 2:19);
- nations shake at their foundations (Hebrews 12:26; Luke 21:26; Psalm 82:5; Isaiah 13:13); and
- mountains (principalities) will be removed (Mark 11:23).

First we heal the body and soul through confession of everything contrary to the Spirit. Then we pray fervently until the Spirit intercedes for us. Then we stand back and watch the power of God released as our prayer "availeth much."

If every member of the body—the church—is healed, the power of God is released through the body (church). This power of the prayer of the righteous is the manifestation of the sons of God who are led by the Spirit of God.

These are the days of the rise of the sons of God who are led by the Spirit! The joint heirs with Christ. The most powerful force on the earth!

Before we can become the most formidable force on the earth, the bride must clean up her garments before the groom's arrival. I believe that the church of the book of Acts, whose constituents can be defined by Mark chapter 16, is the Church of Philadelphia in Revelation chapter 3. The sons of God led by the Spirit of God, the Church of Philadelphia, and the Bride should be equal in number. However, knowing that God is calling His people to come out of Babylon or partake of her plagues (Revelation 18), there are many who have been called, but few will be chosen (Matthew 22:14–16). There are many who are led by the Spirit but do not follow, and many who will not be among the Bride when the groom arrives.

I have been very harsh on Roman Catholicism, but I have a vast number of Catholic friends—as we all do. Half of all Christians and 15% of the global population are Catholic. Please pray with me that they discover the truth about the history of Rome and the papacy. According to authors, researchers, and investigators such as Kevin Annett, Dave Hunt, and others, Rome is the axis and epicenter of global evil and the pinnacle of global power. Their cathedrals are lined with gold that was payment for sin through "indulgences." While Catholics may argue that indulgences are no longer accepted, the culture of tithing to atone for sin continues in Catholicism without condemnation. What could be more insulting to Yehshua than to attempt to pay for sin with money?

The Word, who was with God and was God from the beginning, came to earth as flesh and bone, was beaten, whipped, stabbed, His beard and hair ripped off, hung on a cross to die—without committing a single transgression of the Law—returned to the Father, and conquered death for all mankind past, present, and future. Yet without shame, the church receives a tithe or "Hail Mary" as atonement for sin. "Come out of her, my people!"

This is beyond the facts of the Inquisitions, or that the Vatican was complicit in the Holocaust, financed Germany in the war, and never once condemned Hitler publicly. We've been over this, so I won't go over it again. Just please pray for your Catholic friends and help them as much as you are able. God wants to include them among the Bride and count them as sons of God led by the Spirit of God, to become joint heirs with Christ in the New Kingdom.

I want to share one more thing before moving on from Catholicism. The Jesuits have carefully crafted everything in Catholicism, including the Catholic Bible. For the sake of argument, take a look at the Ten Commandments according to the www.catholic.com online Bible:

The Ten Commandments

1. I am the Lord thy God: thou shalt not have strange gods before Me.
2. Thou shalt not take the name of the Lord thy God in vain.
3. Keep the Sabbath holy.
4. Honor thy father and thy mother.
5. Thou shalt not kill.
6. Thou shalt not commit adultery.
7. Thou shalt not steal.
8. Thou shalt not bear false witness against thy neighbor.

9. Thou shalt not covet thy neighbor's wife.

10. Thou shalt not covet thy neighbor's goods.

At first glance, it seems okay—until you compare it to the King James Version, condensed from Exodus 20:

1. Thou shalt have no other gods before me.

2. Thou shalt not make unto thee any graven image, or any likeness of anything that is in heaven above, or that is in the earth beneath, or that is in the water under the earth: Thou shalt not bow down thyself to them, nor serve them: for I the LORD thy God am a jealous God, visiting the iniquity of the fathers upon the children unto the third and fourth generation of them that hate me; And shewing mercy unto thousands of them that love me, and keep my commandments.

3. Thou shalt not take the name of the LORD thy God in vain; for the LORD will not hold him guiltless that taketh his name in vain.

4. Remember the sabbath day, to keep it holy. Six days shalt thou labour, and do all thy work: But the seventh day is the sabbath of the LORD thy God: in it thou shalt not do any work, thou, nor thy son, nor thy daughter, thy manservant, nor thy maidservant, nor thy cattle, nor thy stranger that is within thy gates: For in six days the LORD made heaven and earth, the sea, and all that in them is, and rested the seventh day: wherefore the LORD blessed the sabbath day, and hallowed it.

5. Honour thy father and thy mother: that thy days may be long upon the land which the LORD thy God giveth thee.

6. Thou shalt not kill.

7. Thou shalt not commit adultery.

8. Thou shalt not steal.

9. Thou shalt not bear false witness against thy neighbour.

10. Thou shalt not covet thy neighbour's house, thou shalt not covet thy neighbour's wife, nor his manservant, nor his maidservant, nor his ox, nor his ass, nor any thing that is thy neighbour's.

In the Catholic Ten Commandments, the Second Commandment has been removed, and the Tenth Commandment has been made into two commandments. The Fourth Commandment regarding the Sabbath is the Third Commandment in the Catholic Bible. And knowing the history of how the Sabbath was erased under Constantine, we can understand why the Jesuits believe it is important not to draw too much attention to it.

But to erase the Second Commandment that instructs us not to have any graven images before us and comes with a curse to the fourth generation for not following it? This is the one they chose to obscure from the Bible? Do you see why I am concerned for my Catholic friends? This practice of bowing to statues has permeated all denominations of the Christian church. Even if you bowed before a cross or figure of Christ, you need to repent for it! It is prohibited by the Second Commandment! Come out of Babylon, my people! Many non-Catholic denominations have a figure of Christ behind the pulpit, and I have seen Christians kneeling before graven images that do not claim to be Catholic.

That's the last beating on that horse and is not the only issue in Christian churches. The Church of Thyatira has many counterparts in modern Christianity. If your church is woke or dei for the gender alphabet LBGTQIA+, remember Yehshua's words:

Notwithstanding, I have a few things against thee, because thou sufferest that woman Jezebel, which calleth herself a prophetess, to teach and to seduce my servants to commit fornication, and to eat things sacrificed unto idols.

And I gave her space to repent of her fornication; and she repented not.

*Behold, I will cast her into a bed, and them that commit
adultery with her into great tribulation, except they
repent of their deeds.*

*And I will kill her children with death; and all the
churches shall know that I am he which searcheth the
reins and hearts: and I will give unto every one of you
according to your works.*

*But unto you I say, and unto the rest in Thyatira, as
many as have not this doctrine, and which have not
known the depths of Satan, as they speak; I will put
upon you none other burden. (Revelation 2:21-24 KJV)*

Pray that you are worthy to escape the things that shall come upon the whole earth, and not destined for the tribulation that the Church of Thyatira will be forced to endure.

Finally, we come to the prosperity preachers: "Ask and you shall receive. Come on up and fill the offering plate, and God will bless you with your own private jet and beach house." In studying the history of the Church of Laodicea, I believe this is the church we can compare the prosperity preachers to today.

*And unto the angel of the church of the Laodiceans
write; These things saith the Amen, the faithful and
true witness, the beginning of the creation of God;*

*I know thy works, that thou art neither cold nor hot: I
would thou wert cold or hot.*

*So then because thou art lukewarm, and neither cold
nor hot, I will spue thee out of my mouth.*

*Because thou sayest, I am rich, and increased with
goods, and have need of nothing; and knowest not that
thou art wretched, and miserable, and poor, and blind,
and naked:*

I counsel thee to buy of me gold tried in the fire, that thou mayest be rich; and white raiment, that thou mayest be clothed, and that the shame of thy nakedness do not appear; and anoint thine eyes with eyesalve, that thou mayest see.

As many as I love, I rebuke and chasten: be zealous therefore, and repent. (Revelation 3:14-19 KJV)

It is unfortunate that the congregations of most churches function as mere social clubs. Many good people gather together, but their faith in Christ is lukewarm at best. If the pastor shares anything too biblical, he risks losing members of his congregation. Losing members means losing revenue, so the sermons are toned down to be more palatable for the "lukewarm" members. The congregations are wealthy and have need of nothing, except to be seen in church and perceived as good people. Most of them are good people, just not on fire for God. The people who are on fire for God have been through hell. The people on fire for God have encountered the devil and know him and have a deep desire to escape his clutches and know the peace that surpasses all understanding (Philippians 4:7). The sons of God led by the Spirit of God are hungry for the truth.

The Laodicean Christians take scriptures out of context and view God and the Holy Spirit as a means to financial gain. They pray to God for their own desires rather than offer themselves for God's desires. I went to the website of one of the most famous Laodiceans—whose name I will not share, but you can probably guess—and they have a long list of prosperity verses to use in prayer for "things." Here are two of them that I want to share to illustrate my point:

I can do all things through Christ which strengtheneth me. (Philippians 4:13 KJV)

But my God shall supply all your need according to his riches in glory by Christ Jesus. (Philippians 4:19 KJV)

In the context of Paul's letter to the Philippians, he had been imprisoned by Caesar Nero and wrote this letter from prison. Paul had a sincere fondness for the church at Philippi, and they likewise for him. In his letter, he warned them to beware of the Judean legalists who were trying to encourage them to return to Mosaic Law. The Philippians had sent gifts to Paul in prison through a man named Epaphroditus. When Paul had finished his letter to the Philippians, he entrusted it to Epaphroditus to deliver. But Epaphroditus became extremely ill and nearly died before delivering the letter. God granted Epaphroditus mercy, he survived, and the letter was delivered. This was spiritual warfare, yet God's plan for the letter prevailed, and it remains in our Bible almost two thousand years later.

While in prison, Paul ministered to the guards, whom he referred to as "those of Caesar's house." When Paul wrote to the Philippians that they could do all things through Christ who strengthened them, and that God would supply all their needs according to His riches and glory in Christ Jesus, it was in the context of having what he needed in prison to complete Christ's mission for "those of Caesar's house". Paul's condition and faith while enduring difficult circumstances inspired the Philippians to spread the gospel and fulfill Christ's mission for them without fear.

Take a look at how Paul begins the letter in chapter 1:

Now I want you to know, believers, that what has happened to me [this imprisonment that was meant to stop me] has actually served to advance [the spread of] the good news [regarding salvation]. My imprisonment in [the cause of] Christ has become common knowledge throughout the whole praetorian (imperial) guard and to everyone else. Because of my chains [seeing that I am doing well and that God is accomplishing great things], most of the brothers have renewed confidence in the Lord, and have far more courage to speak the word of God [concerning salvation] without fear [of the consequences, seeing

that God can work His good in all circumstances].
(Philippians 1:12-14 AMP)

According to Eusebius, Paul was beheaded in public by Caesar Nero a few years after writing this letter to the Philippians.

If we are doing God's work in Satan's kingdom on this putrid earth under the authority of thousands of Neros who lie to us daily at their press conferences, we might be faced with difficult times. But through Christ who strengthens you, you can overcome all circumstances, and everything you need to do God's work will be supplied to you. Maybe that includes a private jet, but don't count on it—and above all, don't pray for it. In the same chapter as the "prosperity verses" that are taken out of context, Paul also says this:

Let your moderation be known unto all men. The Lord is at hand.

Be careful for nothing; but in every thing by prayer and supplication with thanksgiving let your requests be made known unto God.

And the peace of God, which passeth all understanding, shall keep your hearts and minds through Christ Jesus.

Not that I speak in respect of want: for I have learned, in whatsoever state I am, therewith to be content.

I know both how to be abased, and I know how to abound: every where and in all things I am instructed both to be full and to be hungry, both to abound and to suffer need.

I can do all things through Christ which strengtheneth me. (Philippians 4:5-7, 10-13 KJV)

If we can learn to become more like Paul, we can learn to have the mind of Christ. It is almost never easy, but we will always endure. This is God's promise to the Bride.

Meanwhile, in the little Church of Philadelphia, miracles are manifesting daily around the world where the sons of God led by the Spirit are joined in prayer. Stories abound of children being healed of incurable diseases without explanation. There are daily sightings of angels in hospital rooms or near auto accidents, saving lives. Even stories of people coming back from the dead are becoming increasingly common.

Last night I watched a video of a young woman in her twenties who had been raised in a satanic environment and was recognized as an acclaimed witch. I did not recognize her accent, though she was European, possibly French. She had been sick with intestinal problems for most of her life and learned to live with it by simply not eating. Something inspired her to seek Jesus, and she attended a service where she confessed Jesus as Lord and Savior of her life and wanted to be baptized that same day.

Upon being baptized, a demon contorted her body into painful positions, and she screamed in a voice that was not her own. The demon didn't immediately leave her, but she was surrounded by people praying in tongues and holding her hands. After about five minutes of screaming and violent contortions, the demon left her.

The camera repositioned over her head, and the transformation was incredible. She was smiling, looking upward, and resting in total peace. Suddenly, her chin started chattering, and she started speaking in tongues with a calm smile. She continued looking upward—not at the people around her, but I believe she saw her Messiah. I can't even write about it without becoming emotional. It may be the most beautiful baptism I have ever witnessed.

Around the world, Christians are being persecuted, tortured, and killed in countries like Nigeria, Syria, Iran, Afghanistan, China, and elsewhere. Yet people are finding a deep, burning desire to know Yehshua and pursue Him without fear of reprisal. Pray for these people—that they can escape persecution, and that until then, they may do all things through Christ who strengthens them. We are one body, no matter where in the world we find ourselves, and it is imperative that we pray for one another constantly. In the West, we have the luxury of freedom to worship as Christians, but many around the world are not so privileged. May the privileged pray daily for the oppressed, that they may do all things through Christ who strengthens them.

It is tragic that so many churches today believe miracles were restricted to biblical times, and that only Jesus could identify and cast out demons. I have personally witnessed several miraculous events, including expelling demons from my own life. The sons of God led by the Spirit of God are empowered by the authority of Yehshua to do what He did—until the time of His return. If this were not true, why would He have made the statement recorded in John 14:12 (KJV)?

Verily, verily, I say unto you, He that believeth on me,
the works that I do shall he do also; and greater works
than these shall he do; because I go unto my Father.

Either we believe the entire Bible, or we do not. We can't cherry-pick and modify it to suit our carnal desires. The church has been weakened by a multitude of deceptions that have rendered much of the body of Christ ineffective against the sons of disobedience. Another of Satan's achievements has been convincing the church that he doesn't exist, and that miracles no longer happen. Nearly half of Christians fall into this benign category according to Barna surveys.

However, there is a small church lifted up for the sons of God led by the Spirit—who is of little strength—but for whom the gates of Hell shall not prevail against her. He who holds the key of David will decide which doors remain open and which are shut for His little church. Liars and deceivers will be cast down at her feet and forced to declare that she reigns with Him forever.

She will expel demons, heal the sick, restore the downtrodden, and raise the dead. She will patiently reside in the shadow of the Almighty, in her secret place of refuge. In her time of trouble, He will set her upon the Rock, and she will fear no evil. No river will sweep over her, and no flame will consume her though she walks through fire. She will seek justice, defend the oppressed, take up the case of the fatherless, and plead for the widow. The Spirit of God is upon her, and He has anointed her to bring sight to the blind and to free the oppressed from the bondage of sin.

She is the Bride of Christ, and these are the sons of God led by the Spirit of God. They are of one body, with the Bridegroom as the head. The sons of God shall inherit the Kingdom of God and will see Yehshua as He is, for they shall be as He is. They will be joint heirs with Christ, rebuilding that which was destroyed and left uninhabited by the fallen sons of God in ages past. The sons of disobedience will inherit the wrath of God and the kingdom of eternal fire with the prince of death. If you have read everything to this point, you know that the sons of disobedience are the targets of God's wrath—not the justified in Christ (Colossians 3).

The glory of God will forever shine upon His children in their presence, and the sons of God will be pillars in His holy temple. Eden will be restored as it once was, fully and forever. May the sons of God led by the Spirit rise to become a living testimony to Israel and to the world—that the Bridegroom is Yehshua, whom they pierced, the Alpha and Omega, who forever was, still is, and who is to come. He who was dead and is now alive —that all of Israel may be saved in the great Day of the Lord. Amen.

For as by one man's disobedience many were made sinners, so by the obedience of one shall many be made righteous. (Romans 5:19 KJV)

For the Spirit himself giveth testimony to our spirit, that we are the sons of God.

And if sons, heirs also; heirs indeed of God, and joint heirs with Christ: yet so, if we suffer with him, that we may be also glorified with him.

For I reckon that the sufferings of this time are not worthy to be compared with the glory to come, that shall be revealed in us.

For the expectation of the creature waiteth for the revelation of the sons of God.

For the creature was made subject to vanity, not willingly, but by reason of him that made it subject, in hope:

Because the creature also itself shall be delivered from the servitude of corruption, into the liberty of the glory of the children of God.

For we know that every creature groaneth and travaileth in pain, even till now.

And not only it, but ourselves also, who have the firstfruits of the Spirit, even we ourselves groan within ourselves, waiting for the adoption of the sons of God, the redemption of our body. (Romans 8:16-23, Douay-Rheims 1899)

CHAPTER 15

A Present Help in Times of Trouble

God is our refuge and strength, a very present help in trouble.

Therefore will not we fear, though the earth be removed, and though the mountains be carried into the midst of the sea;

Though the waters thereof roar and be troubled, though the mountains shake with the swelling thereof. Selah.

There is a river, the streams whereof shall make glad the city of God, the holy place of the tabernacles of the most High.

God is in the midst of her; she shall not be moved: God shall help her, and that right early.

The heathen raged, the kingdoms were moved: he uttered his voice, the earth melted.

The Lord of hosts is with us; the God of Jacob is our refuge. Selah.

Come, behold the works of the Lord, what desolations he hath made in the earth.

He maketh wars to cease unto the end of the earth; he breaketh the bow, and cutteth the spear in sunder; he burneth the chariot in the fire.

Be still, and know that I am God: I will be exalted among the heathen, I will be exalted in the earth.

The Lord of hosts is with us; the God of Jacob is our refuge. Selah.

—Psalm 46 (KJV)

Once again, Tucker Carlson has inspired me to write. In a recent interview with Alex Jones, Tucker stated that nothing could be more absurd than the rapture theory, citing the beheading of Paul and questioning why anyone should be so privileged to escape death. Whether by beheading, cancer, car wreck, or whatever, we're all appointed to die once (Hebrews 9:27).

I watched my mother take her last breath as she died of cancer. In God's mercy, she was in a coma upon her passing, but for eleven months, she agonized in excruciating pain. She was a Spirit-filled Christian, and dozens of pastors and church members laid hands on her and prayed for a healing that never came. Whether you're beheaded by Nero or you die of cancer, death occurs in the kingdom of death and is almost always painful. However, I believe this age ends with the disappearance of millions of the sons of God who are led by the Spirit. Why? Because the age of Pentecost ends when the last generation bride that is the final wheat harvest is removed. The tares will be burned by the tribulation, while the harvest will be taken to the Father's barn. The wheat that is gleaned from the fields (those who refused the mark), followed by the olive harvest (Jewish people) is who most of the book of Revelation was written for.

If you have never experienced trials, tribulations, suffering, or despair in challenging times, you're either not from this planet or something even stranger. All of us are subject to the conditions of the kingdom of the prince of death and destruction until we are taken away from it to our heavenly kingdom. However, it is worse for some than others, and those people need help from the rest of us. We are one body.

The Wrath of the Lamb at the tribulation is reciprocity for the pain and suffering on earth that has been inflicted on us by the fallen sons of God and their prince of death, satan. Those who do not join the Bride will suffer the wrath of the Lamb during the tribulation for rejecting Him and embracing the deceptions of the prince of death. If wrath is anger, it makes no sense that the wrath of the Lamb would target the Bride. The wrath of the Lamb is the "Day of the Lord."

In fact, I missed an important detail in the last book. In Revelation 1:10, almost every Bible translation renders this verse as "the Lord's Day."

- *I was in the Spirit on the **Lord's day**, and heard behind me a great voice, as of a trumpet. (KJV)*
- *I was in the Spirit [in special communication with the Holy Spirit and empowered to receive and record the revelation from Jesus Christ] on the **Lord's Day**, and I heard behind me a loud voice like the sound of a trumpet. (AMP)*
- *I was in the Spirit on the **Lord's day**, and I heard behind me a loud voice like the sound of a trumpet. (NASB)*

This is an excellent opportunity to demonstrate the problem with certain scholarly commentaries and why we must seek the Holy Spirit when we study the Word of God. Here is from the *Pulpit Commentary*, which I have referenced at times as being an unreliable resource:

> *Verse 10. - I was in the Spirit. I came to be (see on ver. 9) in a state of ecstasy capable of receiving revelations; like γενέσθαι με ἐν ἐκστάσει (<u>Acts 22:17</u>; comp. 10:10; <u>2 Corinthians 12:2-4</u>). On the Lord's day. The expression occurs here only in the New Testament, and **<u>beyond all reasonable doubt it means "on Sunday."</u>** This is, therefore, the earliest use of the phrase in this sense. That it means Easter Day or Pentecost is baseless conjecture.*

You can read for yourself many commentaries that will also suggest it is the same day as the Lord's Supper, or not the abolished Jewish Sabbath. If the Sabbath has been abolished, the millennial temple has a problem because it only opens on the Sabbath and new moons (Ezekiel 46). I had previously assumed that when John said he was in the Spirit on the Lord's Day in Revelation 1:10, he meant the sabbath. I commented to that point in my last book. I was very perturbed with commentaries that declared "beyond all reasonable doubt that it means on Sunday" when there was no Sunday on John's calendar in that era! But I missed something critically important to understand about this verse. It has not been properly translated or interpreted! Here is a more accurate translation that corrects the record of John:

> *I came to be in the Spirit on the Day of the Lord, when I heard a loud voice behind me like a trumpet. (ISV)*

It is not a reference to a day of the week. John is stating that he was in the spirit when he experienced a supernatural event, becoming a witness to the great and fearful "Day of the Lord," i.e., the Wrath of the Lamb. In the Spirit, he physically experienced the Day of the Lord then wrote the book of Revelation afterward. The Day of the Lord has over one hundred prophetic references in scripture:

> ***Alas for the day! for the day of the Lord is at hand, and as a destruction from the Almighty shall it come. (Joel 1:15 KJV)***

> ***Blow ye the trumpet in Zion, and sound an alarm in my holy mountain: let all the inhabitants of the land tremble: for the day of the Lord cometh, for it is nigh at hand. (Joel 2:1 KJV)***

> ***Near is the great day of the Lord,***
>
> ***Near and coming very quickly;***
>
> ***Listen, the day of the Lord!***
>
> ***In it the warrior cries out bitterly.***
>
> ***A day of wrath is that day,***
>
> ***A day of trouble and distress,***
>
> ***A day of destruction and desolation,***
>
> ***A day of darkness and gloom,***
>
> ***A day of clouds and thick darkness,***

A day of trumpet and battle cry

Against the fortified cities

And the high corner towers. (Zephaniah 1:14-18 KJV)

**Behold, the day of the Lord cometh, cruel both with
wrath and fierce anger, to lay the land desolate: and he
shall destroy the sinners thereof out of it.**

**For the stars of heaven and the constellations thereof
shall not give their light: the sun shall be darkened in
his going forth, and the moon shall not cause her light
to shine.**

**And I will punish the world for their evil, and
the wicked for their iniquity; and I will cause the
arrogancy of the proud to cease, and will lay low the
haughtiness of the terrible. (Isaiah 13:9-11 KJV)**

Alas, you who are longing for the day of the Lord,

For what purpose will the day of the Lord be to you?

It will be darkness and not light;

As when a man flees from a lion

And a bear meets him,

Or goes home, leans his hand against the wall

And a snake bites him.

**Will not the day of the Lord be darkness instead of
light,**

**Even gloom with no brightness in it? (Amos 5:18-20
KJV)**

This list could go on to create another book. The "Day of the Lord" is
one of the most prophesied events in the Bible. John was transported through
time to experience its vivid details, wrote about it, and specifically declared

he was "in the Spirit on the Day of the Lord" that had been prophesied for thousands of years. Because of translation and interpretation errors, (written by some that are not led by the Spirit) we missed it. John was not saying he was in the Spirit on Sunday, which was not on his calendar in AD 95, nor would be on any calendars for another two centuries. He was not saying he was in the Spirit on a Sabbath. He was in the Spirit when he experienced the "Day of the Lord"—the Wrath of the Lamb!

In verse 3 of chapter 1 is a promise:

Blessed is he that readeth, and they that hear the words
of this prophecy, and keep those things which are written
therein: for the time is at hand. (KJV)

The reason for this promise of blessing is so the sons of God led by the Spirit of God will bring as many as possible out of the inevitable Day of the Lord, which is reserved for the sons of disobedience (Colossians 3:6, Romans 5:9). In my next book, I will try to get a bit more granular on this revelation shared with John. As horrible as it is, the Day of the Lord does not apply to the Bride, the Church of Philadelphia, who is justified by the righteous blood of the Bridegroom. On the contrary, it is written so the Bride would understand the importance of rescuing as many as possible from the "Day of the Lord," prophesied for thousands of years.

The Day of the Lord and the Wrath of the Lamb are one and the same. John was in the Spirit on the "Day of the Wrath of the Lamb"!

And said to the mountains and rocks, Fall on us, and
hide us from the face of him that sitteth on the throne,
and from the <u>wrath of the Lamb</u>: (Revelation 6:16
KJV)

This verse is early in the tribulation, and already the sons of disobedience recognize that this is the Wrath of the Lamb. Why? Because those who are not the object of His wrath have been removed. It does not take a PhD to understand this, but it does take a PhD to conclude that the

Lord's Day was a Sunday—230 years before Christians were forced to worship on Sundays under Constantine after the Council of Nicea.

No one with a PhD in theology will have read this far, so rest assured, I have not offended anyone with this comment.

Much more then, being now justified by his blood, we shall be saved from wrath through him. (Romans 5:9 KJV)

For which things' sake the wrath of God cometh on the children of disobedience. (Colossians 3:6 KJV)

I have often considered something I once heard Chuck Missler say: that God is looking to see who will step up and partner with Him. He cited the situation involving Abraham when God sent angels to investigate Sodom and Gomorrah. In Genesis 18, Abraham bartered with God— and Abraham won, possibly because his faith was accounted to him as righteousness. Abraham was known as a friend of God (Isaiah 41:8; James 2:23). We should all share in that goal of becoming a friend to God. He desires our participation in the fulfillment of Christ's mission on earth. This is the Bride's mission. Corporate prayer from a healed body of Christ, confronting demons, princes of darkness, and the sons of disobedience is our mission.

Find your mission as part of the body of the Bride. I am writing, and though I struggle with the slow grind of publishing, I know I am called to write and that God's will always prevail. I want to partner with Him in my writing and rely on the Holy Spirit to direct and guide me, while God commands His angels concerning me (Psalms 91).

If we are living for Christ, we know the things we are passionate about, and these passions directly correlate to God's plan for our lives. There is so little time left—please find a way to increase your reward in heaven. There is only one way to be saved, and it is not by works, paying tithes, or, even worse, indulgences. It is by faith in Jesus Christ, who is the one and only door to the Father (John 14:6, 10:9). Yet to increase our reward in heaven can only come by works (Revelation 22:12).

I have become passionate about writing, but I am also passionate about helping the children who are being sex-trafficked around the world, or worse, tortured and sacrificed to satan. We all know the Epstein situation was evil and hundreds of powerful people were and are still involved in the exploitation of children for evil purposes. That it can be swept under the rug by people we thought we could trust should tell you everything you need to know about the world we live in. This world is ruled by the sons of disobedience under the prince of death. I write and share what I have learned and will support those who are dedicated to the rescue and well-being of these children.

Whatever your passion for Christ is, pursue it in what little time we have left before the arrival of the groom. God will sustain you. He will be your rock and your refuge in times of trouble. There is so little time left to accomplish so much.

And he spake to them a parable; Behold the fig tree, and all the trees;

When they now shoot forth, ye see and know of your own selves that summer is now nigh at hand.

So likewise ye, when ye see these things come to pass, know ye that the kingdom of God is nigh at hand.

Verily I say unto you, <u>This generation shall not pass away,</u> till all be fulfilled.

Heaven and earth shall pass away: but my words shall not pass away.

And take heed to yourselves, lest at any time your hearts be overcharged with surfeiting, and drunkenness, and cares of this life, and so that day come upon you unawares.

The budding forth of the fig tree began seventy-eight years ago as of May 2026. Some of the Jews born on or before May 14, 1948, will still be alive when Yehshua returns. There is little time left, so every second counts now.

I hear and read accounts of miracles daily that go unnoticed. A few months ago in Nicaragua, friends and family gathered and prayed for one-month-old Esther Paola Sánchez, who had a deformed heart and would not live without surgery. As surgeons arrived for the procedure, little Esther mysteriously had a new heart, requiring no surgery.

In Ukraine, witnesses have seen bombs explode in midair that were targeting hospitals or schools. In every case, these miracles can be traced back to prayer over those facilities by local Christians.

Of course, the miracles in Israel are amazing, though unreported. During the Hamas War that began October 7, 2023, miracles occurred daily and were seen by hundreds of witnesses. Missiles were turned at impossible right angles and thrown out to sea. Many angels appeared to troops and led them to safety. God neither slumbers nor sleeps where the apple of His eye is concerned. Replacement theologians and anti-Semitists need to keep these verses in mind:

*he that toucheth you toucheth the apple of his eye.
(Zechariah 2:8 KJV)*

*And I will bless them that bless thee, and curse him
that curseth thee: and in thee shall all families of the
earth be blessed. (Genesis 12:3 KJV)*

The communist dictatorship of Venezuela will probably fall before this book is published. Why? Because of an exploding evangelical movement, where small rural churches are gathering in prayer on behalf of the nation.

Can this happen in Laodicean/Pergamos America? Absolutely!

Have you heard the story about the pastor in Nigeria who was raised from the dead?

*Death certificate No. P086/01, issued by the St. Eunice
Clinic at 108 Orlu Road, Akwakuma, Oweri, Nigeria on
30 November 2001, states "Rev. Dan Eke was dead on
arrival at 23:30. No breathing, no pulse, no heartbeat,
eyes dilated and fixed, dead. Transfer to morgue."*

*Pastor Daniel Ekechukwu had been so seriously injured
in a car accident that two doctors declared him dead.
His wife Nneka was convinced that was not the last
word and believed that God would revive her husband.
Daniel's corpse was taken to the morgue, where a
chemical was injected to prepare it for embalming. The
overseer of the morgue was, as he confirmed to The Post
Express, awoken by the sound of singing in the morgue,
despite the fact that only corpses should have been there.
Visibly disturbed, he insisted that the pastor's corpse be
removed.*

*Nneka took her husband's corpse to a church in
Onitsha, where German evangelist Reinhard Bonnke
was speaking. There, according to the report, the
corpse suddenly inhaled and sat up, unbeknown to
the evangelist, who was preaching in the auditorium.
Ekechukwu had been dead for around two days, but
on his revival, his body showed no signs of the fatal
injuries.*[36]

If you want to take an online adventure, conduct a search on "miracles of people raised from the dead," and you will find amazing stories of eyewitnesses—many of them secular physicians—who could not explain what their eyes observed.

I absolutely love *Sid Roth's It's Supernatural* show, where he interviews people who have personally experienced miraculous events. One of the stories I am especially fascinated with is of a five-year-old girl who was swimming and fell from a slide onto the concrete below. Her grandmother, who was in the pool, said it seemed she fell in slow motion, as if she was being laid gently on the ground.

---

36   Telegram Revival Report from CFAN, Reinhard Bonnke, Frankfurt, Germany.

The little girl then experienced an out-of-body event in which she was taken to heaven, met Yehshua and family members, and returned to share her story—with knowledge of things there was no way she could have known at age five.

These are the lyrics of "Days of Elijah," written by Robin Mark:

These are the days of Elijah
Declaring the word of the Lord
And these are the days of Your servant Moses
Righteousness being restored

And though these are days of great trial
Of famine and darkness and sword
Still, we are the voice in the desert crying
"Prepare ye the way of the Lord!"

Behold, He comes riding on the clouds
Shining like the sun at the trumpet call
Lift your voice, the year of jubilee
And out of Zion's hill, salvation comes

And these are the days of Ezekiel
The dry bones becoming as flesh
And these are the days of Your servant David
Rebuilding a temple of praise

Oh, these are the days of the harvest
For the fields are as white in Your world
And we are the labourers in Your vineyard
Declaring the word of the Lord!

Behold, He comes, riding on the clouds
Shining like the sun at the trumpet call

Lift your voice, the year of jubilee
And out of Zion's hill, salvation comes

Behold, He comes, riding on the clouds
Shining like the sun at the trumpet call
Lift your voice, the year of jubilee
And out of Zion's hill, salvation comes

Oh, we give glory to You, Lord (we worship You, Lord)
You're the Lion of Judah
The Lamb who was slain (we worship You, Jesus)

You're the God of Jacob
You're the God of Elijah (Lamb of God)
You're the Lord God of Israel (oh, I praise You, Lord)
You're the Lord God of the universe (You're the Lion of Judah)

You're God of Heaven and earth
Oh, Lord our King and our Redeemer, You are

The sons of God led by the Spirit of God should strive to become "friends of God." Abraham was called a friend of God. Yehshua called the disciples His "friends" (John 15:15). The most obvious characteristic that defines friendship is shared interests. Many people believe they have friends, only to discover otherwise—making true friends our most valuable asset as we navigate the kingdom of death.

One of my greatest mentors, who was like a father to me, once said, "When you're my age, if you can count your true friends on one finger, consider yourself blessed." It is sad that his statement reveals much truth about our fallen state as Christians, when the Second Commandment is akin to the greatest—that we love each other as much as we love God (Matthew 22:36–40).

James makes this statement in 2:23 (KJV):

And the scripture was fulfilled which saith, Abraham
believed God, and it was imputed unto him for
righteousness: and he was called the Friend of God.

He may have been referencing Isaiah 41:8 (KJV):

But thou, Israel, art my servant, Jacob whom I have
chosen, the seed of Abraham my friend.

However, remember that during the time of the disciples, they had far more access to ancient scrolls and texts than we do, such as the book of Enoch and the complete books of Moses, etc. I believe that the book of Jubilees was a valuable resource to the disciples as well.

Joshua 24:2 (KJV) makes this comment about Abraham's family:

And Joshua said unto all the people, Thus saith the
Lord God of Israel, Your fathers dwelt on the other
side of the flood in old time, even Terah, the father of
Abraham, and the father of Nachor: and they served
other gods.

There are many extrabiblical accounts of the life of Abraham, and I won't go into detail here. But it would certainly appear that Abraham's story could fill volumes of books. We know that Abraham lived during the time of Nimrod. The Midrash is an interpretive Jewish rabbinical exegesis of the Torah, developed in response to the Talmud, which itself didn't emerge until long after the destruction of Jerusalem in AD 70. According to rabbinical expansions of the Bible, Nimrod was warned by his astronomers that a man greater than Nimrod would be born. From the time of Abraham's birth, Nimrod became Abraham's arch-nemesis and vice versa. It is believed that to escape Nimrod's intent to kill him, Abraham was taken to Shem and Noah and raised by them for a while.

This is not biblical, and not all of it may be true, but it might close some gaps in determining why Abraham was called the "friend of God" and vehemently opposed idolatry having been born into a pagan family (Terah and Nachor). I first questioned the timeline of Abraham to that of Noah and Shem, only to discover something amazing. Using biblical timelines, Abraham would have been fifty years old at the time of Noah's death. Even more amazing is that Shem outlived Abraham by about thirty-five years! Certainly, it is possible that Abraham, at the very least, would have spent time with Noah. This is how God would pass down the preflood knowledge of Noah to Abraham, the patriarch of Israel. It is also how Abraham would have known not to worship idols as his father's family did.

There is an interesting Midrash account of how Abraham, at around age fourteen, destroyed the idols of the area, even those in his father's home. Abraham's father was supposedly a general in Nimrod's army, and as punishment for this act, Nimrod captured Abraham and threw him into a furnace. Abraham was accompanied by angels and taken away from the furnace, which caused Nimrod to fear Abraham even more. While extrabiblical, I find the possibility that it could be true to be very fascinating.

The book of Jubilees, in my opinion, is a reliable resource. There is a great story in Jubilees about Abraham that I want to share for several reasons, in establishing this "friend of God" status. This is from chapter 11, verses 16–24:

> *And the child began to understand the errors of the*
> *earth that all went astray after graven images and after*
> *uncleanness, and his father taught him writing, and he*
> *was two weeks of years old, and he separated himself*
> *from his father that he might not worship idols with him.*

> *And he began to pray to the Creator of all things that*
> *He might save him from the errors of the children of*
> *men, and that his portion should not fall into error after*
> *uncleanness and vileness.*

And the seed time came for the sowing of seed upon the land, and they all went forth together to protect their seed against the ravens, and Abram went forth with those that went, and the child was a lad of fourteen years.

And a cloud of ravens came to devour the seed, and Abram ran to meet them before they settled on the ground, and cried to them before they settled on the ground to devour the seed, and said, "Descend not: return to the place whence ye came," and they proceeded to turn back.

And he caused the clouds of ravens to turn back that day seventy times, and of all the ravens throughout all the land where Abram was there settled there not so much as one.

And all who were with him throughout all the land saw him cry out, and all the ravens turn back, and his name became great in all the land of the Chaldees.

And there came to him this year all those that wished to sow, and he went with them until the time of sowing ceased: and they sowed their land, and that year they brought enough grain home and ate and were satisfied.

And in the first year of the fifth week Abram taught those who made implements for oxen, the artificers in wood, and they made a vessel above the ground, facing the frame of the plough, 1 in order to put the seed thereon, and the seed fell down therefrom upon the share of the plough, and was hidden in the earth, and they no longer feared the ravens.

And after this manner they made (vessels) above the ground on all the frames of the ploughs, and they sowed and tilled all the land, according as Abram commanded them, and they no longer feared the birds.

Remember in chapter 7, I mentioned that certain creatures can be inhabited by demons. This flock of ravens was a flock of demons using the ravens, and Abraham knew this by the power of the Holy Spirit, rebuked them using the words "descend not, return to where you came from," and they never returned anywhere near Abraham. This is proof to me that Abraham knew the origins of demons from Noah. I shared this in the last book, but I'll share it again. This is from chapter 10, verses 1–5 of Jubilees:

And in the third week of this jubilee the unclean demons began to lead astray the children of the sons of Noah; and to make to err and destroy them.

And the sons of Noah came to Noah their father, and they told him concerning the demons which were, leading astray and blinding and slaying his sons' sons.

And he prayed before the Lord his God, and said:

God of the spirits of all flesh,

who hast shown mercy unto me,

And hast saved me and my sons from the waters of the flood,

And hast not caused me to perish as Thou didst the sons of perdition.

For Thy grace hath been great towards me,

And great hath been Thy mercy to my soul;

Let Thy grace be lift up upon my sons,

And let not wicked spirits rule over them

Lest they should destroy them from the earth.

But do Thou bless me and my sons, that we may increase
and multiply and replenish the earth.

And Thou knowest how Thy Watchers, the fathers of
these spirits, acted in my day: and as for these spirits
which are living, imprison them and hold them fast
in the place of condemnation, and let them not bring
destruction on the sons of thy servant, my God; for these
are malignant, and created in order to destroy.

I believe there is much more to Abraham's story that explains in-depth why he was a "friend of God" as James and Isaiah mentioned. He was obedient to God and chosen in Noah's post-flood procession to become the patriarch of God's chosen representatives on earth (Israel). He confronted false religion, Nimrod, and his father, Terah, and destroyed their idols, without fear of reprisal. He feared only God. He knew who demons were and did not fear them; rather, he rebuked them fervently.

In Genesis chapter 14, he pursued the king of Shinar "Amraphel" until he rescued his nephew Lot. King Amraphel could only have been Nimrod in the context and timeline of this story. Later, he was willing to sacrifice his only son, Isaac, on Mount Moriah, if it was God's will.

Abraham was fearless. He feared his God when no one else did, he hated the idolatry of Babylon, and he was obedient to God. This is why Abraham was called a "friend of God," and we can all aspire to be called the same if Abraham is our example.

There is another example whose name was "Beloved."

◀ 1732. David ▶

David: David

Original Word: דָּוֵד

Part of Speech: Proper Name Masculine

Transliteration: David

Pronunciation: dah-VEED

Phonetic Spelling: (daw-veed›)

KJV: David

NASB: David, David›s

Word Origin: [from the same as H1730 (דּוֹד דֹּוד - beloved)]

Of the forty-two kings of Israel, David was one of the few who never fell into idolatry. David feared God only, exalting the God of Israel above all things. David captured the heart of God:

*But now thy kingdom shall not continue: the Lord
hath sought him a man after his own heart, and the
Lord hath commanded him to be captain over his
people, because thou hast not kept that which the Lord
commanded thee. (1 Samuel 13:14 KJV)*

*And when he had removed him, he raised up unto
them David to be their king; to whom also he gave
their testimony, and said, I have found David the son
of Jesse, a man after mine own heart, which shall fulfil
all my will. (Acts 13:22 KJV)*

Remember that when David played his harp for Saul, he would be relieved of demonic torture for as long as David played. The common theme of the Old Testament friends of God and New Testament friends of Yehshua (God) is to fear God alone and nothing else, confront idolatry and the worship of false gods, false doctrines, and rebuke demons.

Yehshua arrived and, in John 15:15, called His disciples His friends. As the son of the living God, He set the bar high for the sons of God led by the Spirit. Yehshua introduced the invisible fourth dimension of "love" into the basic algorithm of becoming a friend of God.

> *Love bears all things [regardless of what comes], believes all things [looking for the best in each one], hopes all things [remaining steadfast during difficult times], endures all things [without weakening]. (1 Corinthians 13:7 AMP)*

These are the final hours of the last days until the "Day of the Lord." The sons of God led by the Spirit of God are rising up, confronting principalities and powers of darkness, healing the sick, even raising the dead, and proclaiming miracles as we "prepare the way of the Lord," our Bridegroom. We must be worthy of the inheritance that we will receive as joint heirs with Christ. The Holy Spirit is not only our witness but also the Administrator of this estate and Keeper of the bride until the return of the Bridegroom. Now is the time to "be considered worthy to escape these things that shall come to pass" (Luke 21:36) and become deserving of receiving the estate that the fallen sons of God abandoned in their rebellion to God.

> *Later, Jesus appeared to the eleven [disciples] themselves as they were reclining at the table; and He called them to account for their unbelief and hardness of heart, because they had not believed those who had seen Him after He had risen [from death].*
>
> *And He said to them, "Go into all the world and preach the gospel to all creation. He who has believed [in*

*Me] and has been baptized will be saved [from the
penalty of God's wrath and judgment]; but he who
has not believed will be condemned. These signs will
accompany those who have believed: in My name they
will cast out demons, they will speak in new tongues;
they will pick up serpents, and if they drink anything
deadly, it will not hurt them; they will lay hands on the
sick, and they will get well."*

*So then, when the Lord Jesus had spoken to them,
He was taken up into heaven and sat down at the
right hand of God. And they went out and preached
everywhere, while the Lord was working with them and
confirming the word by the signs that followed.] (Mark
16:14-20 AMP)*

The sons of God led by the Spirit of God will encounter horrible circumstances while currently residing in Satan's kingdom. We are the targets of Satan's wrath, not God's or the Lamb's. The "Day of the Lord" is reserved for the sons of disobedience, not the justified in Christ. From the time we are baptized and renounce our citizenship in the kingdom of death under the prince of death, we are the targets of his wrath. The apex of spiritual wisdom is knowing how not to leave an open door to our adversaries. This begins with daily atonement while residing in satan's kingdom.

We're surrounded by the sons of disobedience, so it can be difficult navigating around them while maintaining a loving and compassionate heart. We're all included as Satan's victims, but we don't have to face his persecution if we know how to resist him and his tactics while exercising our authority through the blood of Yehshua.

Always remember David's Psalms while enduring the kingdom of death until Yehshua's return. God is our refuge and our strength. Nothing of this world can substitute God's love. He is always present, more so in times of trouble when we should be pressing in nearer to Him. Become like David, Abraham, and the disciples, never fearing in any circumstances, though the earth be moved and the mountains (principalities) are cast to the sea. When the sons of disobedience rage against us like tidal waves at sea, know that the one who caused the sea at the flood of Noah can calm it. Storms will come violently, but they will always pass. Learn to rebuke the storm, and live for the peace that comes with knowing Yehshua. Our reward will be worth every second of pain and suffering we must endure while in Satan's kingdom. God has already seen to it.

> *But as it is written, Eye hath not seen, nor ear heard, neither have entered into the heart of man, the things which God hath prepared for them that love him. (1 Corinthians 2:9 KJV)*

Sons of God led by the Spirit if God, go out and combat the powers of darkness behind the pedophiles and child sacrifice satanic cults that have been getting away with murder while churches have become social clubs—or worse, LGBGTQIA+ under the influence of "Babalon." God is with us, and if He is with us, who can be against us?

> *What then shall we say to all these things? If God is for us, who can be [successful] against us? He who did not spare [even] His own Son, but gave Him up for us all, how will He not also, along with Him, graciously give us all things? Who will bring any charge against God's elect (His chosen ones)? It is God who justifies us [declaring us blameless and putting us in a right relationship with Himself]. (Romans 8:31-33 AMP)*

As joint heirs with Christ, an enormous estate is awaiting final probate when the sons of God who rebelled are finally judged, as promised in Matthew 25:41. Look up at the night sky full of stars, and imagine that there is at least one of them that is your inheritance when Satan's reign finally ends and God's judgment is complete. Rise to the occasion, and pray to be considered worthy of what we have been promised. "As it is written, Eye hath not seen, nor ear heard, neither have entered into the heart of man, the things which God hath prepared for them that love him" (1 Corinthians 2:9 KJV).

Do not be naive. The sons of disobedience will not give up without a fight. Stay atoned, watch, fight and pray (Matthew 26:41).

Rise up, sons of God led by the Spirit! Prepare the way of the Lord!

Heavenly Father,

Thank You for being our strength and our refuge, a very present help in times of trouble as we restrain the lawless one until the time of Your Son's coming, during these final hours of the Church Age. As Satan rages ever more diligently, may the sons of God led by the Spirit rise up ever more fervently in corporate prayer against the sons of disobedience.

Thank You, Father, that You neither slumber nor sleep where the apple of Your eye is concerned, and all of Israel will be saved in the great Day of the Lord. Thank You, Father, for the gift of salvation and for including us as citizens of the kingdom of heaven with Yehshua as our King. Thank You, Heavenly Father, that we are counted among the sons of God led by the Spirit of God and are soon to become joint heirs with Christ in an expansive estate abandoned by the rebellious sons of God who turned against You in ages past and present. They shall soon be no more according to Your Word and Your will, and we ask, Father, that You bless us with every ability to rise to the occasion and responsibility of the task at hand.

Guard us beneath the shadow of Your wing, that we be constantly vigilant against deception and that no one

*take our crown. May Your Holy Spirit please guide and
direct our paths precisely and without deviation in these
final hours ahead of Yehshua's arrival, as this generation
shall not pass 'til all things be fulfilled, and Yehshua is
seated on the throne of David at Jerusalem when peace
is restored forever.*

*Our Bridegroom deserves the best. Empower us, Father,
that we be the perfect Bride ahead of His imminent
arrival, and our Babylonian garments become as white
robes in your sight.*

*In Yehshua's holy name and by His holy precious
blood, we pray and thank You, Father, for including
us as partners in fulfilling Your will as we witness the
cataclysm of the prince of death and his angels, our
mutual adversaries. May we become worthy of the tree
of Abraham we have been grafted into, and may the wild
branches become known as "friends of God" in this
war against deception, demons, and principalities in the
kingdom of Your enemy, the prince of death.*

*May peace be restored to Jerusalem forever, in Yehshua's
name. Amen.*

Find a great cause and be a pillar of strength and support to them. I
have suggested a few from chapter 9:

Handing the Shame Back - https://www.handingtheshameback.org/
Operation Underground Railroad - https://ourrescue.org/
SOAR (Speak Out Act Reclaim) - https://www.
speakoutactreclaim.org/
Covenant Rescue Group - https://www.covenantrescue.org/

If you know someone in need of legal support, I understand this law firm is doing good work for victims of pedophilia, child sex trafficking, and sexual abuse of children in schools and churches:

Andreozzi + Foote, Sexual Abuse Lawyers - https://www.victimscivilattorneys.com

These are a few examples, but there are more. Covenant Rescue Group is doing some amazing work in training law enforcement at local levels to learn how to identify the signs of child trafficking and apprehend the individuals committing these atrocious crimes. Invite them to your hometown!

Special Thanks

I suppose I should again thank Tucker Carlson, whose comments during interviews continuously provoke me to write.

I have some very special friends who watched over me, prayed for me, and nursed me back to health during my brief battle with cancer. I say brief because many miracles occurred—or I wouldn't be writing this today. When the main tumor ruptured, the infection in my abdomen was so severe that I shouldn't have survived the surgery, much less the cancer itself. I bled internally, and there was not enough of my blood type in the hospital to revive me. But some special friends started making calls and gathered enough blood to at least allow the surgeons to do surgery. My surgeon said, "I've never done surgery on anyone with a hemoglobin level below seven." But he did—and I recovered.

We tend to live our lives in complacency until we are faced with death. Thank you, my dear friends Jimmy and Renee, the King family, Rick and Cathy, the Miranda family, and many others, for your care, compassion, and prayers that kept me on the right path.

I want to leave you with this thought. Remember the prophecy of Hosea 6:2-3. We can calculate the year of the crucifixion from the prophecy of Daniel's 70 weeks in chapter 9. Gabriel told Daniel the clock would start ticking with the decree to rebuild the temple, which occurred in 444BC. The date can be accurately determined by reading Nehemiah 2:1-8 where specific timelines are given. By converting Hebrew years to Roman calendar years this takes us directly to 33AD when the crucifixion occurred. Hosea's "2nd Day" will close 40 jubilees of years or 2000yrs, since the crucifixion on Passover 2033. The current jubilee ends on Nisan 1 of the Hebrew year 5800, or the Roman year March 15, 2040. Something so huge we cannot imagine will occur between the time you read this book and March 31st, 2033. Don't waste any time!

When the sons of God are revealed, they are the Bride, who will join Christ in ruling over the former estates of the sons of God that fell with lucifer. Just as there were stars in heaven named after the sons of God that fell, those stars will soon bear our names. Let's commit ourselves to becoming worthy of what God has prepared for us!

> *But as it is written, Eye hath not seen, nor ear heard, neither have entered into the*
>
> *heart of man, the things which God hath prepared for them that love him. (1 Corinthians 2:9 KJV)*

This book was a bit heavy, but certainly was not a sterile academic exercise! So, a special thanks to any reader who made it this far!

Remember that Hosea 6:2-3 will be fulfilled between the time you read this book and Passover 2033 in this final jubilee. This generation (of May 1948) shall not pass til all things be fulfilled at the close of the age. Let us not be like the Jewish people when Yehshua wept over Jerusalem in Luke 19:41-44 because they were not looking for their Messiah, after Daniel recorded the precise day of His coming in chapter 9! Look up! Get ready to leave it all behind for something far better!

> *The Lord bless thee, and keep thee:*
>
> *The Lord make his face shine upon thee, and be gracious unto thee:*
>
> *The Lord lift up his countenance upon thee, and give thee peace. (Numbers 6:22-26 KJV)*

Until we meet in the air, rise up you sons of God led by the Spirit!